SOCIAL & BEHAVIORAL SCIENCES   Psychology

36-2441   *WM*   RC569   97-45761 CIP

Haaken, Janice. **Pillar of salt: gender, memory, and the perils of look-ing back.** Rutgers, 1998. 332p bibl index afp ISBN 0-8135-2524-1, $26.00

To understand adult recall of childhood sexual abuse, one must grasp the concepts of forgetting and remembering trauma. When a woman alleges incest and the father claims innocence, reliability and sources of error in memory become major concerns. Unfortunately, traditional concepts of memory neglect the influence of social context. Haaken investigates the controversy surrounding these memories; the influence of gender and culture on the reliability of autobiographical memory of early sexual trauma; and what causes close relatives to have conflicting memories of family life. In part 1, Haaken dis-cusses frameworks for remembering, reviews the science of memory, and considers per-spectives of psychoanalysis, feminism, and storytelling. Part 2 takes on the recovering of historical memories and the ways that suggestion and society can color recall. The third section of the book focuses on clinical storytelling and contemporary social dilemmas. This well-written discussion of how storytelling, gender, and culture influence traumatic memories raises fascinating questions and issues for researchers, therapists, and others involved in examining reports of sexual abuse and recovered memories. Not as useful in undergraduate collections.—*S. M. Valente, University of Southern California*

PILLAR
OF SALT

PILLAR OF SALT

GENDER, MEMORY, AND THE PERILS OF LOOKING BACK

JANICE HAAKEN

RUTGERS UNIVERSITY PRESS
New Brunswick, New Jersey, and London

Excerpt from "Lot's Wife" in *Views with a Grain of Sand: Selected Poems,* copyright © 1993 by Wislawa Szymborska. English translation by Stanislaw Baranczak and Clare Cavanagh copyright © 1995 by Harcourt Brace & Company, reprinted by permission of the publisher.

Library of Congress Cataloging-in-Publication Data

Haaken, Janice, 1947–
    Pillar of salt : gender, memory, and the perils of looking back / Janice Haaken.
       p.   cm.
    Includes bibliographical references and index.
    ISBN 0-8135-2524-1 (alk. paper)
    1. Adult child sexual abuse victims—Psychology. 2. Recovered memory. 3. Adult women—
Psychology. 4. Autobiographical memory.   I. Title.
    RC569.5.A28H3   1998
    616.85'8369—dc21   97–45761
                                                              CIP

British Cataloging-in-Publication data for this book is available from the British Library

Manufactured in the United States of America

In memory of my sister
Joan Hawkinson Bohorfoush

Contents

Acknowledgments

My deepest appreciation goes to my partner, Tom Becker, whose keen insights, close readings, and unflagging support have been of vital importance in bringing this project to completion. Johanna Brenner, Norm Diamond, Gerald Fogel, and Friderike Heuer also have provided encouragement and enormously helpful suggestions throughout the stages of preparing the manuscript.

For their generous assistance in reading and commenting on various drafts over the past several years, I thank Larry Bowlden, Marta Greenwald, Maureen Katz, Sharon Lamb, Debbie Nathan, Frann Michel, Astrid Schlaps, Mike Snedeker, Gary Smith, and Julia Watson. For library research and technical assistance, I thank Dina Dickerson, Joyce Kerley, Kathy Hollisey, Pam Livingston, Zoe McClanahan, and Lisa Titan. Also of special importance are my editor at Rutgers, Doreen Valentine, my finest teacher, Victor Wolfenstein, and my mother, Leah Torkelson. And, finally, I wish to express gratitude to my students at Portland State University and to my patients, whose many observations about life are woven into the fabric of my own personal memory.

PILLAR
OF SALT

Lot's Wife

They say I looked back out of curiosity,
but I could have had other reasons.
I looked back mourning my silver bowl.
Carelessly, while tying my sandal strap.
So I wouldn't have to keep staring at the righteous nape
of my husband Lot's neck.
From the sudden conviction that if I dropped dead
he wouldn't so much as hesitate.
From the disobedience of the meek.
Checking for pursuers.
Struck by the silence, hoping God had changed his mind.
Our two daughters were already vanishing over the hilltop.

—Wislawa Szymborska, *View with a Grain of Sand*

INTRODUCTION

Looking Back

Then the Lord rained down burning sulfur on Sodom and Gomorrah from the Lord out of the heavens. Thus he overthrew those cities, and the entire plain, including those living in the cities and also the vegetation in the land. But Lot's wife looked back, and she became a pillar of salt. —Genesis 19:24–26

AS A YOUNG GIRL, I was filled with sadness over the story of Lot's wife, the woman with no name. Who was this woman who became a pillar of salt for the seemingly innocent act of looking back? What was she trying to see, and why was she punished so severely?[1] For women, the act of remembering—of looking back—can feel transgressive, even sinful. Lot's wife defied the commandment not to look back, and her act of resistance serves as a cautionary tale of the consequences of female rebellion. Such an act of defiance also may evoke anxiety over lingering too long at the transformative moments of history. As both a treacherous and a liberatory activity, confronting the personal past involves reconciling competing allegiances and conflicting desires. To do so often involves the violation of cultural taboos.

For women, particularly, the process of remembering—both individually and collectively—means creating representations of the past out of a shadowy historical landscape. In Western traditions, women are more likely than men to be transitional icons, facilitating masculine journeys of exploration and conquest. As wife, mother, daughter, the woman is the one who is left and returned to, a fixed position in a male universe of transformative action. Women are spared and at the same time deprived of grand legends that place them at the center

1

of cosmic dramas. Western cultural legacies offer women few illusions about their importance as agents in the larger order of things.

Given their invisibility within patriarchal legends and lineages, how do we understand what is involved for women in the project of remembering? And, further, what is at stake for contemporary women who collectively challenge the "Word" of the Father(s)? There are both advantages and disadvantages to understanding recollecting as transgressive work. This viewpoint permits careful scrutiny of received truths and opens up a field of possible discoveries. But it also stirs uncertainty about what is real and what is not, and it creates problems in defending what is learned. For women, who traditionally have been denied the authority to define the cultural past, the project of remembering is also a struggle for a new way of looking back. When the master's creation is called into question, so too are his tools—the very methods of arriving at the truth.

We should not be surprised, then, to find that women's efforts to find their place in history are fraught with social conflict and struggle, on the one hand, and ambiguity and confusion on the other. *Pillar of Salt* grew out of my own efforts, as an academic psychologist, psychotherapist, and feminist, to sort through the confusing claims surrounding a controversy that emerged in the 1990s over women's memories of family history. The controversy centers on the veracity of "recovered," or "delayed," memories, typically involving childhood sexual abuse, which became common in the psychotherapies of the 1980s. While much of the heat of the controversy surrounds the issue of whether traumatic childhood events can be repressed or forgotten, the real issue involves the nature of remembering. Further, it involves contestation over the role of women as credible observers and chroniclers of the social terrain. This book uses the recovered memory debate as a window onto a much broader field of ideas concerning memory, storytelling, and the psychology of women. I move beyond the poles of "true" and "false" recollections of childhood sexual abuse and trauma to suggest how women's stories reveal layers of gendered and ambiguous meanings, spanning a wide cultural, literary, clinical, and historical landscape.

THE CULTURAL RECOVERY OF MEMORY

Child abuse, as family historians argue, has a long history of being forgotten and remembered. The women's movement of the 1960s and 1970s gave political momentum to the cultural "recovery" of memory around family violence, with sexual abuse at the forefront of challenges to the private control of men over women and children. Backed by the moral authority of an emerging women's movement, psychotherapists, who were increasingly likely to be women, assisted their female patients in transforming private remembrances into public testimonials. In the clinical encounter and in public discourse, women could now speak of the unspeakable, violating traditional mandates to remain silent. Rarely addressed in the earlier literature on problems of women, incest and other forms of childhood sexual abuse became a common feature of clinical histories reported in the 1980s.

But the late 1980s ushered in a new era of therapeutic discovery. Whereas earlier accounts of childhood sexual abuse were based on continuous memories of abuse, by the late 1980s women with no prior known history of abuse began to "recover" such memories in the course of psychotherapy. The 1988 bestseller *The Courage to Heal* inspired many women, including therapists, with its portraits of anguished journeys into the personal past.[2] These journeys led to new memories of childhood molestation, as did countless other publications and recovery groups in the years that followed. The many problems of women that, as Betty Friedan noted in 1963, "had no name" were now being named as incest.[3] Equipped with lists of signs and symptoms indicating a possible history of abuse, therapists and patients gained new conviction that the source of female disturbances was in a forgotten childhood trauma. What they increasingly found, more than memories of childhood neglect, assault, or developmental "storms and stresses," were primal scenes of sexual violence, with graphic images of family barbarism becoming dominant motifs. Incest and alcoholic rages gave way to stories of child sex abuse rings and satanic rituals. The dysfunctional family was now cast as a battlefield, with women and children as the traumatized survivors of domestic wars.

By the early 1990s a reaction to these dramatic portrayals of family trauma set in. Academics, journalists, and a newly formed organization of parents, the False Memory Syndrome Foundation, were aligned in an impassioned claim that therapists were the malignant source of such horrific memories. Public sympathies were divided, as stories of adults ravaged by childhood sexual abuse competed for the public spotlight alongside portraits of "decent" parents destroyed by false sexual allegations. The courts set the terms for adjudicating claims and counterclaims, with each side armed with professional expertise advancing the truth or falsehood of recovered memories of childhood trauma.

Some feminists characterize the debate over women's memories as a predictable backlash against the movement for women's and children's rights. For many feminists and therapists in the field of sexual abuse, the tendency has been to close ranks around women's allegations, whatever they might be. This solidarity is understandable, if not inevitable. Throughout history, the deck has been stacked in favor of the powerful, and men often have used their power to discredit women by denying or minimizing their grievances. The gains that women have made in achieving credibility—in legal, clinical, and academic arenas—are recent and, therefore, tenuous. In addition, adjudicating claims of sexual abuse, particularly after long lapses of time, is difficult, if not impossible. Sexual abuses typically occur in private, and when material evidence is lacking, the scales of justice tip toward the most believable or credible claimant.

Credibility, of course, is highly linked to social status. Until the 1960s, child abuse, particularly incest, was believed to be extremely rare among middle-class families.[4] Child abuse, *most* particularly incest, is no longer so incredible.

Given this history and what we now know about the widespread incidence of child sexual abuse, why should we challenge the claims of women? Is it not likely that the questioning of women's stories is motivated more by a backlash against feminism, as many recovered memory adherents assert, than by a desire for justice or the "truth"?

The cultural resistances to acknowledging the extent and scope of child abuse form an essential backdrop to this book. But there are other disturbing questions circling around the debate that make it difficult to settle on an adequate version of the truth without further investigation. Why, for example, do so many of the memories women are recovering involve sexual abuse? Women certainly experience other difficulties in the course of development, other traumas, including poverty, neglect, nonsexual abuse, and burdensome domestic responsibilities. Why is sexual abuse such a dominant motif in the distressing childhood stories that emerged in psychotherapy in the 1980s? These questions might be easier to answer if the conflict simply pitted women, as patients, against a male-dominated professional establishment. But women are no longer entirely outside the kingdom. The contexts within which these memories emerge do need to be taken into account, including the role of professional authority in shaping them. How, then, does this clinical context shape the creation of memory? And why do so many therapists now speak more of trauma and dissociation, and less of internal conflict, in framing emotional problems, particularly those of women?

Pillar of Salt examines the cultural and historical dynamics behind this passionate debate, which has polarized academic and clinical communities and divided public sympathies. The book begins with the premise that there is more at stake in this controversy than the literal accuracy of childhood memories or the susceptibility of memory to distortion. Broad currents of conflict and anxiety are palpable, as both defenders and critics of recovered memory advance their positions with moral urgency.

While the debate has been understood as a struggle over the factual basis of allegations of child sexual abuse, this limited approach to the issues overlooks the truths contained in even false accounts about the past. Framing the controversy in terms of true and false memory is sorely inadequate because it misses the range of meanings and partial truths that lie between these polarized, absolute categories. We need an alternative means of entering into the psychological and social meaning of these accounts and of understanding why and how they came to carry such import for vast numbers of contemporary women.

In searching for an image to represent the position of women in the recovered memory debate, I confronted the poverty of female images in my own cultural background. Some feminists have reclaimed pagan-goddess traditions or Greek myths in which female deities vie for power alongside male gods, in which both occupy a space in the cosmology closer to human scale than those in monotheistic traditions. I have chosen the image of Lot's wife because biblical stories were the legends of my own childhood, and they remain a powerful force for meaning making in Western culture.

Freud took the legend of Oedipus to represent the collective conflicts of men. This story of a son's guilt over taking the place of the father also makes central the metaphor of sight. But if men suffer from guilt over what they cannot bear to see in their unconscious desires and, like Oedipus, gouge out their own eyes, women have faced an opposing dilemma. For Lot's wife, the story ends before we know what she has seen. Her fatal rebellion creates a disturbing void, one into which traditional theological interpretations are often projected, but it also may be employed as a metaphor for a generative, symbolic space opened up for feminist analysis. Like Lot's wife, women have their experiences entombed in men's accounts of the past. Unraveling entombed memories is, then, both a creative and a revelatory project.

SODOM AND GOMORRAH

I enter into the recovered memory controversy through the story of Sodom and Gomorrah and the flight of Lot's family because it illustrates the cultural blind spots and moral anxieties associated with sexual storytelling. The story begins with God's displeasure with the people of Sodom and his wrath over their turning away from his commandments. God sends two male angels to the city as messengers, and Lot brings them into his house, feeding and protecting them. When the men of Sodom encircle Lot's household, aggressively demanding that the angels come out that they might "know" them, Lot offers his daughters instead as a means of appeasing the intruders. "I have two daughters which have not known men. Let me, I pray you, bring them unto you, and do ye what is good in your eyes" (Genesis 19:8). The messengers bring God's commandment to leave Sodom, but Lot resists and lingers inside the city. "But I can't flee to the mountains; this disaster will overtake me, and I'll die," he protests (Genesis 19:19). Lot is preoccupied with his own survival and woefully unheroic. But the Lord is as patient with Lot as he is merciless with Lot's wavering wife. As Lot and his wife and two daughters prepare to leave, the angels direct them not to hesitate or to look back. Lot's wife is killed for violating the commandment, and her husband and two daughters continue on to the mountains, where they find sanctuary in a cave. The two daughters plot to get their father drunk in order to have sex with him, in the interest of continuing the surviving lineage. The two sons that result from these incestuous unions, Moab and Ben-Ammi, become the patriarchs of new tribes.

This biblical story continues to be used by conservative, anti-gay Christians as a cautionary tale about the male "sin" of sodomy, even though, as Naomi Rosenblatt and Joshua Horwitz so perceptively point out, it more aptly serves as a sanction against gang rape.[5] Jewish commentaries offer more nuanced readings of the tale than do those in my own Christian background, and there is more tolerance in Judaic traditions for ambivalence in human relations with the Almighty.

Whether denied or rationalized in various theological exegeses, however, this biblical tale remains one of a terrifyingly punitive God and of an honored patriarch who sexually barters his daughters. Lot escapes with his life from the fires of Sodom, and his own sins perish from cultural memory, even as his lineage is preserved. The destruction of Sodom and Gomorrah positions men as both subject to the rule of the Father and as having some power to influence the course of divine actions. It was Abraham who designated his nephew, Lot, as worthy of God's mercy and who negotiated with God on his behalf. God's first impulse was to destroy the entire city in a fit of rage. But Abraham, like the eldest son in an alcoholic family, appeals to the Father's more reasonable side, arguing that the virtuous should not be killed along with the guilty. Lot, as it turns out, emerges as the one man sufficiently virtuous to be spared such a dreadful fate.[6] In the biblical account, the proffered sacrifice of the daughters does not diminish the virtue of the father. Indeed, Lot's offering of his daughters is born of a commitment to a higher principle, that of protecting the messengers of God. Yet the actions of patriarchs are perennially justified as serving some higher good, while the sacrifices of women are subsumed within this dominant justificatory account.

The story of Lot's journey out of Sodom and Gomorrah invokes a vision of parental authority based on submission to the absolute rule of the Father. And it is a story of repression, with the fantasy of an all-good father as the central motif. Like the sparing of Noah's family, the spiriting away of Lot on the eve of a holocaust permits the faithful to preserve the idea of a loving Father. The horror of the Almighty's acts is mitigated by the survival of the "one good man" and his heirs. Their survival symbolizes the rewards of obedience and permits a splitting off of the good father from the rageful, destructive one. Looking back at what the father has done becomes a collective prohibition, but one that women, as symbolized by Lot's wife, bear more harshly than men.

But survivors also suffer from guilt and the defenses that such guilt evokes: those who survive must see themselves as virtuous and those who perish as deserving of their fate. For the surviving patriarchs, there is a triumphant attitude toward the losses of history. The heirs to the Law of the Father—the good men—inherit the right to tell the story and to justify the events of history and patriarchal rule itself. The son who submits to a ruthless father may despise him, but he ultimately inherits the father's rights and privileges. He may rebel, but he can lay claim to an alternative kingdom, if only a woman over whom he may rule.

Women are at the forefront of resisting patriarchal authority because they have been offered fewer compensations for what is given up than have men. If the biblical pillar of salt represents the tears of women and grief over the losses of history, it signifies more generally feminine impotence in the face of those losses. And for the collective daughters of Lot, it marks their entry into a motherless wilderness where the protective side of patriarchy is often illusory.

For many conservative Christians, the biblical account of Sodom and Gomorrah is an authoritative text on absolute evil and the rewards of righteousness. Lot is spared the consuming wrath of God because he is a righteous man. But this fixation on absolutes is blinding. To not be blinded requires that we look at ambiguities in meaning, at how the story is being told, and at who is doing the telling. The contemporary challenges to patriarchal authority brought about by the women's movement require complex readings of the legendary past and alternative ways of looking back.

Adult survivors of incest—whether real or "imagined"—confront daunting problems in charting a new path beyond patriarchal rule. Part of what is at stake is the potential loss of idealized notions of the past, including idealized conceptions of parental authority. As Freud frequently pointed out, parent/child relationships are ambivalent. For children, the realization that love for the parents must be reconciled with hostility and disappointment is anxiety-provoking. Idealization of an all-good father figure means pushing out of mind, or repressing, the hostile, disturbing side of the ambivalence. It means continuing vigilance in warding off negative feelings toward those on whom we depend for survival and a chronic sense of the dangerous consequences of rebellious impulses.

Overt rebellion, however, also has its costs. The devaluation of past objects of dependence can give rise to guilt and fear. For daughters even more than for sons, overthrowing the powerful father creates anxiety about retaliation and a sense of loss and uncertainty. One of the sustaining effects of oppression for women, as opposed to men, is that there is less cultural allowance for female rebellion, fewer valorized images of defiance, fewer prodigal daughters. Nonetheless, women in the modern era have created a large-scale rebellion, historically unprecedented in scope, against exclusive male control over public life. As a result, female "oedipal" struggle against the powerful fathers has entered a new era of possibilities. Much like sons, daughters must reconcile love and idealization, on the one hand, and hostility and rivalry, on the other, as they come to discover new powers and possibilities for displacing the ruling elders.

RE-VIEWING THE PAST

The feminist movement of the 1960s and 1970s legitimized the right of women to find their own voices and to look back on the past with new awareness. As I suggested earlier, sexual violations were a recurring theme in the narratives that surfaced as women refused to remain silent about the private transgressions of men. The sexual abuse recovery movement that emerged in the 1970s and 1980s represented a collective challenge to both actual fathers and symbolic ones.

The belief that feminists and therapists in the field of sexual abuse have gone "too far" in their claims around family pathology underlies much of the literature on the "false memory syndrome." With claims of "denial" competing with charges of "hysteria" over sexual abuse, the possibilities for exploring shades of meaning or the ambiguities of truth telling are reduced. Accused parents and their professional allies present themselves as defenders of the integrity of the family. Adult daughters and their allies argue that the bodily integrity and rights of women and children are at stake. With both sides under siege, any acknowledgment of doubt means losing ground to the other side.

The creation of a negotiated space for reconciling polarized claims is no simple feat. Growing up as a middle child, I have always tended to take the position of the mediator, which can be, itself, an avoidance of conflict. While both sides inevitably contain elements of truth, the middle position is not more truthful simply because it refuses partisan loyalty. And in the struggles between the powerful and the oppressed—in this case, between the claims of men and those of women—the oppressed must be granted a certain privileged vantage point on reality, simply because their voices have been systematically silenced for so long.

From a feminist perspective, however, taking a stand in the memory debate is not reducible to simply "believing women" because there is no singular woman's story. At first glance, the conflict would seem to pit a newly empowered group of adult women against the word of their fathers. Unlike the nameless daughters of Lot, who, in the biblical narrative, are made responsible for the sexual lapses of the father, this new generation of daughters is "naming" itself as incest survivors and placing the blame on the father. But as these adult daughters find their voice, so do their mothers. Many of these mothers are publicly challenging the accounts of their daughters and advancing their own competing version of family history. And their stories must be heard and interpreted along with those of their rebellious daughters. In both contexts, there are deep currents of meaning—subplots, metaphorical conventions, and strategic alliances—embedded in women's storytelling practices.

The stories presented in *Pillar of Salt* contain many diverging elements, with differing cultural motifs shaping the structure of the narratives. In capturing the key elements of these stories, I strive for a third (rather than a middle) position—an alternative to both the literalist approach, which characterizes much of the trauma and feminist literature, and the social constructionist approach, which pervades cultural and sociological theorizing and stresses the structures of interpretation over the lived content of human experience. While this book is informed by the insights of social constructionism, it also is guided by the felt urgency and passion attendant in women's efforts to find new voice.

What does it mean, then, to listen to women's accounts of childhood sexual abuse with a "third ear," and what are the specific barriers confronted by speakers and listeners? Certainly women have been granted some authority in chronicling family life and in regulating sexual matters; indeed, women are the gatekeepers of family and sexuality. Why then are women's stories of childhood abuse and incest now being so aggressively challenged? One possibility is that women who report dramatically altered memories of the past are viewed by men, and even by many women, as excessively emotional and as lacking rational capacities. This project of exploring the credibility of women's memories, then, takes us into deep cultural affiliations among women, emotionality, and hysteria.

Pillar of Salt springs from the passion, conviction, and outrage over individual and social injustices that prompted me to become a psychologist. The training chastens and domesticates such impulses, however, and they can easily be left behind, like the hysterical girl of one's youth. This book looks back on women's "hysterical" traditions and, as a text, attempts to burst the bounds of ordinary scientific discourse. Like the migratory symptoms of the hysteric, it moves across established disciplinary boundaries, borrowing ideas from distant places and reaching for new connections in an uncertain field of inquiry. This by no means is a project of jettisoning scientific insights into memory but rather one of reducing the barriers between science and those human concerns that often are placed outside its borders.

The main focus of the book is not on the factual content and evidential basis of the various claims and counterclaims, although these issues clearly have bearing on the many legal cases that found their way to the courts in the late 1980s. The central purpose here is to understand why women's memories of sexual abuse have become the focus of such passionate public and academic scrutiny and, further, how childhood sexual abuse—so often experienced as a particularly revelatory area of memory—anchors female identity in a new relation to the past.

There are dangers, however, in shifting the terms of the debate from whether sexual abuse actually occurred to the symbolically laden terrain I have mapped out here. Both adult survivors and accused parents are potentially offended by this conceptual turn because they often do agree on the urgency attached to the question of whether incest really happened, if not on the answer. Either these fathers sexually abused their daughters, and are deserving of punishment, or they did not. Variations of this idea abound as the line is drawn in the sand. All positions are suspect in such passionate disputes, including "alternative" positions. In moving away from the main factual claims, there is real potential for avoidance of both conflict and the necessity of taking sides. Moreover, many feminists distance themselves from women's complaints that seem to have a "hysterical" cast for fear of losing credibility.[7] Seeking a more "reasonable" common ground can signify inhibitions against excessive female outrage, a defensive clinging to a more conciliatory position, and a distancing from less "reasonable" women. Granting merit to the arguments of the other side—particularly when that other side has organized itself around a referendum on felt injustices—is similarly perilous.

The suspicion arises in some quarters of feminism that women who are skeptical about recovered memories refuse to relinquish the status of "daddy's girl."[8] The air of collaboration can be difficult to dispel when the accusers and accused have intimate histories and when solidarity among women may be so easily undermined by these binding affiliations across the gender divide. Whether incest survivors or not, we can all be seduced by the powerful fathers and give in to sibling rivalry. Given these pitfalls, the tendency to suppress doubts and to close ranks around a plausible version of the truth is as understandable as it is costly.

CENTRAL ARGUMENTS

One of the organizing principles of psychoanalytic therapy is that the best road from a problem to its source is often indirect and convoluted and, further, that important truths reside at the periphery of what is most readily noticed. In practice, this principle means that expanding self-awareness requires attending to latent meanings, enlisting receptive as well as more active strivings, and engaging both imaginative and cognitive capacities.

The contemporary fixation on the question of the literal truth of memory is itself a phobic reaction to the irrational and nonrational aspects of mind and of the debate itself. Getting at the truth of the debate, as well as to the deeper meaning of recovered memories of sexual abuse, requires a new portal of entry. To recast the memory debate and enter it through a culturally informed psychological framework, four central arguments are advanced.

The Defensive Side of Human Inquiry

First, this book shows how socially transformative insights and discoveries inevitably have a defensive side and how recognition of this aspect of human inquiry is vital to enlarging our understanding of scientific, clinical, and political debates over memory. By defensive, I mean those distortions in human consciousness that emerge in response to managing anxiety associated with "knowing." Sometimes knowing is anxiety-provoking because it unsettles prior beliefs, ideals, or self-perceptions. And sometimes the act of looking and seeing itself is unconsciously associated with aggression and the violation of taboos.

In the field of sociology of knowledge, the problematic role of subjectivity within science has achieved tremendous currency in recent decades. Yet feminists have been more likely to employ this line of critique in stripping science of its pretensions of objectivity than in extending it to feminist investigative discoveries. In "recovering" the nonrational aspects of feminist inquiry into sexual abuse, my interest is not in celebrating irrationality. Such romantic impulses, as vitalizing as they may be, must be grounded in a systematic and careful search for the basis of human knowledge and understanding.

In the feminist-informed field of sexual abuse, the tendency has been to grant an exalted status to subjective, experiential knowledge and to adopt a literalist approach to memory. This experiential/literalist approach could also be described as a naive realism: essence and appearance are conceived as one and the same. From this perspective, recovered memories are considered representations of actual events, and little attention is paid to how meanings are altered in the course of telling and retelling. The storyteller moves the listener through the "eyewitness" account of vivid, experientially realized suffering. One of the limits of this approach is that we are captured—mesmerized, in a sense—by the immediacy of the drama and by the subjective, personal conviction that underlies it. First-person narrators may be unaware of various influences on the telling and interpreting of the story, bound as they are to its particularities and to their own inevitable ego-involvement in the unfolding narrative.

Part of recognizing the defensive side of theorizing, then, involves taking into account ego-involvement in the perspective taken. Women have suffered from too little ego-involvement, one might counter, and are often all too ready to yield to the position of the "other." The female legacy of conciliation and of subjugation to patriarchal authority makes the project of establishing an independent vantage point daunting. To stress the limitations of women's authoritative claims, then, runs the risk of contributing to the censorship of female voice. But to valorize female storytelling and to insist on its inherent truthfulness is to deny women a complex subjectivity.

In theorizing woman as psychological subject, I address various contexts of female development and identity, steering an alternative course between the excesses of theoretical universalism and those of particularism. In addressing theoretical excesses, it is important to recognize both the predominant role white, middle-class women have played in defining the subject matter of female psychology and the relative exclusion of other groups of women. But in rejecting universalism and the very idea of scientific "lawfulness," the recent narrative turn in the social sciences has tended to jettison the search for common patterns and motifs that cut across the cultural landscape. Stories most certainly are created out of specific locales of experience, and a diversity of human stories does undermine the idea of universal truths. There is a creative and necessary tension, however, between the general and the particular, even as there are alternatives to the imperialism of universal Man (or Woman), on the one hand, and a profusion of discrete accounts on the other. By working this ground of the recurring motifs in discourses and counterdiscourses centering on women's personal accounts, my interest is in contributing to a theory of female psychology informed by historical and cultural dynamics. I keenly recognize the potential pitfalls in overgeneralizing and the daunting challenges in attempting to work out translations at the borders of the various disciplines engaged here.

The Return of the Repressed

A second argument, and an extension of the first, is that defensively organized experience creates its opposite: the defensive banishing of emotionally significant aspects of consciousness paradoxically strengthens their power or hold over its latent operations. This notion of the return of the repressed was one of Freud's most important, generative insights, even though it was based on a nineteenth-century hydraulic model of mind (the idea that the force of pressure on an object influences the magnitude of the counterforce). If not taken too literally, the idea that banished thoughts acquire a certain valency through their forbiddenness is a useful one, no less in cultural life than in individual experience. It is part of what is meant in the saying that those who do not know history are condemned to repeat it; emotionally significant elements of experience that are disallowed or denied expression tend to return in a disguised form. As later chapters show, allegations of incest have acquired complex, potent meanings as they have penetrated public consciousness, carrying the emotional power, ambivalences, and distortions born of past cultural silencing. The "return" of forbidden knowledge is never entirely free of a history of repression, and such moments inevitably introduce ambiguity and uncertainty as to what precisely has been discovered.

My cultural use of the idea of the return of the repressed enjoins the related concept of splitting, or the defensive separation of two elements of a conflict. One form in which repressed elements of a conflict may "return" in an interpersonal field of experience is through in-group/out-group struggles, particularly those that assume an all-good (the in group) and all-bad (the out group) emotional cast. In the memory debate, the refusal of each side to acknowledge the elements of truth on the other side paradoxically strengthens the hold each side has over the other. Fascination or preoccupation with one's opponents has various meanings and interpretations, but it includes this tendency for enemy camps to depend on one another for vital emotional functions, including the maintenance of internal harmony. This is not to suggest that there are no real perpetrators or victims in human history, for there most certainly are, nor is it intended to minimize the crucial distinction between good and bad arguments, imagined and genuine foes. There are real differences in beliefs and social interests that divide people, and there are power differences in the social world that need to be taken into account. The powerful have greater access to and control over public audiences and more means available to silence opponents than do the powerless. But it is important to reflect on the nonrational aspects of conflictive engagements, specifically those polarized positions that result from defensive distortions in human consciousness or from limited, rigidified modes of analysis.

Gendered Recollections

A third argument advanced in this book is that remembering is itself a gendered activity. It is a product both of gendered social locations and of those collectively organized fantasies and beliefs about gender that dynamically shape what aspects of the past are likely to be preserved. So, too, gender mediates the accessibility of memory and the anxieties and defenses mobilized in the process of recollecting.

Moreover, gender differences and conflicts infuse disputes over the credibility of memory. Since women have been more associated than men with emotionality, sexuality, and the body in Western thought, these more "primitive" or nonrational aspects of life are more readily inscribed in the storytelling of women. These motifs are both more embedded in female experience, by way of women's social location, and are more readily projected onto female narratives of distress. As receptacles and bearers of emotionally laden cultural knowledge, women have historically been both valorized and villainized. There has been voyeuristic fascination and dread attached to the psychiatric gaze into female mental states, including women's "reminiscences."

My own reading of female autobiographical memory speaks to both the blunting side of female oppression and its generative effects, particularly for those middle-class women who constitute much of the subject matter of the psychology of women. As defined by class and race as by gender, women patients and psychological subjects express the contradictions and tensions of their social location. Incited by an enlarging field of possibilities for advancement, middle-class women express many of the same concerns as have the middle-class male professionals who have probed their states of mind. But unlike their male cohorts, women have confronted a more restricted social world. This restricted field of possibilities perpetually redirects female mindfulness toward an interior landscape, even as it directs women's life activity to the local, familial, and particular. The limited vistas of female self-discovery give rise to creative capacities and strengths, on the one hand, and to inhibitions and disabilities on the other.

This inquiry into the gender dynamics of remembering also extends into the metaphorical conventions of memory. The reservoir of female experience, traditionally located within familial struggles and at the borders between private and public life, generates female idioms and imagery as much as it does a "fund" of concrete experiences. In this realm of the symbolic, incest emerges as an insurgent form of female storytelling based on actual historical trauma. But the very reality of incest, and rumors of incest, creates a generative space for metaphorical truths, for the vivifying of female boundary violations and bodily located threats to well-being.

HYSTERIA AND INTERSUBJECTIVITY

A fourth organizing argument is that women are more severely punished than are men for hysterical reactions and for the errors and excesses of their own emancipatory struggles. In response to such phobic and punitive responses to female outrage, contemporary feminism has adopted its own defensive strategies and reactive disavowal of any problematic emotionality in women's storytelling. I examine the basis of this social anxiety over women's grievances and, further, how recovered memory of child sexual abuse emerges out of the cultural ground available for women to articulate complaints and grievances.

A vital dynamic behind this debate over the credibility of women's accounts is the ancient association of femaleness with emotionality and hysteria. Hysterics, we might add, are suspect storytellers, notorious for generating more heat than light. In the colloquial usage of the term, hysteria refers to emotional flooding, particularly as it undermines the capacity for rational thought. Clinically, hysteria encompasses a range of bodily located, migratory complaints that are assumed to be emotional in origin, complaints traditionally associated with female mental disturbances. In the classical forms of hysteria, intolerable mental conflict is unconsciously converted into a physical ailment, such as the paralysis of a limb. While these classical hysterias are thought to be far less common today than in times past, there is still a thriving psychiatric literature on "somaticized" emotional conditions, still highly associated with women. There is much of the old wine in these new psychiatric wineskins, then, as female distress continues to speak (and to be heard) through the language of the body.

For many modern women, the legacy of hysteria is disturbing, leading to a reactive retreat into overly "scientistic" reinterpretations. Indeed, scientific methods can provide coherence and analytical clarity. In topics that are emotionally charged and febrile, the dispassionate eye of science provides a steadying corrective. But the hysteric so often finds her emotional companion in the obsessive scientific or psychiatric onlooker. Mental health professionals and social scientists have brought their own disavowed anxieties to the project of curing the hysteric, of controlling her labile emotionality.

While one tendency within feminism has been to shun hysteria and its embarrassing associations with female irrationality, another has been to celebrate and exalt it. Many contemporary French feminists, for example, embrace the bodily circumlocutions of the hysteric, making use of this archetype to mock the patriarchal ego ideal and its "excessive" demand for rationality. This romantic revolt against science, rationality, and masculinized emotional control has its costs, however, in a dizzying loss of orientation to reality.

TRANSFORMATIVE REMEMBERING

In shedding new light on the psychological and cultural processes of remembering, *Pillar of Salt* builds on a concept I term *transformative remembering*. There are, by now, more than a dozen terms for memory, some referring to different types of memory and some introducing new theoretical stances toward the same phenomena (see chapter 2). I draw on recent work on autobiographical memory and trauma memory, bridging the language and findings in these fields through a culturally and psychodynamically informed theory.

Transformative remembering refers to the recollection of an event that serves as a psychological marker from an early to a later form of self-knowledge. Since memory may be true, false, or somewhere in between as a representation corresponding to some referent event, the interest here is in mental activity that is judged to be memory, either by the subject or by some observer. Transformative remembering refers to event schema that have superordinate explanatory power, serving as phenomenological anchors in autobiographical recall. With a privileging of the verb over the noun—*remembering* as opposed to *memory*—the motivational and active dimensions of mind are put in the foreground of the analysis.

This book explores various instances of transformative remembering and the contexts that make them personally evocative and self-defining. Some memories may acquire such meaning as contemporary emotional conflicts or cultural dramas permit new insight into the seemingly mundane or banal aspects of a past encounter. The concept of transformative remembering is intimately tied to that of insight, which involves the capacity to recognize new patterns or relationships in previously available information. Events that never were forgotten may assume emergent meaning and emotional vividness in light of nascent awarenesses or newly found possibilities for framing and interpreting the past.

Transformative remembering may be placed along a spectrum from continuous to discontinuous representations of the past. At the continuous end, looking back involves a shift in schema available for interpreting events or for reworking autobiographical recall. New understanding is attached to a previously remembered experience in such a way that it may feel like a new memory. Other forms of transformative remembering take on the character of a conversion experience, with the subjective sense of a radical disjuncture between prior and present knowledge of one's personal history. Phenomenologically, this new memory feels like the forceful return of prior knowledge—like a bolt of lightning. It is as though the "truth" were there all along, hidden behind a screen or disguise, breaking through into consciousness with the forcefulness of its immanent power. These more dramatic, transfigurative moments of insurgent recall are often employed to make sense of a powerful contemporary conflict or dilemma.

My approach to remembering is a dynamic one, as it relates to both psychological and social processes. A state of acute anxiety or conflict motivates a memory search. The past is reactivated, and a new configuration arises out of previous recollections. While the elements of the story may be fact, fantasy, or (most likely) some combination of the two, what is key is the reorganization of the past from a newly acquired vantage point. Religious conversions—as well as "conversions" to political and theoretical worldviews—represent this kind of identity-transforming relationship to the past.

The concept of transformative remembering permits a new path into the thicket of difficulties women face in giving narrative coherence to disturbing, dysphoric states, on the one hand, and arousing, excitatory states on the other. In a sense, the memory controversy is more about emotion, distress, and bodily arousal than it is about memory per se. The activity of remembering stands at the threshold between body and mind like a translator. Put another way, transformative remembering refers to the creative use of the past in redefining the self, with emotion and bodily felt states of arousal serving as a motivational impetus for this process of self-discovery. Beyond this, these powerful, revelatory uses of the past contain possibilities for both insight and distortion. The sexual past, particularly, is a Pandora's box of exciting and dangerous imagery—a container for myriad anxieties and fantasies, individual and collective, which gives rise to transformative remembering and storytelling.

FREE ASSOCIATIONS

For me, psychoanalysis and feminism were the liberatory bridges out of the confining, comforting world of old mythologies. As a child of the 1960s, I had a sense of hope and hubris associated with self-discovery, both therapeutic and political. Trauma was there, but it was not the central motif. Indeed, it was in challenging Freud's theory of the "castrated" woman—the notion that female development was hindered from the start by female "lacking" of the phallus—that a generation of feminist revisions of psychoanalytic theory was launched. Freud, it seemed, didn't go far enough in theorizing the castrated woman. He recognized the "impotence" of women but failed to probe its social origins. In our new use of psychoanalytic tools, we understood the Freudian notion of the traumatized female as a male defense against recognizing both the real assaults on our selfhood and the rebellious desires underlying domesticated feminine identity. The traumatized feminine self, we asserted, was a propagandistic illusion, one intended to reinscribe our sense of frailty. In more recent times, however, conceiving of the traumatic past has assumed a more urgent meaning, moving to the center of feminist theory in registering women's suffering and injuries. Feminists are divided over whether this feminist project of putting in the foreground dramatic ruptures—of powerful, destructive invasions of the self—advances or retards the emancipation of women.

In describing the process of looking back as perilous, I am speaking to the conflicts that emerge among us, as women, in recollecting our pasts and to how sexual abuse narratives reveal a broad terrain of ambiguous threats and dilemmas. The book is about the power of sexual abuse to limit and terrorize women and about the power of allegations of sexual abuse as a tool of resistance. It is about real sexual abuse and sexual abuse as an idea or fantasy. And it is about the potential for progressive movements to bring unanticipated blind spots, particularly as grievances migrate from their original context and acquire social symbolic loading over time.

This project is undertaken in the spirit of asking critical questions and opening up new avenues of inquiry. As the daughters of Lot's wife who, like her, are not afraid to look back, women can claim more ground for interpreting the world than in the past. But this ground must include the freedom to explore the ambiguities and uncertainties that accompany our storytelling and our efforts to create a more authentic history.

FRAMEWORKS FOR LOOKING BACK

Gender, Memory, and Social Pathology

We may safely assert that the knowledge men acquire of women, even as they have been and are, without reference to what they may be, is wretchedly imperfect and superficial and will always be so until women themselves have told all they have to tell.
—John Stuart Mill, *The Subjection of Women*

The scientific-academic mind and the feminine-mystical mind shy from each other's facts, just as they fly from each other's temper and spirit.
—William James, "What Psychical Research Has Accomplished"

IN LOOKING BACK on the past and in identifying those influences most constitutive of the self, we are faced with the dilemma of how to select an interpretive lens for making coherent what we see. The human mind automatically performs part of this task, for it searches for patterns, selecting and organizing perceptual input in such a way that meaningful constellations emerge. Culture, including storytelling practices, also intervenes in the organizational processes of mind and in the sense made of experience. For women, who have been "repressed" in the legends of the past, however, reliance on the conventional habits of mind and culture has been confining. Wariness toward "received truths," whether in science, religion, or folk wisdom, is an understandable response.

Part one of this book takes the problem of women's "recovery" of concealed knowledge—their efforts to create more authentic versions of the past—through various communities of expertise. I explain how scientific psychology, trauma theory, and psychoanalysis—central protagonists in the debate over memory—bring their own insights and blind spots to the project of understanding

emotionally charged remembrances. My choice of these communities of expertise is not an arbitrary one, for it follows the plot development of the contemporary drama over recovered memory. This part begins with the story of the Freyd
family, focusing on the divergent remembrances of mother and daughter and how
such remembrances are employed by the competing sides of the memory war.
This archetypal family feud opens up a much wider window onto interactions
between psyche and society, extending into questions about storytelling, remembering, and the psychology of women. The focus is on stories about the past that
feel consequential for social participants—particularly in their implications for
social relationships and alliances—and thereby are conducive to transformative
remembering. Feminism is introduced as yet another protagonist in contested
recollections, for it aims to renegotiate the terms of social encounters by giving
rise to subversive forms of storytelling.

Chapter 1

FAMILY REMEMBRANCES

A Daughter and a Mother Look Back

IN HER 1991 NOVEL, *A Thousand Acres,* Jane Smiley places a recovered memory of childhood sexual abuse at the center of her heroine's awakening capacity for self-knowledge. Set in a Midwestern farming community, the story unfolds as the struggle of an adult daughter against her authoritarian father, a father whose acquisitions of land over the years, acre by acre, extend to the domination of all life within his reach.

While the youngest daughter, Caroline, has left the farm to pursue a career in the city, Ginny and Rose, the two older daughters, marry farmers. The mother of these daughters of the thousand acres died in their youth, leaving them without distinct memories of her. The tightly woven, monotonous regularity of their rural life falls apart midway through the novel as the father, in a state of drunkenness, hurls insults at Ginny, the more compliant of the two farm-bound daughters. He calls her a "barren whore," rupturing the stony silence that previously had held things in place between them. After the father storms out, the two daughters break a sisterly silence as well, speaking for the first time of incest. Rose, the angry, defiant daughter, has always remembered the father's sexual assaults, his coming to her bedroom at night, and she remembers as well the father's furtive entries into her older sister's room across the hall. Ginny rejects her sister's memories in horror, even as her own restive stirrings work in the other direction, making the once unthinkable now a potential object of consciousness.

We can imagine how someone like Ginny, who holds on to so little outside of her father's reach, may be unable to remember the incest until some decisive shift in the balance of powers has occurred. The father's cruel insults, his final breach of any lingering illusion of filial affection, occur after Ginny has had a brief love affair. This new lover—a farm boy who had left to resist the draft, returning as a prodigal son—signifies possibilities beyond the rule of the father. And it is in preparing a bed for her lover in her own childhood room, a room she had not entered in years, that she begins to remember the incest. Laying on the tidily made bed, Ginny gazes at the ceiling and begins to remember the heaviness of her father's body bearing down on her flesh. The forcefulness of the returning memories assumes a primeval urgency, as violent surges—"mysterious, bulging items in a dark sack"—violate the feminine calm that she had so carefully held at the center of her being. Remembering becomes an aggressive act—like "plastic explosives or radioactive wastes"—and it confronts her with dangerously unstorable knowledge. She becomes, in the act of recollecting, a passive recipient of knowledge—taken, like sex with her father, lying on her back. She also becomes, in this moment of remembering, the aggressor, as the "radioactive wastes" of memory potentiate aspects of herself that would otherwise lie dormant.[1]

Why, we may ask, did the one daughter remember while the other did not? Is it possible or likely for the one daughter to conform so fully to the dictates of the father that she has no independent memory? Is it possible, as a strategy of survival, that a division of labor among sisters becomes embedded in the structuring of recollections—where one remembers and another forgets? And why is remembering experienced as a violent act, as aggressively imploding a prior sense of self?

The context of Ginny's recovery of memory powerfully evokes broad cultural themes. Living under the ironclad rule of a destiny not of her own choosing, within a world with paths as straight and narrow as the vast cornfields on the Midwestern plains, Ginny is denied an independent vantage point. As the oldest and most dutiful child, she lacks a private world of her own, a place of internal reflection and self-knowledge. Does the daughter take hold of the memory to justify her own rebellion? It certainly seems likely that forbidden memories require some form of selfhood in order to be reclaimed and registered in consciousness. Smiley positions Ginny, like the prototypical daughter in many contemporary incest narratives, as moving from an unenlightened to an enlightened state of mind. It is a perilous return back into that room that never was her own to face the father at the threshold.

This chapter enters into the phenomenon of sudden remembrances of sexual abuse through the personal stories of Jennifer and Pamela Freyd, central protagonists in the recovered memory debate that emerged in the early 1990s. This mother and daughter have mobilized competing audiences of allies, and their stories recount the clashing concerns and specific experiences of two generations of women. As protagonists in a larger social-historical drama, they tell stories that transcend the particular and require cultural readings. This chapter examines the competing social strategies and theories of faulty remembering produced by these warring parties in the recovered memory debate. I go beyond the issue of the relative correctness of the two theories to explore their underlying assumptions and the social dynamics fueling the debate. In understanding the scripted character of the drama, we may be better able to grasp the nature of the conflict and what is at stake for various participants.

STRATEGIES FOR LOOKING BACK

In August 1993, Jennifer Freyd, a cognitive psychologist, gave a remarkable talk at a conference in Ann Arbor, Michigan. Freyd's talk was part theory, part personal narrative, and most decisively a reaction to the debate that had recently thrust her onto the cultural stage, a debate that started at a Christmas dinner several years before.[2] For an academic psychologist, having a syndrome or an "effect" named after you is a mark of prestige. But for Freyd the phenomenon that came to be associated with her name—the "false memory syndrome," the title of an organization founded by her parents—was like a scarlet letter. Turning this infamous label into a badge of courage, Freyd laid out her own competing theory of how traumatic childhood events may be forgotten and later remembered, followed by her personal account of the troubling family feud that was by then quite public. Her book, *Betrayal Trauma*, elaborates on the theory presented at the 1993 conference.[3]

Freyd started her talk by emphasizing that her departure from academic prose was necessitated by circumstances not of her own choosing. A distorted version of her story had become common knowledge, she explained, initially through her mother's wide circulation of the "Jane Doe" story—a mother's account of an adult daughter's false allegations of childhood sexual abuse. The article was sent to many of Jennifer Freyd's colleagues, including myself, during the summer and fall of 1991, when she was being reviewed for promotion to full professor at the University of Oregon. A cover letter was attached, dispelling any mystery about the identity of the anonymous family, including that of the daughter.[4] Authored by Jennifer's mother, Pamela Freyd, who holds a doctoral degree in education, the Jane Doe story was published in 1991 in a child abuse journal known for its skeptical stances toward many allegations of abuse. The Jane Doe story also launched the False Memory Syndrome Foundation (FMSF), organized by Pamela Freyd in 1992 as a self-help group for parents who claim to have been falsely accused of child sexual abuse.

The Jane Doe story begins with a daughter's revelation, at the age of thirty-three, that, as a child, she had been sexually abused and raped by her father for thirteen years. The author states that "I am Susan's mother, and I have been trying to cope with that revelation." A dramatic set of events surrounded an aborted family visit over the Christmas holiday of 1990, just weeks after Jennifer ("Susan") entered therapy. In her published account, Pamela Freyd offers a blissful picture of that family gathering at her daughter's home. "As in past years, the weeks before our flight had been bustling with happy conspiratorial coast-to-coast phone calls about secrets for presents and plans for our two grandsons" (154). According to Jennifer Freyd, who rejects this portrait of harmonious family togetherness in her own commentary on the Jane Doe story, her mother was steadfastly oblivious to the mounting tension. In her version of the holiday visit, Jennifer recalls that while her two-year-old son was holding a turkey baster, her father, Peter, explained to all those at the table the technique of artificial insemination used by lesbians. In remembering that same Christmas dinner, Pamela observes that "the chicken was served so that Alex [Peter Freyd, Jennifer's father] did not get a breast" (154). While this observation referred to Jennifer's disregard for his food preferences, it seems an odd comment in the context of the sexual story.

The Jane Doe story continues with "Susan" (Jennifer) fleeing from the house with one of her sons, claiming she needed to take him to the doctor. But this was a ruse. Jennifer's husband intervened after her departure, giving his in-laws their "exit visas." As they were ushered out the door, the senior Freyds learned of the charges against them: Peter had sexually abused Jennifer. In reflecting on their forced departure and the abrupt severing of ties with their daughter and grandchildren, Pamela Freyd voices her outrage. She characterizes the behavior of her daughter and son-in-law as "cruel" and "gestapo-like." "After such humiliating treatment how could we ever speak to our daughter and Steve [Jennifer's husband] again?" (155).

Peter Freyd, a mathematics professor, emerges, ironically, as a minor player in the public accounts of mother and daughter. In her Ann Arbor talk, Jennifer presented an e-mail communication from her father that has an intimidating cast. She cited one example of this response to her expressed resentment over the public tactics of the FMSF: "I assumed that you would know what we would do in a case like this: it is one of the more predictable things I've ever done. (It would be totally out of character for me to keep my mouth shut; even so, I did just that for over a year.)"[5]

How do we judge the motives of these parents, who marshaled the vast array of resources available to middle-class professionals—e-mail, academic journals, newsletters, and the media—to reclaim their lost daughter? Jennifer disputes her father's assertion that the "whole project [is] primarily a way of communicating with our daughters" (the Freyds' other adult daughter, who has refused to comment publicly, also severed contact with her parents). Jennifer counters that her parents' behavior is consistent with long-term patterns of intimidation and boundary violations. She claims that her mother told a psychologist in her hometown of Eugene, Oregon, that "if my sister and I didn't 'stop' doing what we were doing (by which I think she meant our refusing to reunite with our parents), we would be 'very embarrassed.' I responded to this news with profound concern. At the same time my mother was sending me lots of 'I love you' messages; I had implicitly learned that these messages meant that trouble was headed my way" (25).

In turning in her talk in Ann Arbor to the contentious allegations of childhood sexual abuse, Jennifer Freyd focuses on the least disputed elements of family history. In the chronicling of these less contested events we see most clearly a central dynamic in the drama: remembered history is just as disputed as forgotten history. Freyd notes that her father's sexual innuendoes and provocative touching throughout her childhood are minimized by the senior Freyds or are dismissed as normal activities without sexual intent. The daughter, however, weaves these memories, which include her father's own acknowledged history of being sexually abused as a child, into a narrative of incestuous family dynamics.

Jennifer Freyd notes that her alcoholic father's memories are assumed to be accurate whereas her own are assumed to be less credible. Freyd recalls that after her second session with her therapist, who inquired about sexual abuse, "I went home and within a few hours I was shaking uncontrollably, overwhelmed with intense and terrible flashbacks. Am I not believed because I am a woman . . . and am therefore a hopeless hysteric by definition? Is it because the issue is father-daughter incest and as my father's property, I should be silent?" (29). A telling element of the saga, according to Jennifer, is that the Jane Doe story circulated within months after the stormy Christmas visit that culminated in the sexual abuse allegations. Further, the FMSF was incorporated "14 months after I entered therapy and began to face the truth of my childhood." Jennifer portrays her mother's creation of the FMSF as a "frenzied effort to deny my reality" (24).

The tendency of many parents to respond defensively to such accusations is not surprising; such human responses have a long, documented history. However, Jennifer may be expecting too much to insist that her parents accept her "reality" when it involves such a dramatically altered version of family history, one with profound ramifications for all concerned. The explanations that Pamela Freyd and FMSF members offer must be assessed, rather than simply dismissed as the self-protective rationalizations of abusive parents. However intrusive the tactics of the senior Freyds, there are compelling bases to FMSF concerns over therapeutic influences on the process of memory retrieval, influences often minimized by sexual abuse survivors and their allies.[6]

The Daughter's Perspective

For the audience in Ann Arbor Jennifer Freyd's emotionally powerful presentation drew its strength from the movement for women's and children's rights that she frequently invoked in her talk.[7] The issue of how politics and science interact in the pursuit of knowledge is also central to understanding the deeper problems posed by the memory controversy. Women who identify with the clinical project of "recovering" repressed memory implicitly understand that gaining new self-knowledge is a struggle, even an act of resistance. In spite of the difficulties in scientifically establishing the concept of repression—the unconscious pushing out of mind of anxiety-laden material—the term captures a vivid phenomenological and political reality. The term *repression* is based on a model of mind that makes conflict over knowing—conflict between an internalized set of beliefs and emerging competing awarenesses—a dominant motif in efforts to recollect the personal past. And it assumes that the pursuit of knowledge can feel like an act of aggression, one accompanied by guilt over discarded childhood identifications and the allegiances they inspire.

Also of significance, given the history of feminine struggle to achieve public, authoritative voice, was the sequence in which Jennifer Freyd presented her ideas. Starting with her academic credentials and a lucid summary of her betrayal-trauma theory, Freyd's narrative took on a potent significance because her later description of her personal anguish as a self-proclaimed incest survivor stood on the stronger shoulders of science. Her narrative is a modern chapter in the history of women and madness, one where women in the role of experts, with the authority of "science knowledge," acquire legitimacy to speak generally, even universally, about emotional suffering. As novelists, poets, and diarists, female authors remain on the margins of public authority, chronicling the particularities of feminine outrage and discontent. But science aims to generalize beyond the particular. Science, traditionally, has been more intimately tied to a masculine world of lawful effects and technocratic power than have those literary portraits of the human condition mapped out in the humanities.

The specter of the "mad scientist" is the other side of this authoritative legacy. If madness is associated with the feminine and rationality with the masculine—as many historians of mental illness argue—women's efforts to enlist science to theorize about their own madness has an uneasy side. (See chapter 4.) But we should not be too phobic about being "mad scientists." Indeed, the tendency to overrationalize and scientize our efforts to know has, as we will find, unforseen costs.

Reconciling the subjective and objective sides of science is no easy task, however, particularly when the subjective looms too large over the "data" in question. Freyd began her talk with a dramatic account of incidents of child sexual abuse that rocked the Catholic Church in the early 1990s. Frank Fitzpatrick, an insurance adjustor, recalled for the first time, at forty-one years of age, that he had been sexually abused as a young boy by a trusted priest. The allegations of sexual abuse against Father James Porter, subsequently corroborated by about fifty other men and women, are not disputed. This man, who is no longer a priest, finally admitted to the abuse when the evidence against him proved to be overwhelming.[8]

This example was important, implicitly, in setting the stage for Freyd's betrayal-trauma theory because it bypassed some of the contentious, sticky issues in the recovered memory controversy. Not only were the allegations corroborated, but Fitzpatrick's recovery of childhood memory was not associated with psychotherapy or other notable directive influences. He had suffered various emotional ailments as an adult and, during a period of introspection, had remembered the sexual assault that had occurred during early adolescence. This case argues for the possibility that adults may forget painful childhood events and later remember them with considerable accuracy.[9] While such examples are reported in the literature, most accounts of new memories—that is, memories that depart in a significant way from the previously known past—involve the use of "memory-enhancement" techniques, such as hypnosis, guided imagery, dream analysis, and suggestive interviewing, all of which are commonly employed by clinicians and self-help groups involved in "memory work."[10] In the Fitzpatrick case, however, these suggestive influences are muted while the power of spontaneous remembering is vivified.

Drawing on an example of a man's recovered memories of childhood molestation also displaces the gender issues in the debate. This strategy can be important in dispelling some of the sexist biases that cloud the issues—for example, the assumption that women are more suggestible and fantasy-prone than are men. But it does not shed any light on why the vast majority of recovered memories involve sexual abuse, rather than other childhood traumas, and why they are more likely to be produced by women than men.

Freyd draws on ideas from evolutionary, cognitive, and attachment theories to posit an explanation for traumatic amnesia. Rather than beginning with clinical cases or the disturbances that result from childhood trauma, she starts from the other direction. "If a child is abused and betrayed," she proposes, "what would we expect to happen to the *information* about the abuse and betrayal?"[11] The notion that we engage in behaviors that are adaptive for survival is one of those axiomatic assumptions in psychology that has various applications. But in the context of betrayal-trauma theory, Freyd makes use of this idea to explain why a child might continue to behave in attachment-oriented ways toward a caregiver—behavior necessary for survival—while simultaneously encoding knowledge of abusive situations, also of adaptive necessity. She argues that humans are prepared evolutionarily both to engage in attachment behaviors and to detect dangerousness or untrustworthiness in others. These two competing survival mechanisms contend for the attention of the child.

This theory bears a striking resemblance to triaging: a hierarchy of tasks based on surviving and preventing massive trauma takes priority over long-term effects or lower-order injuries. Freyd uses the analogy of a broken leg and differential responses to pain—depending on the presence of aid—to illustrate the survival mechanisms associated with betrayal of trust. If there is another person available to offer help, the injured individual would be expected to experience acute pain and to avoid use of the leg. If the injury occurred in social isolation, the experience of pain would be overridden, and the sufferer would use the injured leg in order to find help. Long-term damage to the limb might result, but the brain processes information according to a hierarchy of survival tasks.

How, then, does this theory explain forgetting and remembering the emotional injuries of childhood? Some evidence supports the idea of traumatic amnesia, particularly temporary amnesia, but provides remarkably little clarity about the conditions under which it occurs or the precise meaning of the term itself.[12] Much of the past is normally forgotten, particularly events in early childhood.[13]

But traumatic amnesia is a pathology of remembering where the emotional impact of events interferes with normal memory processes.[14] It may refer to loss of information associated with an entire class of events, to particular details, or to restricted memory functions. Freyd seems to be referring to what has been termed *robust repression*—the failure to remember an entire class of events, such as that one has been sexually abused. Yet her model fails to explain why many sexual abuse survivors do remember the abuse, apparently finding different strategies of survival than do those who develop traumatic amnesia.[15] Further, children who are victims of severe parental beatings in childhood generally remember them, even though repeated beatings become scriptlike or generic in memory.[16]

Differing or more variable processes may be involved in representing sexual abuses in memory, however, either because they involve the victim in a more intimate and confusing way or because they are less able to be integrated into the concept of the "good parent" or the idealized authority figure. The child who suffers the disciplinary belt may come to believe it is "for her own good," particularly within a culture that endorses such behavior. The child who submits to the father's penis may have more difficulty reconciling the contradiction between formal codes or rules and private parental transgressions of them.

Freyd does not explore the broad continuum of experiences that may be subsumed under the rubrics of betrayal and trauma, nor does she examine the ambiguities associated with these categories. While many survivors of sexual abuse claim that for periods of time they were unable to remember the abuse, it is not clear from these reports whether respondents are referring to actual amnesia or to times when thinking about the abuse was extremely difficult or was avoided.[17] As a discursive strategy, the concept of amnesia underscores the idea that considerable emotional work is involved in making particular past events the object of reflective consciousness.[18] For many self-proclaimed survivors, this concept, as a contemporary idiom, conveys a sense of dramatic discontinuity between domains of self-experience—public and private, past and present. Moreover, Freyd's use of the broken leg as a metaphor may be a means of vivifying the less visible emotional injuries of female development and dramatizing the complaints of chronically silenced daughters. Freyd describes, for example, being encouraged to dance nude in front of her father as a young girl and a kiss that felt sexual.[19] Indeed, ambiguous emotional situations are more difficult to represent in memory than are more clearly defined traumatic ones. The physical analogy, then, of vague aches and pains, which are open to various interpretations, would seem to be more apt than that of a broken leg. Aches and pains stimulate an active search for the source of the difficulty, which may involve both directed effort toward memory retrieval and the arousal of fantasy associations.

The Mother's Perspective

The picture that emerges of Pamela Freyd from her daughter's personal account is that of a controlling woman whose fierce loyalty to her husband blinds her to her daughter's pain. It is a feminine version of Abraham and Isaac, where the daughter's memories are offered up by the mother as sacrifice in a demonstration of fidelity and obedience to the higher Law of the Father. Long before the wave of allegations of sexual abuse based on recovered, or "delayed," memory, such complicity of the mother in the daughter's betrayal had been a dominant motif in the survivor literature.[20] More recent is the direct confrontation of mother and daughter in a public battle, with each making use of scientific and personal discourses in mobilizing public support.

Just as Jennifer Freyd has assumed a heroic status for incest survivors with her personal testimonial, so too has her mother for a competing audience of aggrieved parents. In taking on the psychotherapeutic establishment, Pamela Freyd has emerged as the champion of hundreds of accused parents.[21] Speaking with outraged conviction and certainty of purpose, she has made a career out of citing the flagrant abuses of mental health practitioners. But for many self-proclaimed survivors and therapists in the field of sexual abuse, Pamela Freyd's work in advancing the concept of "false memory" is an act of collaboration, a public relations campaign to cover the tracks of patriarchal transgressions.

The portrait of Jennifer that emerges from Pamela Freyd's Jane Doe story includes common motifs in contemporary women's lives, even as it raises unsettling questions about the hostile side of mother/daughter relationships. Pamela Freyd describes her daughter as a highly ambitious and distraught woman, overwhelmed by the demands of career and motherhood. She speculates that her daughter's stresses, including conflicts with her husband over competing career goals, were at the root of the problem. Jennifer needed a scapegoat for her misery, Pamela suggests, and her parents were a convenient target.

The unifying grievance of FMSF parents is their loss of contact with adult daughters. This loss feels as horrific to these parents as do the allegations of incest. In the first published book of FMSF stories, Eleanor Goldstein begins with a passionate appeal. "Imagine what it is like when the person you have loved, nurtured, idolized—your child—suddenly turns against you and accuses you of the most horrendous crimes imaginable. That is what is happening in the U.S. today."[22] In preserving the ideal of a common set of familial interests and grievances, the FMSF narrative casts the therapist as the prototypical outside agitator. Therapists are perceived as modern pied pipers, taking adult children away from loving parents. As a cultural narrative, this motif mobilizes parental anxieties over abduction of children, over seductive strangers who ensnare vulnerable youth. The rejection of parents on the part of adult children may be particularly hard to bear given the normal expectations for daughters. As the old saying goes, your sons may go away but your daughters never leave you. Daughters may lose identities and names through marriage, but they remain morally bound to a "matrilineal" system of caregiving. Rather than restoring their daughters to health and sanity, FMSF members assert, the mental health community has become a purveyor of the very illness it purports to treat. Just as the lying-in hospitals of the nineteenth century became incubators of disease, with physicians carrying pernicious microbes from the cadaver halls to the birthing beds, modern therapists are cast as unwitting carriers of a modern ailment. A consistent refrain of FMSF parents is that the prior "illnesses" of their adult daughters pale in comparison with the monstrous conditions that emerge through treatment.

A troubling problem for the FMSF and its allies, however, is reconciling this claim that recovered memories are an indication of mental illness and cultlike dependence on therapists with the high level of functioning and professional accomplishments of so many "false memory syndrome" victims. Jennifer Freyd stood before her audience as a vivid example of lucidity and academic achievement. Whatever the form of her putative madness, it was not apparent in her carefully organized talk and warm, amicable manner.

The concept of mental illness has many important social functions, even as it may reify human suffering. In the context of the FMSF narrative, it permits the separation of personhood (the prior view of the daughter) from the disturbing new knowledge that is at the center of a family crisis. Framing the daughter's complaints as a psychiatric condition—as a false memory syndrome—offers an explanation that also holds out the hope of a cure and reunification. The false prophets of therapy have made her ill, but health can be restored through competent professional guidance. As one mother put it, in describing the return of her daughter to the family fold, "she was ill and now she is well again."[23] This concept of a passage through illness tends to depersonalize the problem, however, obscuring the question of what gave rise to such feverish familial anguish.

Now a literal and figurative continent stands between Pamela Freyd and Jennifer, her estranged daughter. The continent of memories that divides these generations of women seems unbridgeable. While it is not possible to establish whether Jennifer Freyd's recovered memories of sexual abuse correspond to factual realities, her narrative is suggestive of the conflicts and dilemmas of a new generation of mothers and daughters. The riveting question of whether this daughter was sexually abused may be, as it turns out, the least crucial one in understanding the memory debate. Staring at the sun too long can be blinding, and we must look to the periphery to perceive the light and shadow, figure and ground, that allow us to make meaning of the picture.

MOTHER/DAUGHTER DYNAMICS

The Freyds are no different from countless other families in their tendency to produce conflicting accounts of the past. As a memory researcher, attuned to the reconstructive aspects of autobiographical recall, Jennifer Freyd concedes that her recovered memories may not be accurate in all their details, even though she remains unmoved from her claim that she is an incest survivor. The central issue, she insists, is her parents' destructive use of their professional authority in publicly challenging her own reality. Jennifer Freyd's personal story also illustrates the threatened loss of femininity for women who resist parental demands. For these angry adult daughters, feminine credentials inevitably become open to scrutiny. How could these formerly loving, caring daughters—FMSF parents ask—behave so cruelly toward their parents? Because child sexual abuse is the one unforgivable parental sin in the eyes of FMSF members, as well as in the eyes of the larger culture, it may be the one allegation that permits a "good" daughter to walk away without looking back.

The legacy of the "good daughter," the deeply ingrained pattern of "oversocialization" of girls, inhibits the expression of anger and strivings for autonomy.[24] In breaking free of this legacy, daughters may construct a memory that vivifies this life-and-death struggle with the seductive powers of childhood. The murky range of boundary violations that commonly occur in the course of female development take on dramatic power when framed through the lens of the sexual abuse survivor movement. The memory of the seductive father who seeks gratification from "Daddy's girl" may become decisive when recovered as a memory of him as pedophile or perpetrator. The seductive power of the father is dispelled, as he is "named" through an antagonistic discourse that permits feminine protest.

The emotional reactions of adult women—as mothers and daughters—clearly become culturally admissible when they are expressed through a narrative of motherly protectiveness.[25] Most certainly, one of the dilemmas of contemporary women is reconciling their egoistic interests and traditional feminine virtues. While self-advancement is generally celebrated as healthy in male development, careerist women are often maligned as lacking in maternal capacities, as not fully human. So ambitious women often run a gauntlet of public condemnation. As eloquent women with rival theories of family history, Pamela and Jennifer Freyd each speak of protecting children. This stance is, in all likelihood, a genuine sentiment they share, even though they differ vastly in their perceptions of those threats that elicit their protective responses. Jennifer Freyd recalls her turbulent emotions during that last visit with her parents over Christmas of 1990 in terms of motherly concern. "I feared for my children's safety. I felt if my parents stayed in the house for 10 days my head would explode—it was a powerful sensation, one that I suppose only comes in psychological crisis."[26] Both mother and daughter explain their outrage as a maternal response, as aggression in the service of protection of children. For Pamela, it is the threat of a malevolent therapist who has emotionally abducted her daughter; for Jennifer, it is the threat of dangerous parents who invade the cherished family that "my partner and I have created—a family that happens to include particularly lovable children."[27]

Beyond the maternal motif, there is a subtext of hostility in this mother/daughter conversation that may be difficult to reconcile with cultural ideals of female nurturance and conciliation. Indeed, this family feud acquires some of its toxic intensity in disputes over Jennifer's professional ambitions. Pamela Freyd claims in the Jane Doe story, for example, that her daughter was denied tenure at her previous university and that, at the time of her recovered memories, was struggling with a sense of professional failure. Jennifer Freyd counters, in her own personal testimonial, that these claims are patently untrue. She was, in fact, so highly accomplished that she was offered a tenured position at the University of Oregon, a clear indication of a robust career. While Pamela presents her own version of this history as an effort to understand her daughter's lapse into emotional illness, Jennifer understands it as a hostile attack on her professional status. Whereas Jennifer weaves the events of the past into a narrative of invasive family dynamics, Pamela constructs a competing account centering on parental concern over how to guide a striving, overreaching daughter.

Part of this ambition, Pamela speculates, involves Jennifer's rivalry with her. "Four women my age have independently suggested to me that perhaps Susan [Jennifer] felt extra stress and inadequacy because I had recently had tremendous professional success. They suggested that she had an image of me that did not include serious, visible success and that this might have been a trigger for the timing of her revelation."[28] In framing the problem in such oedipal terms, Pamela Freyd overlooks the possibility that oedipal rivalry can work both ways. Parents may experience competitiveness and hostility toward their children, and this hostility can be difficult to reconcile with parental love, particularly for mothers.

Both Pamela and Jennifer see in the other's project an unambiguous, bold career move, while their own public role is construed tragically. Pamela Freyd points out that it is difficult for Jennifer to retreat from her allegations because she would have to revise a theory that has become the basis for her career advancement. Too much is now at stake. But is this not also her own situation? No, she counters. "I probably could not get another job again, because most people will still believe in our guilt."[29]

For many families, rivalry between mothers and daughters may be troubling in that there are few cultural traditions through which to manage them. Since women are in the position of preserving relational ties and family cohesiveness, mother/daughter ruptures become uniquely threatening. Pamela Freyd is quite open, though, about her own resentment over the way mothers are cast in the incest literature. She notes that feminists in the field of sexual abuse are all too ready to validate the memories of daughters, while dismissing the recollections of mothers. After seeking consultation with a feminist therapist in her hometown, Pamela was indignant that the therapist rushed to judgment, taking the side of her daughter. First confused and despondent, Pamela Freyd then rose up in righteous anger, drawing on the same feminist insights used by the opposition. "I can deal with rape or incest, I thought, but I cannot deal with being a non-person. Neither my daughter nor this therapist seemed to feel that I was a conscious conspirator in all that was supposed to have happened. Instead there was the assumption that I was 'out of it,' was somehow absent as a sentient human being and was pitiful and of no account. . . . My despair turned to anger and the anger to action. I set as a goal to change this one young woman's view of the situation."[30]

Some of the grievances of women who came of age during the women's movement of the 1970s center on the weakness and impotence of mothers in the face of patriarchal abuses within the family.[31] The sin of the mother was her passivity in silently standing by and failing to protect the daughter. But in the contemporary struggle over family memory, daughters confront a newly empowered group of mothers who resist this characterization. And passivity seems to be the least of the failings of Pamela Freyd, a woman who describes her own worst trait as her "bossiness."[32]

This emergent maternal voice in the incest controversy confronts another cultural legacy, however, one that is more palpably present in the complaints of a more recent generation of abuse survivors. This legacy—one that contains both fantasy and reality elements—involves the prototypical mother who knows no "boundaries" and refuses to recognize her daughter's separateness.[33] This second motif is more dominant than the earlier motif of maternal powerlessness in current mother/daughter feuds over family history. Indeed, the term *FMS* does evoke the image of a feminine hygiene product, a parental invasion of the private parts of the daughter's world. On an unconscious level, daughters may perceive these powerful mothers, rather than fathers, as the dangerous sexual invaders, hidden within a Trojan horse of seductive maternal concern.

As daughters fight for a historically emergent right to be angry and to break free of family ties, the rights of mothers in family feuds are more ambiguous. Pamela Freyd acknowledges that a central issue in the heated controversy over recovered memory is the mother's alliance with her husband against her daughter. Once the accusations are made, the mother must decide whom to believe. For many, the response is immediate and resolute; for others, it is more uncertain and torturous. "One mother spent three months in her house with the blinds shut before she finally sought out the help of the Foundation," Pamela notes in illustrating the depths of maternal anguish.[34] Pamela seems to have been unwavering from the beginning, building theory and support as she defiantly forged ahead in spite of moments of despair.

The mother's own ambivalent responses and process of arriving at the truth seem to be an area of silence, a potential chink in the FMSF wall. If these couples were part of a generation that believed that parents needed to maintain a unified front in handling family quarrels, the prospect of a separate voice for women, as wives and mothers, seems to carry the threat of playing into the hands of manipulative daughters. Indeed, the FMSF literature generally refers to sexual abuse allegations as being made against "the families" rather than against fathers.

Given women's traditional responsibility for preserving intergenerational relations, it is not surprising that the refusal of adult daughters to carry out this responsibility evokes alarm. Yet there is a certain hypocrisy in parental condemnation of these daughters and in the outrage surrounding these women's insistence on breaking contact with families. Even as U.S. culture romanticizes the family as a protective harbor in a storm-tossed world, there is a long-established tradition of leaving kinfolk behind. The immigrant experience and westward migration chronicle this epic journey. Transgressive daughters who "abandon" their parents emotionally may arouse, however, cultural anxieties and guilt over this tradition of undoing binding ties in the process of forging a more independent future.

THE POLITICS OF PSYCHIATRY

To what extent do the phenomena described by the FMSF constitute a genuine psychiatric syndrome, albeit one not yet officially sanctioned by the mental health establishment? Canadian psychiatrist Harold Merskey, a member of the FMSF Scientific Advisory Board, addresses this question in the June 1995

FMSF newsletter. He notes that *syndrome* refers to "a group of symptoms that occur together" or "the sum of signs of any morbid state; a symptom complex."[35] Just as the common cold includes a predictable set of symptoms and progression in their course, psychiatric syndromes present similar groupings.

In medical discourse, the distinction between a syndrome and a disease often includes distinguishing between manifested effects and underlying causes. Syndromes are merely descriptive, correlational rather than causal accounts of findings that go together. When the cause or underlying mechanisms of a constellation of symptoms are not known, the term *syndrome* is more likely to be used than *disease* (for example, the chronic pain syndrome). But Merskey describes the recovered memory phenomenon as a syndrome "principally due to an artificial cause, i.e., induction of ideas by an external person." The insertion of medical language permits, it seems, a specious next leap into causality. This is a necessary step because the entire controversy centers on the "cause" of the symptoms.

Merskey asserts that this syndrome includes "a set of ideas for which there is no independent evidence, complaints based upon so-called recovered memories, and the propagation of hate and hostility." This hate and hostility is part of another feature of the malady: it is a "doxogenic disorder, i.e., it is one due to thinking about the illness and having the thought gives the condition." This symptom complex leads its sufferers to accuse their families, who, in turn, turn to the FMSF for help in dealing with this "particularly nasty syndrome."[36]

In mobilizing around a perceived public health problem, the concept of a syndrome becomes a vehicle for quarantining rebellious daughters and their therapeutic allies. And, in the midst of an epidemic, demands for clarity and careful assessment of evidence can yield to more urgent demands to restore social order. Merskey's medical jargon and circular reasoning provide mere ephemeral comfort for parents, however, because they shed no meaningful light on the real dilemmas of these families.

An array of feminists and therapists have united around the position that the actual agenda of the FMSF is protecting perpetrators and undermining the gains of the movement for women's and children's rights.[37] Anxiety over changing gender roles and the danger of women going "too far" in their rebellion against traditional constraints does run like an insistent subtext in much of the FMSF literature. Goldstein, for example, points out that while both accusing daughters and their mothers are often feminists, their views of feminism are "wide apart." While she targets Twelve-Step groups, New Age psychology, radical lesbianism, and feminism as culprits, Goldstein identifies Ellen Bass and Laura Davis's *The Courage to Heal* as particularly pernicious. Goldstein suggests that the book's graphic depictions of sexual abuse may corrupt the morals of young women. "For a sensitive, troubled, empathic woman these descriptions must be especially disturbing."[38]

Both defenders and critics of recovered memory share the assumption that women are not capable of generating disturbing sexual imagery on their own, nor are they assumed to be inclined toward rebellion without the assistance of an outside agitator. For defenders of recovered memory, a past sexual perpetrator is presented as the sole importer of conflict into the female psyche. For critics, therapists are similarly cast as the violators of feminine innocence, implanting unwholesome thoughts in the minds of hapless female victims. While therapists describe their role in recovering memory as one of merely "bearing witness" to the trauma and protecting patients from destructive parents, accused mothers and fathers present themselves as similarly virtuous in their concern with protecting daughters from malevolent outside influence—that is, therapists.

This counterpositioning of malignant and virtuous authority—a theme on both sides of the memory war—is also central to the discourse on "cults." Both sides in the recovered memory debate have their cults, and each draws heavily on the cult imagery that became popular in the 1970s. The youth movement and rebellions of that era, including the search for alternative forms of community, fueled research on cults. Various experts were trained in recognizing "mind control" and in "deprogramming" former cult members. Since the term *cult* generally refers to a group based on charismatic leadership, the extension of this line of inquiry into therapeutic authority was initially a stretch. Unless one includes parents, teachers, employers, and the clergy in one's definition of cult leaders, therapists would seem unlikely candidates. Yet many of the allies of the FMSF have a longstanding interest in cults, bringing many of the same ideas and preoccupations to contested memories. A number of its professional spokespersons are editorial board members of *Cultic Studies Journal,* published by the American Family Foundation (AFF).[39] The AFF is a conservative organization that views threats to the family, particularly by nonmainstream groups, as the central social problem of our era. Ironically, the AFF distributes information on organized satanic cults, even though the FMSF points to the satanic abuse scare as an illustration of the hysteria of the sexual abuse survivor movement. (See chapter 10.)

One subtext of the current debate over "false memory," then, is struggle over parental authority. The FMSF, in advancing its cause, is able to mobilize broad-based anxieties over the integrity of the family and over the legitimacy of parental authority. Behind the question of the veracity of memories of sexual abuse recounted by adult daughters in treatment are the competing claims of parents and clinicians in interpreting those memories of family experience. Survivors who tell their stories do have more cultural support than they have had in the past, and there is a growing challenge to parental authority from the professional community. Standards and expectations for good parenting have risen, and the right of parents to control their children is no longer considered absolute.[40]

Such advances in the recognition of children's rights mobilize tremendous ambivalence in many parents, particularly in a society where parents, and most particularly mothers, are often blamed for the problems and suffering of their children. Indeed, the discourse on the dysfunction of the family that emerged in the 1980s unfolded in a political context of declining institutional supports for children and families. A strong component of the backlash represented by groups like the FMSF not only is against feminism but is also against professional expertise that blames parents without addressing the lack of social and economic supports necessary for good parenting. One can hear in the anguished and angry responses of parents a strain of rivalry with therapists and helplessness over the loyalty therapists seem to inspire in their adult daughters. Beyond the specific allegations of who did what to whom is an outraged conviction that therapists have taken their daughters away from them.

The issue of how therapists influence the process of memory retrieval is a complex one. There is real potential for therapeutic suggestion to mediate the process of both memory retrieval and the weaving of memories into a clinical narrative.[41] But underlying the debate over therapeutic suggestion in recovered memories of sexual abuse is the unsettling question of why adult daughters would come to redefine their relationships with their parents in such a fundamental way.

SCIENCE AND REBELLION

In his historical analysis of shifts in scientific paradigms, Thomas Kuhn argues that rebellion against authority, rather than dispassionate assessment of evidence, is a motivating force in the reshaping of knowledge.[42] While Kuhn understands this rebellion as a response to the failure of old paradigms to adequately explain a set of phenomena, the issue of the emotional side of science may be equally important. And for women, who have emerged more recently as contenders in scientific disputes, the role of emotion in efforts to know has moved to center stage.

How do we reconcile, then, the authoritative position of Dr. Jennifer Freyd, as credentialed scientist, and that of Jennifer as impassioned incest survivor? It is not simply that she, as incest survivor, is less credible than her father, also a credentialed scientist. Jennifer Freyd emphasizes her own professional accomplishments at "one of the world's best psychology departments, especially in the area of cognitive psychology," her chosen field.

For some, Jennifer Freyd's emotionally compelling personal account gives her far more credibility than do her scientific credentials. Many women may silently feel that the account of Jennifer—speaking from the "soft" science of psychology—is more compelling than that of her father—affiliated as he is with the "hard" science of mathematics. Popular movements, including feminism, often mobilize around a suspiciousness toward science. The elite pronouncements of science are warily regarded as attempts to obscure and mystify commonsense experience and power relationships. Often theoretical language, accompanied by charts and graphs, feels removed from the lived realities of its human subject matter.

Jennifer Freyd, like many feminists in contested areas of inquiry, draws on two competing discourses in bridging this gap. The language of science is humanized, brought closer to the drama of lived life, and her own objective distance collapses as she becomes "one of us"—a victim no less silenced than countless other women who lack the authority to speak on professional podiums. Within feminism, this rejection of distance between subject and object—between the authority to define social reality and the objects of social scientific investigation—is a necessary condition for humane, liberated inquiry.[43] Theories inevitably bear the mark of their creators, and our recognition of the subjective side of science inevitably means critiquing the authority that stands behind it.

But how do women, as professionals and scientists, make use of this critique of science and objectivity in reflecting on their own newly acquired authority? Why are personal accounts so much more compelling and believable than scientific ones? And what are the costs in relying too heavily on emotional appeals and female virtue in countering patriarchal traditions, including those within science?

Women have inherited a problem that has haunted science since the Enlightenment. Is it possible to acquire an objective position, unbiased by moral sentiments or assertions of power? This project of striving for an objective position has had a progressive side in countering prejudices and traditional constraints on inquiry. The demand for procedural and consensual rules for assessing knowledge claims democratizes the pursuit of knowledge (at least for those who develop the procedures, learn the rules, and master the discourses of science). The problem, as critics of science point out, is that these very procedures conceal the operations of power, particularly as the claim of dispassionate objectivity, of speaking from a position of "nowhere," obscures those worldviews and social interests guiding various projects of inquiry.

The critiques of science that rocked academia in the 1970s debunked the notion of objectivity and singular versions of reality.[44] Unlike the more recent drift toward postmodernism, with its fixation on uncertainty and the groundlessness of all knowledge claims, the earlier radical critiques of science assumed that there *were* realities to be discovered. The more ideological believed that there was a singular "truth," concealed behind the veil of dominant appearances. But over time the recognition of multiple perspectives—of diverse truths and means of knowing—gained strength as an emerging progressive insight.

This notion of multiple versions of the past can be a limited form of liberal tolerance, however, a mere coexistence of disparate worlds without meaningful engagement. The celebration of multiple perspectives does not equip us, necessarily, in negotiating competing claims or in distinguishing degrees of truth and falsehood. Undoubtedly all scientific theories may be described as discourses or narratives, organized around various "subject positions," but this stance does not provide much in the way of criteria for evaluating the relative validity of various claims.

The aspect of the Enlightenment that unites those who seek knowledge in the laboratory and those who seek it through the barricade is the idea that finding the truth involves real work. It has to be struggled for, and it requires a capacity for conflictive engagement with others and tools for public discourse. But there is an important difference between the vision of the Enlightenment embedded in less politically conscious, "normal" science and the movement (also traceable to the Enlightenment) toward critical thinking and feminist methodology in the

1970s. Many radicals and feminists in academia dismantled the very procedures of science—as well as those of other dominant institutions—by showing how powerful groups and interests create tools to construct a reality in their own image.

In the sexual politics of the 1970s and 1980s, when disputes over sexual abuse claims heated up, social alliances took precedence over procedural approaches to getting at the "truth." One simply adopted the version of events advanced by the least powerful protagonist, on the assumption that social power and deception go hand in hand. Further, it did seem that when those who had been historically silenced began to speak—when women, minorities, and children found their "voice"—their utterances did have the ring of truth. Advancing the notion that "victims always tell the truth" or "children don't lie about sexual abuse" became an important strategy in overturning preexisting prejudices and in claiming public space for unorthodox viewpoints.[45] And, besides, the available evidence for adjudicating sex abuse claims is often inconclusive. In the private operations of power that women know so intimately, psychic scars may be more common than physical ones, aches and pains more frequent than broken bones. And there are few, if any, witnesses at the scene of the crime. So the public rituals enshrined in legal codes seem ill suited for whole classes of personal abuses and harms.

However, social change does bring new vantage points and new technologies for discovering hidden realities. The battered child syndrome in the 1960s, for example, presupposed the development of advanced X-ray technology that permitted detection of small fractures in children.[46] More important than the technology, however, was the readiness to see what was formerly invisible. The social movement for children's rights—born out of feminism and the "youth" movement of the 1960s—created the impetus for such discoveries. Child abuse was not a fact, ready to be revealed through the expanding frontiers of science or technology. Child abuse was a social concept that emerged from the trenches, and it transformed our observations of parent/child interactions.

In the social sciences, procedures for evaluating claims seem crudely suited to emancipatory knowledge. From the perspective of "normal science," a claim is either supported or unsupported by available evidence. It meets the probability criterion—that two events are causally related by more than chance—or it does not. The problem of how facts are socially negotiated and that of multiplicity of meanings require radically new approaches. Even though some research methods have moved in the direction of "context-dependent" knowledge, incorporating multiple determinants of human action and eschewing general laws of human behavior, the process through which individuals become attached to particular causal explanations of their experience remains methodologically elusive.

What we need, in bridging this gap, is a social science of storytelling. How do we construct stories about the past, and what is the role of fantasy and fact in schematic representations of the personal past? How do we convey a sense of urgency to others, and by what means are emotional responses from others mobilized in eliciting support? How is remembering transformed over time, in response to emerging ideals, concepts, and social alliances? These are among the questions pursued throughout this book.

Both sides of the recovered memory debate enlist the authority of science in mobilizing public support, which is not surprising. Contemporary science is a florid enterprise, offering a wide range of models, theories, and research findings. In a commodity-driven society, science easily becomes yet another supermarket where one may pick and choose from a tantalizing array of choices. Since we now know that science is a competitive game and that research findings often have a brief shelf life, the aura of authority that once surrounded this lofty vocation has been diminished. Social movements also appropriate psychological theories in complicated ways. For example, the campaign to define alcoholism as a disease rather than as a form of moral depravity used science to destigmatize a social problem. In the 1980s, a grassroots literature developed based on the concept of codependence as a feminine malady, wedded to the masculine disease of alcoholism.[47]

So, in keeping with such traditions, generational struggles within the U.S. family are currently being framed in terms of competing syndromes. And it is not surprising that the movement to defend those accused of sexual abuse has been particularly effective under the banner of a psychiatric condition. The sputtering successes of Victims of Child Abuse Reporting Laws pale in comparison with those of the FMSF.[48] This "syndrome" and the foundation that launched it have achieved a remarkable legitimacy given the moral weight of child sexual abuse in U.S. culture.

In spite of Jennifer Freyd's impressive academic credentials, she, like so many professional women, is both inside and outside the kingdom. As outsider, she speaks for the many women who continue to struggle with the powerful fathers, both past and present. As survivors, women face tasks that are perennially daunting in a world still run by more powerful men. But, as insiders, we need to reflect on our own exercise of power. It is here that the idea of feminine virtue—the romantic ideal that women are "closer" to the emotional truths of life than are men (even as they more readily veer into hysteria)—creates particular blind spots. And it is here that sweeping, authoritative theories of victimization may conceal key social differences—including differences among women—in what it means to be betrayed or traumatized. But perhaps by acknowledging an inescapable subjectivity and the contradictory positions of insider and outsider women can address both the sometimes illusory objectivity of science and the moral and social conflicts that underlie the enterprise. The repression of emotional conflict is a man's defensive game. Women are less socially suited for it, perhaps, but exalting emotional knowledge is not an effective counterstrategy.

The dilemmas of the memory debate take us to the heart of science. And if women have more heart, we must also investigate its darker side. In dispelling the mysteries surrounding contested remembrances, it is important to reflect on the problematic uses of our own authority, even as we recognize how readily women's authority is displaced by the more culturally sanctioned pronouncements of men.

The rupture of the patriarchal system of social dependence permits women and children to create a new future and, in so doing, to recollect the past with new self-consciousness. In a sense, the memory crisis suggests a period of heightened awareness of the fluctuating aspects of personal identity. More specifically, it is suggestive of a female selfhood in search of its moorings in the past. A crisis implies that the outcome is not fully determined; it is an unsteady state. Both creative and regressive possibilities inhere in this threatening uncertainty.

CONCLUSIONS

Where are we, then, in sorting through the competing claims of the debate? Even if claims of childhood sexual abuse are used and sometimes abused to legitimize female rebellion, it also is the case that sexual abuses have been historically minimized or silenced. Yet this very silencing may infuse sexual abuse allegations with tremendous emotional valency, generating a wide range of psychological, cultural, and political interpretations. By not foreclosing on the question of whom to believe, we may more effectively work through what is at stake for women in this contemporary struggle to be heard. So too, the project of "believing women" is more complex than it might initially appear in that women do not speak with one voice, nor are the communications of women entirely independent of various attendant translators. While women—as mothers, daughters, therapists, and researchers—are no longer silent, passive participants in matters concerning their own lives and well-being, they remain marginalized in many cases and subject to the authoritative pronouncements of others, including those of other women. In taking power into account, it is important to grant increased space for women's vantage point on the past while avoiding the mystification that accompanies feminist mythologizing. Substituting matriarchal legends for patriarchal ones may feel therapeutic, but it doesn't provide a means of separating illusions and realities, nor does it acknowledge the complex currents in women's lives.

The contemporary gender climate in the United States—subsequent to the women's movement of the 1970s—may be characterized as turbulent and labile, with various cultural currents commingling with a diffuse but still palpably present feminist movement. Gender categories and proscriptions have been destabilized, even as they have not been fully overturned. In the context of countervailing cultural forces, transformative remembering, for many women, is a highly ambivalent project, born of an awakened sense of entitlement and possibilities, on the one hand, and persisting inhibitions and constraints on the other. Women's transformative remembering—particularly stories about sexual encounters—map a cultural battlefield with perpetually shifting borders, even as it anticipates yet-to-be-realized possibilities for human freedom.

THE GHOST IN THE MACHINE

Chapter 2

Emotion and the Science of Memory

I REMEMBER MY MOTHER telling me, in a rare moment of sexual candor during my mid-teens, that if a woman is raped, it is better that her assailant "finish the job." It is better to die in honor than to live in shame and emotional ruination, she seemed to be saying. In pondering this prospect, I felt relieved that my own encounters with local perverts had fallen significantly short of rape, sparing me such a suicidal dilemma. Going all the way, especially under the maniacal control of an attacker, was immutably tragic. There were no exceptions. My sensible mother would never utter such pronouncements about other crimes. She would never say, for example, "If a man breaks into your house, it is better that he burn it down." Sexual crimes were in a category of their own, it seemed, one that marked victims more profoundly than other personal violations, one that stubbornly resisted reparation.

Sometime in my early thirties, I asked my mother about this episode, intent on conveying to her the harmfulness of her implicit message. She countered that she could never have said such a foolish thing. Of course, her memories were no more reliable than mine. Further, her fleeting effort to retrieve a memory of our conversation confronted the emotional force of my indignation as well as several intervening decades of tutoring in feminism by her daughters. So while she once may have made such a statement, her current beliefs gave my accusation an alien quality.

She might also be correct, though. My memory may have been fabricated out of the complex web of my own adolescent fears. Mothers undoubtedly are the objects of countless childish fantasies and internal dramas. It seems to be the fate of our first protector that she is held responsible for the dangers and dis-appointments we endure as we venture out into the world. I may have imagined such a conversation with my mother during adolescence—or later, in retro-spect—to produce clear moral vectors out of the vague, diffuse anxieties of ado-lescence. Yet again, I may have crafted a memory that relied on a series of experiences with my mother, the incalculable, small observations of daily life that cumulatively produce a scripted recollection. Countless raised eyebrows and maternal references to "heathens" and worldly dangers may no longer be recalled as discrete events but may still yield a memory. When these schematic representations are made concrete and are transformed into a story, particular-ities are often reintroduced to flesh out and vivify the narrative.

I remember telling this story initially in a women's divorce group in the early 1970s, as many of us were reminiscing about our mothers. While vary-ing in thematic content, many of the reminiscences served as cautionary tales about the traps set for us in the course of female development. In my own case, I was proud of my capacity to discard my mother's fears of the world—much as I had discarded my girdle a decade prior. My mother lived in a world where women were captive, at the mercy of dark forces beyond their control. Having marched out of domestic confinement, including a recent marriage, I felt bold, sustained by the power of sisterhood, and I had an exhilarating new sense of potency.

Other feminist contexts of memory retrieval might make different use of this memory/fantasy to yield other truths. These contexts illustrate the murky ground where factual and interpretive aspects of memory often converge. Taking the con-versation at face value, many contemporary feminists would assign a political meaning to it, providing a less psychological cast to this mother/daughter encounter, one that would likely prompt further associations of a similar sort. They would agree with my mother's assessment of sexual assault, seeing in her pronouncement a commonplace reality. Sex can be deadly for women, and the freedoms of sexual ventures are easily offset by their considerable risks. Women are readily branded as "damaged goods," even as their male sexual partners escape retribution. My mother's statement simply conveys this sexual code, one not of her own making. Implicitly, she is protectively alerting her daughter to a world of sexual predation and unequal consequences.

From yet another feminist perspective, my mother's cautionary admoni-tion would illustrate the repressive legacy of mother/daughter relationships. The mother, who must rein in her own impulses and curb her own sexual plea-sure, imposes similar constraints on her daughter. "Catastrophizing" conveys the message that the dangers of the world cannot be successfully negotiated. Although growing up and learning from life require some capacity to take risks, maternal anxiety can flood daughters in a way that inhibits exploration of sexual, social, and intellectual possibilities. The mother, as much as the father, can be associ-ated with the administration of rituals intended to achieve this domestication of female curiosity. While maternal fears and inhibitions may well be the result of a patriarchal legacy, the mother can be an active agent in their intergenerational transmission and thus the immediate object of the daughter's rebellious wrath.

Over time, each of these renditions of a memory can assume some importance, providing a new level of insight. The truth of the memory is intimately related to how it is deployed and to the emotional and social meanings that are evoked in the telling and retelling of it. It is in the nature of human storytelling—particularly those stories we tell about ourselves to communicate self-knowledge—that memorable events achieve dramatic force and contain a rich multiplicity of interpretive possibilities.

While this notion of multiple meanings contained in memory is a common theme in literature, it has been at odds with much of the research tradition of psychology. This chapter looks back on the history of scientific inquiry into memory and at what this history can tell us about socially contested recollections. In looking back, I explore the personal side of scientific inquiry and how social alliances and philosophical assumptions shape which accounts of the past are more readily believed. Further, I show how the uneasy marriage of emotion and cognition in the study of memory is embedded in broad social conflicts over gender and is mediated as well by historical shifts in the participation of women in scientific conversations about memory.

SCIENTIFIC INVESTIGATION OF MEMORY

How may the scientific investigation of memory help us settle the dispute between my mother and me over our competing memories? The answer to this question depends on which science of memory we employ—for there are many methods, theories, and findings from which to choose. Further, it raises a related question of how we apply scientific findings to a particular case—how we move from statistical analysis of aggregate findings to the vagaries and specificities of individual life experience.

In *Rewriting the Soul,* philosopher Ian Hacking argues that both sides in the contemporary recovered memory debate rely on the "sciences of memory" that emerged in the late nineteenth century.[1] The sciences of memory, according to Hacking, intervene in the project of preserving the past by substantivizing the hidden, the secret, and translating it into publicly verifiable knowledge. While religion similarly holds the power of explicating the ineffable—the mysterious, the ambiguous, the uncertain—science bridges, even transgresses, this realm of uncertainty in a more radical way. Whereas religion stirs awe before the ineffable, science is essentially antihypnotic in its aim, committed to a project of dispelling the aura of impenetrable mystery surrounding human experience. Both sides of the contemporary memory debate appropriate the authority of science in making public claims concerning private knowledge. Science presupposes a knowable, verifiable "truth" that is open to impartial scrutiny. Whether it takes the form of calling for increasingly reliable tests of memory, summoning charts documenting the neurological effects of trauma, or outlining procedures for avoiding the contamination of memory, the dominant discourse in the war over family recollections, as I suggested in the previous chapter, is a scientific one.

If we grant that science can answer many questions of great human concern, how do we recognize defensive uses of science? Are we able to detect the distinction between illuminating and concealing operations of science, either in its basic operations or in its social applications? Scientists are more equipped than laypersons to identify cheaters, but they may suffer from a certain myopia of their own. While it is important to distinguish between bad science and good science in the sense of how carefully it complies with procedural rules, even solid scientific findings may serve as defensive armor in various unacknowledged struggles over power and authority.[2]

For Hacking, the "deep structure" of the memory controversy is more philosophical than empirical, more fundamentally tied to ingrained cultural ambivalences over psychology's role in secularizing the "soul" than to the technical claims of various contestants. In navigating these cultural currents, Hacking observes that "when life seems parlous and a Western society is about to fall apart, there is a great talk of reviving the soul in its various manifestations, and if not the soul, then the values of the family."[3] However conjured, the soul signifies what is felt to be the stable, enduring core of human existence.

The "soul" that is lost, recovered, and rewritten throughout the history of the sciences of memory, I would argue, is not an abstract, ineffable essence but, rather, is related to those domains of life most intimately associated with women. Western dualisms that counterpose science and art, rationality and emotion, head and heart are deeply inscribed with gender associations.[4] But these oppositional categories are quite dynamic—in the study of memory as elsewhere—and have been subject to various challenges not only by feminists but by other critics of Western thought.

Recovering the "soul" of the sciences of memory, then, means engaging emotion, the body, the familial—areas of life most linked with the feminine. Even though men, like women, have bodies, emotions, and families, these dimensions of experience have been culturally coded predominantly as feminine. The psychology of the unconscious—with its dramatic plots, secret motives, and disguised communications—has an unmistakable affinity with female psychology. Located at the margins of public life and "hidden from history," female psychic spaces are, in fantasy and in reality, socially constructed as domains of concealed knowledge. And as later chapters make clear, this equation of femaleness with veiled knowledge is open to various social and political uses.

Many feminists regard science warily because its claim of objectivity so readily conceals the politics of truth telling and the social dynamics of knowledge production.[5] As feminist psychology expanded its domain of inquiry into family secrets in the 1970s and 1980s, the problem of how private knowledge is converted into public, verifiable findings reached a new level of crisis. One response within feminist inquiry has been to reject science in favor of the personal narrative, which is embraced as closer to "women's ways of knowing." But the jettisoning of science is a costly strategy, just as is an uncritical belief in its social autonomy or revelatory powers.

Models and Metaphors

While a dizzying array of methods and theories circulates in the contemporary memory debate, two competing models are discernible. The first of these—often termed the *storehouse model* or the *old model*—conceives of memory as discrete mental images accumulated over time and subject to decay or erosion.[6] The second of these two prototypes may be described as the *storyteller approach*—the *new model* in that it places memory processes in the context of narratives and social relationships. This approach tends to focus on constellations of preserved knowledge—on how things "hook together"—rather than on constituent elements of memory.[7]

Human interest in the capacities and vulnerabilities of memory has an ancient history, as does interest in enhancing the accuracy of memory. The storehouse model has roots in earlier Western traditions but has a particular affinity with highly competitive, acquisitive societies. Much like capital accumulation, acquired and preserved memory products circulate within a competitive realm of exchange. One image that comes to mind is of the quiz shows of the 1950s and 1960s—fantastic displays of youths with encyclopedic memories reeling off facts with rapid-fire speed. Currents of anxiety over Cold War competition were palpable in these quiz-kid memory performances, as well as jolts of optimism over the prospects of advancement through self-improvement.

Within psychology, the storehouse model of memory operates far less crudely or propagandistically for the most part. The enduring strength of the model, in spite of a long history of critiques, is related to methodological traditions, specifically to the influence of logical positivism. The positivist tradition—the dominant paradigm in social science research—is based on procedural rules for testing the correspondence between a construct and an external or observable phenomenon. This tradition assumes that there is an objective reality that can be established and consensually verified, independent of the subjectivity of observers. While most researchers recognize a distinction between factual claims and interpretive ones, the interdependence of observer and observed tends to be minimized in positivist research. A second principle associated with positivism is that of atomism—breaking reality down into small units disembedded from the system of human meanings and signifiers in which these units operate. In this tradition, a simple, classical memory test might involve presenting a list of words to a subject and later asking how many of these words he or she can recall. While translating research questions into manageable, operationalized variables permits a degree of consensual agreement over the terms of inquiry, it leaves much of what matters about memory behind, like psychic debris on the floor of the laboratory.[8]

We do not want to respond to this methodological narrowing of attention, however, by discarding over a century of experimental research on memory. For one thing, memory research has advanced in far more complex directions than its earliest iterations. Further, the experimental research tradition provides a means of assessing the independent contribution of various factors influencing memory processes, a means of discerning trees within the surrounding forests. Rather than rejecting experimental findings, we want to create a dialogue between various modes of inquiry, attending as well to the metaphorical conventions and social interests underlying authoritative claims of various sorts. From this vantage point, experimental psychology loses its claim of social autonomy and takes a more modest place as one protagonist among many in the conversation about human memory.

As an insistent subtext throughout this history of scientific inquiry into memory, the storytelling model of memory is, itself, periodically remembered and forgotten. The storytelling approach includes a loose cluster of rebellious currents in the field of memory research, particularly those aimed at restoring the human project of meaning making to the inquiry into memory. Emotion, human relationships, and social schema are recurring themes in storytelling traditions, themes that introduce ambiguity and indeterminacy to the research enterprise.

If the storehouse approach has circulated more easily than the storyteller model in the marketplace of ideas, it is because the knowledge it generates lends itself to marketplace practices. The German psychologist Hermann Ebbinghaus is a progenitor of this tradition of laboratory research, with all of its considerable promise and limitations. Mindful of the socially embedded nature of recall, Ebbinghaus devised during the 1880s a method for investigating pure memory, separated from prior knowledge. By studying rote recall of nonsense syllables, Ebbinghaus determined, for example, that the rate of forgetting increases as time intervals between encoding and retrieval widen.[9] The laboratory tradition of Ebbinghaus became paradigmatic in the field, not simply because of its merits within an abstract enterprise of expanding human knowledge or its "masculinist bias" but because of its compatibility with the driving force behind Western industrialism. Throughout much of the twentieth century, experimentalism and behaviorism defined the subject matter of psychology as a discipline, focusing on observable, measurable "units" of responses. As the father of American behaviorism, Robert Watson, stated, the purpose of psychology is to "render serviceable predictions" about "what the human machine is good for."[10]

From the beginning of the sciences of memory, however, there were dissident tendencies in the field. William James, who established the first psychology laboratory in the United States in the 1870s, sardonically described the new scientific discipline's unease with emotion. Beginning with the "internal shadings of emotional feeling" that "merge endlessly into each other," James concludes that "the result of all this flux is that the merely descriptive literature of the emotions is one of the most tedious parts of psychology. And not only is it tedious, but you feel that its subdivisions are to a great extent either fictitious or unimportant, and that its pretenses to accuracy are a sham."[11] While James does not develop a social theory of emotion, he does make central the role of the body in emotional life. The then-prevailing view was that psychological events occur within a temporal sequence moving from sensation to perception, cognition, emotion and finally to bodily arousal. James short-circuits the model by arguing that bodily changes follow directly from "the perception of the exciting fact."[12] Without specifying what makes particular facts "exciting," James is making the still rather unorthodox claim that the body in a sense "teaches" us what it is we feel. We learn to scan and read bodily cues as a means of interpreting our responses to situations.

Rediscovering Emotion in Cognitive Psychology

The dominance of behaviorism in academic psychology throughout much of the twentieth century displaced theories and methods that focused on mind and consciousness. The storytelling model of memory—which approaches preserved knowledge as relational and oriented toward "hooking things together" through narratives—was placed outside the domain of scientific inquiry and within the more ambiguous, "speculative" domain of the humanities. There were important exceptions—for example, in the work of British psychologist Sir Frederic Bartlett in the 1930s. In his classic text, *Remembering,* Bartlett describes his research on the telling and retelling of an old Indian legend entitled "The War of the Ghosts."[13] Bartlett's work on how current emotional needs and social expectations modify the content of the story over time has been more recently "recovered" in the revival of interest in the reconstructive and social aspects of remembering. Mary Douglas, for example, makes use of Bartlett's work to illustrate the perpetual remembering and forgetting in the field of scientific psychology of the social embeddedness of its own subject matter. Turning the scientific "gaze" back onto the investigator, Douglas asserts that "as soon as they [psychologists] know it, they forget it."[14]

In the 1970s, there was an awakening of interest in the storytelling model of memory, but this fledgling development did not emerge in full force until the 1980s and, in neuroscience, until the 1990s.[15] With the revival of cognitive psychology, the mind came back into fashion as a legitimate topic of psychological investigation. Much of the cognitive revolution simply transferred behavioral categories to the study of mind, however, without rethinking the models themselves. Mind and consciousness remained chained to a discourse of discrete events, stimulus-response relationships, and manipulation of variables. Emotion, human relationships, and language remained peripheral players in the theater of consciousness.

In the 1980s, a strong resurgence of interest in the study of emotion shook the world of cognitive psychology and memory research. The work of neurologist and cognitive scientist Antonio Damasio, inspired by the writings of James, is an example of this revolt against dispassionate models of cognition and memory.[16] Damasio begins his critique by stating the classical position: "upstairs in the cortex there is reason and willpower, while downstairs in the subcortex there is emotion and all that weak, fleshy stuff." Without turning this house entirely upside down, Damasio does reconfigure the theorizing in ways that challenge cherished assumptions: "the neocortex becomes engaged *along with* the older brain core and rationality results from their concerted activity" (Damasio's emphases).[17]

Much like theologians arguing over whether Eve was created out of Adam's rib—and by extension suffered the fate of becoming a companionable helpmate or an absolute subject—cognitive psychologists wrestle uneasily with the dependence of higher-order human qualities on their lower-order ancestors. And, similarly, we may suspect that making emotion and cognition equal partners does not level the playing field as much as it would seem. Indeed, research continues to examine the question of whether emotion helps or hinders cognition rather than the obverse, companion question of whether cognition helps or hinders the capacity to feel. I return to this topic later.

Damasio also revisits the old debate over the relationship of emotion to the body, a debate framed in James's time as a question of whether emotion was derived from cognition—the "higher" functions—or from bodily responses—the "lower" functions. James came down on the side of the body, presumably in reaction to the overvaluation of rationality in the field of psychology. The question of whether there was a detectable residue of "pure" emotion, uncontaminated by bodily sensations, was a dominating one of James's day, a question resonating with Victorian sensibilities.[18]

In a field heavily influenced by Darwinian theory since the late nineteenth century, psychologists have traditionally stressed the functional aspects of emotions in fight/flight or other such defensive responses. From this perspective, emotions have adaptive value for the organism, particularly in preparing the body for action. Yet moving from primitive fight/flight or fear responses to the more variegated and subtle emotional capacities that humans acquire in the course of development creates a quandary. In mapping this complexity, Damasio argues that feelings are the conscious manifestation—the experiential result—of a vast network of bodily activity.[19]

One of the attendant controversies involves how we understand the laws underlying the interactions of these complex derivatives of bodily states with mental processes. Once we move from a simple, autonomic conditioning model—for example, Pavlov's pairing of a new stimulus (ringing a bell) with an old one (food) in conditioning a natural response (salivation) in dogs—the array of potential associations between bodily reactions and mental activity becomes immense and unwieldy. The vast number of possible permutations and the ambiguity of underlying natural laws traditionally made psychologists afraid to introduce emotion into their models. The interjection of body and emotion into the study of properties of mind implies an irreducible indeterminacy to consciousness. While fight/flight responses and autonomic conditioning undoubtedly explain some emotional reactions, the origin of much of human affective responsivity is less decisively located. Scientific psychology's anxiety over the messy aspects of bodily sensations that impinge on consciousness is rooted in Western ideals concerning control over the body and anxiety over the dependencies and uncertainties it evokes. Implicitly, Damasio is responding to an ancient fear in Western psychology: once the threshold for diffuse bodily sensations is lowered and emotion floods the research field as a legitimate scientific enterprise, cognition will be drowned in the noisy emissions that result. Impassioned researchers, it is implied, may no longer be able to think amidst all the racket.

In many respects, the debate over memory that came to dominate psychology in the early 1990s was, at base, a debate over emotional distress and other conditions with ambiguous origins. Cognitive psychology intervened to adjudicate competing claims because it seemed to carry the promise of counteracting some of the hysterical reactions surrounding contested sexual memories. But cognitive perspectives tended to "overcontain" the distressing dimensions of the debate by stripping memory of its phenomenological and social symbolic character. The tendency to adopt highly operationalized models of memory permitted investigators to subvert the legacy of phobic attitudes toward emotion, but it also missed much of what was at stake for various participants.[20]

Take, for example, the work of Joseph LeDoux.[21] In demonstrating that emotional responses are integral to a broad range of brain functions, LeDoux implicitly refuses the split between emotion and reason, as well as the placement of emotion within a lower-order (feminine) domain of mind.[22] Yet his focus on locating emotional states, primarily fear, in brain structures bypasses the more vexing problem of how such states are converted into narrative memory. LeDoux's rehabilitation of emotion within cognitive science is achieved through a depersonalized, technocratic discourse of "embodied thought."

This effort to objectify more ambiguous aspects of mind is as noticeable in the trauma literature as it is in the experimental literature, where objectification similarly slides into reification. Bessel van der Kolk, for example, a leading theorist in the trauma field, tends to cite physiological measures—such as changes in the amygdala and biochemistry in the brain—to demonstrate the corporeal validity of psychic trauma.[23] A number of studies do report such effects associated with psychological trauma.[24] Yet van der Kolk's argument that trauma memory is stored in "primitive" areas of the brain, as sensorimotor traces rather than as narrative memory, sidesteps the difficult issue of how such "nonmemory" of trauma is converted into conscious recollections. In enlisting biological models to concretize disturbing mental imagery, van der Kolk turns a blind eye to the social influences mediating their resurrection and transfiguration in consciousness.

Implicit Memory in Cognitive Psychology

As clinicians argued about the factual accuracy of "delayed," or "recovered," memory in the late 1980s and early 1990s, researchers were embroiled in a parallel set of disputes over the very nature and stability of human memory. In clinical settings and in laboratory research, the problem of divisions and subdivisions in the mind's access to knowledge was a central motif. Memory discourse broke lose from its moorings in the Western ideal of the imperial, unified mind.

Yet there was a déjà vu aspect to this "great awakening." In drawing a parallel with the late nineteenth century, psychologist Daniel Schacter describes the 1980s as the Golden Age of memory research—particularly in the study of implicit memory, or "nonconscious," unintentional types of retained knowledge.[25] Much of the heat generated in this Golden Age involved arguments over new categories. But beneath the rather obsessive project of classifying memory subsystems, or "modules," was a profound shift in thinking: the concept of the unconscious, which had been banished from scientific psychology for much of the twentieth century, had been recovered as a legitimate concept.

The "cognitive unconscious" was quite different from the Freudian or dynamic one—an issue taken up in the next chapter—but the growing scientific interest in latent aspects of mind had the effect of relegitimizing the psychodynamic unconscious. As Elizabeth Loftus and Mark Klinger put it, the question was no longer one of whether there was an unconscious but, rather, whether it was "smart or dumb."[26] The Dumb Unconscious (the one preferred by many cognitive psychologists) was much like a factory worker carrying out boring, routine tasks. The Smart Unconscious (the one preferred by many clinicians) evoked the more romantic image of the storyteller or artist, subverting conventional consciousness from below.[27] Since femininity and the unconscious have a longstanding affinity in Western psychology, it is not surprising that many women sided with the smart version, particularly as the debate came to center on disturbing sexual recollections.

Implicit memory bears some similarity to the notion of classical conditioning in learning theory—the acquired association of a response with a cue that precedes it, a habitual response to a stimulus. For example, the subject may experience nausea in response to some food without any knowledge that such learning was acquired because eating that food preceded a bout of illness in the past. Similarly, a child who has been repeatedly beaten may bolt when approached from behind without knowing why. While classical-conditioning principles could be applied to lower- and higher-order animals alike, the idea of implicit memory had the effect of "upgrading" mental processes that occurred outside conscious awareness by demonstrating their complexity.

The experimentally derived concept of implicit memory has been appropriated by clinicians in explaining a much broader range of phenomena than its experimental progenitors intended it to explain. In the 1993 "Statement on Memories of Sexual Abuse," published by the American Psychiatric Association in response to the recovered memory controversy, implicit memory is described as the mechanism underlying various "nonconscious" mental phenomena. "A child who demonstrates knowledge of a skill (e.g., bicycle riding) without recalling how he/she learned it, an adult who has an affective reaction to an event without understanding the basis for that reaction (e.g., a combat veteran who panics when he hears the sound of a helicopter, but cannot remember that he was in a helicopter crash which killed his best friend) are demonstrating implicit memories in the absence of explicit recall."[28]

WOMEN AND MEMORY RESEARCH

Psychological inquiry in the 1980s did come to parallel, in many respects, the tumultuous debates over memory of a century ago, when the specter of divided consciousness—the dissociations implicit in hysteria, amnesia, hypnosis, and dual personality—mesmerized psychologists and psychiatrists. (See chapters 6 and 7.) And in both eras, intense disputes over terminology and nomenclature—over naming things—obscured a deeper social crisis over the nature and continuity of the self.

But the contemporary cast of characters differs in an important respect from its turn-of-the-century counterpart: women now play a leading role in public life, including within science. And while women make use of the same models, theories, and methods as do men, women are more likely to concentrate in the labor-intensive, lower-status areas of the professions, those closer to everyday human concerns.[29] Further, women scientists, like other women in the workforce, often differ from their male colleagues in that they lead "dual" lives. The boundary between private and public, family and work, is more permeable for women, exacerbated by the cultural ideal that women's work must be "interruptible." Interestingly enough, one of the few enduring findings in psychology that approaches "lawfulness"—the Zeigarnik effect—was documented by a woman in the 1920s; the German psychologist Bluma Zeigarnik reported that interrupted tasks were more likely to be remembered than were uninterrupted ones.[30]

It has long been noted that clinical inquiry in the area of recovered memory was deeply influenced by the women's movement. Yet the question of how this same social movement may have shaped experimental and cognitive psychology is less often examined. Until the 1970s, women were a small minority within the professions and particularly within the "hard-science" research wing of both psychology and psychiatry. A wave of women professionals was trained in the 1920s, following the earlier feminist movement. But women's entry in significant numbers into laboratory and experimental research—the most "masculinized" of the psychological disciplines—has been far more recent, similarly the result of an era of activist feminism.[31]

While it is difficult to decisively separate the influence of women from other social influences on a field, it is likely that the influx of women into cognitive psychology did contribute to the more animated, emotionally engaged models of memory that accompanied their arrival on the scene. I am referring here to an aggregate effect of gender on the field, including broader cultural awarenesses brought about by feminism that may impinge "implicitly" on investigators

and on the articulation of new models. It is important to remember that investigators, much like their scientific subjects, may have a propensity to forget the
context of their own discoveries. As feminist scholars so frequently point out,
women, particularly, tend to be forgotten as a source of male knowledge.[32]

Even as emotion achieved new respectability in memory research in the 1970s
and 1980s, there remained a palpable wariness in approaching this ancient
nemesis of cognition.[33] Unlike the literary or narrative turns within feminist
inquiry, some of which have been hostile to science, functioning within the procedural rules of science required different strategies. Marcia Johnson introduced
the term *experimental phenomenology* to describe the bridging of the subjective and
objective dimensions of remembering.[34] But within the highly methodological
milieu of experimentalism, emotion remained the junior partner of cognition.
One of the central debates involved whether emotion hinders or enhances
memory, either during the original encoding of events or in their later retrieval.
While many studies demonstrated that emotion—both positive and negative—
enhances the vividness and intricacy of recollections, there was less agreement
on whether emotionality leads to more or less accurate memories.[35]

What is striking about the debate at this juncture is the shift in metaphors
of memory as emotion comes out of the scientific closet. The entry of emotion
into scientific discourse did subvert conventional beliefs about the stability of
mind and its processes. As we have seen, the most dominant tendency in cognitive psychology and memory research traditionally had been to omit emotion
or to view it as epiphenomenal—that is, derivative of more primary psychological
processes, such as fight/flight and fear responses. Further, in much memory
research, productionist metaphors continued to prevail, perpetuating the old view
that the mind is machinelike in its propensity for efficiency. As computer analogies for memory came into vogue, the mind was conceived as a "global work-
place," where memory subsystems in the brain operated much like assembly-line
workers, freeing higher-level "executives" from routine tasks.[36]

But as researchers moved into the terrain of establishing the positive role of
emotion in cognitive memory, new images of mind were born. While earlier generations of memory researchers bound to the storehouse model employed the
metaphors of the file cabinet and library to capture the bureaucratic orderliness
of the mind, the interjection of emotion into the research field seems to have generated a poetic turn. Even as many cognitive psychologists were captured by computer analogies, others created a profusion of Romantic metaphors in vivifying
and analogizing how the mind retains knowledge. Schacter, for example, draws
on the work of abstract painter Cheryl Warrick, who "treats the canvas as a
metaphor for memory itself, building up layers of paint that visually represent
the layers of everyday experience that accumulate in our minds."[37]

The work of Loftus, an FMSF ally as well as a leading memory researcher, illustrates the contradictory impulses and changing metaphors in the contemporary
field of memory research. As a key protagonist in the recovered memory debate,
Loftus is an actor on the cultural stage, much as are Pamela and Jennifer Freyd.

(See chapter 1.) In approaching Loftus's scientific work as a cultural text, this section explores specifically her use of transitional metaphors. On the one hand, her work is an extension of the traditional view that emotion hinders memory accuracy and cognitive processes. On the other hand, she employs "feminine" metaphors, breaking from mechanistic conventions in the field. Unlike her predecessors, Loftus permits more "hysteria" to leak into her model: "like curious, playful children searching through drawers for a blouse or pair of pants, our brains seem to enjoy ransacking the memory drawers, tossing the facts about, and then stuffing everything back in, oblivious to order or importance."[38] This transitional metaphor preserves the idea of memory as a storehouse—a chest of drawers—while introducing images of an animated messiness. If the brain is like an unruly child, however, it also imposes a certain maternal order onto the mess. Carrying domestic metaphors of memory further, Loftus concludes that "we interpret the past, correcting ourselves, adding bits and pieces, deleting uncomplimentary or disturbing recollections, sweeping, dusting, tidying things up" (20).

While this domestic imagery has an innocence about it, Loftus also stresses its darker side, as she shifts from "cleaning up" to the more sinister idea that "we are innocent victims of our mind's manipulations" (21). Emotion is the master of mental tricks, and it often impairs memory. The brain doesn't function well when it is hit by the lightning bolt of emotion, "shutting down electrical signals and scrambling the memory drawers" (189). The imagery of an electrical storm invading a prior state of innocent chaos has its parallel in the notion of "implanted memory" employed by the FMSF and its professional allies. Under the right conditions—sufficient emotional arousal, confusion, social isolation, or interrogation—people will accept even wildly bizarre ideas and incorporate them into autobiographical memory. Loftus's research has demonstrated that under these same conditions original memories can be overwritten by later revisions that permanently abolish the original mental record. It would seem that malevolent bystanders can take advantage of children at play by getting into their "memory drawers."

While Loftus's research tells a compelling story of the malleability of memory and its vulnerability to social influences, a story supported by other contemporary research findings, there is a strong current of realism in her theorizing.[39] The fidelity of memory to some original scene—which is assumed to be essentially "true" and unproblematic—is the dominant interest; emotional and social variables are introduced as factors that weaken or impair memory. There is also an implicit individualism in this model, in its counterposing of the individual mind and the compromising effects of the social field. The potential for social influences to enhance or potentiate memory in positive ways and the importance of group support in the preservation of collective forms of remembering are missing in this line of research.[40]

Even though Loftus's research does not explore the positive impact of social influences on memory, it does carry an implicit critique of institutional authority, one that registers some sensitivity to oppression. Her work on eyewitness accounts has been enormously important in challenging police procedures and, more recently, mental health interview protocols for obtaining corroborating evidence and for evaluating eyewitness testimony. Interviewers, Loftus has demonstrated, often introduce demand characteristics, unconsciously priming the respondent and reworking the memory. Under conditions of hypnosis or with the use of "memory-enhancement" techniques such as guided imagery, subjects may be less able to separate fact from fantasy, memory from suggestion. New accounts of past events can be constructed that are experienced with the emotional conviction of true memory.[41]

Loftus's work does mirror the thinking on the other side of the memory blockades, however, by holding to the idea of a primary truth, hidden beneath the smoke of memory deception. Whether this primary, original experience is viewed as "recoverable" is a crucial area of difference. But beyond this difference, critics and defenders of recovered memory share a common tendency to focus on memory deceivers on the other side of the fence. In her advocacy work for the FMSF, Loftus does not address social influences and cultural scripts that may shape parents' recollections of past events, such as interactions with other parents or with professionals. The local authorities—whether parents, therapists, or other "experts"—may seem more believable and benign than the foreign ones as each side projects onto the other the problematic aspects of its own emotional allegiances and social influences. For social scientists, the larger issue may be how we understand the cultural fabric of remembering and how representations of the past are mobilized for varying social ends.

STORIED MEMORIES

The further one moves from classical, laboratory tests of simple memory tasks to personally meaningful events with complex narrative structures and motivational properties, the less adequate is the old storehouse model. In the recent literature on autobiographical memory, the recall of factual events becomes intertwined with imaginative processes. Yet the new doctrine that memory is "reconstructive" rather than "reproductive" introduces a radical uncertainty into the scientific study of memory. Once judgments about the correctness of memory shift from its direct correspondence to an external event to the idea of reconstructive processes, the project of scientific psychology seems to lose its footing as an enterprise distinctly separate from the humanities.

Working against the current of research in the 1980s that stressed the unreliability of memory were investigators who preserved the idea that autobiographical recall does retain a general fidelity to actual events. As Schacter points out, memory systems have evolved to preserve information quite reliably for the most part, even though these systems are demonstrably error-prone.[42] The pioneering work of Ulric Neisser tended to be cited as a counterforce to extreme reconstructivism, even though he was very much part of the reconstructivist turn.[43]

In the early 1980s, Neisser introduced a distinction between verbatim recall of conversations, on the one hand, and, on the other, "gist" and "repisodic" remembering, which refer to the ability to recall the underlying ideas or themes of a conversation. This distinction suggested a middle ground between the poles of true and false accounts of external events, even though it failed to satisfy either side in the controversy that emerged concerning recovered childhood memories. In the late 1980s and early 1990s, deciding on the "gist" of sexual abuse memories confronted a thicket of problems, particularly as these memories came to be adjudicated in the legal arena.

Through different investigative routes, however, many clinicians and researchers arrived at a common discovery: emotion and autobiographical memory have a natural affinity because the art of storytelling depends so heavily on dramatization and the use of affective cues. A good storyteller is able to create a mood and arouse emotional interest and to present an animated account of events. Even when an event is understood to be autobiographical—that is, factually true—there is a certain social license for elaboration and dramatic emphasis in transforming personal experience into an emotionally compelling tale.[44]

While some researchers have upset the conventions of the field by asserting that all memory is storytelling,[45] others remain faithful to the positivist paradigm, carving out a role for emotion and storytelling within the methodological conventions of the discipline. Roger Brown and James Kulik's "flashbulb studies," first published in 1977, illustrate this positivist trend and the blind spots of many memory researchers who venture into collective storytelling.[46] Among other questions, subjects were asked where they were when they learned of John F. Kennedy's assassination—a publicly verifiable event with a similar emotional impact on large numbers of people. Brown and Kulik found that most people held vivid memories of where they were at the time. In other words, emotion heightened the vividness of memory. Emotion allows the organism to produce memory for long-term storage—a mechanism the researchers termed "Print Now!"—since learning from even single events can be vital to survival.

While they rehabilitate emotion within the field of memory research, Brown and Kulik achieve this victory by overly concretizing emotionally vivid remembrances, reducing them to mere snapshots. Just as the concept of implicit memory was transmuted into the idiom of body memory in clinical discourse, the research on flashbulb memories seemed to legitimize the clinical concept of flashbacks—of vivid, mental imagery associated with past traumatic events. Not surprisingly, most research does show that emotional events are remembered better than are neutral ones, particularly over a long period of time.[47] Yet emotionally vivid events do not necessarily produce accurate memories. Indeed, even the posttraumatic flashbacks of Vietnam veterans are not so much a reliving of actual combat experiences as they are a convergence of anxieties, fantasies, and factual occurrences.[48]

Underlying this discourse on emotion and the mental traffic in memory is the idea that forgetting can be as important as remembering.[49] Contrary to the commonly held belief that most registered experiences are preserved "somewhere deep in the mind," one of the most durable findings in the past hundred years of memory research is that much memory is permanently lost over time. There is an adaptive aspect to human forgetfulness. If we were able to recall too much of the past, it would fail to take on the quality of distant, faded experience that no longer requires immediate attention.

COLLECTIVE STORYTELLING

There is an alternative way of approaching the seeming human tendency toward error-proneness in evaluating the accuracy of autobiographical remembrances, for both the subject and for listeners. It may be that judging the authenticity and genuineness of the storyteller is more important, in many human contexts, than is the factual accuracy of the story. Many of the scientific examples illustrating the reliability of memory systems focus on physical objects and properties of the environment.[50] But social interactions require different forms of remembering and different strategies for communicating retained knowledge. Stories are important forms of interpersonal exchange, conveying information about internal concerns and desires even as they stimulate states of mind in the listener. Since emotional cues serve such important attachment functions, the motivational intents behind a story may assume greater importance than does its correspondence to actual events.[51]

In the 1970s and 1980s, a number of psychologists departed decisively from the conventions of the field—from the view of memory as a lawful, biological substrate of individual minds—and began to situate the activity of remembering in social contexts and narrative practices. Jerome Bruner describes the cognitive revolution in psychology as opening up more uncertain, unstable areas of mind, less readily incorporated into scientific models of lawfulness. He comments that "the essential self gave way to the conceptual self with hardly a shot fired."[52] Yet the debate over whether recovered memories are "true" or "false" may be a delayed effect of this revolution—the shot that was finally fired as skirmishes in the discipline gave way to open combat.

Within this more recent narrative turn in psychology,[53] few theorists have addressed issues of power and domination in storytelling, even though there is some recognition that a distribution of "storytelling rights" often structures social narration.[54] Peggy Miller argues that contemporary storytelling approaches to memory continue to neglect the cultural scaffolding of transmitted accounts of experience. She notes, for example, that working-class and poor parents are less likely than middle-class parents to "censor" stories of emotionally charged experiences, such as fights or wife beatings, because such stories are understood to convey to children the extreme hardship of life and strategies of survival.[55] Building and sharing a common stock of stories is the basis of affilial ties, establishing vital markers of personal identity and group inclusion.[56] As family therapists frequently note, the stories families tell reveal a mythic past of ideals, hopes, and fears as much as they do a historical one. Not all family members participate equally in the creation of "cobiographical" memories, however, so we may want to attend carefully to whose stories get told, as I do in subsequent chapters.

Efforts are being made within the scientific margins of the memory controversy to understand social-motivational aspects of remembering. David Middleton and Derek Edwards, for example, introduce the concept of the rhetorical organization of remembering and forgetting, which is "about contested pasts and plausible accounts of who is to blame, or to be excused, acknowledged, praised, honored, thanked, trusted and so on, that occur as part of the pragmatics of everyday conversation."[57] Once again, these observations suggest that inferences concerning underlying motivations may be more important in everyday assessments of memory than is the fidelity of the report to a past event.

Subversive Stories

One of the interesting aspects of the collective memory of the Kennedy assassination, hovering in the shadows of the flashbulb studies, is the motif of distrust of official storytelling.[58] Insurgent movements, throughout history, have had an affinity with the idea that the hidden story is more truthful than is the publicly authorized one. While narrative approaches to memory often draw on the idea of social scripts in storytelling, they pay little attention to resistances to official stories. As the Kennedy assassination so vividly demonstrates (and as we have found in the vitriolic debate over interpretations of clinically recovered memories), cultural accounts are not simply passively absorbed by a captive populace, nor are all authoritative "scripts" equally endorsed.

The proliferation of Kennedy-assassination conspiracy theories suggests that memories of emotionally powerful events can take on a life of their own as they move from the limited context carved out by the flashbulb studies (memory for place and circumstance in learning of an emotional event) to that of making meaning of disturbing knowledge. Jerome Bruner argues that this most important problem in human psychology—how we make meaning out of experiences—remains peripheral to psychological research, in part because meanings, in the broadest sense, go beyond a mere correspondence between an external object and its representation in mind to include complex imaginative, constructive properties of mental life.[59] Bruner suggests that distressing or arousing experiences "demand" a story, and that imposing a narrative structure on emotionally charged or salient events is a means of managing them. Our emotions serve as triggers or cues, prompting us to continue to attend to a situation until a mental "gestalt," or schema, is fully formed. Further, emotional events elicit psychological interpretations—speculations on motives, states of mind, as well as potential consequences and courses of action.[60]

Memory researchers have failed to complete the gestalt of the particular collective memory problem of the Kennedy assassination. Obsessing over the details of memory accuracy may blind investigators to dramatic effects at the periphery of their vision. The profusion of conspiracy accounts of the assassination suggests that the search for meaning—for an acceptable story—is a complex social and psychological process.

Narrative strategies for making sense of dramatic events often draw on cultural scripts and skeleton stories transmitted from one generation to the next. But cultural legends are also modified and transformed over time in response to social change and new ideals. The Kennedy-assassination conspiracy theories have the elements of older legends and simultaneously register more contemporary concerns. The death of a virile leader may arouse a collective sense of vulnerability, one evocative of childhood dependencies. Some theorists place Kennedy as victim in a Shakespearean drama, where the powerful generals betray the noble king. The valorization of the fallen hero protects against feelings of vulnerability by preserving an idealized mental representation that offers solace. This capacity to create a sustaining, internal imago of the lost, beloved object is quite integral to the experience of hope and psychological renewal.[61] It is a means of creating meaning out of unpredictable loss and out of the terrifying finality of death.

Common memories—with their shifting plot structures, scripts, and schema—mark generational boundaries as well as other social boundaries, enunciating the formative experiences that are felt to be constitutive of group identity. The drama of the assassination plot and the valorization of Kennedy in collective memory evokes the historically transformational meaning of the period in which he was killed. The era—the early 1960s—was the dawning of a new age, one of social protest and challenges to established authority. In looking back, Kennedy's assassination signifies a much broader constellation of epochal events. His death also may signify, in retrospect, the tragic losses of subsequent heroes—Martin Luther King, Jr., Malcolm X, Robert Kennedy, and John Lennon—also gunned down in their prime. Preserving the memory and searching for the hidden betrayals and the conspiracy behind the throne are symptomatic of public distrust of institutional authority and of a collective sense that the state no longer operates protectively or benignly.

Women and Transformative Remembering

If we approach recovered memories of sexual abuse in terms of narrative structure—leaving behind the question of the factual correspondence between a memory report and its external referent—a picture emerges of the struggles of many contemporary women. Many recovered memory narratives resemble the heroic narratives of men, while introducing different protagonists, plot structures, and denouements. In the sexual abuse recovery movement, the subtext is mourning a lost male protector. The betrayal/trauma theory of Jennifer Freyd employs this idea of traumatic loss and a felt absence of adequate restorative possibilities. (See chapter 1.) The restitutive process seems to unfold, however, around the project of de-idealizing the powerful father in memory—even as it places the daughter as emergent protagonist in cultural history, as a force with which to be reckoned. The rejection by many women of conventional accounts—including many of the explanations offered by the science of memory—grows out of a sense that many of the dominant legends and cultural scripts falsify women's experiences.

The sexual abuse recovery movement signals a shift in the authority granted female storytellers—a redistribution of "storytelling rights"—even as it mobilizes ancient suspicions over the reliability of women's tales. One of the most powerful "master narratives" that emerged out of the contemporary women's movement was that of childhood sexual abuse. Its rich generativity spanned a vast domain of female emotional experience, from everyday insults to dramatic violations of the self, and this generativity formed the basis for a new kind of oppositional storytelling. Yet since memory accuracy emerged as the criterion for legitimacy—for being taken seriously—the project veered in the direction of anchoring new awarenesses and insights in concrete past events and in uncovering memory of discrete traumas. While there is certainly a place for such operationalized definitions—for concrete, factual claims about harms endured—the broad thematic contours of women's experience centering on emotional distress, bodily violations, and storytelling conventions were obscured in this battle over facticity.[62]

Roger Schank and Robert Abelson describe various "skeleton stories" that provide coherence to the cultural transmission of knowledge.[63] The "betrayal legend" is one such story, encompassing a broad range of human concerns and moral dilemmas. But is human history merely the recycling of old tales, as Schank and Abelson imply, or does it give rise to new protagonists and plots?[64] In deepening our understanding of storytelling, how do we put flesh on the bones of skeleton stories, specifically those of women? Throughout much of history, women have been denied a public stage for the casting of their own dramas and have been silenced concerning the private knowledge they hold. As Schank and Abelson point out:

> This phenomenon of the untellable story is familiar to psychoanalysts. They typically regard the dangerous content as repressed, and not available to consciousness. With this view, one of the goals of analysis is to undo repression and enable the patient to have insight into the hidden motives. We prefer to think that untold, negative autobiographical experiences are partially conscious but surrounded by confusion resulting from many unsuccessful attempts to edit and tell them, leading to the absence of useful indexes.[65]

While the storehouse model has leaked into this theory in problematic ways, specifically in the use of the filing cabinet metaphor, many psychoanalysts would agree with much of the argument. The aura of mystery surrounding the concept of repression, with its associations of dramatic upsurges of alien knowledge from the bowels of the unconscious, has little to do with most actual psychoanalytic approaches to repression. (See chapter 3.) Yet Schank and Abelson's vocabulary of "useful indexes" and functional filing systems is too removed from the personal vicissitudes of memory, too mechanical as a metaphor, to capture much of what is at stake in preserving the personal past.

In "recovering" the unconscious from scientific psychology's own past, cognitive psychologists often intervene in the uncertainties it evokes through an overly rationalistic discourse. Memory researcher John Kihlstrom and his colleagues, for example, offer, in place of the "hot and wet" Freudian unconscious, which is "hallucinatory, primitive, and irrational," a cognitive unconscious that is "kinder and gentler than that and more rational and reality-bound."[66] Yet for rebellious storytellers who feel all too bound by conventional realities, the visceral appeal of the hot and wet unconscious, as against scientific psychology's cool and dry one, may vivify more powerfully the messy aspects of life, so often borne by women.

CONCLUSIONS

This chapter began with a mother/daughter conversation—my example of a dispute between my mother and me over a childhood recollection—as an illustration of how various contexts for remembering shape constructions of past encounters and the insights that may be drawn from them. Scientific inquiry into memory, particularly the storehouse model, is generally at odds with this notion of multiple perspectives. Further, the traditional emphasis in science on memory accuracy—the correspondence between a memory report and its referent event—obscures this problem of competing vantage points on the past.

In approaching this remembered mother/daughter conversation from the vantage point of research psychology, I must concede that my confidence in my own version of the story tells us nothing about its accuracy, even though it may reveal a great deal about its importance to me as a subjective memory. Personal investment in the certainty of a memory is important to attend to, even though memory confidence is often quite wrongly interpreted as an indicator of memory accuracy. As an interpersonal strategy, however, confidence may be related to "storytelling rights," to struggles over who is to be believed. Emotional cues convey the felt authenticity of the story, evoking responsive states in the listener.

Scientists make use of passionate appeals no less than do other human actors on the cultural stage in expressing personal conviction concerning the felt import of their findings. And, in the recovered memory debate, social alliances and worldviews shape which victim stories are readily believed. For clinicians, sudden remembering is likely to make as much sense as gradual remembering because psychotherapy has a certain affinity with the idea of dramatic discovery. For researchers, emergent knowledge is more likely to be understood as incremental. Dramatic discoveries, whether personal or scientific, must meet a higher standard of proof than do those consistent with prior, lawful knowledge. This principle is most certainly a defensible one. Yet psychological science also may operate defensively. The readiness of science to foreclose on ambiguous states by imposing its own categories on unstable aspects of mind may contribute to the rebellion against science so evident in clinical discourse on "body memories."

Stories may be employed for multiple purposes, depending on the demand characteristics, or "prompts," of the social situation. There are myriad possibilities, as well, for "indexing" stories in the mind—that is, for referencing the thematic composition of autobiographical recall. A recollection of a spanking in childhood, for example, may illustrate parental concern for a child's welfare, childhood terrors, or frank abuse. Clearly the vantage point matters, but humans are capable of multiple perspectives on and interpretations of life events. At the same time, the telling of a story inscribes its format in memory, sometimes replacing previous versions of the tale.

The next chapter explores further the cultural context of disputes over memory, focusing on the question of whether trauma memories are qualitatively different from ordinary memories and the attendant question of whether "normal" science is relevant to understandings of trauma. Navigating the terrain of contemporary trauma theory lays the groundwork for the analysis of trauma narratives in Part 3, narratives that captured center stage in popular and mental health culture in the 1980s.

THE TRAUMA MODEL

Chapter 3

Insights and Hysterical Blind Spots

AS I ENTERED ADOLESCENCE in the early 1960s, I became a master at simulating various illnesses for the purpose of staying home from school. I would sit on the couch, sipping juice in my bathrobe, with my mother standing at her ironing board, and, after the morning soaps, we would watch *Queen for a Day.* Four or five time-worn women would tell their grueling stories, each reporting hardship after hardship that she had endured. One would describe losing a son to leukemia, followed by a husband's heart attack and a foreclosure on their home. Another would present her saga of taking care of four children with cystic fibrosis while working nights at a convalescent home to make ends meet. As contestants in the lineup took their turns, each wearily conveying the unremitting misery of their lives, my mother and I would weep sympathetically. We would then cast our private votes as the applause meter registered the audience's selection of the day. The host of the show would wrap the regal robe around the stooped shoulders of the lucky winner, placing a crown on her graying hair. The prizes generally included a washer-and-dryer combo or a freezer.

As a spectacle of womanly virtue, *Queen for a Day* was an unintended parody of both the American dream and the Cinderella story, even as it honored such cherished fairy tales. While these women had lost out in life, being a winner in this pageantry of suffering required a certain art in storytelling. The queen for the day typically stood out from her competitors not by the sheer magnitude of her travails but by her capacity for storytelling. Singing for her supper meant projecting a pitiable but winsome image of feminine stoicism, one without any trace

60

of anger or bitterness. There were, as yet, no movements to support open rebellion against such unnecessary suffering, no public discussion of health care as a basic human right or the indecency of banks, foreclosing on poor people. The stories were isolated personal tragedies—acts of God—and as such the audience did not have to endure the discomfort of feeling implicated in them.

Today we would call these women survivors, and we have more categories available for registering their suffering. There are no applause meters in the contemporary displays of women's trauma, but there is still a strong echo of them in the selling of tragedy. Throughout the 1980s, as social services were being reduced and U.S. society was getting meaner, trauma stories became best-sellers, increasingly graphic in their tales of childhood torture and family barbarism. And still there was a pervasive public silence concerning the mundane suffering of daily life and the mounting, wearisome responsibilities of countless women.

Listening to speakers at a 1996 conference on sexual abuse and trauma, I remembered those women on *Queen for a Day* and the humiliating spectacle made of their pain. In workshop after workshop at this conference, I had the sense that something at the heart of the problem of human agony was being overlooked, that the steady stream of horror stories and the prevailing manner of talking about them were unreal.

Part 3 of *Pillar of Salt* will explore a contemporary clinical genre of trauma stories and the historical and cultural motifs that weave through these narratives. In setting the groundwork for this critical reading, this chapter looks at the premises and social dynamics of the trauma therapy movement. Beginning with an analysis of the trauma/dissociation model, the critique moves from the progressive contributions of this model to a discussion of its downside. In addition, I explain why feminist-informed therapies have embraced the trauma model so uncritically and what the costs are of an overreliance on this model of mind. I argue that a hysterical current runs through the trauma model, in both its clinical and its social applications.

I realize, of course, that my use of the term *hysteria* has the ring of heresy. In the mental health field, the trauma model emerged out of the ashes of hysteria, transcending the psychiatric specter of disturbed female minds that operated in some mysterious tandem with female bodily functions.[1] The modern trauma survivor, unlike her sisters of yesteryear, who were diagnosed as hysterics, is viewed as responding rationally to her situation, never excessively, and her symptoms plot no more than the course of her externally imposed injuries. Therefore, to reclaim the idiom of hysteria, a term that has been used to silence women in the past, can feel like a retreat from ground hard won and tenuously held, particularly in the contemporary climate of backlash.

Yet there is something amiss in this contempt for hysteria—in the rejection of emotional excess and irrationality—that is so evident in clinical discourse on female unhappiness. Hysteria is not inherently a female condition, even though women may carry the lion's share of emotions that are culturally designated as excessive or abnormal. Male hysteria is not likely to be recognized or understood as such, primarily because hysteria, as both a clinical and a colloquial term, is so embedded in gender assumptions.

At the base of hysteria is a battle for recognition, one that women must wage in a way that does not alienate their audiences. The art of presenting suffering in a palatable form, in a manner pleasing to the ears of powerful others, is, after all, a feminine craft born of social necessity. In defending the authenticity and reality basis of female complaints, feminists and trauma therapists may tend to overlook the various conscious and unconscious strategies employed by women in their efforts to be heard and seen. Such strategies are not merely "attention-getting" but rather communicate real emotional pain and deep, unmet longings.

The jettisoning of old categories and the creation of new ones—the "renaming" of the problem—can seem like a greater advance than it is, particularly if the new language obscures important history. The previous chapter probed the difficult project of converting mental states culturally designated as "feminine"— the intimate domain of emotions, bodily arousal, and familial plots—into the language and categories of science. In pursuing a path through clinical storytelling, it would seem that feminine grievances and remembrances may fare better. In contrast to the experimental subject, the clinical subject has greater control over the thematic content of her stories and over what claims may be made on professional listeners. Once liberated from the victim-blaming vestiges of psychiatric culture, women would seem to enjoy considerable freedom in the modern clinical encounter.

Converting hysteria into posttraumatic stress disorder or dissociative identity disorder—as many mental health practitioners have done—may gain ground on one front, particularly in locating a chain of disturbing mental events in an originating, external cause.[2] But this discourse of trauma has had significant costs, particularly for women, who are most often pronounced as trauma survivors. The question taken up here concerns the form and extent of selfhood that "survives" the tremendous heat generated by trauma interpretations of female experience. If high levels of dissociation suggest both a history of trauma and extreme vulnerability to suggestion,[3] the mental life of "survivors" may register the marks of both past and present authoritative influences.

The nature of present influences is explored in this chapter, with the social influence of the trauma model itself as the focus of investigation. By understanding the trauma model as a product of a social field—one that includes clinicians' own culturally mediated anxieties and conflicts—we may be better able to recognize the defensive implications of the theory as well as its generative potential.

THE TRAUMA PARADIGM

In less than two decades, large areas of the field of psychotherapy underwent a remarkable historical reversal. A late-nineteenth-century model of mind and psychopathology that had been essentially jettisoned by mainstream psychiatry after the turn of the century was reclaimed. Dissociation, as propounded by Pierre Janet, whose thinking shaped Freud's seduction theory in the 1890s, emerged as the basis of the contemporary trauma model. Janet argued that the mind's capacity to dissociate—to separate off from normal consciousness a traumatic memory trace—is activated by events that are excessively arousing and inescapable. Like an encapsulated cyst, the traumatic memory is sealed off behind a protective shield—an amnesic barrier—but erupts into consciousness when that shield breaks down. Hysterical symptoms signaled the compromised functioning of these protective mechanisms and the consequent flooding of consciousness by a "fixed idea," the dissociative residue of an undigestible psychic trauma. Janet used hypnosis to therapeutically reduce this amnesic barrier and to access and transform the pathogenic memory.[4]

The trauma/dissociation model gained tremendous currency in the mental health field in the 1980s, bridging different schools of psychotherapy in a common clinical project aimed at the recovery and abreaction, or emotional release, of trauma memory. Heralding this trend of the 1980s, psychoanalysts Richard Ullman and Doris Brothers urged therapists "to return to the paradigm of psychic trauma"—that early theoretical crucible of psychoanalytic investigation that Freud abandoned with his relinquishment of seduction theory.[5] This paradigm shift is advanced as a corrective to a history of psychotherapeutic silence concerning the social origins of human suffering. As such, it enlarges clinical investigation beyond the narrow confines of the inner or intrapsychic world to encompass a broad realm of tragic events that leave their indelible marks on the human psyche. By recognizing the unique suffering of survivors of politically organized torture and of violence, including family violence and sexual abuse, psychoanalysis restores the social-reformist dimension of its legacy, one that was central to its early vitality as an intellectual movement.[6] The trauma paradigm signifies a unified effort to "bear witness" to human cruelty and to "break the silence" around professional collusion in such villainy.[7]

The concept of psychic trauma has been progressive in normalizing psychiatric conditions that historically have been viewed as reflecting some form of personal dysfunction. The contemporary trauma model represents a revolt against biological psychiatry, with its traditional emphasis on pathological symptoms as deficits, as well as a reaction against Freudian psychoanalysis. While the assumption that pathological symptoms had an original adaptive value has been a tenet of psychoanalytic thinking historically, trauma theory goes much further in asserting the "internal wisdom" and essential "normalcy" of the patient's symptoms in light of the magnitude of what has been endured.[8]

FREUDIAN STORYTELLING

In responding to Ullman and Brothers's call for a return to the early trauma paradigm, we may benefit from revisiting the psychiatric ground Freud claimed and later relinquished. One of Freud's first insights—which continues to have tremendous heuristic value in studies of mind—was that psychopathological symptoms communicate meaning. They tell a story. Hysteria involved converting mental anguish—the unspeakable—into the language of the body, or the mimetic. Further, Freud and his colleague Josef Breuer recognized that such bodily communicated stories required a new mode of listening, a means of translating seemingly inchoate images, gestures, and speech into normal, rational discourse.[9]

Initially using hypnosis and, later, free association, Freud and Breuer entered into the inner worlds of their female patients, enlisting them as collaborators in this clinical project of inquiry. The past trauma that women began to speak about in these clinical conversations included a range of losses, daily insults, and blunted aspirations. In their early formulations concerning the etiology of hysteria, Breuer and Freud suggested that hysterical illness offered an escape from the suffocating domestic responsibilities of women.[10] While Breuer maintained that hysterical symptoms elude precise or singular etiological origins, Freud pursued the path of sexual memories. Indeed, many of the recollections of sexual abuse uncovered in the course of psychoanalysis emerged after considerable coaxing on Freud's part, as he pressed for more compelling explanations for hysterical symptoms.[11] As his women patients shook with emotion, particularly in describing sexual scenes, Freud became convinced that he had arrived at the original source of hysterical illness. In a series of papers on the etiology of hysteria published in 1896, Freud took the position that hysteria was a direct result of childhood sexual assaults and seductions, a kind of excitation that overwhelmed the child's nervous system.[12]

Overdetermination and Countertransference

By 1897, Freud had jettisoned seduction theory. In one sense, this retreat has been rightly described as Freud's failure to confront a difficult social problem.[13] Yet Freud had compelling reasons for reassessing seduction theory, however overdetermined such reasoning may have been by social conventions. The multiplicity of traumatogenic scenes and multifaceted symptoms generated by his women patients seemed to defy a simple cause-and-effect relationship. His early associational model, linking a hysterical symptom to a primary, traumatogenic event, failed to adequately explain these clinical phenomena and the extent to which the body itself was the focus of disturbance in hysteria.[14] The concept of overdetermination—of multiple causes—came to displace the idea of a singular origin or source of psychopathology.[15]

Freud's theoretical shift did not involve a complete renunciation of the importance of external factors in neurosis, but it did involve a movement toward a primary focus on unconscious fantasy in the reworking of childhood memory and on the hysterical illness as a disguised enactment of unbearable conflict. Further, Freud came to the view that hysterical conditions associated with early sexual experiences were often retroactive trauma, as adolescence and early adulthood mobilized sexual awarenesses and moral anxiety, both of which infiltrate the process of remembering.[16] And, indeed, in the context of Victorian morality it is not surprising that the process of uncovering the hysteric's secrets was infused with erotic, forbidden meanings. Many of these patients may have been abused and traumatized by sexual encounters, but Freud correctly recognized that sexual desire felt transgressive for many women, disturbing to such a degree that even minor sexual incidents or states of arousal could feel overwhelming.[17]

Women's sexual confessions could also be arousing and overwhelming for male listeners. Freud realized—first in developing the concept of transference and later in developing the idea of countertransference—that the patient's communications had an impact on the listener. As a profession grounded in science, psychiatry could incorporate the problem of transference more readily than that of countertransference. Analysis of transference involved approaching the patient's complaints as living history. The patient made the past present by imagining that (unconsciously responding as if) the analyst was some loved or hated person of childhood. Initially thought to be an obstacle to treatment, the transference was later understood to reveal the core relational dilemmas of early life, the effects of which continued to operate unconsciously in adulthood.[18]

The concept of countertransference, however, required a radical departure from turn-of-the-century scientific thinking. This term—which is among the more subversive in the psychoanalytic tradition—stripped the scientific observer of any pretense of an impartial, superordinate position of knowing. Clinicians were required to take their own subjectivity into account. For the early generations of analysts—eager to establish the scientific foundation of their authority—the process of understanding countertransference, primarily through the training analysis, was conceived as a rite of passage, a domain to be conquered in the acquisition of male authority.[19] But for others, particularly for a contemporary generation of therapists schooled in feminism and the countercultural movement of the 1960s, understanding the subjective side of clinical authority was extended into a less hierarchical approach to the therapeutic relationship.[20]

This progressive vision of clinical listening runs the risk, though, of masking problems of authority and of oversimplifying what is at stake. The problem that Freud confronted—in recognizing that the patient's stories have various unanticipated effects on the listener—is no less problematic today than it was for Freud. It may be that Freud was a bad listener—particularly of women—but this castigation of Freud may also be used defensively by contemporary therapists to fortify the distance between his failings and their own.

Concealed Knowledge

Beneath the heat of the controversy over therapeutically recovered traumatic memories is a deeper and more perplexing problem concerning the relationship between psychiatric conditions and translators of those conditions. In psychiatry, all mental disorders are constituted, in part, through the system of signs and discourses created by professionals, whose authority lies in their capacity to convert irrationality into rationality. This conversion process operates in a double sense, both in making comprehensible, scientifically, a disordered state of nature and in bringing under control, clinically, a "disordered" subject. Whether we are speaking of hysteria, multiple personality, or schizophrenia, mental disorders are not ontologically independent entities, autonomous of the system of signifiers in which they circulate.

Yet hysterical conditions, including contemporary variants such as the dissociative disorders, have served, throughout the history of psychiatry, as the site for clinical conversations about this problematic tension between subject and object, observer and observed. The fact that hysteria is so deeply rooted in the "mysteries" of the female body—indeed, its etymological roots are in the Greek word for the womb—establishes a framework for using this condition to relay social tensions over knowledge and to enact cultural anxieties over emotions, the body, and sexual difference. The hysterias signify the dilemmas of the "modern subject," then, not because of properties inherent to hysteria, as an illness in the psychiatric sense, but because hysteria serves such functions in contemporary discourse. As Michel Foucault observed, the "hystericization" of the female body was the nexus for the production of "knowledge power" in the nineteenth century and for the "sexualizing" of the soul.[21] Hysteria—associated with the body and "excessive" emotional states—symbolized the gap between the known and the unknown, and the elusiveness of "man's" efforts to control nature, including human nature.

Freud intervened in the mystery by regarding hysteria as a mimetic condition, where the mind makes use of the body to communicate the "incommunicable." In converting mental conflict into the language of the body, the hysteric unconsciously enacts the pathogenic drama that gave rise to her illness. But this very ineffability of the hysterical drama—its transcendence of ordinary speech—permits a broad range of interpretations.[22] To his credit, Freud recognized the considerable risk of unconscious suggestion—that is, that physicians may introduce meaning that is more a function of their own mental processes than of the patient's illness.[23]

In the late nineteenth century, fascination with latent personalities, concealed intelligences, and hidden potential was endemic in the fledgling fields of psychology and psychiatry. Freud did not differ from his intellectual peers in his interest in scientifically establishing the basis of latent realms of mind. Nor was his theorizing unique in arguing that trauma was a cause of hysteria.[24] More important—and of relevance to contemporary debates over psychic trauma—was his discovery that children create stories and theories about the world, including about their own origins, relationships, and suffering, and that these stories continue to play a vital role in adult mental life. Infantile logic pervades adult consciousness, emerging during psychopathological conditions such as hysteria but also during dreams, waking fantasies, and everyday human interactions.[25] While Freud believed that women were less able than men to repress the infantile origins of consciousness, he also asserted that men too were subject to such infantile forces.

As chapter 2 established, there is a long history of cultural splitting and hierarchizing of rational and emotional, conscious and unconscious, and of managing cultural ambivalences about such processes of mind through gender categories. One response of contemporary feminism has been to refuse the cultural position of "receptacle" for male, disavowed irrationality. The trauma model—which recast many of the predominantly female mental conditions as trauma disorders in the 1980s—was midwife to this enterprise. This normalizing of psychiatric disorders, however, redeems the psychiatric subject by implicitly accepting cultural unease with "abnormalcy." To be anointed with this newly redemptive label, the patient must produce evidence of trauma of sufficient magnitude to account for the symptoms or emotional distress at hand. Without such evidence of trauma, the sufferer slips back into the ranks of the mentally disturbed. And, in the 1980s, the plight of the mentally ill, as well as the more banal pathologies of daily life, met with increasing cultural indifference.

The emotional heat generated by the debate over recovered memories of childhood abuse may itself be a hysterical reaction to the interpersonal demands of storytelling. Trauma and hysterical reactions are linked not only because trauma causes hysterical reactions but because they mutually reinforce the idea that human experience often exceeds the expressive capacities of ordinary language. Trauma stories—whether accounts of actual tragic events or symbolic tales of human suffering—demand a departure from ordinary modes of listening. Trauma confronts us with the ineffable aspects of human experience and marks the ground where ordinary language no longer adequately imparts meaning.[26] Further, trauma stories collapse the social distance between everyday people and experts—between basic human responses to suffering and professional interventions in suffering.

What lessons are to be drawn from Freud's listening errors? He may, indeed, have retreated from seduction theory because it implicated respectable, bourgeois men in the problems of their daughters, as feminist critics have argued. But Freud also began to reflect on the possibility that he had unwittingly influenced the course of clinical storytelling in his effort to find evidence in support of his sexual theory of neurosis. This possibility was a vital insight, one which has been lost by many of Freud's critics. Further, although it is likely that many psychiatric conditions, including some cases of hysteria, do have their origins in discrete traumas of childhood, it is also the case that sexual anxieties of more ambiguous origins pervade human experience. Women, particularly, suffer from the effects of sexual repression as much as from the effects of sexual abuse, a theme revisited throughout this book.

PSYCHOANALYSIS AND PSYCHIC TRAUMA

We may view the affiliation of hysteria and trauma through yet another lens, less bound to the medical model or the search for cause-and-effect relationships. This alternative lens, which approaches stories as discursive modes of engagement, permits a new point of entry into the longstanding affinity between trauma and hysteria. Rather than putting trauma stories into true and false piles—plausible and implausible—I consider how the trauma narrative is employed in social contexts and how stories of palpable human suffering acquire new meanings over time in their telling and retelling. In unraveling this cultural entanglement of hysteria and trauma—as related storytelling practices—it is important to understand how the concept of trauma has evolved in the history of psychiatry. In tracing this history, this section looks at how the concept is over-determined by the historical and cultural dynamics that shaped its clinical meaning. As psychic trauma comes to stand for a range of experiences that disrupt previous modes of being, it also comes to be associated with the idea of transformation of the self.

From a psychoanalytic point of view, psychic trauma refers to any developmental event or crisis that overwhelms the ego's integrative capacities, compromising subsequent adaptive structures. Trauma may take the form of a discrete event, such as the loss of a parent or birth of a sibling, or chronic strains and stresses, such as neglect or abuse. What is crucial is not simply the magnitude of any "shock" to the system but the availability of psychological structures—particularly object relational (self in relation to other) representations derived from early attachments—that permit a relatively nonpathological integration of disturbing experiences.

Psychoanalytic and trauma theorists would agree that the structure of the self, developmental processes, and internal and external object relations combine to mediate the effects of disturbing events.[27] But a key distinction lies in assumptions concerning whether or not the subjective experience of an event is a reliable indicator of its objective reality. More specifically, can we infer the precise type or degree of harm endured from clinical "clues" such as bodily disturbances, dreams, intrusive imagery, or other symptomatology?

Schools of psychotherapeutic thought differ in how they interpret such ambiguous dysphoric states, including differences in their readiness to infer past trauma. The most theoretically unifying premise of the trauma paradigm is that acute subjective distress is a response to an unbearable reality. Psychic trauma is a state of internal crisis in response to an overwhelming external event that threatens existing mental structures. In Freudian ego psychology, the mind is an active agent in the defensive transformation of events. The trauma paradigm, in contrast, reduces the ontological gap between a psychologically powerful scene and the mental record of it. In viewing mental images as direct derivatives of external events, the trauma paradigm is positivistic, even though it is simultaneously romantic in its emphasis on a dramatic rupture that destroys a prior state of harmony and innocence.

Conceiving Early Trauma

Beyond the historical shift toward a more social psychoanalytic model and a more environmental theory of psychopathology, there has been a subtle shift within psychodynamic thought in conceptions of the prototypical traumas in human experience and in the moral cast assigned to them. In Freud's formulation of the primal scene, the trauma of discovering adult sexuality revolved around inevitable, developmental crises.[28] The immaturity of the young child produced misconceptions concerning what she or he had furtively discovered. Learning about adult sexuality generated frightening fantasies. Was father killing mother or was she devouring his penis? Such fantasies abounded in the sexually curious and fertile mind of the Freudian child, and these imaginative constructions of reality were thought to be determinative, in and of themselves, of later disturbances. The human mind was conceived as a place where complex, symbolically encoded meanings are produced. From Freud's point of view, psychic trauma was more often than not an accident of nature, the unintended consequence of curious children misconstruing adult actions. The cultural silences and prohibitions surrounding sexuality made bodily intimacies a particularly receptive ground for the seeds of neurotic conflict.[29]

In the post–World War II period, the prototypical trauma in the psychoanalytic literature centered on early separation and loss, particularly for institutionalized children. Once again, much of the trauma endured by children was understood as the unintended result of cultural practices. The literature on trauma in the 1940s and 1950s followed in the wake of the displacements caused by war. René Spitz and Anna Freud worked with orphaned children, and the new emphasis on emotional abandonment and maternal loss may also have been intimately tied to the experiences of psychoanalytic theorists, many of whom had lost their "mother country" through war.[30] Object relations theory emerged out of the investigation of traumatic disruptions in early attachments and contributed to the shifting of psychoanalytic investigation from oedipal (father-centered) to pre-oedipal (mother-centered) phases of development. With this turn, maternal pathology assumed a more dominant place in the clinical investigation of adult emotional problems.[31] This trend in psychoanalysis both shaped and registered changing standards of parenting. Beyond the basics of physical care, love, and discipline, a vast domain of crucial subtleties opened up in the maternal management of the child. In a remarkable postwar paper on trauma and the recovery of memory, Ernst Kris noted that clinical attentiveness to specific childhood recollections is highly linked to the constructs historically available to the therapist.[32] The traumatic significance of an early memory of emotional loss, for example, depends on "our general knowledge of the impact of separation on children."[33]

The historical realities of human trauma gave rise to new narrative and metaphorical conventions. British psychoanalyst Ronald Fairbairn, for example, traces the infant's psychic war with the mother back to the birth experience. His seminal papers on object relations theory shaped the reworking of Freudian ego psychology during the war years.[34] This theorizing, shaped by the rise of fascism and world war in Europe, is symptomatic of the cultural loading of the maternal body in explaining the insecure attachments of the modern subject.

Drawing on the work of child psychoanalyst Melanie Klein, Fairbairn sees the infant as unhappily struggling to repudiate its earliest identificatory tie even as it desperately attempts to retrieve it out of a state of terrifying aloneness and isolation. (See chapter 4.) There is a current of dark Romanticism in his writings, with the journey from intrauterine to extrauterine life serving as the prototype of a violent rupture of a prior state of unity. In this passage, taken from Fairbairn's essay on war neuroses, the global specter of death and slaughter likely over-determines the symbolic loading of the birth experience as a representation of psychic terror at the deepest level.

> It requires little imagination to appreciate that the experience of birth must come as a profound shock to the child accustomed, while *in utero,* to a blissful state of absolute identification; and there is good reason to believe that birth constitutes not only an extremely unpleasant and painful experience, but also one fraught with acute anxiety. . . . This being so, it can be readily appreciated that separation-anxiety will always retain the impress of the birth trauma by which it was originally evoked. . . . It is not implied, of course, that any conscious memory of the birth trauma is retained; but that the experience is perpetuated at a deep mental level and is capable of reactivation under certain conditions may be inferred from a number of psychopathological phenomena.[35]

While romantic in its undertones, this concept of birth trauma differs in crucial ways from contemporary currents of trauma theory. Fairbairn's maternal body is the agent of trauma, but it is not intentional in its destructive agency. The infant's ability to take hold of the "satisfying, good object" in defending against the terrors of infantile dependence is contingent on the real soothing and responsive capacities of the mother. But the Fairbairnian infant, like the Klein-ian one, begins life at war with its primary object, aggressively destroying and guiltily repairing this powerful other. Mothers may, indeed, attack, frustrate, and abandon their infants, but the infant also attacks her, projectively making use of her to defend against its own considerable aggression.[36]

In the 1960s and 1970s, Donald Winnicott's concept of "good-enough moth-ering" advanced a more contented portrait than Fairbairn's of the maternal/infant pair. Winnicott's image gained currency in psychoanalysis because it seemed to steer a middle course between the ideal of serenely attuned mothers with their hothouse infants, on the one hand, and the specter of the insatiably hungry, attacking (Kleinian) infant on the other. Winnicott's infant was more libidinal than aggressive, more object-seeking than object-destroying, and it was also more resourceful in making use of the environment. His concept of transitional objects and transitional spaces directed analytic attention to the infant's capac-ity to reach outside the maternal object to secure a footing in its struggles against dependence.[37]

The emerging feminist movement, which was accompanied by dramatic increases in the number of working mothers, likely contributed to this shift toward more flexible models of infant development. As a pediatrician as well as an analyst, Winnicott was attuned to the dilemmas of parenting and to the infant's own adaptive capacities. One aspect of the "adaptable infant" was its readiness to make creative and growth-producing use of frustration by mobilizing the available resources of its social environment. Theoretical swings between the resilient, capable infant and the fragile, vulnerable infant came to characterize the postwar period, with the feminist movement bringing to light the political dimensions of assumptions concerning the infant's "basic" needs. The nature and extent of the young child's needs were highly contested—within psychoanalysis and among various disciplines—as were the ramifications of early maternal responses for adult psychopathology. The shift toward an environmental psychoanalysis carried considerable, unanticipated freight for feminist theorizing. As the "environment" came to be exclusively defined as maternal responsivity, object relations theory shifted the axis of pathogenic influence from the oedipal, triadic constellation of mother/father/child to the pre-oedipal, dyadic union between mother and infant. While trauma could be located anywhere in human social experience, clinicians schooled in object relations theory overwhelmingly located pathological ruptures of psychic structure in maternal failures.

The object relational trend in theorizing was not simply a sexist fiction born of the psychoanalytic imagination. Rather, it mapped determinative social realities. As nuclear families are normatively constituted in the modern era, the mother is the primary object of the infant's early ambivalent strivings, and she is the first object of the infant's identifications. Psychic structures build on this early relational tie, with its relative frustrations, gratifications, and holding capacities. While mothers may bear the psychological weight of the most primitive of psychic conflicts—of idealized longings and primitive rage—it is in part because they stand at the terrifying threshold of consciousness itself. At the same time, we may recognize how object relations theory minimizes various developmental and social influences beyond the sphere of maternal responsivity, including the impact of fathers on development.[38]

Murderous Mothers

In contemporary trauma theory, family dynamics unfold around a quite different cast of characters than that presented by Freud, Klein, and Fairbairn. Even as Klein and Fairbairn departed from Freud in their emphasis on the pre-oedipal world of the mother, they shared Freud's view that the infant was an active agent in the psychic drama. The work of Leonard Shengold, an American psychoanalyst schooled in object relations theory and the trauma/dissociation model, exemplifies the contemporary reframing of psychic trauma. His widely read text on childhood abuse and trauma, *Soul Murder*, charts the course of a psychoanalysis aware of the pervasive effects of family violence, most particularly of sexual abuse.[39] Signaling the trend within trauma theory toward a moral vision of psychopathology, Shengold's model of trauma centers on the willfulness of parental destructiveness. Yet the patients Shengold describes as victims of soul murder are not, as it turns out, the survivors of overt parental violence. These psychoanalytic patients are highly functional adults who suffer from the ordinary range of inhibitions, conflictive relationships, and dysphoric moods commonly seen in an analytic practice. Their initial portraits of family life fall within the expectable range of losses, frustrations, and pathogenic experiences, so that the term *soul murder* takes on a highly metaphorical meaning.

The use of this metaphor is, however, symptomatic of the apocalyptic theorizing that has come to characterize the trauma field. It also signifies the difficulty of negotiating the boundary between what Donald Spence terms historical and narrative truth.[40] Shengold initially charts his own course through this contested terrain of childhood memory by acknowledging the high level of uncertainty and ambiguity attached to the project of "lifting repression." Yet early caveats are soon abandoned as Shengold pushes back the frontiers of consciousness to reveal increasingly grisly childhood scenes. A striking feature of the history of Shengold's patients, uncovered through analytical investigation of early memories, is that most suffered from sadistic sexual abuse by their mothers. The maternal/infant dyad emerges as a totalitarian state, with the infant as prisoner of a diabolical female guardian. One case illustrates a recurring theme in his text. "The child was forced to share the mother's distorted, narcissistic view of the world. . . . The child could not be allowed a view from outside her mother's domination. Efficient dictators appreciate the importance of propaganda and brainwashing. Psychical isolation, especially that separating the victim from loving and caring people, is part of the brainwashing technique used in concentration camps."[41]

This passage illustrates a historically emergent trope within the trauma paradigm: the concentration-camp victim as archetype of a broad range of human experiences with cruelty (a theme in chapter 8). Certainly there are such authoritarian, destructive mothers (and fathers), and soul murder may aptly serve as a metaphor for the effects of malevolent, destructive parenting. The idealization of family life in Western culture, with its sentimentalized portraits of convivial togetherness, does conceal the cruelty—both overt and covert—parents regularly inflict on children. Yet this reactive theorizing—this effort to expose the malignant bad concealed behind the fig leaf of the good—brings it own distortions to the project of creating more authentic versions of the past.

Where consistently similar parental images emerge in the therapeutic process, we may suspect that these images carry a surplus loading—the unacknowledged freight of the therapeutic journey itself. Put another way, consistent emotional themes in clinical material may reveal unexplored areas of countertransference, or unconscious reactions on the part of the therapist. Interestingly enough, Shengold concludes his book by noting that "there is an inevitable (and usually predominant), health-giving degree of seduction provided by the mothering figure's bodily care [which is] reflected in the universal fantasies of having been seduced" (309). In this concluding remark, Shengold seems to be making reparations to the mother who relentlessly haunts the previous chapters as a ruthless murderess.

Much like trauma therapists generally, Shengold makes little analytic use of the idea that children may misinterpret maternal ministrations, as he recovers a Pandora's box of early sexual intrusions and pernicious overstimulation. Bathing, dressing, sleeping, enemas, and other erotically ambiguous encounters with the mother emerge as definitive scenes of malevolently motivated psychic assault. The general line of interpretation Shengold pursues is that the arousal of feelings in the transference threatens to "revive the overwhelming incestuous excitement" of parental overstimulation (128). Almost without exception, Shengold traces symptoms back to a seductive mother, the "sphinxlike" soul murderer in childhood, the destroyer of early sexual innocence.

DISSOCIATION VERSUS REPRESSION

One of the more confusing areas of the trauma and recovered memory literature is in the use of the terms *repression* and *dissociation*. Often used interchangeably, the terms are actually based on differing understandings of what the mind "does" with material that is outside of conscious awareness. Rarely mentioned in psychiatric training prior to the 1980s, the concept of dissociation has assumed enormous importance in clinical understandings of psychological functioning. Referring technically to discontinuities in memory, affect, or identity, dissociation—both normal and abnormal—may be employed to encompass various unstable, fluctuating mental or interpersonal phenomena.[42]

One of the significant developments in the trauma literature over the past few decades has been in the movement to infer trauma from clinical indicators alone and most commonly from dissociative states. As characteristic symptoms such as hyperarousal, hypervigilance, and emotional flooding came to be linked with known trauma, clinicians began to infer trauma when a similar symptom complex—or subset—was present. Once amnesia was added to the symptom list of trauma, along with hypermnesia, a clinical floodgate opened for inferring hidden trauma. The assumption, however, that dissociative states, memory gaps, and other clinical symptoms are reliable indicators of severe past trauma is an enormous leap. Dissociation, in and of itself, is not associated with psychopathology. In other words, people dissociate for various reasons, and the relationship between even extreme dissociation and trauma has not been empirically established.[43]

Dissociation is a valid construct, one with indisputable relevance to understanding some reactions to trauma. But in the trauma therapy movement, this term encompasses such a broad array of fluctuating phenomena that it may serve, conceptually, as a Ouija board in clinical practice. Sudden reversals, stops, or turns in the clinical narrative, as well as almost any unanticipated reactive state, may be labeled dissociation. The model holds the potential, then, for registering reactivity of any kind and for such reactivity to loop back into the model as evidence of trauma. If trauma produces dissociation, then dissociation may be viewed as indicative of hidden trauma. Among the pitfalls here is the readiness to infer trauma from a broad range of clinical indicators and to neglect other developmental processes and conflicts not specifically derived from past trauma.

Dissociation is sometimes confused with Freud's concept of repression in that both terms refer to unconscious forgetting.[44] In clinical discourse, both terms are used to describe normal defenses that may be employed so massively that they impair functioning or reality testing. In his review of the history of the concept of dissociation, psychologist Ernest Hilgard is careful to note the distinction between the two concepts and their related meanings in designating defensive processes of mind, even as he attempts to preserve their compatibility as useful clinical constructs.[45] Repression refers to what Hilgard terms "horizontal" divisions in consciousness—that is, Freud's topographical layering of the "system conscious" and the "system unconscious." The repression model posits that events with affect-laden, personal meaning are never passively registered in memory but rather are filtered through motivational states and psychic structures. Internal demands on the ego, such as impulses and fantasies, are the primary source of unconscious forgetting and of various splits within the ego. In other words, the defensive process is organized intrapsychically, primarily in relation to anxiety-provoking internal events. As the child enters adolescence, for example, new moral capacities and preoccupations collide with intensified sexual awakenings, and these conflicting pressures heighten the meaning of sexual encounters. Freud viewed trauma as often retroactive in that symptoms did not always emerge "on impact" but rather through the arousal of memory in the context of later moral anxieties, such as during adolescence and early adulthood.[46]

While many psychoanalysts believe that repression may be lifted under clinical conditions, such as hypnosis and free association, it is generally assumed that the ego continues to disguise unconscious material. The unconscious is thought to be an inferred agency of mind, understood through its derivative expressions—for example, through dreams, fantasies, slips of the tongue, or free association. These "roads" to the unconscious require attentiveness to the mental transformations of psychic experience, through displacements, reversals, substitutions, and condensations.

Hilgard characterizes dissociation as "vertical" splits in consciousness, with the unconscious remaining more accessible than in repression and with divisions expressed through alternating states of awareness or identity. In other words, dissociation permits movement in and out of walled-off areas of the mind, whereas repression implies a "deeper," less accessible unconscious. Under conditions such as hypnosis or other dissociative states, split-off areas of mind, such as traumatic memories, are thought to directly surface in consciousness.[47]

Not surprisingly, the two models sensitize practitioners to different phenomena, even as they offer differing frameworks for understanding and interpreting the dizzyingly complex array of material that may arise in clinical situations. The dissociation model assumes an unconscious that is far more ready-at-hand, more transparent, than the Freudian unconscious. With the dissociation construct as a fundamental tool of clinical investigation, analysis tends to proceed in the direction of accessing a relatively nonproblematic, though concealed, mental record of events. The repression model, however, tends to heighten clinical attentiveness to problems of interpreting what is understood to be irreducibly ambiguous or opaque in meaning.

THE POLITICS OF THE UNCONSCIOUS

The etiological uncertainties of psychotherapeutic work took on new urgency in the 1980s as trauma claims did battle in the courts and in popular discourse and as therapists were informed of their legal and ethical obligations to report suspected child abuse.[48] Many therapists took increasingly authoritative positions, even when clinical indicators were vague. The rush to deduce child sexual abuse—or even satanic ritual abuse—from scant clinical evidence was a response to cultural pressures for certainty, coupled with the mandate not to repeat the "Freudian error." To err on the side of validating real external trauma was better than to err on the side of the symbolic.

The heightened attentiveness among clinicians to indirect indicators of trauma—and particularly to disguised presentation of sexual abuse—seemed to absolve the collective sons and daughters of Freud from the sins of the father. If, like Oedipus, the previous generation of therapists symbolically gouged out their own eyes, it fell to the next generation to cast off this hysterical blindness. To register on the side of uncertainty was to express a woeful lack of moral courage; to fail to see where clinical signs pointed was irredeemably myopic.

Yet distinguishing extreme trauma from various forms of "empathic failure" or other early relational disturbances—based on clinical indicators alone—is often impossible. Clinically, they may manifest themselves in similar or disparate ways. While therapists may claim that it is possible to assess the nature of early trauma from clinical material (the transference or specific symptomatology), our ability to establish the primary or original cause of the patient's current distress is limited.[49]

The revival of the trauma paradigm in the 1980s was also driven by the social movement to recognize specific events in childhood as having inevitable consequences. The notion of trauma as sustained injury has been appropriated by feminist therapists and clinicians in the field of abuse because it counters the cultural legacy of denying or minimizing the injustices that women, particularly, endure. The assertion that "regardless of its form and the child's response, incest is a devastating experience and leaves a devastating mark on its victims" finds a responsive chord among women patients and therapists who resist the traditional injunction to suffer silently or to minimize what has been endured.[50]

While this claim of "inevitable effects" of sexual abuse has been strenuously challenged in recent clinical research, it remains a legendary truth because it operates collectively as a refusal to be appeased.[51] By shifting the focus from women's own emotional reactions or interpretations of events to the inexorable effects of the events themselves, the legacy of victim blaming is resisted. As a self-organizing belief, however, this assertion has its downside. The notion that psychological devastation inevitably results from objectively abusive experiences may predispose participants, within various contexts of interpretation, to anticipate psychic shattering. This is not so far from the idea that virginal women are "ruined" by early, culturally unauthorized sexual experiences as well as by sexual abuse. The effects of psychologically and politically regressive beliefs concerning sexual contamination, particularly in relation to women's bodies, can be difficult to untangle from the direct effects of sexual abuse. The use of trauma metaphors in the service of vivifying emotional suffering may be a Trojan horse. Under the guise of validating female injuries, the old idea of an inherent feminine vulnerability can be imported into the therapeutic field. The therapist who assumes that psychic devastation follows from particular life events may be operating under the sway of an archaic fantasy: that an original female "castratedness"—a primal "wound"—leaves the feminine psyche perpetually vulnerable.

THE TRAUMA MODEL AND
MENTAL HEALTH CULTURE

The trauma model does not so much reclaim the notion of psychic trauma—a term that has always been foundational in psychoanalytic thought—as it concretizes and localizes the source of human suffering within an apocalyptic metapsychology. Feminist psychiatrist Judith Lewis Herman, for example, draws on the trauma prototypes of war and rape to describe a dramatic rupture that leaves survivors in a state of inconsolable loss. "Wounded soldiers and raped women cry for their mothers, or for God. When this cry is not answered, the sense of basic trust is shattered. Traumatized people feel utterly abandoned, utterly alone, cast out of the human and divine systems of care and protection that sustain life."[52]

The dramatic urgency of a shattering experience obliterates everything prior, in Herman's theorizing, including ego capacities. However, this same moment of acute necessity—of extreme crisis—can legitimize the interventions of whatever authorities are at hand. And it is the influence of therapeutic power—the role of the practitioner in shaping the emerging trauma material—that tends to be "repressed" by trauma therapists. While the trauma model may be mobilized to break through a deadening cultural insensitivity to human suffering, it also may be advanced defensively in countering scrutiny of therapeutic interventions in that suffering.

Within the mental health professions, the trauma model occupies an important position at the border between psychoanalysis and related therapeutic approaches. The clinical concepts of the unconscious, motivated forgetting, and the developmental view of psychopathology draw on the psychoanalytic legacy and form core elements of most psychodynamic approaches. These ideas are elaborated in various directions, blended into highly eclectic approaches in some quarters and taken up in more intensive ways in others. Strictly psycho-analytic approaches, however, are associated with a cohesive system of ideas or school of thought and a more formally structured mode of training, including a training analysis.

Psychoanalytic theory underwent somewhat of a revival in the mental health professions in the 1970s and 1980s, as institutes began to train nonphysician therapists or "lay" analysts. The Division of Psychoanalysis was formed within the American Psychological Association, signaling a historically unprecedented rapprochement brought about by a renewed receptivity within the profession to "depth" psychology. With the "cognitive revolution" in psychology, the mind came back into fashion, and this coup against behaviorism ushered in the revival of interest in "nonconscious" mental processes. (See chapter 2.) Psychoanalysis became less balkanized with the entry of nonphysicians into the folds of the institutes, although the practice of formal analysis—three to five times a week on the couch—declined precipitously. Long-term psychotherapies of various modalities came under siege as third-party coverage was reduced. Within this climate of pragmatic and cost-effective criteria for evaluating treatments, psycho-analysis and related approaches were on the defensive, even as their ranks within the professions were swelling. The effect of these countervailing forces was a height-ening of passions, as psychodynamic approaches were demonized by some and valorized by others.

Indeed, reports of Freud's death and resurrection seem to cycle endlessly through American culture, as do seasonal shifts in the fortunes of psycho-analytic institutes. As a highly specialized, privileged, and expensive mode of train-ing and treatment, psychoanalysis emerged as an object of intense ambivalence for those who staked their claims on the margins of this embattled tradition. Many psychodynamic practitioners not formally trained in analytic institutes—social workers, psychologists, counselors, and some psychiatrists—forged an auto-didactic, pragmatic path through the world of psychoanalytic thought.

These tensions between psychoanalysis and its ambivalent allies in the mental health field provided a key impetus for the restoration of the trauma/dissociation model. During the 1970s and 1980s, Henri Ellenberger's book on the history of the concept of the dynamic unconscious achieved wide-spread influence in the field.[53] In his overview, Ellenberger takes the bold step of reducing the significance of Freud's contributions and elevating those of Janet. Ellenberger implies that Freud, overstating the originality of his theory, appropriated Janet's ideas concerning the traumatic origins of splits in consciousness.

The contemporary revival of Janetian dissociation—as the "true" soul of the psychodynamic tradition—has taken place within a context of expansion and dilution of psychoanalytic training, on the one hand, and a hostile cultural cli-mate toward depth therapies on the other. Rejection of Freud and all things Freudian serves a unifying function in demarcating the new terrain from the old regime. Over against the "bad" Freud, Janet came to be viewed as the good father of the psychodynamic past and its rightful progenitor.[54]

This collective splitting of the good and the bad in the psychodynamic past may be a reaction to ambivalences born of palpable pressures on clinicians. Psychoanalytic work has always been difficult to reconcile with the exchange values of the marketplace. It is labor-intensive activity with an uncertain outcome and, as such, is easily displaced by lower bidders. But if one tendency is to escape into the narcissism of theoretical abstractions removed from concrete, visceral suffering, a reverse tendency, also problematic, is to reify and lionize emotional suffering. As economic and institutional supports for exploratory psychotherapy collapse and managed-care schemes colonize the field, the tenuous status of psychoanalytic work is further strained.[55] The emerging professional and existential crisis finds expression in what might be termed *theoretical revivalism*. Like religious revivalism, the trauma movement involves a return to an early, transformative discovery as antidote to the current crisis and its associated assaults on collective well-being. It also involves a reawakening—a revitalizing of the power of ideas to transform and mobilize—against a backdrop of real and imagined threats.

The "feminizing" of the mental health field has emerged as midwife to this reinvigoration of depth psychology. As women have come to numerically dominate the mental health professions, the encroaching critique of labor-intensive therapies takes on a gendered character.[56] For female clinicians, securing professional authority in a competitive market is no cakewalk. It means elevating therapeutic work above the profoundly devalued maternal labor of everyday life while defending women's "ways of knowing" within male-dominated professions.

The work of psychoanalyst Alice Miller, based on object relations theory, has been quite influential in the movement to return to the trauma paradigm and to the assertion of a "maternal" authority in the mental health field. She counters the classical Freudian and Kleinian emphasis on the aggressive drive and its derivatives—that is, the importance of understanding defenses and symptoms as derived from anxiety over impulses and fantasies. Miller stresses instead the therapeutic necessity of emphasizing parental failures and the reactive nature of hatred.[57]

The trauma model also has contributed to the currency in mental health culture of the metaphor of body memory, an idiom that encompasses an ambiguously defined domain of emotional states and somatic symptoms. In the previous chapter, I argued that the "repression" and "recovery" of the topic of emotion in the history of psychology is intimately tied to gender dynamics as well as to Romantic revolts against rationalistic, mechanistic models of mind. The term *body memories* may mystify activities of the mind, and its ascendence in contemporary mental health culture similarly signals discontent with prevailing models of the mind. The "wisdom of the body" has an intimate companion in the purported "wisdom of the child," that capacity for authenticity, spontaneity, and relatedness that is often thwarted along the path to adulthood. Miller's work echoes this romantic valorization of bodily knowledge and disenchantment with pure reason. "The truth about our childhood is stored up in our body, and although we can repress it, we can never alter it. Our intellect can be deceived. . . . But some-day the body will present a bill, for it will accept no compromises or excuses, and it will not stop tormenting us until we stop evading the truth."[58]

While Miller's psychoanalytic theorizing has an ecclesiastical tone, with the unconscious positioned as righteous judge, it is a reaction to the legacy of emotional distance and moral "neutrality" within psychoanalysis. A Swiss psychoanalyst acutely sensitive to the silences surrounding the Holocaust, Miller is taking the professions to task—presenting them with the "bill" for untallied, unnoticed suffering. The body is, in a sense, a metaphor for the power of history to reassert itself in a disguised form and for the silencing of victims.

But when victims do begin to speak, how do we understand the various processes that impinge on the stories that get told? Interestingly enough, Miller's most significant and influential contribution, *The Drama of the Gifted Child,* focuses on the more ambiguous, diffuse complaints of highly narcissistic indi-viduals rather than on psychic or physical assaults in childhood.[59] The distur-bances she analyzes emerge out of seductive, subtle engagements with parental authority. The family pathology dramatized centers on intense, unremitting parental pressure on children to perform and on lack of parental empathy for the child's emotional fears and longings. Miller's portrayal of cultivated "gifted-ness" in children is a poignant indictment of tendencies quite common in middle-class families, where performance demands create later adults who lack a sense of spontaneity, empathy, or vitality.

In a society where changing social structures leave many feeling motherless as well as fatherless, there is a growing public responsivity to an explicitly nur-turant clinical authority. Herman suggests that the belabored warriors of mod-ern life cry out for "their mothers" even prior to appeals to "God" the father. Within the analytic priesthood, the rejection of the patriarchal and the embrace of the maternal is evident in what Heinz Kohut terms experience-distant versus experience-near analytical positions. The experience-distant position, associ-ated with the Freudian stance, is emotionally remote and analytical, whereas the experience-near position is empathically attuned and palpably present.[60]

The critique of phallocentric theories and paternalistic practices within the professions has been progressive. Nonetheless, it is important to be aware of the defensive aspects of "uterocentric" and maternalistic modes of inquiry. In correcting for the unresponsive, masculine authorities of the past, therapists may overidealize what is experienced as their own more benign and nurturant authority.

GENDER DYNAMICS AND CLINICAL PRACTICE

While many trauma therapists note that dissociative disorders are highly correlated with gender, they pay little attention to gender dynamics as they relate to clinical interventions or interpretations.[61] So too, the recurring finding that females are more likely than men to develop dissociative disorders suffers this same "repression" in the trauma/dissociation literature. It is as though disembodied, neutered subjects engage one another through this clinical field of fragmented awarenesses. What are the implications, for instance, of labeling a patient "borderline"—a diagnostic term that gained widespread currency in the 1970s and 1980s, also highly associated with women—versus using the more contemporary dissociative-identity category?

In bridging psychoanalytic and neodissociative traditions, psychiatrist George Ganaway refracts dissociative states through the lens of the borderline diagnosis.[62] Many clinicians in the trauma field most certainly would consider this revisionism a retreat.[63] Unlike the vast clinical literature on borderline conditions, which chronicles the rocky course of treatment through the various subterfuges of emotionally consuming patients, the literature on dissociative disorders maintains a respectful tone and even a valorized stance toward female pathology. But this admiration is based on an insistence on the woman's normalcy, which is concealed beneath the disguise of madness. Dissociative patients, unlike their borderline sisters, suffer from "real" trauma memories intruding on their consciousness, presumably uncontaminated by destructive impulses or disturbing infantile conflicts.

What is the meaning of this recasting of female disorders that exhibit unstable, clinical characteristics and that tend to be destabilizing for the clinician? Does the recovery of a concrete moment of violation and the unambiguous identification of a parental aggressor serve to anchor the therapist, relieving him or her of painful uncertainty and guilt? Further, does the concept of a dissociative disorder redeem and dignify women's suffering by eliminating the older idea of a manipulative, seductive femininity and replacing it with the more contemporary one of a fragmented but rational self?

Many therapists influenced by feminist insights understandably welcome this historical shift toward locating the source of female disturbances within an external set of events imposed on the psyche through a discrete sexual assault that exerts a powerful pathogenic effect through the deferred action of the trauma memory. This model offers a corrective to the cultural tendency to view females as more prone to mental disorders, as well as a counterweight to the idea of a dangerous, hidden aspect of the female self. However, neodissociationism may easily operate as a defensive reaction. It intervenes in the "dangerous" obscurity of the female psyche, substituting the illusion of transparency for a threatening opacity.

As interactive, intersubjective phenomena, dissociative states may be the expression of a hysterical relaying of disturbing knowledge. The patient, engaged in a therapeutic model that makes shifting, fragmented states a prized indicator of trauma, embraces a communicative strategy that is both spellbinding and concealing. The rhythmic utterances and fluctuating mental states of the dissociative patient may be a means of unconsciously titrating revelations that would otherwise overwhelm the therapist. Dissociation, then, may be the product of a mutual field of engagement, ambivalently looking and not looking, anxiously approaching and retreating from some felt dangers within the domain of yet-to-be-revealed experience.

The therapeutic valorizing of the female psyche, based on the remembering of discrete, vivid trauma, offers little space for confronting the mundane, repressive side of female development. In inferring sexual trauma from ambiguously disturbing mental imagery, therapists may reinforce women's fears of their own imaginative processes, and they may overlook the impact of sexually repressive traditions on female desires.

While a number of authors in the trauma field note the link between conservative religious upbringings and sexual abuse,[64] exploration of the influence of religious ideas and practices on sexual imagery tends to be neglected. Janet Liebman Jacobs, for example, notes that for girls "raised in religious households where rigid definitions of sin and godliness prevail, it might be the devil who enters the child's bedroom and from whom she is not safe."[65] Yet as vague dreams and images are transmuted into recovered memories in Jacobs's clinical account, giving concrete form to the shadowy images of a repressive childhood, the devil and dad become one and the same. In gaining "memory," the realm of the imaginary and the symbolic becomes concretized.

As all disturbing awarenesses associated with the body are shunted into the trauma paradigm, even masturbatory pleasures of childhood are recast as abusive enactments. Jacobs describes the recovered memory of one survivor who recalled erotic fantasies involving the "ouch ouch body man"—fantasies that included her sister who shared the same bedroom. While the survivor notes an element of uncertainty attached to these images of the "ouch ouch body man," who "could have been my father," Jacobs weaves such accounts together to construct a one-dimensional, unambiguous tale of sexual trauma.[66]

As those identified as trauma survivors find their voice, piecing together fragments of experience and translating them into a narrative, meaning is inevitably constructed. Since the trauma model is concerned primarily with where memory is stored in the mind rather than on its transformations over time, dissociative states are often used as a kind of Geiger counter for hidden trauma. Integration of the dissociated fragments is the central aim of treatment rather than analyzing the various meanings that may be assigned to emerging material. There is little emphasis on how other aspects of development or self-experience mediate memory of disturbing events beyond fragmentation.

Take, for example, the phenomenon of "spacing out." Many theorists in the trauma field have reported higher levels of spacing out during stressful events among those who are later diagnosed with posttraumatic stress disorder.[67] Just as attention deficit disorder currently captures a broad, heterogeneous group of problems, some of which are likely related to the unengaging quality of many schooling experiences, dissociation casts a similarly wide net. One patient of mine, a young woman of eighteen at the onset of treatment, exhibited dissociative states that would place her in the middle range of the dissociative continuum. Her early sessions, full of disruptive stops and starts and moments of spacing out, began with her most pressing concern: to talk about the meaning of life as she was attempting to understand it. Her dissociative states seemed to be related more to communicative impairments in her family, however—to a diffuse sense of purposelessness and emotional detachment that pervaded family life—than to any discrete childhood trauma. In her family, bouts of shouting were punctuated with extensive silences. Television was the primary window to the world, hypnotically soothing the disquieting states of this troubled but in many respects highly "functional" family. The difficulties of this intelligent and thoughtful young woman were intertwined with what emerged as a lack of vital connection, a profound sense of aloneness and isolation.

My point is that dissociative states may be indicative of far more than trauma. The therapeutic preoccupation with the recovery of trauma memory engages women, paradoxically, in a quest that reaffirms their fragility and invisibility. Both therapist and patient assume that women's untold stories are more important than the remembered ones and that the unrevealed drama provides the key to the kingdom. There is a real possibility here for the trauma story to become a kind of Gothic fairy tale or a Cinderella story with the prince as the perpetrator. The reversals are important, but the narrative elements are the same: the fantasy of discovering the missing object (the memory, the phallus) that will make women whole.

CONCLUSIONS

Freud's Hegelian insight that the demons and gods we create are made in the shadow of our own image has been significantly eclipsed in the contemporary revival of the trauma paradigm. For certain, this Freudian insight has a long history of being employed to conceal the operations of real power and actual demons in the world. But we currently seem to have a reverse problem, as the demonic is progressively externalized and concretized in clinical theorizing.

While the Freudian view, with its emphasis on intrapsychic conflict, is associated with an emotionally distant, authoritative therapeutic stance, this characterization minimizes its advances in broadening the scope of conceived human suffering. The humanistic side of the classical tradition is seen in its respect for psychically generated suffering. Hysterical suffering was no longer understood simply as manipulative attention getting: the suffering of the hypochondriac was no less "real" than that of the arthritic; the hallucinatory terror of the psychotic no less torturous than that of the trauma victim.

Subjective reality, we might conclude, is one aspect of material existence and ontological knowledge that is intimately related to—but not perfectly correlated with—objective reality. So too, the tragedies that humans endure—particularly at the hands of powerful others—can profoundly alter self-capacities but in complex, highly variable ways.

In negotiating the meaning of disturbing events, human consciousness is prone to two opposing sorts of social defenses: one involves denial and minimization of disturbing sources of knowledge and the other involves elaboration and amplification of them. Human history is replete with examples both of minimizing actual threats to well-being—denying evil and destructiveness—and of creating threats out of the internal workings of the imagination. We live in a world of gods and devils that are a product of internal anxieties and fears as much as they are reflections of benevolent and malevolent external forces. The distinctions humans make between what is internally generated and what is externally imposed, what is understood to be more literal and what more symbolic, are bound up in complex psychological, cultural, and historical processes.

Trauma theory has advanced an important corrective to the history of denial in the mental health professions and has confronted this most problematic human tendency. As an approach to psychotherapy, it heightens awareness of the external sources of human suffering. But the model "represses" the second of these two problematic human tendencies—the tendency to imaginatively elaborate on reality and to project internal threats onto the external world. If we are too fearful of human imagination, too fearful of irrationality, we may live in perpetual dread of vital areas of internal life.

Freud once said that the purpose of psychoanalysis is to transform neurotic misery into everyday unhappiness. His point was that psychotherapy is very limited in the "cures" it produces, even though it can make a real difference in the capacity for vital engagement with life, including engagement with life's problems. Many trauma therapists seem to have reversed Freud's dictum. In advancing an ambitious project of recovery, the trauma paradigm seems to have converted everyday unhappiness back into hysterical misery.

Chapter 4

PSYCHOANALYTIC FEMINISM

Bridging Private and Public Remembrances

IT WAS 1975 and the battle over the legalization of abortion was still a recent memory. Emboldened by this victory yet fearful of losing ground, feminists throughout the United States expanded the frontiers of the struggle. In clandestine groups around the country, women gathered to teach each other cervical self-exam, menstrual extraction (a euphemism for an early abortion procedure), and folk remedies for various female ailments. We formed clinics where consciousness, health advocacy, and woman-centered care were revolutionary concepts, manifestos in a guerrilla war with the medical establishment, which was felt to be the apotheosis of patriarchal power.

I had witnessed many gynecological exams during my first career as a registered nurse and had, of course, submitted to this annual procedure as a patient. Yet the female body remained for me, as it did for most women, a dark mystery, with its endless production of secretions, disturbing sensations, and lumpy, folding fleshiness. Peering into this intimately familiar yet alien land was a subversive act, a violation of an ancient taboo. Women were to be "looked at," to be "done to," but were prohibited from looking and doing.

It was now 1976. A dozen or more of us—two or three regular staff members at the women's health center and the rest newcomers—met weekly in a dingy room in a West Central Los Angeles office building. A poster of a hirsute Wonder Woman was taped to the wall—a bold cartoon figure with raised arm extended defiantly into a clutched speculum—emblazoned with the words "WITH MY SPECULUM, I AM STRONG!" Amidst the raggedy, stuffed chairs and coffee-stained rugs, we gathered in a circle on the floor to talk about our common experiences as women within the health system. Taking out the box of shimmering, clear plastic speculums, one of the leaders then slipped off her panties and inserted the moistened instrument, inviting group members to observe her cervix. Moving to counteract the inevitable wave of feminine modesty, the second staff member joined in, asking others to take their turns in this group ritual of self-discovery.

Through our speculums we opened up a new vista of self-knowledge. As the muscular, vaginal walls were separated, a moist, bulbous protrusion came into view. My first association on seeing this hidden part, I silently confessed to myself, was that it looked much like the end of an erect penis. As a graduate student in a psychoanalytic institute at the time, I struggled with the competing lenses of feminism and Freudianism.

Being both politically and psychologically minded, I began to think about what it was we were *really* searching for when we peered into our own and each other's dark passages. To pose such questions at the time—to suggest that there may be a nonrational or overdetermined dimension to this project—would have been an act of betrayal. To assume the position of participant-observer, of one who stands outside the system of meaning in order to gain a new vantage point on it, would be to step outside of a solidary fold.

These ritualized group experiences were clearly a kind of spectacle, one infused with the sexual experimentation of 1960s and 1970s counterculture as well as with the show-and-tell of latency-aged group explorations. Yet in contrast to the hustling atmosphere of much of the sexual revolution, these women's self-help groups created a sustaining cultural bridge that most of us had been denied in the course of development. We were both seizing the phallus—as the speculum became the symbolic equivalent of the powerful, penetrating male member—and claiming unauthorized cultural space for self-discovery and mutual exploration.

We were looking for something, of course, that could not be found at the end of a speculum. The activities were invested with surplus meaning, with magical significance that blinded us to the complex aspects of power, sexuality, and female selfhood. Taking control over our bodies was too concretely understood as a struggle over the body as personal property and too bound to biologistic ideas of femaleness. Yet even though self-exam became, for me, a bit reminiscent of the laying-on of hands at revival meetings, these feminist gatherings were nothing short of transformative.

This women's self-help movement bore little resemblance to the women's recovery groups of the 1980s, where talk of dysfunctional families, love addiction, and early sexual violations was the feminine vernacular of an emerging group consciousness.[1] Unlike these psychotherapeutic groups, the earlier feminist versions of self-help envisioned the female body as the immediate terrain of emancipatory struggle. While the sexual abuse movement advanced this same struggle, it became, in the 1980s, more centered on demonstrating the damage inflicted on women than on asserting their intactness.

This chapter develops a framework for rethinking some of the recurring themes in female psychology, particularly links between the body, fantasy, and women's disturbing states of mind. Psychoanalysis and feminism are uniquely suited for this project, for each grants priority to the body in explaining conflicting aspects of human consciousness. Although psychoanalysis and feminism have a long history as warring companions, they find common ground in their mutual fascination with bodily states and the tension between public and private conceptions of the self.

As a psychology of secrets—a theory of hidden knowledge revealed through narratives—psychoanalysis creates a more hospitable stage and a more receptive audience for female storytelling than does the highly operationalized world of scientific psychology. In contradistinction to much of cognitive psychology, which stresses the mechanisms of memory, psychoanalysis asserts a narrative coherence to mental life. From a psychoanalytic perspective, repression is not simply understood as interference in the mental retrieval of information but, rather, signifies human conflict concerning self-knowledge. A central question underlying scientific and clinical discourse on the unconscious, one taken up in the previous chapter, involves whether the unconscious "tells a story"—that is, whether intelligible patterns of meaning may be deciphered from processes of mind operating outside of conscious awareness. Used heuristically and in a less reified way than we have seen in the recovered memory debate, the idea of repression sensitizes us to the drama and conflicting currents of consciousness.

Yet psychoanalysis, too, whether in the context of clinical practice or in cultural theory, requires that we examine how the stage gets set and who directs the drama. While psychoanalytic theory may be enlisted to probe the deeper currents of female conflicts and desires, granting women a fuller, more complex subjectivity, this tradition of theory also carries its own repressive legacies and blind spots. But, in correcting for these problems, many contemporary psychoanalytic feminists have tended to leave the symbolic meanings of the body and sexuality behind in an effort to assert a more authoritative female voice. As a result, the subversive potential of a feminist reading of psychoanalysis—and of women's experiences—has been blunted.

In recovering this subversive potential, this chapter enters a domain that has perpetually haunted feminism: that of fantasy and the symbolic loading of the body. Prototypical "dangerous" fantasies are explored, specifically those related to sexuality and aggression. Psychoanalysis permits us to understand how fantasies, at the individual, social, and cultural levels, are created from the inside out—that is, how they are shaped by processes of mind—whereas feminism sensitizes us to how fantasies are structured from the outside in—that is, constructed by social and cultural forces. In working both sides of this equation, I explain how the image of sexual invasion is a particularly potent one for women and suggestive of a broad landscape of possible interpretations.

FEMINISM AND PSYCHOANALYSIS

Rebellion has always been at the center of psychoanalytic storytelling as the dynamic counterpart to repression, yet this theme is subject to various cultural and political choreographies. Freud's oedipal drama, for example, may be employed to tell quite divergent stories about the formative dramas of childhood, even though it does put in the foreground the child's ambivalence toward the father. The young child does not initially love the father, in this drama, but comes to this position only through various defensive transformations. According to Freud, cultural idealization of father figures—for example, in the religious sphere—operates defensively, specifically in warding off hostility toward this early destroyer of infantile pleasures. More conservative traditions of psychoanalysis come down on the side of the father (and a more "reasonable" superego), granting the child (or child part of the adult) its mighty revolt against paternal authority but ultimately guiding the subject toward the relinquishment of infantile protests and their defensive disguises. But radical and feminist psychoanalysts create a different denouement to the narrative, more readily taking the position of the child in exposing the debilitating emotional costs of repressive paternal demands. From this subversive perspective, the neuroses that emerge out of the patriarchal family are understood to take the form more often of inhibitions, a readiness to comply with authority, than of irrational resistances to the demands of literal or symbolic fathers.[2]

Part of the appeal of psychoanalysis and the basis of its wide influence in disciplines outside of psychology is that it offers a method for understanding storytelling. In both its clinical and its cultural applications, psychoanalysis understands autobiographical memory as a means of organizing and structuring the self through narrative—through tales about the origins, dilemmas, and strivings of the self. The history of psychoanalytic inquiry into hysteria—pursued in detail in chapter 7—is of particular interest as a feminine narrative because it bridges cultural and developmental dimensions of female identity, extending from normal to pathological states associated with women.

While feminism has been at the forefront of contemporary critiques of psychoanalysis, it also has been, paradoxically, at the forefront of its revival in the social sciences and the humanities. My own approach draws on contemporary currents within psychoanalysis, weaving together ideas drawn from Freudian, object relations, and intersubjective theories, as well as from Kleinian and Lacanian traditions. My use of the psychoanalytic tradition is based on a critical and cultural view of theory, specifically as seen through the lens of feminist analysis. I am, admittedly, an ambivalent daughter of psychoanalysis, engaged in a love/hate relationship with the forefathers.[3]

Many feminist critics have argued that Freud was unable to see women outside a framework of "failed" manhood—that is, outside the idea that females "lack" the requisite capacities (for example, the phallus, cultural signifier of masculine entitlement) to forge a path through the stormy vicissitudes of development via identification with the powerful father(s). As feminists, we are more able than Freud to see women, to unravel the chain of signifiers around the nineteenth-century female hysteric and the medieval witch.[4] We now recognize how readily male fantasies and anxieties infiltrate representations of women. But how do we apply a feminist critique during an era when women have achieved some degree of authority—as theorists, patients, and practitioners—in decoding the meaning of their own stories? Part 2 of this book turns to the cultural dimensions of female storytelling and to the historical dynamics shaping their plots and subplots. But this chapter establishes a mode of listening to stories by and about women and of understanding how fantasy and external reality interact in female narratives centered on the body.

THE FANTASY OF THE MADWOMAN

In Jean Rhys's 1982 novel, *The Wide Sargasso Sea,* a different perspective on the past is used in telling the other side of the story of a character in *Jane Eyre,* Charlotte Brontë's Victorian Gothic novel centering on a love affair between a servant, Jane Eyre, and her master. In Brontë's novel, the master's crazy wife is confined to the attic, occasionally escaping at night to wreak havoc in fits of revenge. By the end of the book, the master has recovered from cruel streaks in his own nature as the love between master and servant blossoms and triumphs over Victorian propriety, on the one hand, and the "madwoman in the attic" on the other. Rhys's novel reverses perspective, telling the story of this woman in the attic, of her own losses and betrayals in being forced from her home in Jamaica and swindled by her husband's family. The madwoman in the attic is the unarticulated other, the frightful legacy of colonial oppression that masters keep closeted away, a legacy that perpetually threatens to unsettle a bourgeois world devoted to order and containment.

Sandra Gilbert and Susan Gubar use this image of the madwoman in the attic as a metaphor for the dilemmas of nineteenth-century women writers.[5] Positioned on the margins of public life, women found that the act of writing was infused with phallic, transgressive meanings. This "return of the repressed" in the form of a resistive female voice gave rise to various patriarchal reactions, including the charge of hysteria. Indeed, one of the predominant themes in late-nineteenth-century clinical case studies (a theme revisited in chapter 7) is the intimate affinity between intelligence or intellectual ambitions (or both) in women and hysterical illness.

What are the dilemmas of contemporary women who emerge from the attics of history? One of the problems of the sexual abuse survivor movement, discussed in chapter 3 in the context of the trauma model, has been how to advance awareness of the collective injuries endured by women—and the emotional devastation that has resulted—while preserving a stance of basic rationality and agency. The judgment of madness does undermine, sometimes even erases, the subject's authority to evaluate reality and to speak convincingly about it. Yet collective moments of "madness" may produce their own kind of truth. Individual women may be quite rightly described as mad, but a picture may be assembled from the various pieces to tell a lucid story.

We are accustomed in the West to thinking of madness as a dysfunction of the individual mind rather than as an interactively created condition. It is useful in many instances to approach madness as a localized or individual state; certainly psychotherapy requires such a close engagement with an individual life story and its specific vicissitudes. Social or mass madness requires a different vantage point, however, in order to bridge the effects of mind and of society. The basis of this group psychology and how it may differ from individual psychology is an undertheorized area, even in those critical traditions that extend the range of social influences beyond the domain of the family. Take, for example, Elaine Showalter's historical analysis of mass hysteria. While Showalter makes salient the role of cultural scripts in channeling ambiguous emotional complaints into medically or psychiatrically legitimized "syndromes," her analysis paints the terrain with too broad a brush, overlooking vital differences in the various conditions she reviews. Clinical narratives that capture the historical moment are variable in meaning, and understanding them requires attentiveness to their social and psychological specificity.[6] How do we understand incest tales as a group phenomenon? Are they, as many critics argue, a modern-day example of mass hysteria?[7] There may be elements of madness in the incest recovery movement, but this insight does not take us very far in explaining the group dynamics involved or the source of the madness. Since incest does commonly occur and, further, there is a long history of dismissing women's complaints as hysterical, it is not readily apparent where madness intervenes in this movement. Incest stories do have a solidaristic function for women, so we want to be careful about how we import pathology into the social-diagnostic picture.

Further, there is the question of who is really mad, those women who hold contested memories or their disturbed observers. Women's emotional reactions are often regarded as suspect and are readily associated with instability and madness. Women who insist on speaking and being heard are, in a sense, reversing a legacy of female "boundary violations" by men through their own transgressive speech, forcing their words into unreceptive ears. In response to this unsettling situation, those forced to listen have their own hysterical reactions. Projecting this hysteria onto women, experiencing their speech and emotions as excessive, may be the first line of defense for recalcitrant listeners.

To adopt a social-psychological perspective on madness does not obviate the role of individual pathology. Particular individuals and groups assume positions in cultural life depending on specific vulnerabilities or capacities as well as on the vicissitudes of personal history. Yet we can also see how various illnesses and syndromes, whatever their material or immediate causes, may be taken up over time in social symbolic ways, acquiring new meanings as they traverse the cultural landscape.

So how do we recognize the legacy of the "madwoman in the attic"—women driven quite insane—while asserting a sober, authoritative voice? In remembering the collective past, is it possible to parcel out the madness that rightly belongs to women and that which has been imposed, that which may belong to men? Feminist theorizing evidences a profound ambivalence in responding to these questions. As rule violators, madwomen are often honored as resisters in the war against patriarchy. Their sanity is in their absolute refusal of normalcy, their rejection of the Law of the Father and of his symbolic order. At the same time, there is often an insistence on the essential normalcy of madwomen, an assertion that the problem is one of misrecognition, of irrational diagnostic judgments about women. In the aphorism of Phyllis Chesler, "women aren't mad, they're angry."[8] Today we would add an intermediate category between the clinical and the political, the category of posttraumatic stress disorder, which recognizes a pathological state as a normal response to an abnormal situation.[9]

Can we have it both ways? Can we recognize both elements of rational resistance, disguised as madness, and instances of genuine insanity that run through women's collective history? It is easy enough to understand how both may be true, how culturally imposed and actual madness may be associated features of human experience, exacerbated by social marginality or by other debilitating life events.

When the social psychology of female madness is considered, however, the complexity and uncertainty attached to such questions become more pronounced. From the medical displays of hysterical fits in the late nineteenth century on through the contemporary talk-show circuit of women claiming to be multiples or satanically abused, public fascination with the madwoman has been unabated. There is a parallel riveting interest in the male psychopathic killer, a sickness of perverse detachment. Female madness is more eroticized, however, closer to the realm of the pornographic. We may grant the madwoman an enlarged cultural space for telling her story while still posing the question of whose troubles and conflicts she is enacting, her own or those of her rapt observers. As many of the sexual stories women are telling in clinical settings devolve into Gothic tales of sexual barbarism and orgiastic cults, this question has become an urgent one.

FANTASY AND FEMINIST CLINICAL PRACTICE

In the early feminist awakenings of the 1960s and 1970s, the idea of female bodily resilience mesmerized the women's movement. We learned to get up, dust off our skirts, and move on with a sense of intactness after an unsatisfying or abusive heterosexual encounter. Fighting back, in events such as Take Back the Night, often took the form of reclaiming social and cultural spaces as well as taking legal actions. Group legal and legislative actions (class-action suits, petitions, legislative and institutional reforms) provided a kind of holding ground for our various stories and experiences, a unity out of differences. In consciousness-raising groups, women spoke of rape and incest, often tearfully, but there was a cultivated matter-of-factness and outrage in much of the group talk, even as a broad range of emotions and stories were registered.[10]

The feminist theorizing of the 1980s tended to foreclose on the ambiguities of female disturbances and sexual anxieties, proclaiming them as evidence of sexual trauma. To some extent, the new focus on sexual abuse, displacing an earlier emphasis on sexual repression, marked a deep generational divide within feminism, particularly in reconciling two competing conceptions—or dominant narratives—of the concealed effects of women's oppression. One of these narratives centered on the notion of repressed female desire; the other centered on disguised or hidden injuries. And, in feminist clinical practice, trauma stories captured center stage, "repressing," in a sense, alternative readings of female disturbances of desire.

Incest, as a motif in feminist critiques of the patriarchal family, has followed this same trajectory. There has been a shift from the early feminist clinical literature on sexual abuse, which situated abuse within a broad configuration of repressive relationships in the patriarchal family, to contemporary approaches based on the trauma/dissociation model. (See Chapter 3.) In understanding the implications of this transition, Judith Lewis Herman's work is important because it bridges these two traditions of feminist inquiry. More specifically, it illustrates a set of problems confronted by feminist therapists in reconciling the legacy of sexual repression, on the one hand, and that of psychic injuries on the other.

Herman's early book, *Father-Daughter Incest,* published in 1981, combined psychodynamic and feminist thought and shaped feminist discourse on sexual abuse during the early 1980s. Her second book, *Trauma and Recovery,* published in 1992, is a significant departure from her earlier formulations and adopts the trauma/dissociation model. *Father-Daughter Incest* is based on an analysis of two groups of women: incest survivors and daughters of "seductive fathers." In describing commonalities between the two groups, Herman notes that patriarchal family dynamics include both an eroticized father-daughter relationship and intense anxiety over sexuality. "Bodies, particularly women's bodies, were considered dirty."[11] She also describes the tendency of women in both groups to idealize the father. The daughter's conflictual relationship with the father included guilty gratification in displacing the mother as the father's primary love object, as well as fear and helplessness in response to his sexual interest in her. In contradistinction to the idealized relationship with the father, the relationship with the mother was marked by pronounced hostility and rivalry. "Mothers were often suspicious and resentful of this special relationship. . . . The mothers' resentment made the daughters feel guilty but could not entirely extinguish the pleasure they derived from their favored status. Some even exulted in their mothers' mortification."[12]

In *Father-Daughter Incest,* the emotional suffering of daughters runs along a continuum from overt abuses to subtle, erotically toned invasions of childhood.[13] Herman's continuum implicitly allows for a range of interpretations of father/daughter relationships. In her more recent book, these more nuanced aspects of family dynamics and more conflictive themes in women's relationships—both familial and therapeutic—are notably minimized.

Within feminism, trauma stories also have become a unifying vehicle for expressing female disturbances within a narrative that wards off exploration of potentially disunifying differences. In the recovery literature, therapists and other group members are repeatedly described as bearing witness to the trauma, which often depends on the recovery of trauma memories. Herman states in *Trauma and Recovery* that while members of trauma-focused groups are encouraged to choose a concrete goal to achieve, most members focus on the recovery of trauma memories or the telling of the trauma story. Herman doesn't consider the possibility of group pressure to produce a trauma memory or the influence of therapists on the retrieval of memory.[14] The subsuming of a broad range of experiences and symptoms under the rubric of trauma provides a unifying basis for group identity but forecloses the exploration of many aspects of female experience, including conflict among women. Herman's description of the groups illustrates this avoidance of conflict. "The work of the group focuses on the shared experience of trauma in the past, not on interpersonal difficulties in the present. Conflicts and differences among group members are not particularly pertinent in the group; in fact, they divert the group from the task. The leaders must intervene actively to promote sharing and minimize conflict."[15]

The potential of the trauma memory to serve as a kind of psychological container for the disturbing side of female experience, including conflict with other women, is heightened by this focus on the recovery of the trauma memory. Through the story, women are able to speak about the forbidden: sexuality, aggression, rivalry, and fantasies of submission and domination. Because all these feelings are assumed to be derived from the trauma, the retrieval of the trauma memory becomes essential to the validating and normalizing of women's responses.

Although Herman notes that sexual abuse stories may stir sexual responses in therapists, particularly in male therapists, discussion of the evocative power of the trauma story in recovery groups is limited to its overt meaning as a testimonial. Implicit in her analysis is the assumption that women are not aroused by such stories, nor do they experience voyeuristic interest in such dramas. Herman does recognize, however, the potential for the retrieval of trauma memories to reenact the original trauma for the patient. "The patient may imagine a kind of sadomasochistic orgy, in which she will scream, cry, vomit, bleed, die, and be reborn cleansed of the trauma. The therapist's role in this reenactment comes uncomfortably close to that of the perpetrator, for she is invited to rescue the patient by inflicting pain."[16] The potentially invasive aspects of "inflicting pain" and the possibility that the patient's emerging memory is a symbolic communication of her own position in relation to an intrusive therapist are not considered. Herman is more likely to describe the therapist's interventions in heroic terms, just as the survivor is described heroically.

The negative meaning attached to fantasy in the sexual abuse literature contributes to its destabilizing effects in psychotherapy. Patient and therapist may unconsciously experience anxiety over any fantasies that go beyond reenactment of the trauma, so that all disturbing mental images are interpreted a priori as "flashbacks." This tendency is particularly problematic in that sexual fantasies are as much (perhaps more) a source of shame for women as are revelations around sexual abuse. In constructing memory as a literal representation of past events, the mingling of disturbing events and their fantasy elaborations is closed off, as are the inhibitions imposed on female sexual storytelling.

The use of the trauma model may also "contain" political conflicts within feminism. The focus on retrieval of the trauma memory places the perpetrator securely in the past. As some women achieve authority within public life and yet find themselves continuing to be subjugated to powerful men, it may be less dangerous to confront the "dead" fathers of early childhood than the living ones. The trauma model also unifies women in a common project that evades differences between those who have achieved authority and those who are subject to that authority. It defends against the struggle to recognize the various and divergent grievances among women, including the ways in which women may be implicated in the suffering of other women. And, further, it permits political mobilization around the most unifying issue within feminism: child sexual abuse. Given the history of anxiety over sexuality in the culture, particularly when the image of the innocent child is invoked, there are tremendous gains that follow from the victory—gains that are harder to achieve on other grounds. But it is a pyrrhic victory at best.[17]

AGGRESSION AND FANTASY

Freud has been castigated by many critics for dismissing his patients' accounts of early sexual violations as "mere fantasies," a phrase that continues to echo in feminist writing as a reminder of the prototypical father's tendency to dismiss or trivialize the word of the daughter. Yet Freud's choice of terms may have been defensive in a double sense. The history of patriarchy includes male terror of female fantasies—women's passions, imaginations, and ideas—as much as it does denial of female capacities for rationality.

Child psychoanalyst Melanie Klein went further than Freud in probing the primitive currents of infantile fantasies and the ways in which they work their way into adult mental states. Kleinians stress the mind's readiness, from the earliest moments of consciousness in infancy, to project its own considerable aggression outward onto the objects of consciousness. In part, the infant is the creator of its own maternal fantasy images, as fluctuating, "part-object" representations of the mother are managed through defensive splitting of the "good breast" and "bad breast." Experientially, these fantasy objects are grounded in the early discovery that the maternal object who gives pleasure also frustrates, that the mother the infant loves is also the one it hates.[18]

Like the phallus, the good breast and the bad breast are signifiers, neither reducible to nor entirely autonomous from their biological and social referents. Most fundamentally, they are fantasies, although actual experience modifies their intensity and rigidity as mental representations. Spanking, forcing children to eat food against their will, or emotional neglect intensify infantile paranoid anxieties, as parental harshness hinders the child's capacity to modify its own primitive representations of self and object. The child may introject, or psychologically absorb, parental aggression, which, alloyed with the child's own aggressive fantasy objects, is reprojected back onto the external object. This theory suggests that the image of the devouring monster is a projection of the child's own frightening impulses, modified (amplified or diminished) by internalized aspects of its relational world.

If taken too literally or exclusive of other dimensions of development and culture, Kleinian theory does lapse into subjectivism, for there is little emphasis on the actual environment or conditions that shape elaborations of primitive fantasy objects. While Klein was the "mother" of British object relations theory, many who share her interest in early attachments found her psychic world too inhospitable. American psychoanalytic feminism has found non-Kleinian object relations theory more congenial, in part because this tradition locates human destructiveness within the context of environmental failure.[19]

Even in the best of childhoods, however, consciousness emerges out of divisions within the self born of ambivalent discoveries. The infant discovers that need of the "good mother" evokes a companion vulnerability to her destructive side. Splitting of the earliest object of dependence into all-good and all-bad representations is one of the earliest, most primitive defenses, in that the creation of an idealized maternal imago serves as protective fantasy against its hostilely toned opposite.

In its refusal of the harmonious constructions of the mother/infant pair that came to dominate much of object relations theory, Kleinian theory registered the implacable emotional demands of mothering.[20] A Kleinian perspective emphasizes the mother as fantasy object and as projective container for disturbing currents of psychic experience. Further, Kleinian theory is not as pessimistic concerning human progress as it might seem, for it also stresses the restorative aspects of the developing capacity for guilt. The child's nascent awareness of its own capacity to affect the object of its dependence, initially through the fantasy of having destroyed the "good mother" in the discovery of her absence, is the basis for what Klein terms the "depressive position." Klein's developmental trajectory centers on the child's strivings for reparation, which provides the impetus for both modification of aggression and developed capacities for mutuality.

How does this theory of development help us understand the disturbing side of fantasy? Kleinian theory sensitizes us to those aspects of fantasy that diverge most dramatically from adult logic and external reality. While many fantasies coalesce around actual experience, primitive "flights" from reality are also pervasive in human experience. Folk culture is rife with Kleinian motifs. From fairy tales and vampire legends through science fiction, adults and children share a common fascination with the nightmarish side of consciousness, with eating the other and being eaten by the other. Children's fairy tales are rife with oral aggression and splitting of the maternal object: Snow White's fatal poisoning by the apple, seductively offered by the disguised evil queen; Hansel and Gretel's ordeal of being fattened for the oven by the old woman in the forest. Christianity, as well, is based on cannibalistic imagery—eating the body and drinking the blood of Christ. Such motifs are mediated by particular cultural and historical anxieties that shape their elaboration;[21] but Klein suggests that the persistence of primitive, paranoid anxieties in human fantasy indicates how deeply rooted they are in psychic structure. We may also recognize in Klein's torture chamber of childhood some of the terror of human consciousness and the costs of various defenses employed in its management. Many of these costs are born by women, who have been the objects of particularly virulent witch-hunts and other forms of scapegoating.[22]

We do not have to reach back far into historical memory for examples of such paranoid/schizoid fantasies. Indeed, Kleinian motifs infused clinical storytelling during the 1980s, as recovered memories of father/daughter incest devolved into Gothic tales of cannibalistic childhood orgies, with a demonic mother displacing the sexually invasive father as the central villain. Many of these "deeper" memories, recovered under hypnosis and other clinical conditions conducive to regression, may have less to do with actual past events than with primitive currents in the human imagination, including, for women themselves, the fantasy image of the malevolent, devouring mother.

FANTASIES OF DOMINATION

Appropriating a text despised by most feminists, the psychoanalyst and feminist Jessica Benjamin revisits Pauline Réage's *Story of O*, published initially in France in 1954, making use of it to tell a tale of female development under patriarchy.[23] Benjamin brings a Hegelian/psychoanalytic interpretation to Réage's sordid tale of a woman who willingly submits to brutality at the hands of her male torturers in an isolated castle, men who press the limits of her physical and emotional endurance in order to achieve in her a state of "enlightenment." Benjamin's female protagonists—including the masochistic O—are demanding something and attempting to retrieve a sense of selfhood in their acts of submission. Even though this story is offensive to many women, particularly in its positioning of the heroine as "willing" victim, Benjamin makes use of it to explore a complex female subjectivity. Domination, she insists, is not simply the imposition of power on a passive subject but, more often, enlists the subject in its creation and maintenance.[24]

While Benjamin counterposes erotic domination and authentic mutuality, implicit in her analysis is some appreciation of the way in which primitive impulses and fantasies work their way into a range of human encounters. In collapsing the distinction between the religious and the pornographic, between the saint and the sexual slave, Benjamin attempts to capture the deep structure of human complicity in domination. In both sacred and sexual contexts, she argues, submitting to the will of a powerful other involves an active desire for mutuality and recognition, even as it risks collapse into a state of irreparable isolation.

The master/slave relationship, according to Hegel, is one of mutual dependence, where each position, understood by Hegel as equally masculine, is a constitutive necessity for the establishment of the other. The master knows himself as such only through the slave, who, while being subject to the master, is in a paradoxical position of power over him. The master recognizes in the slave not only affirmation of his masterfulness but a reflection of his own dreaded dependence. Any self-assertion on the part of the slave threatens the master with the terror of abandonment and with the possibility of power reversals. Consciousness of his need for the slave threatens a loss of the master's selfhood, constituted as it is on the basis of an autonomy that exists only to the extent that it is affirmed by an other. The oppressed tend to know their oppressors better—have greater knowledge of their personhood—than the oppressors know their subjects because the slave must come to terms with his or her dependence, with the contingent basis of being, in a way that the master never does. One of the genuine costs of rulership is paranoia, a phobic dread of the other that leads to a preoccupation with the fortification of borders, emotionally and materially.[25]

One way to make use of Benjamin's intersubjective theory is to analyze the patriarchal unconscious, showing how dominant institutions collaborate in the infantile fantasies of men. As Carol Tavris points out, abused women are more likely to be labeled mad than are their abusers.[26] But how do we interpret the infantile elements contained in women's stories? Further, what does a feminist psychoanalytic reading of these stories permit us to understand of the complex currents of feminine desire?

In working at the boundary between the imaginary and the real, it is possible to veer too readily in one direction or the other. Indeed, Benjamin sidesteps the broad range of potential interpretations and social uses of women's stories even as she reclaims fantasy as a determinant of female sexuality. It makes a difference whether the *Story of O* is read as a work of fiction, an allegory of female development under patriarchy, or a literal account of the physical and sexual terrorizing of a woman. There are areas of convergence, but the distinctions do matter. If we read the story as a fantasy, we are working within the realm of what Winnicott terms transitional spaces—the domain of exploring and working through possible versions of reality, a domain where we have some control over the various positions assumed and the outcomes of the drama.[27] If we read the story as an account of actual abuse, we have fewer degrees of freedom, both in how we understand the story and in our moral responses to it. In fact, fantasy and reality are intertwined in all narrative accounts, suggesting that the same story always contains multiple levels of meaning.

The question of how we decide on the true meaning of the story—and its literal or symbolic elements—is not merely an academic or philosophical one. Anne Rice's vampire novels, for example, may be read as part of the incest survivor literature if we take her many references to incest literally, or they may be understood as meditations on the dynamics of guilt and emotional surrender.[28] Further, even the literary work of known incest survivors is open to multiple interpretations and political uses. Dorothy Allison's *Bastard out of Carolina* is a gripping autobiographical account of incest, but it is much more than that. It also is a poignant coming-of-age story of a lesbian girl, a story set in rural America, inscribed as deeply by the experience of growing up poor as it is by the trauma of sexual abuse. In her essays, Allison refuses to pathologize her own aggressive lesbian sexuality—a tendency in contemporary feminism—and asserts, instead, the contradictory, even existential, currents of female sexual desire.[29] Some of these currents are undoubtedly shaped by early sexual violations. But to view sexual fantasies that deviate from domesticated versions of femininity as merely derivatives of childhood abuse is to strip the female subject of her complexity. It is to accept too fully the idea that woman is a mere echo of patriarchy, without psychological substance or moral conflicts of her own.

As a story of actual events, sadomasochistic (S/M) dynamics also include a range of meanings for women. In abuse situations, there is often the possibility of reversals, and women may experience a moment of omnipotence in being the object of the desperate, infantile dependence of an abusive male partner.[30] As a negotiated sexual encounter, S/M sexual practices may carry other psychological meanings. The masochist may fluctuate between the position of indestructible maternal object and that of infant at the center of maternal ministrations. The "bottom" position in S/M practices is the most sought after since it is the sadist who must orchestrate and monitor the activity, in perfect attunement with the desires of the masochist.[31]

In my clinical experience, women who identify with sexual rebelliousness, with exploring the outer limits of sexual experimentation, are sometimes drawn to S/M practices. Most of these women are not interpersonally masochistic (or sadistic), nor do they lack a sense of self. More often, they have some sense of being emotionally impenetrable, of a "thickness" that permeates connections with others, as one patient of mine put it. This same patient grew up in an isolated rural setting with parents who seemed to be quite depressed and withdrawn. The rituals of bondage and controlled pain during sex with her woman lover felt like a form of bundling, less an expression of passivity than an active receptivity toward a palpably present other.

One of the perennial difficulties in feminist incursions into sexual storytelling, particularly as seen through clinical theory, is that the body so readily gets left behind as a realm of fantasy. Even Benjamin's nuanced reading of the *Story of O* suffers this fate—that is, a "repression" of the subtextual, conflicting currents of female desire. In making use of it as an allegorical tale of female lack of subjecthood under patriarchy, Benjamin downplays important narrative elements of the story, including its ending. At the conclusion of the *Story of O,* we learn that the true object of O's desire is a woman, and that O does not so much lack desire as she is fearful of its intensity. O's submission, we may infer, is born out of more than simple selflessness. She falls under the hypnotic spell of her captors because she identifies so strongly with their fantasy: woman as sexual object is frightening because she is "excessive." As Benjamin points out, O concurs with the master that she, like the maternal object of childhood, must be "beaten back" by the phallus. But in this story of ritualized containment, female excesses may be readily disguised as absences, and woman as O may appear to be more vacant than palpably present.

Benjamin's outlook on the human condition, much like Klein's, is not as pessimistic as it might seem. In approaching the Western idea of the absolute, autonomous (male) self as a regressive cultural fantasy, Benjamin does preserve the ideal of true autonomy, based in the capacity for mutuality and knowledge of interdependence. Infants, she points out, do display curiosity about their social world, seeking out genuine engagement with an other. Societies organized around domination and social hierarchies, however, tend to recapitulate the master/slave dialectic on individual and group levels. Women, particularly, suffer the fate of the masochistic O, not in finding pleasure in pain but in searching for a recognition that perpetually eludes them.

This intersubjective approach to psychoanalysis may be enlisted to explain the interactive dimensions of conditions associated with women and how fantasies of domination work their way into a range of gendered encounters, including therapeutic ones. When the idea of S/M encounters is extended beyond the realm of the explicitly pornographic, eroticized domination may be understood as a narrative structure or subtext within a broad range of female stories chronicling the dilemmas of the self.

FANTASY AND FEMALE DEVELOPMENT

Because stories have multiple meanings, it is important to take into account the various currents and subcurrents of female sexuality in such tales. Further, we need to have some means of separating the psychological residue of past sexual violations from other conflictual themes in female development that may work their way into remembered stories, including incestuous ones. If one tendency in feminism has been to excessively pathologize such stories, another has been to excessively celebrate all "unruly" expressions of female desire.[32] In the bipolar world of feminist sexology, there are notable swings between a depressive loss of vitality, on the one hand, with sexual abuse as a monotonic drumbeat, and a manic flight into the delights of polymorphic perversity on the other. Not surprisingly, the second tendency has always been more readily marginalized within feminism, even though it is clearly a reaction to the first tendency.

One way of approaching the normal and the pathological dialectically is to look at how various developmental struggles are mediated by gender dynamics that shape the outcome of the conflict. Submission and bondage, as motifs in some sexual fantasies and sexual practices, express normal as well as pathological conflicts in human experience. Young children regularly engage in games of escape and capture—and often squeal with delight in being swept up into the arms of an adult as the child is taking flight. At the same time, forced tickling and being held down too long or too hard are among the more commonly disturbing experiences of childhood, even though readily dismissed as benign horseplay. There is a vital interplay in human development between the wish to be contained or held by an other—even submitting to the will of that other—and the desire to escape such control. The one side of the conflict is organized around knowledge of dependence on a more powerful other; the second side is born of strivings for separateness and independence.

In the course of female development, however, this interactive dynamic of closeness and distance, containment and freedom, is more often circumscribed. As Benjamin so effectively argues, the girl encounters a series of cultural roadblocks in achieving a unified and substantive sense of self, as does the mother. When women lack social recognition, mothers are limited in their ability to confer recognition to daughters. The cultural devaluation of girls and women and the lack of a secure sense of self that results make the daughter perpetually vulnerable to the seductions of patriarchy, literally or symbolically. Holding on to so little of her own, she seeks recognition from a powerful male other. But the recognition she finds is in serving as Echo to the lonely Narcissus.[33]

What are the implications of this gendered plot for understanding the dynamics of contemporary women? The drama of gender development and stories of the female self, told and retold over the generations, have a disturbing sameness. But there are also subversive female stories, sometimes smuggled in through a dominant narrative. It is important to recognize the dominant motifs while remaining attuned to the complexity of the subtexts and to unexpected twists in the narrative. From a feminist perspective, there is potential for veering either in a depressive direction, as cultural traditions weigh so heavily on our efforts to dismantle them, or in the direction of manic flight from these same sobering realities.

While I make use of psychoanalytic feminist ideas about female development throughout the book, I also emphasize the unstable, fluctuating aspects of gender identifications, an instability that opens up the possibility for social change. Female identity in the contemporary period continues to be constituted through the matrix of power imbalances within the family and the larger society. But it is also in a state of flux.[34] A profusion of images and fantasies, unstable and unintegrated, is more constitutive of the contemporary gendered subject than is the more stable, dichotomous world of gendered subjects of a century ago. The contemporary female subject is less likely to be repressed than to be dissociated. Repression, as I argued in chapter 3, suggests an underlying

associative unity of the self, even as aspects of the self are split off from awareness. Dissociation, however, implies fluctuating, unstable states, and a subject who
has access to various images, memories, and affects but lacks the capacity to make
integrative use of them.

THE BODY EGO AND THE RELATIONAL EGO

In the stories that will be analyzed in part 3 of the book, two
motifs emerge as clinical indicators associated with trauma. The first motif
involves difficulties in the regulation of emotion and states of bodily arousal, and
the second centers on problems in integrating self and object representations,
which interferes with the development of a stable sense of identity and autobiographical memory. Both these clinical motifs, or problem areas, are widely
believed to be the result of trauma. Further, sexual abuse is thought to be particularly productive of dissociative phenomena—disruptions in the mind's capacity to integrate memory, emotion, and identity.

While difficulties in integrating subjective states are demonstrably related to
the effects of trauma, such difficulties are also embedded in mundane aspects of
female development in patriarchal societies. Indeed, this same set of motifs is decipherable in the psychoanalytic literature on female development. One theme
involves impulse/arousal regulation (the body ego) and the other involves inter-
personal/boundary regulation (the relational ego). Freud first introduced the concept of bodily zones as the basis of early ego development through the oral, anal,
and phallic phases.[35] Object relations theory extended this embodied theory into
the mode of care giving, with holding, touching, and gazing displacing Freud's
primacy of the oral zone.[36]

From an object relations point of view, the parent's (typically the mother's)
capacity to empathically regulate the infant's bodily needs, maintaining a vital
balance between restrictive holding and freedom of movement, is crucial to early
ego development. The interpersonal world provides the necessary containment
and support for the expression of arousal states, so that body ego and relational
ego interact, ideally, more or less integratively.

One of the recurring themes in the psychology of women, however, centers
on the dissociation of the female self and body, with the body experienced as an
alienated realm of disturbing sensations and as a site of invasive encounters.[37]
For many girls, discovering the meaning of their own ambiguous sexual stirrings
involves confronting a minefield of threats. It may involve literal sexual invasions,
which preempt the possibilities for making creative use of the body as a source
of pleasure and fantasy. Or it may mean incorporating terms such as *slit* and *hole*
into an imagined female generative space that feels perpetually vulnerable to
vaguely perceived threats. As a result, one line of defense in female development
may be dissociative distance from the body.

For boys, as well, the body ego emerges as a gendered zone of sensations.
The cultural world of American boyhood—dominated by war games and action-

oriented toys—defines the masculine self as a site of heightened arousal. Teachers and parents tend to respond to boys more often than to girls, in both positive and negative ways.[38] Boys are granted more latitude for aggressive, sexual, and antisocial behavior, while also eliciting more controlling and punitive responses from adults. Girls, however, are generally less visible to adults, less likely to stimulate intense, interpersonal engagement. In that the cultural world of female development circumscribes the exploration of intensive states of arousal and offers less provision for sexual and aggressive sensations, there is less space—intrapsychically and interpersonally—for integrating such states into a sense of self.[39]

Under these conditions, female development has a propensity toward the projection of various fantasies and impulses that are not readily integrated into female selfhood, just as male development tends toward the projection of passive affective states, such as dependence and vulnerability. Once again, this process of projection is an intersubjective, unstable process where various participants engage in the exchange and transfer of "hot" emotional goods.

On the positive side, girls may acquire more cultural support than boys for accessing interior life because they have fewer avenues available for externalizing of emotional conflict. Girls also employ this contained inner-directedness in creative ways—for example, in writing and in keeping diaries or journals. This de-eroticized sensuality also permits a level of physical freedom in female relationships that is virtually absent in male relationships. Touching and hugging are more normative in female friendships, as are verbal expressions of affection and tenderness.[40] Female development encourages a broader range of affective states than does male development; these states are more attenuated for girls, more diffusely associated with the body and primary drives (in Freudian language, they are more aim-inhibited.)

Gender differences in the regulation of impulse/arousal states are mediated by the sexual division of labor and by the social meaning of the sex difference. The cultural world of male development tends to heighten arousal states, whereas that of female development tends to diminish them. Women are more engaged than men in caregiving responsibilities, and more attenuated, nuanced responses to social cues may be acquired in the course of engaging in this form of work. In caring for dependent members of the group, women develop a greater capacity to "read" the emotional language of others and to bridge the verbal and nonverbal worlds.[41]

A further implication of this gender difference is that male development in patriarchal societies allows for more "forgetting" of the other than does female development. A woman patient of mine put it succinctly: "My husband doesn't have to remember as much as I do about the kids or the family because when he forgets things he doesn't feel bad about himself like I do." Women's role as "emotion managers" centers on the cultural task of holding and maintaining social knowledge, particularly social knowledge associated with dependence needs.[42] A vital part of this caregiving work is the capacity to protect the object of dependence—men as well as children—from conscious awareness of the extent of their dependence on women.

The considerable constraints on women, derived from both their oppression and the binding claims of caregiving responsibilities, extend into the pleasure "economy" of a society. Female "altered states"—that is, loss of normal ego controls over the body—seem destabilizing, on a societal level and for women themselves, because of the domestication of femininity. Until the 1960s, prohibitions on female alcohol and drug consumption codified this double standard. Historically, female states of rapture, of intense arousal, have been more readily transported into the religious realm, channeled into the imagery of saintly piety as well as into hysterical illness (a theme pursued in part 2).

The other dimension of this problematic foreclosure of female development, one attended to more consistently by psychoanalytically oriented feminists than the impulse/arousal dimension, concerns self and object representations, or self-in-relation. Nancy Chodorow, for example, suggests that normative female development produces more flexible ego boundaries and greater preoccupation with relational concerns than does male development. Masculinity, Chodorow argues, is organized defensively in counteridentification with the mother of early childhood, creating a perpetual readiness in boys and men to take flight from the "feminine" states of dependence and vulnerability.[43]

The central problem of gender development is not so much overall differences in human relationality but, rather, differences in the range of interplay permitted for engagement and disengagement with an other. In that the social world of female development is less permissive of social disengagement, less forgiving of unresponsivity, girls are often deprived of the conditions of separateness that are the basis of a bounded sense of self. The cultural ideal of the eternally accessible maternal (and sexual) object works against female disengagement and undermines possibilities for developing stable mental representational processes and for using fantasy in the consolidation of the internal world. Once again, dissociative distance may be a means of managing perpetual intrusions on female psychic and social spaces.

Some of this female fragmentation and relational embeddedness is connected to enlisting others for purposes of self-containment, however. In my own clinical experience with women, a recurring developmental motif involves the discovery—remembered as part of puberty or early adolescence—of being "too big." Too big may mean a literal sense of towering over boys, or it may refer to taking up too much psychological or social space. A range of associations often flow from this "fixed idea," including the fantasy that female emotions, desires, bodily states are generally excessive. The link between hysteria and femaleness feels intuitively all too real for many women, not because of any biological predisposition to madness but because this cultural fantasy of the excessive female is so deeply rooted in female psychic experience. Women may stop fantasizing altogether, fearful of arousing more internal states than they can effectively manage.

THE PSYCHODYNAMICS OF FEMINISM

What are the implications of these conversations between psychoanalysis and feminism for understanding what is to be done about the suffering of women? Certainly, the project goes beyond "recovering" memories of sexually abusive fathers, although this is one moment of vital feminist discovery. But, more broadly, how do we take patriarchy and its defenses into account, resisting reductionist or one-dimensional portraits of self and other?

Not surprisingly, traversing the rational and the irrational, fantasy and reality, has been more difficult in the immediacy of feminist political campaigns than in the more socially removed area of feminist aesthetics. For some feminists, literature and art are the site where the female body and selfhood can be claimed, aggressively destroyed, lovingly mourned, and revived within the coordinates of a more fluid symbolic universe. Jeanne Perreault describes this engagement with the body in women's writing as a project of redefining self-as-object, a site of conflicting, emerging identities where "'I have a body' struggles with 'I am a body.'"[44]

In feminist projects such as *Bad Girls,* a collection of artistic works by women, culturally idealized representations of the female form are violated, with the brush serving as the phallic agency denied women in representing themselves. Images of devouring female orifices and phallic breasts violate everyday sensibilities, implicitly confronting male castration anxieties, which make such imagery seem obscene. These Bad Girls refuse the position of reassuring mirror, of maternal container for masculine uncertainty, by asserting the forbidden and by mocking the patriarchal unconscious.[45]

As feminists traverse the ground from the poetic to the clinical and the political, from the admittedly imaginary to the "real" world of concrete emotional suffering, the female body seems to become too present as its borders are sharpened in feminist theory. Similarly, memory becomes too concrete and historically localized. In other words, an exploratory, creative space of meanings between the body and the knowing female subject seems to readily collapse; it is as though the body-as-self is too present for women in clinical and political theory, too dominating, to feel like a symbolic space for the free play of fluctuating meanings.[46]

Psychoanalytic feminists operating within the literary sphere—where the theater of mind could be taken seriously as a metaphor—have been able to refuse such partisan loyalties, for they have been less embattled, more removed from the front of feminist resistances to sexual abuse than those operating in the political sphere. Not surprisingly, Freudian feminism thrived in the 1980s as a vital enterprise in the humanities, even as such a marriage of traditions was felt to be an unwholesome one, an anathema, by many psychodynamic clinicians who were informed by feminist critique.

French Psychoanalytic Feminism

Many of the French psychoanalytic feminists have moved boldly into the quicksand of fantasy by anchoring the sexual difference—and the

opposition of mind and body, masculine and feminine—in the Western Enlightenment's pathological dread of the maternal body and the dependencies it evokes.
These theorists resist decisive answers to the question of the precise source of the
hysteric's suffering, even as they locate it in the problem of the female body under
patriarchy.[47]

As theorizing that admits to, even cherishes, the ambiguity and uncertainty
of language, French feminism contrasts starkly with the psychic realism that is
more common in psychoanalytic feminism on the American side of the Atlantic.
French feminists call for "wild" theorizing, substituting traditional phallic talk
within the academy—talk of penetrating arguments—with labial talk of unstable,
rhythmic speech. For the French psychoanalyst Hélène Cixous, this feminism intervenes in the uneasy tension between psychoanalysis and science, calling for their
final divorce and for a surviving "poetics of theory."[48] Remembering is, most defiantly, understood as transformative in that the most determinative moments of
the past resist the sharp outlines imposed by scientific discourse.

Sublimating the gynocentrism of radical feminism into this French playground of language, one of Luce Irigaray's more influential works, entitled *Speculum of the Other Woman*, revisits Freud's theory of female sexuality and the
Oedipus complex, submitting it to a feminist critique.[49] Unlike the laser-beam
gaze of the cervical exams I described at the beginning of the chapter, Irigaray's
speculum opens up a much larger vista of meanings to be negotiated, extending
into the Western Enlightenment. Yet paradoxically, both projects—one highly
concrete and the other enormously abstract—meet at points, circling around the
question of what is wrong with the female body, what is it that women lack.

For French feminists, this question takes them down the path of many postmodernists in challenging the very foundation of Western rationality. Unlike some
of the postmodernists, however, Irigaray and Cixous do not settle for atomistic,
alienated speech acts. They are more the Romantics, in the sense of recovering
a lost language, a bodily articulated knowing of the world. From this perspective, hysteria has less to do with childhood trauma than with the agonizing search
for voice. It is more a problem of the body as a whole for women than of any
discrete, momentous acts in violation of it. "Body memories"—physical sensations invested with disturbing, psychological meaning—do not "tell us" a specific story of past injuries; our unarticulated achings remind us that we are
embodied beings and that our histories have been denied us.[50]

The Dialectics of Fantasy and Reality

Feminism seems to be particularly prone to assertions of unambiguous meaning attached to the body—a body that "speaks itself"—when it
becomes joined to the clinical project of recovery or cure. Psychoanalyst Jane
Gallop addresses this difficulty "in accepting the body as metaphor" within
contemporary feminism and its "demand that metaphors of the body be read
literally."[51] And yet, in retrieving the female body as a site of complex meaning
making, as not reducible to women's historical bodies, we inevitably confront the

problem of fantasy. This confrontation can feel more dangerous than liberatory, however, more fraught with risk than ripe with opportunity. It is one thing to analyze phallocentric fantasies inscribed on the female body; it is quite another to consider how the body is, for women themselves, also a domain of real and imagined terrors. In the realm of the political and the clinical, "playing" with images of the sexual difference is felt to be a boy's game, one where, much as we learned on the playground, girls are easily burned.

Between the two extremes of hysterical poetics and clinical realism, there may be ways of engaging fantasy and material reality more dialectically. As Adrienne Rich so passionately describes it, breaking free from idealization of the father means struggling with the female self in relation to his world.

> For years I struggled with you: your categories, your theories, your will, the cruelty which came inextricably from your love. For years all arguments I carried on in my head were with you. I saw myself, the eldest daughter raised as son, . . . the eldest daughter in a house with no son, she who must overthrow the father, take what he taught her and use it against him. All this in a castle of air, the floating world of the assimilated who know and deny they will always be aliens.
>
> After your death I met you again as the face of patriarchy, could name at last precisely the principle you embodied. I saw the power and the arrogance of the male as your true watermark; I did not see beneath it the suffering of the Jew, the alien stamp you bore, because you had deliberately arranged that it should be invisible to me. It is only now, under a powerful, womanly lens, that I can decipher your suffering and deny no part of my own.[52]

Rich envisions a complex project of closures and openings, of engagement and distance from the father, and of identifications and counteridentifications with his world. This transition from father worship to a more substantive female selfhood requires a strong women's movement, without which female rebellion can easily devolve into illness. Yet in retrieving an authentic sense of self, out from under the shadow of the powerful fathers, women inevitably confront confusion and ambivalence over what belongs to men and what is their own, including the content of their fantasies.

CONCLUSIONS: TRANSFORMATIVE REMEMBERING

What are the implications of these lines of psychoanalytic reasoning for recasting the debate over recovered memories of sexual abuse? First, normal female development under patriarchy does potentiate several problems associated with clinical remembering. Where women lack social recognition or a secure sense of self, they may be vulnerable to clinical suggestions that override historical experience. If femininity is organized around heightened receptivity to the other—around mirroring functions—we must take into account the resultant permeability of female psychic spaces to the invasive responses of others, including those of therapists. Second, sexuality is fraught with anxiety for many women, both as a result of overt sexual violations and as a consequence of sexual repression. The female body is the locus of imagined terrors for women as well as actual historical assaults or harms endured, each of which speaks to one aspect of women's oppression. By focusing exclusively on memory of sexual violations and by neglecting the problem of sexual repression, clinicians fail to grant women full recognition. No less problematic in feminist-informed therapies has been the daughter's desire for the father. If feminism "represses" fantasy and oedipal longings, finding no place for them in enlightened discourse, there may be an inevitable return of the repressed in hysterical storytelling.

In its more progressive expressions, therapeutically and politically, transformative remembering involves a reflective and creative engagement with the past, a past that is understood to be modified through shifting, emerging capacities for "holding" more valencies of self and other representations than was formerly possible. This psychoanalytic feminist approach to remembering inevitably raises uncertainties about the relationship between fantasy and reality, self and other, madness and lucidity. Gender is a dynamic category, subject to historical change and alternative interpretations. Psychoanalytic theory sensitizes us to the overdetermined character of gender—the myriad unconscious conflicts and fantasies that work their way into the gender divide.

French hysterical poetics introduces an alternative to the clinical realism so evident in feminism in the United States, particularly as this poetic view of the unconscious resists the idea of concrete locations or causes of female suffering. But like the hysteric herself, this feminist tradition may suffer a loss of acuity, a diffuseness of perspective, through its widening of the theoretical lens.

Nonetheless, we may make use of psychoanalytic poetics, just as we made use of Kleinian theory, as a corrective to problematic tendencies in contemporary feminist theory. As we continue to understand the social field of female storytelling, attending to multiple meanings and interpretations, we may want to remember that the legacy of women's oppression includes the foreclosing and forbidding of many dimensions of personhood. It is not enough to reject hysteria as a condition affiliated with feminine suffering, recasting it as a masculine defense against female "excess." As important as this insight is in reworking the social dimensions of hysteria, it does not grant women the generative power of fantasy or unruly desires. Further, it does not allow for the real possibility of female madness or emotional suffering born of conditions that often elude identification of a precise origin.

PART II

RECOVERING HISTORICAL MEMORY

Sexual Storytelling, Hypnosis, and Hysteria

From father I got my bearings, the seriousness in life's pursuits; from mother the passion for life, and the enjoyment of spinning fantasies.
—Johann Wolfgang von Goethe, *Zahme Xenien*, pt. 7

Women have served all these centuries as looking-glasses possessing the magic and delicious power of reflecting the figure of man at twice its natural size. . . . The looking-glass vision is of supreme importance because it changes the vitality; it stimulates the nervous system. Take it away and man may die like the drug fiend deprived of his cocaine.   —Virginia Woolf, *A Room of One's Own*

IN THE INTRODUCTION to *Pillar of Salt,* I made use of the psychoanalytic idea that an indirect path is often more useful than a direct one in getting to the source of a problem. This part takes us on such a diversionary path in cutting a wider swath through modern Western history than was undertaken in part 1. There is a purpose to this journey, specifically in helping us to understand better the cultural origins of the contemporary genre of clinical stories explored in part 3. I use the term *transformative remembering* in describing this genre of subversive stories about the female self, stories that diverge from dominant cultural scripts and conventional narratives.

One of the intriguing discoveries I made in investigating the history behind the recovered memory controversy was that women's sexual stories, hypnosis, and hysteria seem to have a long-standing affinity with one another. I began to wonder why they have emerged historically as a constellation of concerns—as a family of affiliated preoccupations—within psychology. Also, I began to attend to what is old and what is new in the contemporary debate over women's communications from "beyond the normal," including what such communications reveal about a historically changing female subject.

This part begins with women's storytelling through folktales and legends, tracing the theme of overt and subtextual incest through to the contemporary genre of sexual abuse narratives. My main argument is that the reality of sexual abuse and incest in women's collective history gives rise to the legendary and social symbolic use of the idea of intimate invasions of the self. Chapters 6 and 7 pursue the theme of intimate invasions of the self as this theme emerges in the history of hypnosis and hysteria. In tracing the steps of some of the early pioneers of the mind, I focus on the role of women as protagonists in the theater of consciousness. Further, this part anchors ideas about the self and "concealed knowledge" in larger social and historical dynamics, forces that shape the storytelling conventions available for creating an internally coherent narrative out of fragmentary imagery and disturbing states of mind.

Chapter 5

SOCIAL REMEMBERING AND THE LEGENDARY PAST

WHEN I WAS A STUDENT at the University of Washington in the early 1970s, my dad occasionally took me to school after stopping by for morning coffee and a visit. On one of these occasions, as we pulled up to the parking booth at the entrance of the campus, my dad initiated a conversation with the attendant. As cars lined up behind our old Buick, Dad explained, "I'm taking my daughter here to the university." The attendant looked back blankly as he handed Dad the yellow drive-through ticket. Dad continued, seeming not to notice the attendant's impatient glance at the expanding trail of drivers waiting for their own parking tickets. "You know, I didn't go to university myself; I went to the college of hard knocks." I sunk into my seat in embarrassment as Dad chuckled out loud, lingering over what felt to him to be an amazing observation. He was truly awed by what his children were able to do in the world, even as he was awed by his own accomplishments. The son of Norwegian immigrants and a high school graduate, he had worked his way up the corporate ladder during the boom years of postwar economic expansion. He alternated between envious admiration of and outright contempt for "Harvard MBA" types. Schools of higher learning were sacred places in his eyes, and he often said that a college education was "something they could never take away from you." I never understood who "they" were, or what things they could take away more easily than college degrees. As a child, I always found these pronouncements vaguely related to the Great Depression, which tended to be confused in my mind with the Dark Ages.

At a social gathering many years later, I was telling this story about Dad when my sister Joanie, also at the gathering, accused me of memory theft. "That didn't happen to you," she charged with obvious indignation; "it happened to me!" After we reviewed the relevant history, the informal jury of our peers decided in her favor. As it seemed, I had indeed unconsciously appropriated her experience and felt it to be my own. As my younger sister, she had learned early on to monitor my tendency to dominate, to claim more than my share of family goods. So this story about a story became, for her, an illustration of sibling domination.

Memory researchers refer to this phenomenon as source amnesia—forgetting the source of acquired information. It is a common type of memory error, even though for most practical purposes autobiographical memory is fairly accurate and reliable.[1] Most of our memory errors are not detected or challenged as mine was by my sister. Yet simply characterizing this minor episode as source amnesia or "false memory" misses an important aspect of remembering. I had woven my sister's memory into my own because it vivified a shared set of experiences with our dad. He was known to be a storyteller of the old-school type, and to hold the attention of his audience, including his children, long beyond the time allotted him by social graces. Joanie's story must have impressed me, at the time I heard it, as prototypically "Dad," as illustrative of a cluster of related traits: his penchant for "holding up the line," reverence for education, and endearing but embarrassing displays of self-mockery. I had my own memories of these aspects of him, but hers seemed to elegantly combine a number of them.

In the Western tradition, we are accustomed to thinking of memory as a property of individuals and to assume a proprietary stance toward personal recollections. College degrees have become a highly inflationary form of currency in recent decades, but memories may be the one thing "they can't take away from you." The sexual abuse recovery literature often displays reverence toward the memory record, as well as a strong belief in the foundational truths it reveals. In a society where values are unstable and in flux, autobiographical memory may be felt to be a "text" that is incontrovertibly knowable and claimable. An unfortunate embarrassment and defensiveness pervade defenders of recovered memory as they respond to the mountainous evidence that remembered events may not always be factually correct. The recognition that memories may be "implanted" or shaped by various social influences seems to compromise their status and to undermine the grievances they so often carry.

Like the biblical house built on shifting sands, social alliances and political movements built on personal recollections risk dissolution when confronted with the uncertainties of memory. While it is important to preserve the rich specificity of individual memories, we also need categories for thinking about collective remembering. We need memory metaphors, legends, and myths, even as we recognize how and where such memory products may merge into autobiographical recall. In some situations factual aspects of memory do matter in evaluating truth content, but an excessive preoccupation with facticity often blunts the capacity to listen and to comprehend.

Feminists in the field of sexual abuse generally are at war with the idea of incest stories as fantasy and legend. To introduce such terms is to suffer a retreat, it is implicitly feared, into the dark ages of prefeminist thought, when women's accounts of abuse were dismissed as hysterical ravings. But an alternative approach to this problem of legendary truth grants legends some revelatory meaning in reconciling the particularities of individual experience and collective efforts to derive meaning from them.

For collective meaning making, the truth of incest legends does not rest on the veracity of each individual account—indeed, some accounts may be mistaken or exaggerated as the extraordinary is employed to give poignancy to the ordinary. Rather, the question of the truth of the legend centers on whether there is a pattern in feminine experience in patriarchal societies that would give rise to such a legend and make it truthful, even if not every reported case is factual. As Bruner has suggested, stories generate "a map of possible worlds in which action, thought, and self-definition are permissible (and desirable)."[2]

With the decline of an activist feminist movement, women seem to be fighting patriarchs one at a time, memory by memory, as the facts of a contested past are reviewed by science or the courts. By "recovering" the social dimension of remembering, however, we may be able to recognize broad motifs that shape a collective past while still preserving the wealth of differences and variations within this collective project. Enlarging our understanding of remembering in this way to include group processes of recall allows us to put the problem of "source amnesia" in a new light. The "source" of a remembrance may not be readily or immediately located in discrete events in an individual past but rather may be found in the complex web of converging group experiences. Exploring this area, which has been peripheral to scientific inquiry into memory, engages us in the question of how social identifications are forged through storytelling.

Chapter 2 established that emotional arousal does heighten memory processes, although it does not necessarily produce more accurate recall. A useful idea from this line of research is that emotional arousal—excitement, anxiety, fear, surprise—creates a readiness to remember, a motivational framework for the encoding of experiences.[3] Such moments of readiness contain the potential for misremembering as much as for vivid recall of actual events. Further, social influences on autobiographical memories, particularly emotionally significant ones, are potent and far-reaching in their effects. Whether we are talking about how parents interpret the screams of a child, how therapists interpret depressive withdrawal, or how cultures interpret bizarre behavior, the underlying issue is the dependence of humans on some explanatory framework in making emotional states communicable and memorable.

As argued in chapter 2, humans do not absorb, spongelike, the cultural schema or interpretations available to them. There must be some congruence between the preexisting beliefs and experiences of a group and its incorporation of a social message. In the 1980s, when the incest survivor emerged as a spellbinding storyteller, much of her power resided in the receptivity of her audience to her transformative message. Many women were moved by this archetypal adult daughter's refusal of her father and his seductions. And many of us queried our own murky recollections, asking ourselves anxiously, "Could my father have sexually abused me, even though I don't remember?"

As feminists mobilized politically to defend women's emergent memories of childhood abuses, however, the broad range of possible meanings contained in such memories was collectively "repressed." As I argued in chapter 4, much of the feminist discourse on sexual abuse and incest has collapsed the cultural space between fantasy and reality in an effort to collectively awaken from a narcotizing slumber. The dreamlike states associated with fantasy often feel dangerously regressive, as they threaten to overcome the fragile collective ego boundaries of our recently won accomplishments. Yet we may benefit from such temporary "regressions in the service of the ego"—even suspending the reality principle for a moment in order to enlarge our understanding of various cultural forces that work their way into our consciousness. Individual incest survivors may, indeed, find this a treacherous regression. Yet collective projects of remembering must find room for such regressions—and for forbidden questions—if they are not to suffer the reimposition of silences of their own.

This chapter explores women's resistive storytelling, where incest and sexual injury emerge as central motifs. I explain how imagery of father/daughter incest operates in fairy tales and legends and how feminist reinterpretations of such legends are shaped by broad cultural forces impinging on storytellers and their audiences.

ENCHANTING STORIES

Throughout the modern period, women have been excluded from much of the storytelling that takes place in public life. Working against this dominant motif, however, is the subtext of woman enacting her own mesmerizing influence over her audience. Here she stands in the tradition of Scheherazade, the heroine of *The Arabian Nights,* who enchanted the powerful king with her learned tongue, subduing his homicidal madness through her skills as a storyteller.[4] The king, who sexually possesses a virgin each night only to have her murdered the next morning, is wreaking revenge on his unfaithful wife. Scheherazade, enlisting her sister as accomplice, outwits the king and perpetually defers her own death, bringing about the salvation of both other Muslim virgins and the soul of the maniacal king. This story represents the power seized by women through their capacities to enchant, their ability to outwit patriarchal authority through seductions of the tongue.

In her analysis of *The Arabian Nights,* Karen Rowe claims that Scheherazade's power to instruct is derived from three sources of knowledge attributed to women: "the knowledge of sexual passion, the knowledge of healing, and the wisdom to spin tales."[5] Yet we must be mindful of the horrendous constraints imposed on these female powers of influence—for example, the lethal consequences of our heroine's failure to please. Further, the feminine power to heal a wounded manhood generates its own kind of madness, as the life force of women is consumed by this dominating project. We may find inspiration in the bravery and cleverness of Scheherazade, but her fate is tragically chained to patriarchal authority, even as she seductively undermines it.

Nonetheless, this hypnotic embrace across the gender divide does create social tension between the "official" stories, most often authored by men, and the unofficial, subversive stories of women. When women achieve new freedoms, we would expect female storytelling to change as a result. In shifting the focus from a female subject vis-à-vis her male translator to women's collective storytelling, we also introduce a different audience. When women are the rapt audience of female storytellers, the gender dynamics of recollections must be understood in terms of the mesmerizing aspects of familiarity and commonality as opposed to the voyeuristic appeal of otherness and difference.

Resistive Storytelling

In recovering the "matrilineal" roots of the feminine imagination, Gilbert and Gubar look back at the emotional illnesses of nineteenth-century women writers and at how women transformed a world of immobility, invisibility, and stifling constraints into a thriving subculture of literary achievements.[6] In asserting the phallic authority of the pen, Gilbert and Gubar suggest, women writers struggled to overcome a cultural castration that preceded the threatening act of creativity. Whereas many male writers were guiltily conflicted over how to wield the mighty pen, women suffered the more diffuse and paralyzing condition of shame, which is less amenable to such "sublimations."[7]

How do women transform the diffuseness of their inhibitions and discontents through the representational materials available to them? And how do they create unpleasing stories without the threat of banishment? From the nineteenth century to the present, women's stories have been cast through the twin legacies of purity and defilement, the angelic and the demonic. As Sherry Ortner observes, woman, as signifier, stands both above and below culture.[8] She embodies both the transcendent principle—the apotheosis of purity—and the subterranean principle: devouring, cunning, and more primordial and lawless than men if left unchecked.

The destruction of demonized representations of femininity has been more urgent for some feminist writers, while destroying sacralized images has been more urgent for others. Before we can create, Virginia Woolf instructs us, women must "kill" the "angel in the house."[9] Finding literary voice inevitably means eradicating the corsets that have bound the feminine imagination. There has been an inescapably fertile union between the demonic and the feminine in women's creative work, Woolf implies, one that confronts the repressive mother—the angel in the house—even as it resists the powerful father. Unlike angels, devils are serious contenders in cosmic struggles over power, a mythic theme that emerges in the satanic ritual abuse narratives discussed in chapter 10.

If women can be culturally reduced to devils as readily as to angels and, by traversing these two poles of the cosmos, excluded from the earthly realm of authority, how do women find a means of asserting cultural authority and of finding an authentic voice? This project involves a rereading of the old tales as much as it does the creation of new ones. And Gilbert and Gubar suggest that fairy tales dramatize most directly the cultural terrain that defines the female subject, a subject framed through the competing representations, particularly pronounced in the nineteenth century, of the angel-woman and the monster-woman.

In turning next to images of women in fairy tales, I look at how the feminist recovery of incest motifs in the classical canon emerges as an effort to overturn this pernicious female duality. Further, uncovering father/daughter incest in the folkloric past, as a concealed subtext, is itself a subversive act. It inverts the classical female protagonist's dilemma over the danger encountered, transposing the danger from distant forests to the home—that is, from highly exteriorized to interior spaces. In this reversal of positions, the protector who defends against the wolf at the door becomes, himself, the predatory wolf. Finding the incestuous father in the fairy tale, however, does not simply settle the score, nor does it restore order to the land. This exposure of the patriarchal "devil in the house," like the killing of the maternal "angel," generates its own dilemmas, even if we renounce the illusion of happy endings.

Fairy Tales and Feminist Disenchantment

There is a profound lament in much of the folklore literature over the loss of the art of storytelling in the modern era. Many of our cultural stories are fragmented, dissociated from their origin or any coherent system of meanings. Active, communal storytelling has been significantly displaced by passively experienced consumption of manufactured narratives, particularly those on television. The dominant stories told in religious traditions and Western myths of progress and manifest destiny have been rightly challenged by critics of these traditions and rejected as mythic untruths. With the decline of countercultural legends and the social movements inspiring them in the 1960s and 1970s, cultural storytelling seems to be in a state of crisis.[10] And, perhaps in response to this perceived crisis, storytelling has become a riveting concern and an area of generative theorizing in academia, capturing a range of disciplines.[11]

For many of us, shaking off the hypnotic spell engendered by childhood legends is a motivating force behind the search for a forgotten past of folk knowledge. Many stories outside of the dominant religious and political traditions have survived, of course, even though their origins may be lost and the realities that gave rise to them may have changed. Yet within the canon of surviving folk literature—stories told by common people to create and transmit meaning—the virtual disappearance of many women's stories is uniquely lamentable.

How does feminism make use of storytelling in reinterpreting the legendary past, re-viewing it through its own transformative lens? In *Woman Hating*, Andrea Dworkin describes the obstacles for women in disentangling themselves from the entrapments of folklore. "When one enters the world of fairy tale one seeks with difficulty for the actual place where legend and history part. One wants to locate the precise moment when fiction penetrates into the psyche as reality, and history begins to mirror it. Or vice versa. Women live in fairy tales as magical figures, as beauty, danger, innocence, and greed. In the personae of the fairy tale—the wicked witch, the beautiful princess, the heroic prince—we find what the culture would have us know about who we are."[12]

Dworkin's critical reading is too one-dimensional, however, reducing the threatening power of such stories to a simplified message that may be more readily discarded than more nuanced interpretations. Since the nineteenth century, subversive retellings of classical fairy tales have found their way into the Western canon, even as new tales have appeared that reverse, transform, or dissolve oppressive social roles.[13] As Maria Tatar and Kay Stone point out, clever heroines and dimwitted male protagonists populate the folkloric canon, and these fairy tales tend to be lost in feminist critical readings of dominant motifs.[14]

Feminist folklorist Ruth Bottigheimer intervenes in this dispute by demonstrating how the widely circulated German canon, though riddled with ambivalences, imposed a consistent pattern of silence on female protagonists, as female utterances were reduced in the text in a literary act of castration.[15] Further, the European canons varied in the moralizing content of folktales. While the neighboring Danish genre permitted heroines acts of bloody revenge on their sexual captors, the German tales promoted the ideal of feminine humility. "In *Grimms' Tales* girls and women are always supposed to obey prohibitions set by good figures, but male characters move with considerably more freedom among these prohibitors. Prohibitions set by a malevolent figure may be ignored by girls and boys, women and men alike. Implicit prohibitions, on the other hand, are regularly honored by women and contravened with impunity by men."[16]

A feminist mode of storytelling does alter the transmission of tales in its opposition to "received wisdom" about women under patriarchy. Recovering rebellious currents in women's past storytelling is part of this subversion of conventional knowledge. Ideally, it is an antihypnotic project, one of dispelling illusions, of waking up from the slumber induced by patriarchal authority. The kiss of the prince is displaced in the feminist narrative of Sleeping Beauty by the sobering and sustaining embrace of sisterhood.

But even radical breaks with the past still carry the presentiments and prefigurative tendencies of prior eras. Feminist storytelling may simultaneously fortify and destroy conventional wisdom. Consequently, feminist storytelling faces a range of strategic dilemmas, both in how to represent women's experiences within available, preexisting traditions and in how to create new stories, less encumbered by inhibitions and constraints. In a sense, women's stories never really are their own (nor are men's), separable in any integral sense from various impinging cultural influences. Further, women, including feminists, may collectively create counterlegends that remain too fully under the hypnotic sway of older motifs.

Recovering Old Wives' Tales

The orally transmitted tales of the "foremothers" are a barely discernible echo in the published canons and in their various modern permutations. Prior to the industrial revolution, storytelling was the principal means of remembering, of preserving and transmitting cultural knowledge, and it was stitched into the very fabric of women's lives. While many European folktales survive within the ghettoized world of early childhood, both women storytellers and the tales they told were once the center of adult cultural life. "Spinning yarns" was an activity that mesmerized the community, as men and children gathered around women at their spinning wheels as they wove regional stories into local ones and narratively embroidered on the dilemmas of the day.

There are surviving remnants of many old wives' tales and some have been recovered from history, primarily by feminist folklorists. The Donkeyskin tale is one such legend in the feminist apocryphal canon. In Irish communities a version of the Donkeyskin tale that has all but disappeared elsewhere continues to be told.[17] Circulated widely in parts of Europe from the fourteenth through the seventeenth centuries, the legendary story centers on a princess named Dympna, who flees the incestuous demands of her father, the king, upon the death of the beautiful queen. As the story unfolds, the king rationalizes his incestuous lust by consulting with his evil advisors, who convince him that such an unlawful union is for the good of the kingdom. Under the guidance of her own, more virtuous advisors, the brave and defiant daughter finally flees into exile under the cloak of animal skins. Most versions of the fairy tale trace the journey of the rebellious princess into a neighboring village, where she is discovered in her state of humble reclusion by a noble prince. Some versions of the tale end happily, with the incest taboo preserved. But others trace the path of Dympna to a brutal ending when her father, pursuing her into exile, cuts off her head.

In European hagiography, the martyred virgin is canonized and becomes the patron saint of the insane.[18] Beginning in the fourteenth century and spreading outward from Belgium throughout Catholic Europe, a cult of Saint Dympna arose, with the rapacious father often represented as a pagan Turk.[19] Woven into the Christian narrative of a female virgin martyr, we may observe, are broader tensions over competing empires and shifting cultural boundaries.

In recovering this dying legend from folklore history, Marina Warner suggests that the casting of Saint Dympna as spiritual interventionist for the mentally ill reveals a deep affinity between madness and incestuous transgression in late medieval thought, extending into the fifteenth and sixteenth centuries. In the ancient parable of Lot's daughters, preserving the bloodline transcended the violation of the incest taboo in the hierarchy of values; but early modern Europe witnessed a renewed concern with the incest taboo.[20]

Other determinants of these shifting legendary tales and their implicit transformations in social values suggest the many levels on which such stories may be read. The reinscribing of the incest taboo and the daughter's right of resistance also mark the crisis of patriarchal rulers throughout Europe. Stories of wicked kings abounded, with their moral transgressions marking the course of their ruinous destiny. Even legends bearing a close affinity to an immediate historical truth resonated with rebellious currents. Take, for example, rumors circulating widely in Europe in the late fifteenth century concerning Pope Alexander VI and his incestuous relationship with his daughter, Lucrezia Borgia, a union that many historians believe produced one of the pope's heirs.[21] Lucrezia, who, as legend has it, was the embodiment of sexual desire, was not without her own allies in her struggle against the combined power of the state and the church. The historical question of the actuality of the incest may be separated, then, from the question of how such stories—whether true or not—galvanize supporters. The spread of tales of resistive daughters may depend less on the factual merits of claims than on their capacity to stir related grievances—a kind of kinship of storytelling practices—particularly in insurgent movements to topple powerful patriarchs.

In his original recording of the Donkeyskin tale in the late seventeenth century, Charles Perrault concluded with a prophetic verse: "the tale of Donkeyskin is hard to believe, but as long as there are children, mothers and grandmothers in the world the memory of it will not die."[22] The survival of stories, however, depends on the power of the storyteller. By the eighteenth century, women's tales of the unlawful desires of fathers had faded from collective memory.

Beginning in the eighteenth century, as the Donkeyskin tales began to drop from the official folkloric record, a corollary trend toward the moral exoneration of fathers took hold, one that continued into the following centuries.[23] As women lost control over the craft of storytelling, female rebellions were displaced by narratives of passive submission and transformation through romantic love. The virginal girl comes to stand for an undefiled state of human nature, and her virtue rests on her beguiling defenselessness.[24] The domesticated good girl is framed in opposition to the bad mother, who assumes a more pronounced position as the source of evil and of unbridled possession of the daughter. Seductive expressions of domestic villainy in these modernized fairy tales are now moralized as the sinister work of women—the wicked queen or evil stepmother—which must now be set aright by the all-good father.

The early versions of the ancient tale of Cinderella, however, have her fleeing into household work, destitute and alone, to escape the sexual advances of her father. Much like Dympna, the heroine has been chosen as sexual substitute for the departed mother, a fate that drives the daughter into exile.[25] While conspiring mothers figure prominently in these older tales, their actions are often placed in the context of the sexual betrayals of husbands. Early versions of Sleeping Beauty, for example, center on the rape of a princess under a spell by a king wandering through the forest; his outraged wife later takes revenge by killing the twin children produced through this transgressive union.[26]

The more modern tales of virtuous maidens did emancipate femininity from its prior position in medieval Christianity, albeit through a form of cultural splitting. The primitive fantasies associated with female sexuality were split off in the fairy-tale canons into the desexualized, negative image of the malevolent old witch and the equally desexualized, positive image of the virginal maiden. Such icons operate repressively—in both the political and psychological sense—in that active, sexual, and aggressive elements of the feminine are dissociated from goodness. The good daughter and good mother came to achieve a highly delimited moral authority, realized within a framework of domestic duty and the upholding of the Law of the Father.

Nonetheless, there was a progressive dimension to these redemptive albeit domesticated images of femininity. The virulent misogyny and paranoid fear of women, expressed in church-sponsored massive executions of women accused of witchcraft in the sixteenth and seventeenth centuries, had waned by the eighteenth century.[27] And, with the passing of the season of the witch, the Evil Temptress, with her malevolent powers, was transformed into the Angel of the House—the nineteenth-century asexual woman, perpetually virginal in her states of mind. In European fairy tales, this woman was the mother who dies at the beginning of the story, a common convention in the published canons, setting the stage for the girl's abandonment as she falls under the malevolent influence of a wicked stepmother or evil queen. The reign of the evil witch in fairy tales and legends represents not only the psychic residue of infantile splitting as defense against ambivalence toward the mother, but a cultural elaboration and reinforcement of such splitting. Specifically, the legitimizing of maternal authority in the nineteenth century depended on collective defenses against any strong sexual or aggressive currents in maternal experience or in female desire.

How do we understand the social basis of such transformations in fairy tales—and more specifically the waning of sexually controlling fathers as a motif? Certainly the reconfiguration of these narratives was related to the repression of the female storyteller, as Warner argues, but it may also be related to broad shifts in kinship structure and social definitions of childhood. In addition to the eradication of incest in the fairy tale, other direct expressions of sexuality were eliminated. Further, there is a certain continuity in the fairy-tale canon, from the eighteenth century on, in the "familializing" of power relations. The modern fairy tale situates human struggle as a process of emancipation from parental controls, whether direct or implied, whether expressed through the controlling father or the malevolent mother. Jack Zipes describes this prototype of the modern socialization process, which runs through the Grimms' fairy tales. "Initially the young protagonist must leave home or the family because power relations have been disturbed. Either the protagonist is wronged, or a change in social relations forces the protagonist to depart from home. . . . The wandering protagonist always leaves home to reconstitute home."[28]

This normative socialization process contains elements of ancient traditions, with their ritualized rites of passage from childhood to a larger social world. But the modern tale departs from these traditional tasks of social development by stressing the radical rupture of early attachments and the emancipation from primary social bonds as a condition of personal happiness, particularly for the male. The ideal of a reconstituted home, according to Zipes, reflected the aspirations of a rising middle class, individuals whose prospects for expanded fortunes depended on mobility and on extricating themselves from a web of kinship obligations.[29] Childhood longings for union with parental protectors (oedipal and pre-oedipal) are threatening in this prescriptive social order, signifying the enormous obstacles to be overcome in achieving individuation, particularly for sons.

While traditional societies invoke the incest taboo in mapping the complex genealogies of possible marriages within the kinship system, the incest taboo within the modern nuclear family is both more invested with psychological meanings and more subject to violation. Freud's casting of the incest taboo as central player in neurotic dramas was not, as historian Michel Foucault observes, an idiosyncratic choice.[30] The bourgeois family created "a perpetual incitement to incest" through its intense preoccupation with the regulation of emotion and sexuality. Further, as the community and larger kinship system loses its authority to enforce social codes, the private, moral authority of parents—particularly of fathers—stands as the primary arbiter of private morality. And as a number of feminists have suggested, those who make and enforce the rules are freer to violate them than those who do not.[31]

Although the early period of urbanization and industrialization undermined and fragmented previous community and kinship structures, the emergence of the modern patriarchal family marks a localized struggle over emotional and sexual control of children.[32] By the eighteenth century, the bourgeois ideal of the socially autonomous family places the father as the presiding authority, with the mother as junior partner.[33] The decline of communally based knowledge, where the skills and crafts of women contributed to survival, and the ascendance of a public realm of production controlled by men transformed the female art of storytelling. Confined to the world of childhood, women's narrative commentaries lost their public authority. Not surprisingly, with the publication of fairy tales and the emergence of a canon in the eighteenth and nineteenth centuries, the Donkeyskin tales drop from the record, leaving only scattered oral remnants behind.

RECOVERING LEGENDS OF INCEST

Modern suspicion of women's tales of incest have the echo of an ancient wariness toward female moral exhortative speech. But, beyond the historical repression of female storytelling and contemporary moves to subject women's stories to inquisitorial scrutiny, there is the question of the relationship between stories and their factual content. Since father/daughter incest is perpetually repressed and "rediscovered," with its rediscovery serving as a banner in a broad movement for women's and children's rights, how do we understand the relationship between the literal and the legendary, the actual and the symbolic elements of incest tales? And can we recognize old motifs—such as those recovered in the Donkeyskin tales—while discerning new ones that deviate from the discursive practices of the old wives' tales of the past?

One way of subverting ancient legends is to rearrange elements of the story, reversing characters or roles within a standard plot, undercutting the narrative resolution, or parodying the conventions that underlie its moralizing message. In other words, the subversive use of fairy tales is not limited simply to retrieving them from history or to celebrating a golden folkloric past. Further, incestuous tales, like fairy tales generally, are both culturally localized—highly specific in their vernaculars—and enduring in their flexibility and openness to multiple interpretations.

Jean Goodwin, a feminist and leading practitioner in the field of sexual abuse, employs the legend of Saint Dympna to represent the plight of incest survivors.[34] In Goodwin's storytelling, the virtue of the daughter is restored and the villainy of the father is established. Yet the moral order that is portrayed through Goodwin's reclamation of the Donkeyskin tale is decisively puritanical, infused with Christian piety. The beautiful princess's father, we learn, "was a cruel man and a pagan. As Dymphna [sic] grew older, she understood that the Queen disagreed with the King about many things. For one thing, the Queen was a Christian, and Dymphna too began to learn Christianity from the hermit Gerebernus who lived in a hut in the forest" (189).

Goodwin's chaste vision of female heroism carries through to the story's tragic denouement. After the death of the queen, "the pagan King's mood became even blacker" (190). After the father pursues the daughter into exile, cutting off her head, we learn that the daughter joins her mother in heaven. The King turns into a howling animal and Dympna into an angel, with Saint Dympna perpetually haunting the father, who is possessed by demons. As patron saint of the insane, Dympna has the power to slay the demons conjured by the father. Goodwin's version of the tale employs the Christian ideal of heavenly rewards for earthly piety and self-sacrifice. Her use of the tale, like much of the Christianizing of European tales originating in a pagan cosmology, absolutizes the moral boundary between virtue and villainy.[35]

Rewriting the Transgressions of the Father

So what are the elements of the old legend—the Donkeyskin story that we recovered—that are decipherable today? The daughter's own rebellious sexual stirrings are hardly a discernible echo, even in the psychoanalytic interpretations of fairy tales—interpretations that, paradoxically, are acutely sensitive to the theme of repressed desire.[36] Generally, the period of sleep—in Snow White or Sleeping Beauty—is understood to signify the latency period between early childhood and adolescence (a modern term for early adulthood), culminating in the sexual awakening of the young girl as the prince facilitates her transition into maturity and the attendant severing of family ties.

This normative process does not allow for the active struggle of the girl, even though dangers clearly abound in her passage from childhood to the protection of a father surrogate. In both reality and in fairy tales, fathers and father figures may indeed circumvent this journey of feminine self-discovery as the girl is transferred from one masculine agency to another. Father/daughter incest is barely repressed in surviving folkloric narratives, as the girl is expected to find and marry a man older, smarter, bigger, and more powerful than she. While the boy may also transfer his love for the mother onto an eventual sexual substitute, he more actively than the girl represses this original tie, particularly his dependence on a powerful woman.

Cultural storytelling, from fairy tales to novels and Hollywood films, continues to express uneasiness over female rebellion, particularly rebellion that threatens familial ties. The defiance of the daughter against patriarchal authority requires moral justification that goes beyond the legendary conflicting interests of sons and fathers. In the received legends, sons may rise up against fathers out of a complex set of motives—both righteous and malevolent—but since the son is ultimately required to take the father's place, to assume the throne of familial power, redemption of the son is a necessary narrative convention. There are far fewer prodigal daughters who return home from their flight of defiance more beloved for their acts of courage. And, in attempting to break from this legacy, the new generation of incest survivors, of self-appointed prodigal daughters, seeks redemption by establishing that the moral transgressions of the father are sufficient to justify the daughter's stake on freedom.

In the Donkeyskin tales, the father's incestuous desire operates as a compelling justification for the daughter's resistance because it highlights an unlawful breach of her body. It dramatizes the father's violation of normal codes regulating male access to female sexuality and an insurgent female moral authority. Yet this very insurgency mobilizes hysterical public reactions, subsequently internalized by women. Whatever meaning we assign to the circumscribed authority of women in private life, the hidden, prepublic aspects of this female authority permit the projection of paranoid fantasies onto it. Male suspicion of the "hidden," "deceitful" motives of women is a collective paranoia exacerbated by the division between private and public domains and the relegating of women traditionally to the private domain.

As legends, tales of father/daughter incest give voice to the daughter's private knowledge of both the actual and the symbolic father and of a newly discovered capacity to expose the public father through private knowledge of him. The feminine position of keeper of secrets, based on the ideal of femininity as passive container and receptive womb, is reversed. By casting the father as transgressor, the one who gives cause for resistance, the daughter seizes the Law of the Father, using it against him. She relinquishes her position as sacred feminine vessel of privatized meanings and becomes a Pandora's box of disquieting, threatening knowledge. Contemporary allegations of sexual abuse and incest are indeed battle cries, turning the tables of history and serving as legendary tales of female resistance.

Ann Sexton stands in this feminist tradition of subversive storytelling in rewriting the story of Sleeping Beauty by placing daddy in the role of prince. In her poem "Briar Rose (Sleeping Beauty)," a spell is cast on a young princess.[37] Following the story line of the fairy tale, Sexton's Beauty tragically fulfills a prophecy in her fifteenth year when she pricks her finger on a spinning wheel and enters a trance. After a hundred years, she is awakened by the kiss of a prince. But Sexton's heroine becomes an insomniac and a secret addict, as fearful of the discovery of her habit as she is of sleep. Each time she falls into a state of slumber, the trance repeats itself, only to be broken when she cries out "Daddy! Daddy!" The poem ends, like a fairy tale, with a cautionary message, for it is not the prince but, rather, daddy who hovers "drunkenly bent over my bed . . . circling like a shark; my father sinks upon me, like some sleeping jellyfish."[38] Sexton subverts the classical tale, as Sleeping Beauty awakens to a terrible knowledge. The mask is ripped from the face of the prince to expose the incestuous father, and we now learn the true reason for her insomnia.

Archetypal Stories

In the sexual abuse survivor literature, incest both stands as one among many sexual violations and serves as archetype of abuses of patriarchal power. Just as stories of clerical abuse of children galvanized rebellion against authority within the Catholic Church in the 1980s, recovered memories of father/daughter incest recount unambiguous breaches of authority. And, in both the religious and familial contexts of these illuminations of fatherly sins, sexual abuse of children comes to stand for something beyond itself.[39]

While exposure of men's dirty sexual secrets does signify a crisis in their ability to exercise absolute power, it may also represent cultural ambivalences of a more complex sort. Historically, when progressive movements are losing ground to conservative forces, the sexual violation of children stands in for other unspoken transgressions. Losing ground in the movement to overturn papal proscriptions against abortion and against women and gays in the clergy may lead to a transfer of these political energies to a more unifying moral terrain. It is more possible to arouse moral outrage over the sexual abuse of an innocent child by a priest than it is to mobilize moral outrage against this same priest's repressive doctrines on women and homosexuality. Exposing the hypocrisy of the holy Fathers—how they violate their own moral codes—can be a means of establishing a chink in the wall. At the same time, creating a chink in the wall can easily become a substitute for tearing it down and building a new structure.[40]

Since sexual violation of the body of a child evokes public revulsion and horror and signifies as well the corruption and degradation of protective institutions, the allegation of paternal incest conveys the sense of a profound cultural crisis. Statistics circulated widely in the late 1970s and 1980s showed that one in three women was the victim of child sexual abuse and one in four was the victim of incest.[41] Even though these numbers have been challenged, on the basis that definitions were either too broad or too vague, almost no one has returned to the prefeminist claim that incest is "rare, perhaps one in a million."[42] Even critics of the incest recovery movement feel compelled to pay homage to the gains of feminism in raising awareness of the widespread occurrence of child sexual abuse and to affirm that it is, indeed, a tragic social problem.

Yet the earlier period of exaggerated claims of sexual abuse and incest did unify women around a pervasively felt reality; the invasion of female spaces, either bodily or emotionally, was discovered to be deeply normative, and moving from childhood to adulthood meant relinquishing boundaries rather than consolidating of them. Women could speak up about violations from the perspective of the innocent child—either their own children or the "child within"—more easily than in the thicket of morally suspect, mature sexual encounters. Demonstrating the absolute innocence and nonculpability of women in cases of date rape, sexual harassment, or domestic violence was an onerous challenge. Winning sympathy for child victims—particularly victims of incest—was far less daunting.

In addition, given the diffuse and pervasive effects of gender, as well as other determinative life events, locating the source of feminine troubles can be similarly daunting. Identifying a moment in time, a momentous rupture of innocence when the girl was cast out of the kingdom, provides a means of both containing and transforming a diffuse and pervasively gendered past. The troubles of growing up female are located in an identifiable source and a time when virtue and villainy could be decisively uncoupled, setting the stage for a subsequent rebellion.

Diversity in Storytelling

In his analysis of how history reworks memory through literary representations, Richard Terdiman argues that nowhere is memory more fraught with emotional conflict than in intergenerational relations—in the tributes owed by children to their parents. "The stories a culture tells about parents and children frame, as if in microcosm, the culture's conception of the inevitably problematic inheritance, of the present's perplexing relation to the past."[43]

Once familial sexual abuse emerges as a political category and assumes a central place as a leitmotif in female collective resistance, it may be employed in various contestations over authority. Since sexuality often evokes forbidden longings, female struggles to emancipate from patriarchal control may be symbolically expressed through an eroticized familial story. Sexual abuse allegations may acquire social symbolic meaning over time as they gravitate from their original entry point in public consciousness.

But sexual motifs in women's storytelling also are shaped by other aspects of cultural history. The project of emancipation from familial constraints is more ambivalent for many women of color, who experience acutely the illusory aspects of feminine "autonomy," than for white women. Confronting the powerful fathers may be more problematic when father and daughter share a common history of oppression, including racist stereotypes of "oversexed" dark-skinned people. Sexual violations may be difficult to disentangle from the web of social forces that crush the spirits of parents and children alike.[44] In describing the dilemmas of black women incest survivors, Melba Wilson suggests too that the taboo against "putting our business out in the street" is stronger than the incest taboo.[45]

The social sciences provide sparse findings and even sparser insights into the particular abuses black women have endured. But although the voices of women of color in the survivors' movement and literature are few, incest and sexual abuse are powerful themes in literary explorations of black women's lives. Fictional storytelling allows for the holding of denser, richer experiences than those representations that circulate in the social science literature. The social science and mental health literature tends to decontextualize abuse, often reducing it to psychological variables. Black women writers, however, are likely to place private enactments of violence within a broad dehumanizing context.[46] In Toni Morrison's *The Bluest Eye,* for example, the rape of Pecola by her father, Cholly, dramatizes a violence that neither begins nor ends with the broken body of the young girl. While the narrative forcefully conveys the horror of the rape, trauma emerges out of a larger constellation of destructive experiences and unbearable losses that grip both father and daughter. The designation of perpetrator—the one who is responsible for destroying the spirit of this black girl—never settles resolutely on the shoulders of the defeated father but shifts and turns within a broad drama of racist brutality.

In addition to Morrison's novel, there is by now an entire genre of novels—including Maya Angelou's *I Know Why the Caged Bird Sings,* Alice Walker's *The Color Purple,* Joan Riley's *The Unbelonging,* Opal Palmer Adisa's *Bake Face and Other Guava Stories*—where incest emerges as a painful part of black women's legacy. Through these novels, Wilson writes, "I began to think of myself in a whole new way—as someone, if you will, whose experience counted for something. Began to feel that those everyday, ordinary things—which help to make up mine and the collective fabric of all black women's lives—were important to remember, record and pass on to those who came after. But even more importantly, here too was my experience of incest" (41).

The candid portrayal of sexual abuse in *The Color Purple,* including father/daughter incest, stirred intense controversy in black communities when the film was released in the early 1980s. In interpreting Walker's novel and in reframing the controversy, the Brixton Black Women's Group in London writes, "It is not like a story because you instinctively feel the truth of it. . . . But like most stories you know it is derived from Every Black Woman."[47] Walker's novel probes the cultural dynamics and contingencies of existence that set the drama of women's lives in motion, closing off some possibilities while opening up others. In this context, incest is Every Woman's Story, not because every woman has experienced it but because it occurs within a common matrix of binding situations. Sexual abuse is deeply wounding, in part because other destructive forces are at work that undermine efforts at self-restoration.

SOLIDARITY AND SEXUAL STORIES

Sexual tale telling is an inhibited affair for most women.[48] Men tell tales of sexual prowess and conquests, and these tales have often been the basis of male solidarity against the frightful power of the "feminine." Conventional narratives do grant women some authority as domesticators of male sexuality—as representatives of familial obligations, binding commitments, and the necessity of sexual constraint. This female socialization project, like Beauty's task, centers on the taming of unruly masculine desires.

If men establish social bonds through tales of sexual potency and conquest, how do the sexual tales of women build solidarity? Further, since women have had less cultural license to tell sexual stories than have men, how does this legacy of inhibitions operate in the storytelling that emerges? Part of the answer is that women, and particularly middle-class women, have had fewer stories to tell because they are granted less social freedom and mobility than men. Traditionally in Western industrial societies, injunctions against female sexual experimentation were based on the necessity of protecting and maximizing feminine sexual capital. Protecting inner spaces against phallic intrusions has been a condition of feminine virtue and the currency of upward mobility. Selling too soon or too cheap could mean a precipitous depreciation of value in the marriage market. As authority over women was transferred from fathers to husbands, the negotiation of sexual rights and obligations gave wives far fewer degrees of freedom than husbands.

The double standard has always implied a further cultural split between the "good" and the "bad" female object of desire. If women were "good"—sexually circumspect—patriarchy would protect them.[49] Women who ventured across the sexual boundary became the objects of masculine ambivalence. The female sexual rebel was simultaneously exciting and dangerous. Outside the protective arms of patriarchal codes, "fallen women" became receptacles for primitive masculine reactions and conflicts concerning women. As "damaged goods," female sexual outlaws, whether labeled sluts, prostitutes, or lesbians, shared a common fate as socially condoned objects of male rage.

While white women may suffer severe penalties for violating moral and sexual codes, black women never were as protected by the embracing arms of patriarchy. But the rage of black women extends beyond this differential treatment—their more fundamental lack of protection—to the complicity of white women in racist storytelling. White women's outrage over sexual abuses, their conviction that this is the worst of crimes against humanity, may easily overlook the racist history of sexual allegations. When Susan Brownmiller's groundbreaking book on rape was taken up by feminists, with rape emerging as the prototype of women's oppression generally, some feminists criticized her ahistorical understanding of sexual violence and her failure to address the racist history behind allegations of rape.[50] Black women were less inclined than white women to reflexively "believe the victim" given their own cultural history strewn, as it was, with lynchings and castrations of "oversexed" black men.[51]

Jacquelyn Dowd Hall responded to this controversy in the early 1980s by recovering this forgotten memory in feminism, probing the complex interpenetration of sexual and racial imagery in U.S. history.[52] Hall chronicles this gruesome history, with the lynching of Emmett Till in 1955 for whistling at a white woman serving as reminder of the persisting expressions of racist sexual violence. She explores the use of sexual allegations as a tool in racial oppression, a violent psychodrama enacted to fortify the control of white men on two fronts: the post-Reconstruction mobility of blacks and the perceived threats of turn-of-the-century feminism. By presenting themselves as the defenders of female chastity, white men were able to control daughters and wives by inscribing the world outside the family as rife with sexual violence. This racist portrait of sexual violence served to displace tensions within the bourgeois family, as wives and daughters chafed under the rule of powerful husbands and fathers. Similarly, the sexual double standard, including sexual assaults by property-owning men against black women, could be projected outward as black men were targeted as the threat to the sanctity of the family.

In the 1980s, there was a decisive shift from rape to incest as paradigmatic of women's sexual oppression. In reviewing this history, Louise Armstrong suggests that incest, even in its early entry into popular consciousness, tended to be more psychologized than rape, ushering in armies of mental health professionals who influenced the contours of the sexual abuse survivor movement.[53] Armstrong laments the depoliticizing of sexual abuse that followed from the movement to treat incest as a "special case"—as more psychologically rooted than other forms of domestic violence. But there may be a deep affinity between incestuous abuse and the anxieties of many middle-class women who shaped feminist politics in the 1980s. The prototypical rapist had always been associated in the popular imagination with the terrors of public life, and folktales of rape often operated as a cautionary tale against female ventures across social boundaries. The idea that protection of females within the family was often illusory took hold as a unifying motif early on within feminism, fortified by findings that women are harmed or killed more often in their homes than on the streets.[54] Shifting the ideological ground from stranger rape to date rape, marital rape, and other violations within the context of intimate relationships was part of a broad struggle to achieve emancipation from domestic confinement and to dismantle psychological and social barriers against women entering into public life.

Incestuous abuse—whether at the hands of fathers or various father surrogates—also captured more of the intimate side of the operations of power than did rape. Incest acquired a powerful social symbolic function within feminism, not only as a means of legitimizing the passage out of the suffocating constraints of the family but also as a potent signifier of seductive, patriarchal authority. As women increasingly entered the paid workforce in greater numbers in the 1980s, the prototypical cautionary tales of the past, including those offered during previous periods of feminist struggle, confronted more complex social realities. The borders between private and public domains for women were blurred as women wrestled with new freedoms within a world of abiding constraints.

Yet the ambivalences and complexities of eroticized power relations were anxiously re-repressed within much of the storytelling that took place in the sexual abuse survivor movement. Nonetheless, the latent meanings and expressive possibilities in storytelling may be at least as compelling as the overt plot line. Stories of father/daughter incest emerged as more captivating than accounts of rape because they arise out of a context of intimacy. Just as Freud's early trauma model, seduction theory, suggested a confusing, guilty state of arousal associated with a premature sexual experience, contemporary trauma narratives center on the father's betrayal of the daughter's trust.[55] The dilemmas women faced in the

1980s in responding to an increasingly complex cultural terrain, where women were no longer relegated entirely to the private domain, may have created anxieties over how to effectively manage the conflicting, erotic aspects of power. As a symbolic tale, the contemporary incest story feels universal to many women, both because it is all too common and because it evokes a sense of complicity, of feeling entranced by oppressive encounters.

Sexual abuse survivorship extended beyond childhood incest, of course, even though the fuzzy borders of the concept of sexual abuse may have precipitated the emphasis on incest as prototype. As sexual abuse enlarged in the 1980s to include a broadening array of experiences—from various degrees and forms of incest (and other childhood sexual contacts with older persons) through date rape, marital rape, and sexual harassment in adolescence and adulthood—the precise and differing meanings of these experiences were collapsed in the unifying appeal of survivorship. A leading figure in the survivor movement, Wendy Maltz, includes in her own version of this lengthening list "disparaging remarks about one's gender."[56] In the welcoming arms of the sexual survivor movement, Maltz's estimate that 30 to 40 percent of women are victims of child sexual abuse are grossly conservative. Since sexual abuse has become emblematic of the oppression of women generally, more "realistic" estimates should hover just under 100 percent.

What is gained and what is lost in this enlarging category of bodily located harm? This expanded lens does advance understanding of the pervasiveness of sexually coded forms of oppression and the various ways in which women come to experience their bodies as objects of male domination, in private and public life. Since the more subtle or ambiguous forms of bad treatment girls and women endure so readily fall below the threshold of cultural awareness—indeed, hardly register—dramatizing abuse may be the strategy of resistance most readily available. The downside of this unity, however, is that it may be difficult to collectively remember other painful or difficult experiences that shape female selfhood and social identity. In contemporary literature on child abuse and trauma, incidents of inappropriate touching overshadow in importance other childhood assaults, such as whippings and emotional cruelty. Chronic neglect—which is the most common form of maltreatment that children, and particularly girls, endure—is particularly difficult to find represented in the collective narratives of memory.[57] In the project of remembering, it may be easier to struggle against a demonic presence than against a perniciously absent one.

This area of relative silence is not surprising given that there is far less agreement in the culture that physical discipline—spankings, whippings, slaps—is as harmful to children as is sexual abuse. Further, because physical assaults of children are likely to be understood as "for your own good," it may be difficult to claim these incidents as abusive. The memory of this same "for your own good," whispered in a girl's ear as her stepfather fondles her breast, may be more readily detected as a lie, particularly once this girl grows up and moves beyond his reach.

Unlike other harms of childhood, secret sexual alliances may be uniquely destructive because they do feel bound up in complex emotional needs, including the desire for physical contact and pleasure. Perhaps even "minor" incidences of sexual abuse may be distressing because they may arouse confusion between "good touch" and "bad touch," between loving and harmful attention. Creating and sharing stories transforms these disturbing private recollections, as does the enlistment of others in emotionally managing them.

CONCLUSIONS

Collective remembering, throughout much of human history, has taken the form of fairy tales and myths, stories that transport everyday experience into the realm of the imaginary. Traditions of female storytelling—of "spinning yarn"—were silenced in the transition to the modern, folkloric canons, as women lost control over the social production of tales. Stories of sexually possessive fathers and resistive daughters fell from the record as the mother emerged as the malevolent influence and daughters were sexually chastened and sanctified in modern revisions of ancient fairy tales.

The historical reality of incest and sexual trauma has given rise to its generative possibilities in storytelling practices. Yet the creative use of sexual imagery fares better in the world of women's fiction than in political and clinical discourse. The contemporary incest survivors' movement did turn private remembrances into social testimonials, as women refused to remain the guardians of the fathers' secrets. Exposing the father's secrets, however, did not inevitably free survivors from their own sexual inhibitions or from the traditional female role of sexual gatekeepers. While courageously resisting patriarchal control, sexual abuse survivors tended to endorse a traditional view of women as sexual innocents, defiled by male lust, with the father representing the original violator.

Feminism has opened up cultural space for the reclamation of older legends, even as it reworks them according to emergent possibilities and ideals. The recovery of the old wives' tales—legends of defiant daughters and cautionary tales of sexually controlling fathers—is an important corrective to cultural repression. Yet virtuous heroines throughout much of the history of folkloric storytelling must establish a morally compelling case against the father as a condition of their freedom. And it is not surprising that feminist storytelling often conforms to this limited plot line of ancient tales. Even feminist storytellers confront the deeply ingrained cultural habit of spiritualizing and sanctifying the path of feminine redemption. In this Christianized myth, the angel woman is created out of the rib of the devil woman, even as this new Eve is perpetually haunted by the old one. In both their idealized and their demonized forms, however, many of the tales about women have not as yet fully awakened from a narcotizing cultural slumber, a theme I pursue in the next chapter through the history of hypnosis.

Chapter 6

HYPNOTIC ENCOUNTERS

Eroticized Remembering and Altered States

ONE OF the lesser-known stories of late-nineteenth-century scientific explorers of the psyche involves Gertrude Stein, the American poet and novelist whose intellectual roots were in experimental psychology.[1] Stein was one of those intrepid interlopers into science, part of a generation of women whose restless minds penetrated male bastions of knowledge. For Stein no less than for other women of her generation, it was an era of intense struggle, of awakened female strivings set against a daunting array of cultural obstacles.

Male reception of women into academia was not uniformly hostile, however, even at Harvard, where Stein studied as an unofficially admitted student. In her autobiography, Stein tells the story of her research on automatic writing at Harvard in the 1890s under the guidance of her beloved mentor, William James, father of American experimental psychology.[2] This research probed the psychological basis of what had emerged in the mid-nineteenth century as a female spiritual craft, one that held lifelong fascination for the Romantic empiricist James. Spiritualists and mediums, who were predominantly women, used automatic writing as a means of communicating with the dead. Entering a trance state, the medium displayed extraordinary powers of eloquence under the guidance of the "visiting" spirit.[3]

In Stein's day, the secular conversation over such dramatic enactments concerned the question of whether the powers of the medium were more akin to hysterical illness or to enhanced intelligence—whether such altered states signified advanced or regressed human capacities. Stein entered James's charmed circle of students at Harvard when the heat of the controversy centered on the boundary between hysteria and normal fluctuations in consciousness. In his effort to bridge the normal and the clinical, James set out to demonstrate that normal subjects showed some of the characteristics of hysteria, specifically in the tendency toward "double" personalities. Adopting the techniques of automatic handwriting and the planchette (a device much like the Ouija board), which he had observed in his frequent visits to seances, James devised experiments to test, under controlled laboratory conditions, the powers of the medium. He sought to establish the process through which the personality split, releasing a latent personality operating outside normal consciousness.

For Stein, however, these experiments revealed effects less readily noticed by her mentor or male colleagues. Stein tells a fascinating story about the social psychology of the experiment, but she tells it from the subject's perspective, introducing a radically divergent standpoint on the laboratory setting. In an 1894 paper, she laments that "this vehement individual [the subject] is requested to make herself a perfect blank while someone practices on her as an automaton." Stein describes the apparatus "strapped across her breast to register her breathing," and she builds a narrative through the theme of female bondage to a voyeuristic male gaze. This feminine position is both self-negating and arousing, blunting the subject's responses while stimulating fantasies of latent possibilities within her. Stein's experimental report on automatic writing anticipates her later literary style, with its use of circularity and repetition: "Strange fancies begin to crowd upon her [the subject], she feels that the silent pen is writing on and on forever. Her record is there she cannot escape it and the group about her begin to assume the shape of mocking fiends gloating over her imprisoned misery. Suddenly she starts, they have suddenly loosed a metronome directly behind her, to observe the effect, so now the morning's work is over."[4]

Standing at the cultural border of a feminine, enclosed world that was breaking out of its nineteenth-century corset, Stein was attuned to the cultural constraints on female expressivity. Automatic writing enacted a gender code, one where female subjects both capitulated to and subverted the silences imposed on them. For Stein, the specter of female automatons scribbling incoherently before an audience of rapt observers mimicked social conventions. But in the more dramatic setting of the seance—one where women had more control—automatic writing allowed women to claim extraordinary powers, even as they demurred from claiming authorship of their own mystical utterances.

A central theme in contemporary literature on recovered memory and sexual abuse is the revelatory power of the trance, the potential of hypnotic states to reveal formerly concealed truths. Much as in Stein's day, battles over the validity of recovered memories in the 1990s extend into differing beliefs concerning techniques for accessing latent aspects of mind.[5] Women have made various uses historically of the concepts of hypnotic states, concealed selves, and hidden knowledge. Since the mid-1980s, therapeutic claims concerning extraordinary revelations—such as psychic phenomena, past-life regression, and reports of alien abductions—weave through many of the clinical narratives on hypnotically recovered memory.[6] For critics of recovered memories of childhood sexual abuse, these highly implausible assertions underscore the antiscientific, deluded thinking that has come to dominate some quarters of the mental health professions.[7]

Focusing on these extreme claims, however, obscures a deeper source of tension between scientific explorations of mind, on the one hand, and the lived experience of women on the other. There is a certain affinity between feminism and beliefs in "occult" psychological processes because women have themselves been hidden from history, operating behind a screen, as it were, of masculine assumptions and fantasies. Indeed, any project of progressive social change requires a capacity to transcend mundane reality, to probe for deeper meanings, and to uncover hidden potentialities. At the same time, it is important to recognize the possibility for the idea of a "hidden" reality to become a container for various projected anxieties and fantasies and for presiding authorities to import their own preoccupations into the mental domain that is discovered.

Feminism is largely an antihypnotic project, invested in dispelling illusions and in collectively awakening from the seductions of patriarchal authority. This antihypnotic project subverts eroticized forms of domination, the prototype being a male hypnotist holding Svengali-like control over a dreamy-eyed female subject.[8] In conventional storytelling, the hypnotist exerts mysterious power over his subject as she readily submits, relinquishing her will to his directives.[9]

We can readily see how a feminist analysis would take aim at the hypnotist, stripping him of his real and imagined powers and exposing the stage work behind the act. But we are on more uncertain ground when we approach the hypnotic as a feminine craft, particularly given the history of prejudices and paranoia concerning female "occult" powers. By stepping back from the heat surrounding various contemporary claims—specifically those involving the use of hypnosis in uncovering forgotten memories—we may be able to establish a new point of entry into the dilemmas of women as storytellers, particularly in their efforts to break out of the binding constraints of conventional tales.

This chapter examines key historical periods in which cultural anxieties over sexuality and gender are enacted through a clinically orchestrated hypnotic encounter. Several questions guide this inquiry. First, why have debates over the nature and therapeutic value of hypnosis so often included contested claims of a sexual nature? Does hypnosis reveal histories of concealed sexual abuse or does hypnosis arouse the erotic imagination? Second, why is the trance state so often associated with the subversive, where the "mesmerized" subject is feared to have fallen prey to corrupting influences? In tracing the social history of hypnosis, this chapter explores the many cultural uses of the trance state and its "feminization" in modern Western societies.

Each era of therapeutic discovery involves an engagement with the intimate domain of the self—what used to be called the soul—which the woman patient, as the cultural embodiment of privacy and interiority, personifies. The role of modern, psychiatric authority in penetrating this domain mobilizes cultural anxieties over the shifting boundaries of masculine and feminine domains of identity and over the nature of authoritative incursions into the intimate aspects of private life. While a range of historical and cultural factors mediate understandings of hypnotic phenomena, the interest here is in how gender dynamics infiltrate clinical interpretations of such "exceptional" states, which are thought to reveal a hidden realm of the personality.

MESMERISM

While Jean-Martin Charcot is most often associated with the creation of a new psychiatric discipline, separate from its neurological predecessor, the infamous Friedrich Anton Mesmer may represent psychiatry's own repressed past. Mesmer, whose brief charismatic influence in late-eighteenth-century France ended in his banishment from the medical establishment, combines the scientific aspirations of the Enlightenment and the counter-Enlightenment sensibilities of the Romantics. In addition, Mesmer, far more than the staid neurologist Charcot, evokes the scandalous undercurrents of psychiatry.[10] Much like the situation today, the struggle in Mesmer's time over the legitimacy of various competing authorities was woven into the fraying fabric of historical change. His cure of hysterical fainting—the illness de rigueur of bourgeois women—combined the mechanical methods of the new science of electricity and magnetic fields and the eighteenth-century fascination with astrology, with its pre-Christian, mystical cosmology. Today, we would characterize Mesmer as a New Age healer; his eclectic blend of nouveau science and mysticism took hold within a culture ripe in receptivity to transformative ideas.[11]

For Mesmer, the French Revolution was a cultural bridge between a mechanistic tradition in science and a more vitalistic vision, Romantic in its undertones. Mesmer asserted that the human body contained a fluid called animal magnetism, which passed through an axis from head to toe. When this magnetic fluid was out of alignment, symptoms such as hysterical fainting occurred. He believed that he was able to harness this invisible force in achieving a cure.[12]

This new mind cure soon proved to be scandalous, as Mesmer was accused of seducing a prominent young woman suffering from hysterical blindness. The Pied Piper of the day, Mesmer stirred sufficient alarm within the medical establishment that magnetism (hypnosis) came to be regarded by both medical and clerical authorities in France as a highly dangerous practice, tantamount to charlatanry. Indeed, the term *hypnotism,* coined by the British physician James Braid in 1842, was introduced to separate the procedure and its companion condition from the legacy of magnetism. But if hypnosis was analogized to the innocuous state of sleep, its erotic associations remained an undercurrent in psychiatry, lingering on like a bad dream.

In their history of clinical hypnosis, Jean-Roch Laurence and Perry Campbell show how debates over hypnotizability were intertwined with the emergence of modern psychiatric authority.[13] At the vortex of passionate historical controversies over mesmerism, however, is a contest over gender codes and sexuality. As the debate progresses through the technical and procedural reasoning of science, more refined at each historical juncture, the sexual and gender subtextual themes become more disguised, embedded, as it were, in the text of cultural memory.

Within the context of the tumultuous political currents of the revolutionary period, female sexuality was the site of competing claims over authoritative influence. In the 1780s, a number of the more vocal critics of magnetism suggested that mesmerized women were dangerously vulnerable to abuse, a claim that may have had some basis to it. One anonymous observer reported his own views of such scandalous practices. "Can a young man who takes in his arms a woman with irritable nerves, rubs her vertebrae, her diaphragm, her stomach, her nipples, her navel region, produce a revolution in the subject he is massaging, as the Indians would say? Yes, assuredly; if the imagination is triggered by fear and hope, or by a sensual delirium that cannot be described by any word of our language, the subject will feel a dangerous lack of constraint and the physician will be able, with a guilty boldness . . . I have to stop here."[14] Common "decency," it seemed, prevented the author from continuing, but his concern with revolutionary stirrings in the breasts of women may reflect more about the times than it does any inherent properties of magnetism as a psychological phenomenon.

Whereas some practitioners sought to domesticate magnetism by keeping it within the security of the family and trusted physicians, others sought to legitimize it by deeroticizing its effects. The "animal" was deleted from the term, as many healers embraced a more aesthetic magnetism. In the process of gaining respectability in France, practitioners came to stress the meditative, quieting aspects of mesmerism—what came to be called somnambulism—over the bodily arousing encounters orchestrated by Mesmer and his colleagues. The "mesmeric crisis"—characterized by passionate fits—yielded ground to a sedate vision of altered states. In reaction to charges of licentiousness and to concerns over the sexual abuse of magnetized women, magnetists advanced the argument that this treatment could access "man's" spiritual nature.

As magnetism lost its intense aura of orgiastic pleasures and sexual surrender, physicians in early-nineteenth-century France began to document the increased memory capacity of somnambulant patients. The concern with dissoluteness and loss of moral control, particularly in magnetized women, shifted to an emphasis on heightened capacities, notable among those with magnetic abilities.[15]

Just as Descartes sought to remap the clerical domain of authority in claiming the (animal) body as a site of scientific investigation separate from the sacred realm of the (human) soul, medical practitioners in the late eighteenth century confronted this same moral authority in extending their own domain of influence. Much as Western discourse on recreational drugs, historically, is embedded in broad social concerns over pleasure and loss of control, reactions to the phenomenon of hypnosis are similarly a kind of cultural Rorschach card. In contests between the church and medicine, the controversy centered on whether the mind's capacity for altered states could be harnessed as a force for spiritual development (the province of the church) or for bodily healing (the province of medicine). In late-nineteenth-century disputes over hypnotic phenomena, taken up below, women's altered states became a battleground for competing authorities within the culture. Women were rarely in a position to articulate the meaning of their own newly discovered consciousness and exceptional states, dependent as they were on presiding male translators.

FEMALE APPROPRIATIONS
OF HYPNOTIC STATES

As mesmerism fell into disrepute in France in the early nineteenth century, never able to successfully overcome its associations with unruly sexuality, its exportation to the United States proceeded in a spiritual direction. The erotic aspects of mesmerism—of socially induced altered states—were less overt on the American side of the Atlantic. Initially, Charles Poyen, a French follower of Mesmer and an abolitionist, embarked on a lecture tour in New England in 1836, where he drew large crowds riveted by his magnetic healing methods.[16] But it was ecstatic revivalism—the Second Great Awakening—which swept New England in the 1830s as a cultural force, that created a fertile social-psychological climate for the spiritualist and mesmeric movement that emerged in the mid-nineteenth century. In rejecting the darkly deterministic Calvinism of the First Awakening of the eighteenth century, spiritualists were captured by the progressive ideal of self-transformation through accessing the mind's hidden potential.

Women were a palpable presence in nineteenth-century magnetic healing (a forerunner of the contemporary alternative health movement), but they were a dominating force in the overlapping spiritualist movement of that same era. Historians trace the origins of spiritualism to 1848, when rumors spread throughout industrial New England of two teenage girls who could communicate with the dead. In a rural town in upstate New York, neighbors gathered to listen to raps on the walls and furniture in a farmhouse owned by the Fox family—a house that had long been thought to be haunted. The mother of Margaret and Kate Fox, girls of twelve and fourteen, provided the "code" to translate mysterious rappings that occurred only in the presence of these two girls. Through the rappings, the Fox girls claimed to have made contact with a peddler who had been murdered in the house years before.[17] The Fox sisters would not be granted so much as a footnote in history had their mystical encounters not been advanced by an emerging movement of spiritual seekers, looking for new signs from the beyond. The sisters left their haunted family home to live with an older sister in neighboring Rochester, where local reformers took a keen interest in their experiences.[18]

Feminists and socialists figured prominently in the spiritualist movement that emerged in the 1850s, as communication with gentle, departed souls displaced the hellfire evangelism of their youth. So, too, as white abolitionists were exposed to African traditions, such as ancestor worship and animism, the conservative Christian doctrines of their childhood were converted into a transformed vision of spirituality. As Janet Oppenheim describes it, the spiritualists embraced "an essentially occult view of the universe, an animistic vision of closely interconnected parts all bearing the mark of cosmic soul, or world force, or ultimate spirit."[19]

As the medium entered the trance state, so too did her audience. Soon after spiritualism took hold in the United States, it spread to England, where it similarly captured feminists and other social reformers.[20] Mediums also entranced psychologists, most notably James, who spent much of his career investigating and writing about psychic phenomena.[21] But many nineteenth-century physicians and psychologists regarded mediums and spiritualists as lunatics, an attitude overdetermined by a general wariness toward the suspension of "normal" consciousness. As one physician put it, the medium offered a despicable display of "emotional incontinence."[22] Since this wariness was not extended to religious phenomena generally, it may have been further overdetermined by the subversive political context of mediumship and magnetism.

Nineteenth-century social constructions of the trance state were also deeply inscribed with prevailing gender assumptions. While men were as attracted to spiritualism as women, the leadership of mediumship was highly feminized, offering a new dialect for the nineteenth-century cult of true womanhood. Since spiritualists assumed that the capacity for entering trance states—the condition required by spirits in order to reveal themselves—necessitated a purity of mind and heart, women were thought to be particularly effective mediums. Drawing on the mesmeric language of electrical currents and energy fields, these unorthodox practitioners invested the cosmos with gendered energy. Femininity was associated with "negative" (receptive) currents and masculinity with "positive" (active) ones in the new "spiritual telegraph." Optimal conditions for visitations by spirits at a seance included a careful balance of positives and negatives in the circle, with the female medium serving as the center of receptive energy.

The spiritualist movement embraced the idea of latent possibilities within the mind that could be realized through a mystical, transformative experience— an idea that also was at the vortex of the Second Great Awakening of the 1830s.[23] In nineteenth-century revivalism, inner promptings could be embraced and received as gifts of the Spirit; these promptings were not bound to the guilt-ridden self-scrutiny of earlier Protestants. For spiritualists, who rejected any idea of hell or damnation, the journey into the beyond was guided by a benign and friendly cosmos.

The actual guides in this spiritual movement—the mediums who interpreted messages from the dead—were most often women. The craft of mediumship required little in the way of formal religious training, from which women were excluded. Yet the mystery surrounding the craft and the association of mediumship with revelatory knowledge made the medium a potent symbol of self-transformation. Female mediums such as Achsa White Sprague, Fannie Davis, Cora

Hatch, and Laura de Force Gordon migrated across the unstable political landscape of the United States, gaining enthusiastic followers.[24]

Like the clinical hysterics who followed, mediums enacted a psychodrama
that was both conciliatory toward, and resistive of, nineteenth-century gender
conventions. While some spiritualists and mediums were political reformers, most
claimed power from the dead rather than for the living. In its familial expressions—its intimate seances or table-turning sessions—female mediumship
stopped short of undermining the power of men in public life. Yet mediums did
orchestrate the ritual transgression of gender boundaries through the spirits that
came to occupy them. As Sonu Shamdasani has noted in describing the late-
nineteenth-century seance, "Women became men and men became women.
There was no limit to who one could be or to how many."[25]

In the 1870s, the spiritualist movement was at its height in the United States,
attracting as many as eleven million followers.[26] At this historical apogee,
mediumship had advanced from simple yes-no responses to automatic writing
and, finally, to full-scale materializations of spirits. Some mediums were reported
to be able to produce various appendages, termed ectoplasm, that extruded from
material draped around their bodies.[27] Unlike the clerical exorcisms of earlier eras
or the psychiatric demonstrations of hysteria that would follow, these dramas were
choreographed by women in the dim-lit parlors of the seance and, by some, on
the public stage of the lecture circuit. Women could transform themselves, even
embracing what was ordinarily forbidden. Alex Owen describes this enchanted
female world as one where "young girls [who] entered . . . as models of deco-
rum . . . indulged in assertive, antagonistic, and sometimes violent displays."[28]

Seances were also occasions for intimate touching, as the benign movement
of the spirits unraveled Victorian propriety. As materializations became the ultimate realization of mediumship, probing and caressing the materialized spirit
became part of the ritual. Eroticism depends heavily on context and on how physical touch is interpreted and understood. The nineteenth-century cult of feminine virtue, as a subtext of mediumship, permitted considerable physical contact
among women even as it stripped women's intimacies of overt sexual connota-
tions.[29] Yet as master of disguises, the medium could assume the more robust,
sensual personage of her double, the spirit "guide" who assumed control of her
body during the trance state. As James put it, the "two wills"—the spirit and the
medium—"might strike up a partnership and stir each other up."[30]

For some spiritualists, mediumship became a vehicle for stirring up audiences
through the women's rights lecture circuit. Speaking publicly meant overcoming inhibitions and intense social disapproval, and the trance state seemed to facilitate a new kind of oratory for women. In anointing the female medium,
Elizabeth Cady Stanton and Susan B. Anthony claimed that "the spirits of the
universe may breathe through her lips."[31]

Most mediums were not political agitators but came to be known as mind
healers and advisors who provided solace for grieving families. The writing of Elizabeth Stuart Phelps, whose enormously popular *The Gates of Ajar,* published in

1868, was widely read, signaled a new genre of spiritualist women's guidance literature.[32] In her novel, the spirit world offers consolation to grieving families who lost sons and brothers in the Civil War. It raises the specter, as well, of dreamlike glimmerings of the beyond that reduce the vast distance separating the living and the dead. From spiritualism's early inception, the most common reason for consulting a medium was the death of a child, and the emotional power of such experiences led many to become actively engaged in the spiritualist cause. Messages from dead children and other relatives tended to be highly reassuring since spiritualists rejected any notion of hell or damnation.

A highly spiritualized female authority in the nineteenth century rose on the grave of the Old Eve, the carnal, oversexed Temptress who first tormented Adam and, later, the early Puritans. While the redemptive femininity of the nineteenth century permitted women to claim a maternally based moral authority, the residue of the Old Eve was palpable in the "gynopsychiatry" of that same period.[33] Physicians located mental disorders in the female reproductive organs, an idea that flourished during the nineteenth-century expansion of medical science. For spiritualists and mesmeric healers, the recovery of a sexualized femininity was constrained by this vestige of paranoia toward the female body within the medical professions, on the one hand, and its demonized forerunner in Calvinism on the other. In the context of prevailing sexual codes that were so costly to women and that offered so little pleasure, it is understandable that women spiritualists would concede the sexual ground and transport their own hypnotic states into a spiritual realm. They sought, through the authority of a virginal-mystical goodness, to assert a culturally unauthorized social influence, even as this expression of influence remained inhibited by nineteenth-century gender codes.

CLINICAL HYPNOSIS

As women employed hypnosis to enchant audiences on both sides of the Atlantic, assuming a spiritualized authority through the trance state, physicians engaged in their own spellbinding performances. Jean-Martin Charcot, the charismatic lecturer and administrator of the Salpêtrière hospital in France, is credited with relegitimizing clinical hypnosis in the 1870s as he reworked the medical mapping of the boundaries between normal and abnormal states. Charcot's famous Tuesday morning lecture series, in which he used hypnosis to induce symptoms in his favorite women patients before audiences of rapt observers, is now legendary. Charcot is often described as a skilled diagnostician whose careful, detailed descriptions and riveting demonstrations of hysterical symptoms boldly introduced the dispassionate gaze of science on the unsettling mysteries of this predominantly female condition.[34] In demonstrating that some of the symptoms of hysteria could be simulated during hypnosis, Charcot concluded that hysterics lived in a kind of permanent somnambulant state as a result of a shock to their nervous system. In exploring this early ground of traumatic dissociation, Charcot distinguished between "dynamic amnesia," where memories are recoverable under hypnosis, and "organic amnesia," where memory is entirely lost.[35]

Charcot and another French physician, Hippolyte Bernheim, were the central protagonists in late-nineteenth-century debates over hypnosis and hysteria. The role of suggestion in hypnosis was at the center of a dispute that arose between adherents of the Salpêtrière school, led by Charcot, and adherents of the competing Nancy school, led by Bernheim. The Nancy school emphasized the influence of suggestion on the manifestations of hypnotic states, stressing the potentially dangerous, seductive powers of the hypnotist.[36] While late-eighteenth-century and late-nineteenth-century controversies over therapeutic influence on hypnotized women did not include debate about contested memories, the sexual meanings of hypnotic states were very much at the forefront of concerned medical minds.

If suggestion operated not only in the administration of the cure but in the very manifestation of the hysterical condition, as Bernheim asserted in his criticisms of Charcot, we may also suspect that this same phenomenon of suggestion exerted influence on its audience of observers. Like medieval clerics searching for the mark of the devil on the bodies of accused witches, the new medical priesthood was mesmerized by its own subjects. The hypnotic spell worked both ways, and this recognition ran counter to the scientific ideal of dispassionate objectivity as well as to the priority of masculine over feminine, mind over emotion, in the hierarchy of Enlightenment values.

In mapping the stages and zones of hysterical conditions, Charcot was able to express conventional concerns and preoccupations with sexuality within an emotionally detached, medicalized discourse. Through his demonstrations of hysterical fits, Charcot imported into the clinical field myriad Victorian sentiments and anxieties over female sexuality. In late-nineteenth-century social thought, "normal" women (that is, bourgeois women) were regarded as predominantly asexual, with the maternal instinct asserted to be analogous to the male sexual instinct. At the same time, deeper anxieties over the "hypersexuality" of women—the other side of the cultural denial of female sexuality—broke through this repressive medical discourse. One follower of Charcot, E. Chambert, introduced the term *erotogenic zones* in describing the acute arousal states achieved by hysterics, which echoed the "mesmeric crisis" of the century prior.

> If one touches very lightly for a second, part of the breast, or any other erogenous point, the patient quivers, her face flushes, and quite rapidly, her face, her attitudes, her words, her movements indicate without a doubt the voluptuous sensations that she is experiencing, and over which she has no control. The effects that we just described are even more pronounced *if the patient is hypnotized.* In such a state, it proved sufficient to blow lightly on the palm of our patient to trigger both a sexual orgasm and a complete re-enactment of the coitus.[37]

Just as the sight of a lady's ankle could arouse titillating speculation on the part of Victorians, hysterical neurosis became a screen onto which male longings and fears could be projected. For some observers, the sexual arousal associated with the hypnotic state was linked with what was believed to be a tendency for women to make false sexual allegations, directed particularly toward the hypnotist. The aroused female subject, overcome by the effects of the treatment, could easily confuse the situation, particularly when an active imagination combined forces with a state of bodily excitation.[38]

Victorian society did not allow much latitude for women to directly challenge male authority. Adherents of both the Salpêtrière and the Nancy schools agreed that highly hypnotizable subjects were prone to memory errors born of an overactive imagination. While they shared a belief that hysterics could be skilled liars, they squared off on the question of whether hysteria was a unique psychological condition, separable from its neurological look-alikes (the position adopted by the Salpêtrière school), or a variant of the normal state of hypnosis and a condition shaped through suggestion (the position of the Nancy school). Bernheim, who defined suggestibility as "the aptitude to transform an idea into an act," argued that every individual is suggestible to some degree and that Charcot's hysterical "phases" were artifacts of hypnosis.[39] Actually, Bernheim's position is more compatible than Charcot's with contemporary thinking in that Bernheim recognized the interpersonal dimensions of hypnosis, particularly how practitioners may unconsciously cue the patient.[40]

Beyond the central areas of dispute and competing positions, a peripheral debate was carried on in Charcot's time over whether virtuous women would submit to or resist the influence of the hypnotist.[41] While one line of medical inquiry attempted to locate the precise stage of hypnosis when women would be unable to resist a sexual overture, others asserted that even a skilled hypnotist would not be able to override the character of a truly chaste woman. To settle this question empirically, a series of experiments were devised to determine whether a women could be convinced to kiss her experimenter during a hypnotic state or through posthypnotic suggestion. While the results were never conclusive, they were mobilized to advance the idea—one that remained pivotal in preserving the respectability of hypnosis far into the twentieth century—that there were limits to the effects of hypnosis, particularly to the hypnotist's ability to subdue the moral character of the subject. Yet undercurrents of anxiety over sexual arousal and surrender, particularly as they related to gender codes, were to move further beneath the "surface" of these debates, only to emerge in a disguised form in contemporary disputes over recovered memories of sexual abuse.

THE DYNAMIC UNCONSCIOUS

Hypnosis played a key role in the development of the concept of the dynamic unconscious, although schools of thought carried this inquiry in divergent directions. Before their bitter disputes, Freud, Breuer, and Janet shared, in the early 1890s, a common set of ideas concerning hypnosis and hysteria. Drawing on Charcot's concept of dynamic amnesia, they used hypnosis to recover a forgotten past and to therapeutically alter the course of this "recovered" past's effects on the mind.

Mediums also shaped the development of the dynamic unconscious, as male professionals sought to break the spell induced by this female expression of social influence. Indeed, a teenage girl, a self-described medium, captured center stage at the historically momentous meeting between Freud and his U.S. colleagues in 1909, during his only trip to the United States. On that occasion, Freud, Carl Jung, and Sandor Ferenczi met at Clark University with American luminaries in the field of psychology.[42] Other than the teenage girl, women were excluded from the meetings, a policy protested by a number of incensed women psychologists.[43]

Psychologist G. Stanley Hall, the president of Clark at the time, later recounted the dramatic moment when the psychological basis of female mediums was revealed. After months of interviewing the girl, Hall was embarrassed when Freud uncovered the romantic motive behind the fanciful inventions of this young medium. "Now the whole situation stood forth in a new light. An erotic motive, of which there had hitherto been no hint, appears to have been the dominant one throughout."[44] In ferreting out the "real motive"—a girlish infatuation—Freud triumphed over the medium. As Hall pointed out, mediumship permits women to violate strict moral codes while disavowing such transgressive impulses.

Even as he was persuaded by Freud's interpretation, Hall, having spent a great deal of time with the young woman, offered his own insights on mediums; in many respects they are more incisive than those of Freud. Prior to Freud's interpretive victory, Hall had portrayed this adolescent girl as socially isolated and as philosophically inclined. Her mediumship enunciated a world she envisioned but could not directly inhabit, and it enlarged her ego by "widening experience."[45] She and her mother, who were shunned in their small town because of the mother's "estrangement" from her husband, formed an enclosed and enchanted world of their own, which was centered on exploring the girl's "budding" spiritual gifts. Hall summarizes the conditions that had been so conducive to her nascent mediumship: "rich fantasy, stimulated by the warmest maternal sympathy, favored the highest flights of fantasy, and the world of imagination grew inversely and more or less as a surrogate of the normal expansion of interests which were lacking in the environment" (147).

Does one interpretation of the story serve as well as another? From the perspective of a psychology of women, demystifying mediumship led to further contradictions. On the one hand, as turn-of-the-century psychologists began to stress the "double consciousness" of female mediums, the various personages that occupied them during a trance state could be recognized as latent aspects of the women themselves, including culturally repressed capacities and desires. On the other hand, the clinical investigation of mediumship stripped the medium of her magnificent social power, as the tricks of her trade were exposed. Once mediumship was clinically interpreted as a disguise, an operation of the ego itself, interest in the phenomenon declined, leaving these female impersonators without an audience. As Hall confessed in his "obituary" on mediumship, "The next generation will be hardly able to believe that prominent men in this [generation] wasted their energies in chasing such a will-of-the-wisp as the veracity of messages or the reality of a post-mortem existence" (154).

Yet moving from the spiritual to the erotic dimensions of female altered states opened up a problematic front in dynamic psychiatry, just as it had for Mesmer a century prior. Inevitably, perhaps, employment of scientific authority to probe the intimate depths of psychic experience, assisted by the mystifying tool of hypnosis, would breach the professionally constituted boundary between practitioner and patient. And this patient, a role initially played by adult daughters of strict, Victorian bourgeois families, was the very embodiment of privacy and propriety and the repository of moral virtue. Whatever the extent of sexual abuse in the histories of these women, speaking intimately to men and revealing hidden aspects of their lives were inexorably riddled with sexual, transgressive meanings. The trance state, then, was an early site of culturally charged revelations.

In his autobiography, Freud notes the unsettling emotional power of the therapeutic journey.[46] He describes his own response to a hypnotized patient, an experience that was decisive in his abandonment of hypnosis as a therapeutic technique. "As she woke up on one occasion, she threw her arms around my neck. The unexpected entrance of a servant relieved us from a painful discussion, but from that time onwards there was a tacit understanding between us that the hypnotic treatment should be discontinued. I was modest enough not to attribute the event to my irresistible personal attraction, and I felt that I had now grasped the nature of the mysterious element that was at work behind hypnotism" (27).

And what was this mysterious element, this sexually arousing aspect of hypnosis that perpetually haunted practitioners of it? Freud's brief intrigue with hypnosis, a procedure he claimed to have never been particularly good at, ended in what he felt to be a resolution of the mystery. For Freud, hypnosis directly accessed a deep psychic reservoir of repressed sexuality and infantile yearnings. He substituted free association for hypnosis as a more neutral tool for accessing unconscious processes. Since hypnosis was so laden with seductive meanings and since it bypassed the patient's voluntary control over revealed material, Freud came to the conclusion that it was countertherapeutic and highly "suggestive" (20).

Beyond these quite legitimate, astute observations, we may recognize in Freud's reactions to his hypnotized patient an anxiety that lingers on in psychoanalysis, even as the profession followed Freud in turning away from this controversial procedure. This anxiety centers on several murky distinctions. First, if the clinical encounter "mimics" in its hypnotic influence an earlier pathogenic one, how do we decisively separate what is present and what is past, those desires and wishes originating in the immediate context and those springing from the past via the transference? Second, if the clinical encounter is a uniquely intimate, erotic exchange, subordinated to therapeutic aims, how do we distinguish between such therapeutic "seductions," often described as rapport, and more pathogenic enactments of domination and submission? Hypnosis may have exacerbated the problem of erotic influences within the therapeutic encounter, even eliciting them, but it did not create them anew, nor did its cessation eliminate their effects.

HYPNOSIS AND GENDER CODES

After the heat of clinical disputes abated in the 1890s, hypnosis fell into disfavor, particularly in Europe, until the First World War.[47] During this period of revitalized interest in hypnotic technique, a new cast of characters came to dominate the psychiatric stage. Hypnosis as a treatment had been established through clinical work with female hysterics, and its extension to the conditions of men, primarily shell-shocked soldiers, confronted considerable social obstacles. In her analysis of this historical period, Ruth Leys poses the questions of precisely how hypnosis effected a cure and of how the process of cure was understood within the context of war-related trauma.[48] For her, the contradiction psychiatry faced at the time in its treatment of shell-shocked soldiers was in responding to cultural anxieties over gender codes, on the one hand, and in therapeutically subverting them within an acceptable framework of scientific rationales on the other. Hypnosis, to be an effective treatment, had to be carried out in a manner that allowed a "feminine" release of emotion while disentangling this procedure from its associations with eroticized seduction. As Elaine Showalter points out in describing this same historical juncture, hysteria had to be "masculinized" in extending it to the infirmities of men, just as did hypnosis as a treatment.[49]

Male hysteria posed a dilemma for professionals, who were generally averse to social controversy or direct challenges to convention. Like the Vietnam War, the First World War generated widespread resistance, among recruits as well as others, and psychiatrists treating war-related conditions were under pressure to separate "malingerers" from the genuinely incapacitated.[50] A psychiatric typology was generated to achieve this end, even though the profession was divided over the scope of the insanity of war and the extent of generalized madness it created.[51] In the psychiatric backwaters of the war, where triaging meant nursing an injured manhood and returning the salvageable back to the front, hypnosis proved to be an effective technique for treating war-related psychic trauma.

Leys takes the position that hypnotic recovery and the working through of traumatic memory was, in the context of the war effort, an engagement more fundamentally with emotion than with memory.[52] It is not simply that traumatic memories and their affective derivatives are stored in the brain, only to be detoxified and integrated into consciousness through the therapeutic actions of hypnosis. Rather, Leys insists, hypnosis provided a technical tool for the ritual expression of emotion that would otherwise be deemed pathological for men.

Since hypnosis raised troubling concerns about both passive longings in male patients and eroticized dependence on the hypnotist, the entire procedure had to be reframed in order to facilitate the rehabilitation of wounded manhood. The solution was to emphasize the technical over the interpersonal aspects of hypnosis and to stress the control that remained within the hypnotized subject. In effect, the erotic/feminine associations of hypnotic control, of entering into the mind of a submissive subject, were "repressed" in a hyperrationalized discourse. As psychotherapist Paul Dubois put it in his scathing criticisms of clinical hypnosis in the early twentieth century, "The object of treatment ought to be to make the patient *master of himself;* the means to this end is *the education of the will,* or, more exactly, *of the reason.*"[53] Hypnotic states, then, may be choreographed along various cultural pathways, even as they repeatedly raise uneasy questions concerning the nonrational aspects of mind.[54]

HYPNOSIS AND THE COUNTERCULTURE MOVEMENT

In his history of the concept of dissociation, research psychologist Ernest Hilgard locates academic psychology's contemporary revival of interest in divided consciousness and hypnosis in the counterculture movement of the 1960s.[55] While this movement may be interpreted as a form of intergenerational rebellion, where contestations over lifestyles and conceptions of society were central, it was also a struggle with patriarchal authority, within academia as well as within the broader culture. "In the 1960s a substantial fraction of people, particularly the young, fed up with technology and contemporary society, turned inward to discover the range of human potential in other ways. These other ways included experimentation with psychedelic drugs, meditation, Eastern religions, [extrasensory perception], and occultism. Much of this searching lay outside the scientific establishment, but it did not leave the scientists unaffected."[56]

Hilgard notes the parallel between this contemporary period and the late nineteenth century, also a time of social upheaval that transformed psychology as a discipline. In both eras, the social sciences emerge as a site of contestation over human nature and its capabilities. While, from the late nineteenth century on, technological forces and industrialism drove the discipline toward mechanistic models of mind and behavior, critical and Romantic traditions resisted such historical imperatives, calling for a reenchantment of consciousness.

Hilgard's observation that interest in altered states originated in the counterculture movement of the 1960s stops short of explaining the implications of this historical insight. Dominant American values, many of which originated in the Enlightenment and during the rise of capitalism, privilege the active (masculine) over the receptive (feminine) mode. Productiveness, pragmatism, and utilitarianism share this valuing of activity and mastery over pleasure seeking or sensuous activity, which interferes with these aims. In reconciling the psychologies of East and West, distinctions pursued by Robert Ornstein in *The Psychology of*

Consciousness, published in 1972,[57] Hilgard argues that active and receptive modes of consciousness coexist in all cultures.[58] Hilgard draws on the paradigm of dissociation to explain a wide range of mental and social phenomena based on splits in consciousness, from trance, fugue, and drug-induced hallucinogenic states to possession states and multiple personality. Some of these states are more ephemeral while others are more sustained; some are more private and others more socially elaborated. Hilgard attempts to reduce the cultural divide between the Western Enlightenment and competing worldviews, rejecting the idea that hypnotic or highly "receptive" states are more "primitive" or "regressive" than ordinary cognitive states.

In countering the hierarchy of values that dominates Western psychology, Hilgard rejects the commonly held view that biological or cultural evolution proceeds from "primitive" possession states, implicitly passive, to more active cognitive processes. Under the influence of the Enlightenment, those aspects of mind associated with passive and receptive states became understood in more secular ways, but they also became more pathologized. Multiple personality and hysteria, as well as the dissociated states associated with spiritualism and hypnotic suggestion, supplanted the possession and trance states of earlier societies.

Active and passive, instrumental and receptive, are gender-laden terms, linguistic dualisms that privilege the masculine over the feminine. Those attributes most prized by the culture tend to be masculinized; those attributes most devalued or marginalized tend to be feminized. As conceptual and linguistic systems of meaning, gendered subjects are both constituted, in the empirical sense, and constructed, in the ideological sense, through discursive practices. Women are more likely to produce vivid imagery during self-hypnosis than are men, and they score higher on measures of absorption—that is, the ability to sustain investment in imaginative processes.[59] However, many studies of hypnotic susceptibility fail to show sex differences.[60]

The close affinity between femininity and hypnotic susceptibility continues to operate as a cultural fantasy, however, because women are socially constituted in the "receptive" position. (See chapter 4.) As a cultural signifier, woman is the receptive container for the male imagination, repository of disavowed male anxieties over vulnerability and loss of control. Gender oppositions, then, are both "real" and imaginary, both constitutive of subjectivity and an ideological veil that conceals the subject's "true nature." Males are seen as more "active" whereas females are seen as more "receptive" in their orientations to reality, yet each of these terms predisposes or potentiates observations to conform to these expectations. Belief in the stability of gender categories creates socially constituted defenses against the contradictory, fragmentary, and overlapping dimensions of gender identifications.[61]

One of the consistent findings over the two hundred years of scientific inquiry into hypnosis is that 15 to 20 percent of the population is highly hypnotizable—often described as "grade five hypnotizables"—in that they readily enter a deep trance state and experience posthypnotic amnesia.[62] These subjects, viewed historically by psychiatry as dependent, suggestible, or hysterical individuals (prototypically feminine), are rehabilitated in neodissociationist theory.[63] Hilgard resists the pathologizing of both dissociative states and cultural phenomena associated with altered consciousness. While he concurs that hypnotic states produce a readiness to accept the suggestions of the hypnotist, Hilgard adds that suggestion alone provides "a very limited characterization of the total alterations that hypnosis produces."[64] He shifts the discourse on hypnosis from the zombielike submission of the subject to the enriched capacity for imagery that the hypnotized subject experiences. The hypnotic state permits an intense absorption and focusing of attention, facilitated by the suspension of ordinary cognitive controls and reality monitoring.

Drawing on the research of his wife and collaborator, Josephine Hilgard, Hilgard describes "hypnotic virtuosos" as exhibiting high levels of imaginative involvement.[65] As a caution against excessive confidence in hypnotically recovered memory, Hilgard emphasizes that hypnosis heightens access to both memory and fantasy. Highly hypnotizable subjects are able to immerse themselves in a role or dramatic enactment of a past scene and to transcend the ordinary boundaries between internal and external reality. Throughout human history, creative individuals, mystics, and shamans have displayed this capacity for entering deep trance states.[66] Such authoritative uses of the trance state have been highly restricted for women, however, and more readily pathologized in them than in men.

CONTEMPORARY AMBIVALENCES

Just as hypnotic states have been valorized throughout history, invested with mystical, revelatory meanings, they also have been demonized. Similarly, the influence the hypnotist achieves through establishing "rapport" with the subject has been alternatively minimized and vastly exaggerated. The hypnotist is an archetype of social influence—in psychoanalytic terms, a transference object. The image of the hypnotist arouses the impulse to yield, to give up control, to be taken over—infantile longings that are as cultivated in normative feminine consciousness as they are phobically denied in masculine consciousness. Leaders in religious movements mobilize these same longings, just as they direct adherents toward particular interpretations of hypnotic states—for example, in the liturgies accompanying prayer. But the hypnotist makes conscious these processes of influence in that awareness of the suspension of normal ego controls and critical consciousness is integral to what subjects understand to be occurring. Because particular states of psychological immersion are associated with vulnerability to the power of others, phobic reactions to such states are understandable, particularly given Western valorizing of mastery and autonomy. Loss of volitional control is anxiety-provoking, arousing deep unease over dependence, which may be expressed in a phobic attitude toward hypnotic states or hypnotists or both.

It is true, as defenders of hypnosis so often point out, that everyday activities such as reading a book, daydreaming, and meditating contain elements of the hypnotic.[67] But the anxiety associated with the hypnotic state centers on its interpersonal expressions, specifically on the related phenomenon of suggestibility.[68] Here, cultural anxieties about social influence in general infiltrate the discourse on hypnosis, creating a readiness to invest hypnotic encounters with dangerous powers.

The position of woman as prototypical hypnotic subject is, in part, a cultural fantasy born of the patriarchal imagination. For women, one strategy of resistance has been to make active use of this cultural fantasy by claiming exceptional powers through the trance state, a theme revisited in part 3 of this book. But in retrieving the "hypnotic virtuoso" from the ranks of the hysterics and thereby redeeming the feminine imagination, specific vulnerabilities associated with this readiness to lose critical consciousness may be easily overlooked. As I argued in chapter 4, female development under patriarchy has a tendency toward problematic foreclosures of intense states of arousal and a muting of personal boundaries. Women's work, as well as cultural representations of the psychic states of women, contributes to the idea that female spaces are perpetually interruptible, subject to the incursions of others. In making use of the trance state as a mode of resistance, as a defensive means of disengaging or distancing, it is understandable that women would be more likely to divert the trance state into the spiritual realm than into the erotic. Throughout much of Western history, women have found the erotic a more treacherous ground for rebellious strivings than they have found the spiritual.

There is both an impulse/arousal dimension to hypnotic phenomena and an interactive dimension, and these two dimensions interact in complicated ways. We need not deny the importance of the hypnotic in interpersonal experience—Freud recognized it as the core experience in falling in love—in order to value critical consciousness. Psychological health depends on the capacity to move between the hypnotic and the antihypnotic—to make creative use of alternating moments of immersion in and distance from objects of consciousness. On an interpersonal level, this involves a capacity for deep mutuality as well as for aloneness, for engagement in as well as disengagement from an other. One aspect of self-awareness includes recognizing when and how we are being hypnotized, as well as having a means of regaining critical consciousness.[69]

Psychotherapy and Hypnotic Influences

In the psychotherapeutic situation, beliefs about hypnosis operate on a number of levels. Over the past few decades, there has been a tremendous increase in the use of hypnosis to "enhance" memory or to access repressed memory.[70] In other words, therapists and patients often share a belief that the past may be revisited or directly "remembered" through formal hypnotic procedures. Critics argue that while memory may be enhanced in some situations, hypnosis also heightens internally generated imagery, or fantasy, even as it makes it difficult for the subject to distinguish these two forms of memory activity.

Another area of contested claims concerns whether the formal induction procedures associated with hypnosis are uniquely risky. Many critics of recovered memory point out that a broad range of clinical techniques not explicitly identified with hypnosis may achieve similar problematic effects, including a heightened vulnerability to suggestion. Guided imagery, the use of therapeutic massage, and other imagery-generative techniques run the same risk.[71] Even free association, the technique Freud substituted for hypnosis, invites imaginative engagement with the inner world. An important difference in the use of these various therapeutic practices, however, is in how the clinician makes sense of the material that emerges. In the psychoanalytic tradition, access to fantasy is believed to be as vital in understanding mental life as is access to "buried" memories. (See chapter 4.)

It seems quite likely that an interaction of social context, subjective states (including beliefs), and social influences contributes to the production of hypnotic conditions. Fatigue, distress, and confusion do make individuals more susceptible to incorporating uncritically the ideas of others into their own states of mind, with less ability to discern the "source" of this new knowledge. Social isolation and leading interview techniques may heighten these effects. A number of critics of clinically recovered memory have drawn parallels between police interrogation procedures and clinical interviewing, both of which may be guided by an active search for a particular kind of "confessional" knowledge. With sufficient persistence and persuasive appeals, individuals may come to believe all sorts of claims, and they even may confess to crimes that they have not committed.[72]

There is a subtext of cultural anxiety operating in this debate, however, specifically in the wariness toward those aspects of mind not readily anchored in external, verifiable events. Since hypnosis is so commonly defended on the basis of its potential for enhancing memory, its role in heightening access to fantasy tends to be cited by critics in refuting the practice. For many defenders, the discovery that hypnosis is associated with the human imagination and with the "nonrational" aspects of interpersonal exchanges arouses keen embarrassment.

Therapeutic Influence

Since psychotherapy, like many other culturally legitimized forms of expertise, does explicitly "influence" the patient's states of mind, how do we distinguish between beneficial and harmful hypnotic influences? If therapists were to explain and explore the vast domain of potential suggestive factors in the clinical encounter, a virtual paralysis would result. Indeed, the expectancy of a helpful experience in psychotherapy is one of the more predictive factors in therapeutic outcome.

Permutations of this conflict abound, specifically over how important it is that the patient understand the theory or reasoning underlying the treatment or, correspondingly, how important it is that the therapist's interpretation, if it is demonstrated to be effective, is really the correct one. Both patient and therapist may be under the influence of factors that escape notice. Yet the difference between shamanism and psychotherapy, each of which may relieve suffering through some form of suggestion, is that the explanations offered by psychotherapy are presumably verifiable in the scientific sense. Hypnotic suggestibility may operate in many contexts, but science is understood to be essentially anti-hypnotic. Although psychotherapy may be accompanied by myriad rituals, with their various placebo effects and instances of superstitious learning, the "enlightened" practitioner is obliged to understand such processes. It is not only that the treatment "works" but that the reasons for its efficacy are grasped and can be articulated by the practitioner. The practitioner, at least, must not be hypnotized by the effects achieved.

There is yet another dimension to hypnotic influence that operates as an undercurrent of conflict in this clinical discourse. As I noted earlier in the chapter, hypnosis, ever since animal magnetism, has been associated with female sexual surrender. Given this association, formal and informal hypnotic induction procedures may mobilize, for hypnotist and subject alike, sexual fantasies as well as other sexually related material. By disavowing the seductive meanings attached to the hypnotic situation, clinicians and patients may confuse the "source" of the material that emerges. Freud recognized this potential confusion and subsequently abandoned the use of hypnosis.

But if we extend our understanding of hypnotic influence to a wide range of intimate encounters and subtle differences in hypnotic susceptibility, this problem is not so readily transcended. Entering the mind of another can evoke associations of sexual surrender, stimulating both receptive modes of sexual longing—the desire to be taken over by a powerful other—and associated anxieties, including realistic fears, particularly among women, that hypnotic situations create a vulnerability to abuse.

Revisitations of the Occult

In a choreography reminiscent of the table rappings that emerged in the early expressions of mediumship in the nineteenth century, many U.S. hypnotherapists in the late twentieth century dramatize their powers through riveting displays of altered states. And, like spiritualists of a century ago, many therapists conceive of the female mind as receptive and innocent, with sexual and aggressive "spirit memories" overtaking it against the will of the subject.

The work of leading hypnotherapist D. Cordyon Hammond illustrates these trends.[73] In his description of a method of age regression used for the purpose of abreacting (emotionally releasing) incest memories, Hammond begins with the induction of a trance state. In the case example he presents, Hammond instructs a female patient to return to the incestuous scene that she has remembered occurring at the age of four and to experience the feelings that were dissociated from consciousness at the time. We do not learn how this memory was obtained—whether it was a continuous or hypnotically recovered memory. Much like Janet, Hammond assumes that the memory is the starting point in a chain of pathological processes. Going to the source of the problem means neutralizing the "toxic" memory through suggestion. This process is analogous to exorcism in that the client is presumably emancipated from the torturous memory that has possessed her.

Hammond recognizes, however, that the patient may resist his suggestions and that a careful procedure for "checking" her acceptance of therapeutic interventions of this kind must be instituted. Just as the table rappings conjured up by nineteenth-century mediums gave material expression to what were felt to be the sentiments of the spirits—initially limited to yes and no replies—Hammond's use of ideomotor signals crudely tracks the subject's unconscious compliance with or resistance to his directives. By raising one finger to indicate yes and another to indicate no, the subject is able to communicate with the hypnotherapist while remaining in a deep trance state.

Beginning with a series of queries, Hammond then offers a suggestion to this modern medium of trance communication: "Now that you have released all those old, outdated feelings, is your unconscious mind now willing to let go of all those old, out-of-date feelings, so that they'll no longer influence you?" If an ideomotor signal of yes is obtained, the therapist may continue with the next suggestion. "You can now let go of all those old feelings of anger, and hurt, and fear, and guilt. Just let go of all those outdated feelings, and when your unconscious mind can sense you letting go of them, your 'yes' finger will float up again." After gaining assurance from the subject that she is, indeed, willing to relinquish the dead spirits of the past, Hammond proceeds to establish the precise intents and migrations of these restless ghosts. "And I want to ask, can your unconscious mind now sense that all men are not like your father?" After a positive response, "Good. You can now understand that all men are not like your father. And do you realize that your husband is not like your father?" After a positive response, "Good. That's right, you can now appreciate that all men are not like your father. And you will begin to see men as individuals now, perceiving them as distinct individuals. All men are not like your father, and your husband isn't like your father. And you are free now; free to relate to men as individuals; and free to relate to your husband as an individual. And those events that we've worked through will no longer influence how you think or act or feel. You are free now."[74]

Hammond does not report the percentages of acceptances or rejections obtained through these therapeutic suggestions nor the procedures for managing recalcitrant "spirits." Yet just as mediums moved from simple table rappings to the more complex communications of automatic writing and somnambulant speech, Hammond moves from ideomotor signals to inviting his female subject to verbally interact with him. By using the sound of her own voice to induce a deeper trance state, her verbal communications allow the hypnotherapist to "tailor the input" and to avoid "operating blind" (20).

This hypnotherapist does seem to be operating blind, however, even as he accesses and transforms what he perceives to be the inner reality of the patient. Hammond addresses the patient's potential doubts concerning these procedures by advising practitioners to cultivate "trance ratification." Even highly "talented" hypnotizables may not always believe that they have been hypnotized, he points out, so they often require a "convincer." In the tradition of mesmerism and spiritualism, proofs of the reality of the metaphysical realm were a dominating concern, as various devices were fashioned to amplify the occurrences, such as the planchette. In this same spirit of scientific faith, Hammond recommends that "you provide from time to time a trance ratification experience for your patients." By poking the skin with a needle or clamping a piece of flesh with a hemostat, the hypnotist dramatically demonstrates to the patient her hypnotic insensitivity to pain. While this ritual is intended to demonstrate the "incredible power of your unconscious mind to control your feelings and your body," it also seems to have the effect of ritually subduing any lingering uncertainty in the patient's mind concerning what precisely has occurred between them (19).

CONCLUSIONS

The story of Gertrude Stein with which the chapter began reminds us of the dilemmas women perpetually face in interpreting their own exceptional states. In her autobiography, Stein describes with evident pride her own "failure" to produce automatic writing as a subject in the laboratory research at Harvard. She reports James as saying, in response to a student who complained that Stein was an outlier in his own experiment, that "if Miss Stein gave no response, I shall say that it was as normal not to give a response as to give one and decidedly the result must not be cut out."[75] While she came to reject the phenomenon of automatic writing—as logical, organized activity operating outside of awareness—Stein nonetheless found the experiments fascinating for what they revealed about what she termed the "bottom nature" of human personality.[76] Automatic writing, she concluded, revealed less about latent intelligences, in the ordinary sense, than it did about cyclical, rhythmic, prelogical patterns of speech. Rather than proving that the hysterical and the hypnotic reveal reservoirs of coherent mental activity, Stein insisted on a psychology that recognizes the vital intermingling of primitive and complex processes of mind.

How do we listen to women's communications from "beyond the normal"? If the aim of science is to demystify, how should we listen to awesome accounts without stripping them of their vital meaning? The trance state is, it seems, ambiguous and heterogeneous in its effects, subject to various social choreographies. Since the French Revolution, periods of social change and mass mobilization in the West have opened up possibilities for rethinking latent aspects of mind. While cultural fantasies do mediate the experience of the trance state, its expressions my be either creative or debilitating. On the creative side, hypnosis may be viewed as an artifact of the human imagination engaged in a project of self-transformation. And we can see how women, whether as patients or as practitioners, may embrace the revelatory power of the trance state in breaking through cultural barriers. Yet the vital project of accessing female "hidden" potential confronts the lingering problem of the hypnotic aspects of the therapeutic encounter and of patriarchal culture itself.

On a cultural level, hypnotizability is associated with the "feminine" (passive) receptive modes of consciousness because women are more likely than men to be placed in this subject position. Entering into the trance state can be dangerous for women, not only in the context of manipulative or controlling therapies but in the broader context of spellbinding beliefs. Among defenders of hypnosis as a tool for recovering memory, we may recognize a suspension of critical awareness concerning how the practitioner shapes the "revelations" that unfold.

But there is a parallel culture of belief operating among critics who may exaggerate the powers of the hypnotist based on nineteenth-century notions of female purity of mind. In making a villain of the hypnotist, who is suspected of "implanting" dirty thoughts in the virtuous minds of hapless women, women's own use of the trance state to express the forbidden is readily overlooked. Further, loss of cognitive controls, along with its attendant anxieties, is pathologized within this psychodrama. The trance state provides the occasion for female spellbinding performances that would otherwise not be permissible, a theme pursued through stories about clinical hysteria in the next chapter.

HYSTERICAL
Chapter 7   # HEROINES

AS McCARTHYISM reached a feverish pitch in the early 1950s, Aldous Huxley published *The Devils of Loudun,* a novel about hysteria and demon possession in an early-seventeenth-century French convent and based on historical events.[1] The story centers on the tragic fate of Father Grandier, a rebellious priest whose refusal to accept the vow of celibacy makes him the scapegoat for battles raging within the church. The handsome priest's amorous relationships with many of the women of Loudun also make him the object of considerable envy in the town, as his exploits become the subject of unbridled gossip.

Charges are brought against Grandier after strange behavior is reported to be occurring at the local convent. As daughters of noblemen, the nuns of Loudun typically enter the cloistered life less for devotional purposes than for respectability. Having failed to achieve a favorable marriage, these women of the gentry find sanctuary in a religious vocation. The dreary orderliness, hard work, and monotony of the convent create, however, a state of perpetual, unfulfilled longing.

Sister Jeanne, a highly intelligent woman who has a physical defect that makes her unmarriageable, displays as well the unseemly trait of ambition, a trait that, nonetheless, leads her auspiciously to an appointment as proprietress of the convent. As events unfold, the sister is plagued by nocturnal longings—increasingly centered on the notorious Father Grandier—which leave her in a state of daily disquietude. Obsessed with this priest, whom she knows only through titillating rumors, the sister turns her longings to bitter hatred when Grandier rebuffs her request that he serve as the convent's confessor. As the story continues, Sister Jeanne is joined by her equally aroused novitiates, who circulate tales of the father's visits at night, his carnal entries into the cloisters. In restoring the good name of the convent, Sister Jeanne enlists a local cleric, and they conspire to formalize charges of witchcraft against Grandier.

A series of exorcisms is conducted on the hysterical sisters, as local clerics arrive on the scene, each pursuing his own political ambitions. The exorcisms become a riveting public spectacle; thousands of people arrive in Loudun to observe the orgiastic proceedings. As the pious clerics administer colonic enemas to the swooning nuns and probe their bodies for the marks of the devil, fainting spells and sexual dreams give way to more ribald behavior. The proprietress and her sisters descend into frenzied states of wanton exhibition and outright blasphemy. This is further evidence of the work of the devil, and even the nuns concur that their utterings and gyrations are most decisively demonic. While some observers of this holy circus suspect fraud or hysterical illness, even issuing pamphlets condemning the entire proceedings, the presiding clerical authorities prevail in their charges of demon possession. Father Grandier is sentenced to death and executed, even though many remain convinced of his innocence.

The demonic fits of Sister Jeanne persist for five years after the death of the priest, requiring an endless series of exorcisms to drive out the lingering presence of the Tempter. When a third protagonist, Father Surin, arrives on the scene as chief exorcist, a new approach is adopted. Anticipating the movement toward the "moral management" of the insane that emerged a century later—the use of gentle, moral prodding and humane treatment—Surin becomes genuinely interested in relieving Sister Jeanne of her demons. Moved by her diabolical fits, he spends increasing hours with the sister, intent on entering into her tortured mind. Like a psychoanalyst, he intuitively senses that the old method of purging the victim of her spirits only inflames the febrile state of the possessed. For Surin, the answer lies in gentle cajoling and in achieving an alliance with the virtuous side of Sister Jeanne. This, rather than torturous exorcisms, is Surin's strategy for combating the malevolent forces that have overtaken his female charge.

Sister Jeanne is resistive to this new approach, however, even as she responds warmly to the attentive but naively blind Father Surin. Huxley's portrayal of the two fathers—Grandier and Surin—is ultimately more sympathetic than that of the aspiring Sister Jeanne. While Surin lapses into a melancholic state of self-imposed privation, searching for a spiritual enlightenment that perpetually eludes him, Sister Jeanne embarks on a road-show display of her stigmata, the specious proof of her miraculous recovery. Surin and Sister Jeanne both meet their deaths never having confronted the source of their guilty consciences, Huxley implies, but Surin remains, like Grandier, somehow more noble than the sister, who dies a bitter, self-seeking imposter. The sins of the fathers are not overlooked in this tale of social hysteria, but they remain more historically contingent, more humanly comprehensible, than those of the tormented proprietress.

How might we understand the role of women as hysterics in such epic expressions of group madness? We may begin by wondering who is the true hysteric in this account. Is it the sexually repressed Sister Jeanne or her sexually repressed exorcisers? There is, decidedly, a folie à deux operating in the text, with the female protagonist bearing the weight of an uncontrollable force that the more powerful protagonist contains. They play their respective parts in a spectacle of conjuring and dispelling the demonic.

One feminist reading of *The Devils of Loudun* would suggest that whatever authority Sister Jeanne has acquired is circumvented by the Law of the Father. The text both represents this dilemma and operates as a paranoid, masculine defense. Her position in the narrative is that of suspect female storyteller—a bitter gossip—who wields her limited authority vindictively, lashing out at the innocent priest, the object of her frustrated desires. Most of those burned as witches during this era were women, so we may wonder about this portrayal of a fiendishly hysterical nun, even though it is quite clear in the text that male authority registers madness in a more concealed form.

How do we rework such stories of hysterics, exposing the various defensive disguises that operate in the male retelling of them? While there is a tendency within feminist theory to substitute heroism for hysteria in combating disparaging portrayals of women, this seems not to be an adequate answer. If we agree at all with Huxley's assessment of history—his caution against emotional excess and frenzied crusades—feminism must take into account the irrational aspects of its own project, as well as the irrational aspects of female subjectivity generally. Huxley is palpably phobic about group, hypnotic experiences, seeing in them the most dangerous aspects of human quests for self-transcendence. While he recognizes how "herd intoxication" and "crowd delirium" may be manipulated for political purposes, he overlooks the advances that may be achieved through group passions and commitments. Yet social movements of various kinds often do repress the irrational currents of their own history.

This chapter explores the relationship between female hysteria and historical dynamics, working toward a more complex portrayal of several notable "hysterical heroines." In taking into account the various impulses that may compete for domination in these women's hearts and minds, both the tragic and the inspiring elements of their lives come into relief. An additional theme is the competition between clergy and psychiatry historically in constructing the meaning of female altered states—what Huxley terms the "ecstatic"—and the difficulties women have encountered in interpreting their own consciousness, both creative and maddening, over against the preemptive interpretations of prevailing male authorities.

MYSTICAL STATES

We learn early on in Huxley's novel that both Sister Jeanne and Father Surin are inspired by the sixteenth-century Christian mystic Teresa of Avila, whose writings on contemplative prayer stirred passionate controversy for several centuries. Sister Teresa, who has a contemporary avid following as well, argued that the receptive, meditative states of nonliturgical prayer allow for greater communion with God, enlarging human readiness for true spirituality. In her many writings, she was preoccupied with the meaning of altered states of consciousness—of ecstatic experiences and "active recollection."[2] Some of Teresa's sixteenth- and seventeenth-century critics, suspicious of any wandering images that may come to occupy the mind, disputed the value of unstructured prayer. This wariness may be, indeed, the lasting hallmark of Western consciousness—a profound uneasiness over mindfulness that is not directed toward knowable, manageable ends, just as we have seen in the scientific debates over hypnosis. (See chapter 6.) Running as an insistent subtext to Huxley's novel is a long-standing controversy over whether there is anything of value in such exploratory ventures into the beyond. As long as they are solitarily pursued, Huxley cherishes the fleeting glimpses that may emerge of the transcendent, once the "shell of the ego has been cracked and there begins to be a consciousness of the subliminal and physiological othernesses underlying personality."[3]

More thoroughly secular theorists than Huxley reject such paths as utterly illusory. Many contemporary theorists would characterize Sister Teresa's contemplative prayer, and the ecstatic states she sometimes experienced, as an example of hypnosis or dissociation. Hypnotic states, these theorists would argue, provide access not so much to a transcendent realm as to the imaginative possibilities that emerge from a state of intense absorption. (See chapter 6.) The mystic is able to disengage sufficiently from distracting stimuli—both internal and external—to achieve a condition of focused awareness. The use of drugs, self-flagellation, rhythmic chants, as well as other mediums of focused attentiveness, may achieve similar results. Further, historical periods offer varying interpretations of these results. If "sex, drugs, and rock and roll" were the hypnotic group experiences of the 1960s, they were soon displaced by the religious and clinical elaboration of dissociative states in the more conservative 1980s.

With the advent of the scientific revolution, the older cosmology—where human actions were governed by occult forces—was reduced to the more controllable universe of natural causality. The paradigm of illness—advanced by modern scientific medicine—stripped the lunatic of her threatening spiritual powers, ushering in a new cast of characters to manage feminine rebellion. Witches, contemporary psychology textbooks typically assert, were actually mentally ill, suffering from the bodily articulated neurosis of hysteria. While this transformation of meanings may have once provided protection from the witch hunters, this is not inevitably and eternally the case. As always, there is an unanticipated cost of this revolution, one borne more harshly by women than by men.

The mystic invoked in Huxley's novel, Teresa of Avila, made use of the modern paradigm of illness when she thwarted the officials of the Spanish Inquisition gathered at her own gate in the sixteenth century. Sister Teresa insisted that the nuns in her convent, rumored to be suffering from strange fits, were not possessed by the devil as charged but rather were "as if sick."[4] Her successful employment of illness as metaphor acknowledged both the authority of the Inquisitors and the church's demand for absolute submission to its doctrine.

At the same time, her use of illness as metaphor was a strategy of resistance in that it transformed the meaning attached to suspect behavior. As a Christian convert of Jewish descent, as well as a woman and a mystic, Sister Teresa was a transitional figure whose unorthodox sense of the contemplative life put her perpetually under the watchful eye of the Inquisitors.[5] In a period when converted Jews could be burned for the slightest evidence of faltering faith, Sister Teresa employed Christian doctrine to advance an even more pious, exalted version of that faith. Part rebellion, part devout supplication, her ecstatic states served a revivalist aim; they never were invoked to challenge clerical authority directly, but they subverted the chaste, cloistered Christianity she inhabited.

For women, the legend of the mystic, like the later legend of the hysteric, is most certainly less enslaving than that of the witch.[6] The curatives of modern psychiatry are, in key respects, more redemptive than the salvation offered through the confessional. Psychiatry is most enlightened when brought into historical relief against the dark ages of ecclesiastical persecution of women witches. But the medicalizing and "psychiatrizing" of suspect states of mind carry their own considerable costs.

HYSTERIA AS ILLNESS

Freud recognized the destabilizing uncertainty attached to scientific advancements, including his own. In a lecture he gave at Clark University in 1909, Freud addressed the struggle within medical science over the nature of female complaints as well as the heretical implications of mental states that resisted normalizing medical explanations.

> Thus the recognition of the illness as hysteria makes little difference to the patient; but to the doctor quite the reverse. It is noticeable that the attitude toward hysterical patients is quite other than towards sufferers from organic diseases. He does not have the same sympathy for the former as for the latter. Through his studies the doctor has learned many things that remain a sealed book to the layman. . . . But all his knowledge——his training in anatomy, in physiology and in pathology—leaves him in the lurch when he is confronted by the details of hysterical phenomena. He cannot understand hysteria, and in the face of it he is himself a layman. This is not a pleasant situation for anyone who as a rule sets so much store by his knowledge. So it comes about that hysterical patients forfeit his sympathy. He regards them as people who are transgressing the laws of his science—like heretics in the eyes of the orthodox. He attributes every kind of wickedness to them, accuses them of exaggeration, of deliberate deceit, of malingering. And he punishes them by withdrawing interest from them.[7]

Feminist historians emphasize the gendered cast of this modern scientific "gaze," both medical and psychiatric. The reclassification of women from the stigmatized status of witch to that of hysteric may have liberated them from persecution, but it signaled the emergence of a more seductive relationship with paternalistic authority. Freud, patriarchal ally and translator of hysterical utterances, became the object of bitter feminist wrath in the 1970s and 1980s, in part because of the treacherous intimacy created through the psychoanalytic "confessional."[8] Further, the union between feminism and psychoanalysis has itself felt incestuous for many feminists, as rejection of Freud has come to assume a symbolic significance within feminism. (See chapter 4.)

Chapter 6 explored the fascination female altered states and hysterical illness have held for male clinicians for several hundred years, beginning with the magnetic cures of Mesmer during the era of the French Revolution. There is both a sameness and an endless variability to psychiatric accounts of the hysteric—like the elements of a legend told and retold, with local customs introducing variation, concealing the deeper narrative structure of the myth.

The history of psychology is replete with case studies of such mysterious female conditions. In *The Principles of Psychology,* William James describes one such case—that of Lurancy Vennum, a girl of fourteen who would have been thought to be possessed, James suggests, in an earlier era.[9] After suffering hysterical fits and spontaneous trances, during which she "was possessed by departed spirits of a more or less grotesque sort," Lurancy announces to her family that she is animated by the spirit of a neighbor girl who had died in an insane asylum in 1865, twelve years prior. After Lurancy pleads to be reunited with her "family," her parents allow her to live in the home of the departed girl. These neighboring parents, who are spiritualists, take the girl in, believing that Lurancy is temporarily in heaven while their daughter, Mary, has returned to them. Lurancy so effectively takes on the identity of this deceased daughter that all who observe the situation are convinced of this spiritist explanation for her behavior. After fourteen weeks, Lurancy occupies her own body again, instructing her foster parents to take her home.

This portrayal of a dramatic nervous illness during early adolescence is extremely common in the nineteenth-century case literature on female hysteria.[10] In this case, the girl finds a bridge out of her developmental crisis by turning to the grieving neighbors. The psychological significance of this move toward individuation is mediated by the way in which her madness is framed. In accepting the girl's behavior as evidence of her extraordinary powers, perhaps out of their own wish for reunion with their lost daughter, these transitional parents assist Lurancy in framing and containing her madness. After the girl returns home, she is described by her mother as "smarter, more intelligent, more industrious, more womanly, and more polite than before."[11] The mother goes on to attribute her daughter's cure to this spiritual respite with the neighbors. The mother, too, was in a state of acute crisis, desperate for relief from her daughter's nervous illness. The intervention in this case offered both mother and daughter a period of emotional distance, without recourse to an asylum, and a means of assigning positive meaning to the daughter's febrile states of mind.

What might have been the course of this illness had Lurancy had available a different discourse, a more secular and psychological interpretation of her deteriorating nervous condition? One of the "transitional" ideas that animated nineteenth-century discourse on madness was that of the creative illness. Shamanistic traditions employ this idea of transformation through a pyrrhic encounter with an underworld of both treacherous and anointing powers. Many psychologists and psychiatrists at the turn of the century endorsed the concept of the "mythopoetic" unconscious—of latent, creative powers that were released in trance states or in hysterical conditions. As Henri Ellenberger laments, the mythopoetic unconscious was displaced by the dissolutive unconscious, as psychiatry and psychology became normalized as applied science in the early twentieth century.[12]

In these competing constructions of the otherness of mind, there is the dilemma of how we reconcile the creative and the debilitating aspects of women's madness and of the contradictory role of psychiatry in bringing about a cure. A number of feminist historians have recast the legend of the hysteric, resurrecting her as a rebel rather than restoring her to sainthood.[13] As Showalter suggests, the bodily dysfunctions of Victorian women diagnosed as hysterics were a form of prepolitical protest, a means of communicating their social paralysis and outrage through the disguised language of their anaesthesia and migratory sensations.[14] As an extension of this point, it is worth noting that several of the most famous "daughters" of dynamic psychiatry were able ultimately to get up off their backs and become militant activists in the cause of women's rights. In the next section, I examine the transformations of one of these daughters of psychoanalysis, Anna O, who went on to become an organizer in the German women's movement.

HEROIC HYSTERIA

The case of Anna O has been the subject of immense scrutiny within psychoanalysis because it was presented as the prototype of hysterical illness in Freud and Breuer's *Studies on Hysteria*, published in 1895.[15] Yet feminists valorize Anna O not as the first daughter of psychoanalysis but as the prototypical survivor who rebels against this powerful tradition. The relationship between Anna O and Breuer, her doctor, introduces the problem of female ambivalence toward the father in his role as a developmental bridge as well as feminism's own ambivalence toward psychoanalysis.

Anna O—whose real name was Bertha Pappenheim—was born in Vienna in 1859. The daughter of wealthy, Orthodox Jewish parents, her experiences were typical of women of her social class. After attending a Catholic girls' school, she was prevented from attending university or from earning her own livelihood. Breuer attributed Anna O's hysterical symptoms to the boredom and puritanical strictness of middle-class domestic life rather than to any specific childhood trauma, a clinical view that departed significantly from that of Freud's seduction theory.[16]

In traversing the psychiatric and political periods of Pappenheim's life, Ann Jackowitz claims that Pappenheim became increasingly ill during the course of her treatment by physicians.[17] She became addicted to morphine and chloral, drugs initially prescribed to relieve her pain and sleeplessness but which later contributed to the hallucinatory states that plagued her during the active periods of her illness.[18]

Pappenheim initially found her own voice, however, in conversations with Breuer, who saw her twice a day for one and a half years, with few exceptions.[19] Breuer's respect for this famous hysteric is evident in his clinical reports. "She was astonishingly quick, extraordinarily intelligent. She had a thirst for knowledge, a penetrating intuition, but nothing beyond a high school education. She suffered from convulsions and hallucinations; yet in her lucid moments gave remarkable descriptions of her insane fantasies."[20]

A death in the family, particularly of a parent, was a common theme in nineteenth-century case histories of hysterics and of women suffering from "double consciousness"; it was as common as child sexual abuse is in the clinical histories of women in the contemporary trauma literature.[21] Pappenheim was passionately attached to her father, whom she cared for during his year-long illness. While she suffered various symptoms during this period, she fell acutely ill after his death in 1881. Breuer, who was the family's physician, clearly became a father substitute, yet one who was able to recognize in the daughter's madness an enormous generativity—a capacity for creativity and self-expression. He was also a maternal figure for Anna O, for she would permit Breuer alone to feed her during her anorexic periods. In a sense, Anna O's fierce attachment to Breuer signifies the daughter's search for the nurturant side of the father—the "breast" behind the "phallus"—which breaks through the strict emotional division of labor within the patriarchal order. It was not only forbidden sexual desire for the father that troubled the hysteric (as Freud came to believe) but the wish to know and be known in a deep sense.

Breuer was a new kind of paternal authority, one who listened attentively to this woman patient, finding meaning and coherence in what others deemed childish gibberish. Anna O, who coined the term "the talking cure," was creating a new language, resisting the symbolic world of the dead father. Anna O engaged the empathic Breuer in what she described as the "private theater" of her imagination, although his role in her translocation from the private parlor to public life is still disputed.[22]

In feminist portrayals of Pappenheim's personal transformation, Anna O sheds her hysteria, like so much dead skin, and emerges as enlightened warrior for women's rights. Thus, a feminist countermythology is born that turns the tables on history—history stacked so heavily against women—finding in Anna O's early hysterical ravings the precursors of the later, revolutionary Pappenheim.

Jackowitz notes the tragic and inspirational dimensions of her life. "Bertha Pappenheim was a remarkable woman. She led, I believe, an ironically fulfilling yet tragic life. First, a debilitating illness, then a miraculous recovery, followed by a career in which she institutionalized her anger at men and her concept of motherhood."[23]

In looking back through the lens of contemporary feminism, we find the hysteria legend transfigured into a human-origin legend. In creating a new mythology, out from under the shadow of the patriarchal texts, Jackowitz takes the position that Pappenheim essentially cured herself: "Having suffered desperately for the first thirty years of her life, Bertha Pappenheim miraculously recharged her life."[24] Biographer Melinda Given Guttman concurs in this celebratory portrait of Anna O's transmogrification from debilitated hysteric to "a heroine who practiced lifelong psychic and spiritual self-healing."[25]

A second subtext—one less dominated by the magical thinking of self-creation myths—situates Pappenheim's transformation in the transition from father worship to female relational ties. This trajectory reverses the developmental progression under patriarchy, where girls and boys move from the world of the mother—associated with dependence and vulnerability—to that of the father, which carries the promise of mastery and autonomy. Boys are the direct heirs of masculine entitlement and control, as compensation for the traumatic loss of the earlier tie to the mother. But girls are stopped at the threshold of adulthood, having to exchange whatever feminine currency they possess in negotiating their dependent fate in a world ruled by men.

In creating a new, feminist legend of a daughter's "recovery" from father worship, we might weave the facts of the case into a revised leitmotif, themes that run through the work of biographers Jackowitz and Guttman. As a young woman, on her developmental entry into a repressive, patriarchal symbolic order, Anna O loses her capacity to speak in her native language of German. Her speech becomes incomprehensible following the death of her father, whom she served as nursemaid. She faints, overcome by an alien internal impulse that she barely discerns, much less comprehends. While Breuer, as her officially appointed healer, is enchanted by the "fairy tales of her imagination," he is unable to break the spell.[26] She wanders in the wilderness of illness for half a decade, supported and seduced by the false promise of father substitutes, until she comes to her senses. Anna O finally leaves the world of the powerful fathers behind, moving with her mother to Frankfurt, where she recovers the sanity latent within her madness. Here she is able to fully articulate the source of her rage and anguish. In 1899, Pappenheim published a play entitled *Women's Rights,* as well as a translation of Mary Wollstonecraft's *Vindication of the Rights of Woman.* Pappenheim also established the first home for wayward girls in Germany and became an active campaigner in the movement for women's rights.

This kind of reworking of historical texts is a common and vital part of any liberatory movement. A current of ambivalence, however, runs through feminist accounts of Anna O's relationship with Breuer. In addressing this issue, Jackowitz stresses Breuer's ultimate failing of his prized female patient and the illusory aspects of his early nurturant position. And she draws on the official history to make this case. Breuer, as the psychiatric legend goes, was called to Anna O's home during an emergency one night, as they were concluding their intensive treatment. When he arrived, Anna O was in the throes of a hysterical pregnancy, exclaiming, "Now Dr. B.'s baby is coming."[27] Breuer fled the scene, shaken by this unexpected "regression" in a patient he had declared to be cured.

Through the lens of contemporary sensibilities, we might wonder what may have happened between Anna O and Breuer that gave rise to this hysterical pregnancy. More likely than literal sexual seduction, however, is that Breuer had fallen in love with Anna O. Because he was unable to acknowledge his growing desires, it was left to Anna O to "carry" these disavowed feelings in the feminine imagery available to her. Pregnancy signifies the inequality of erotic encounters, where women bear more directly than men the consequences of any form of transgressive desire.

The flight of the father figure in the face of hysterical sexual desire may have contributed to Anna O's lingering terror of her own sexuality. For Pappenheim, who died a virgin, sexuality remained a dominating fear, even as she bravely pursued a "a life I had to conquer."[28] Finding an outlet for her passion in the crusade against sexual abuses of women, Pappenheim was able to commit herself to a cause with "holy zeal."[29] Historian Henri Ellenberger concurs with this assessment, describing the case of Anna O/Bertha Pappenheim as an illustration of "creative illness," similar to the transformational states of shamans and mystics.[30]

For women who are deprived of heroic legends the political retrieval of Bertha Pappenheim from the annals of psychiatry is a vital project. Like individual memory, collective legends combine facts and wishes to create meaning out of the past, marking the landscape of human destiny according to historically emergent possibilities. But was Anna O really cured of her hysteria? And if so, was she healed by Breuer or by relinquishing the fantasy of a medical cure and going on to engage in direct political action? The explicitly political portrayal often emphasizes "the double" within Anna O, a recurring theme in female hysteria.

These two alters—the crazy and the sane—conceal the tension between madness and rationality, however, and this romanticized counterposition of feminine selves may operate as a feminist myth with its own crucial blind spots. Take, for example, the political work Anna O undertook, which has led a number of feminists to "canonize" her.[31] As Jackowitz points out, Pappenheim's most passionate political cause involved mobilizing against the "white slave trade."[32] Campaigning against the white slave trade was the central project of the League of Jewish Women, an organization of fifty thousand members at its height in 1929. Pappenheim was active in the league, traveling extensively throughout Europe and the Middle East to speak out against prostitution and illegitimacy. She, like so many feminists of her generation, recognized the double standard that operated in laws governing sexuality and the central place of sexual and reproductive control in women's lives. The campaign against the white slave trade permitted women to storm male sanctuaries, stripping the fathers of their hypocritical robes of piety. "The merchants and the merchandise are Jewish," Pappenheim charged, moving on to assert that the synagogues participated in these organized sex rings.[33]

Jackowitz finds inspiration in this fully empowered period, as Pappenheim's transmogrification from hysteric to activist reaches its apogee. But it is not entirely clear how much basis there was to the white-slavery issue; many historians have concluded that claims were vastly exaggerated and served to screen other social anxieties. The campaign against the white slave trade is an example of "moral panic," where collectively felt fears concerning social dislocation and instability coalesce into a symbolically compelling mythic narrative. Like many other legends, this narrative was based on some actual incidents as well as real social problems that were elaborated and amplified by latent tensions in the culture. In the aftermath of the First World War, economic and social dislocations did contribute dramatically to prostitution and illegitimacy, and the antislavery movement provided a morally compelling rhetoric for confronting these dislocations.[34]

Ironically, the Jews were the target of Bertha Pappenheim's conspiracy theory. The cosmology behind many conspiracy theories, which date back centuries, is virulently anti-Semitic. The notion that an international cabal of Jewish bankers controls the world continues to find fertile soil in the economic dislocations and uncertainties of today, just as it did in Europe in the 1920s. Pappenheim was horrified that the Nazis later used the propaganda of her crusade for their own racist and anti-Semitic purposes.[35] The specter of swarthy men abducting blue-eyed, virginal girls is rife with populist appeal. In casting themselves as the official protectors of homeland and hearth, rulers often exploit moral anxieties and preexisting cultural grievances and prejudices.

One interpretation of Pappenheim's transformation is that she simply became a politically empowered and delusional hysteric who sublimated her sexual anxieties into a narrow political program. And there is some truth to such a characterization. But this reading misses the complex interplay of rationality and irrationality in human affairs and of the continuing legacy of patriarchal oppression that undercuts female authority, even at the moment that women find "voice."

By denying the elements of madness in Bertha Pappenheim's conspiratorial politics—and by erasing from feminist memory the racist elements of the white slave trade narrative—we accept a problematic set of premises. In asserting her complete recovery from madness, we have stripped our heroine of her complex humanity, including the inevitable distortions that run through her newly recovered vision. The separation of the sane and the insane, as a modern boundary for establishing the terms of reasonable civic discourse, must be challenged on the basis that this boundary is, as Freud and Klein repeatedly argued, a costly illusion. It blinds us to our capacity for self-deception and to the troubling uncertainty attached to rational action.

THE HISTORICAL EVOLUTION OF HYSTERIA

One way of challenging the illusion of masculine, rational agency is to turn the hysteric around, looking back at her audience, rather than turning her inside out, as sane woman simply cloaked in the garb of madness. We may then understand something of the fascination she holds for the medieval clerics as well as for the psychiatric legions that followed in a new era of masculine inquiry into female mental maladies.

The first published account of hysteria appeared in 1859 in France. A physician named Paul Briquet described a condition predominantly affecting women, one that eluded medical explanation.[36] While he claimed that catalepsy was equally common among males and females, the more heterogenous condition of hysteria was twenty times more frequent among women.[37] The distinctive feature of the disorder was that symptoms were migratory, with each "cure" leading to a new, apparently unrelated manifestation of the illness. Today, Briquet's syndrome—a psychosomatic disorder—is estimated to affect 10 percent of adult women.[38] In Briquet's time, medical inquiry into ambiguous female complaints confronted a veil of uncertainty. And modern physicians crossing the border into feminine, bodily located distress continue to encounter a minefield of unstable sexual codes.

In Briquet's day, the search for the source of women's migratory ailments led to countless surgeries and medical procedures. S. Weir Mitchell, also a pioneer in this female terrain, described hysteria as "the nosological limbo of all unnamed female maladies. It were as well called mysteria."[39] In the 1860s and 1870s, the hysteric "evolved" in medical science as the site of her madness traveled from the reproductive organs—where "ovarian reflexes" were thought to stimulate the various anaesthesias of the hysteric—upward to the central nervous system. George Miller Beard discovered a new syndrome in the late 1860s; termed *neurasthenia,* it literally meant "weakness of the nerves."[40]

Beard's recasting of hysteria opened up yet another frontier in modern medicine. Like defenders of the diagnosis of posttraumatic stress disorder in the 1980s, Beard departed from the medical model to locate the pathogenic source of hysterical ailments in a debilitating social order. The competition and strain of modern industrial life, Beard reasoned, sapped individuals of nervous energy, leaving them in a state of emotional exhaustion. Neurasthenia was much like the chronic fatigue syndrome of the 1980s, as speeded-up work schedules and the intensified demands of the "double day" found expression in vague medical complaints and exhaustion, particularly among women.[41]

In the 1860s and 1870s, neurasthenia differed from hysteria in that hysteria was assumed to be more common in the lower classes.[42] Neurasthenia was a more aesthetic mental infirmity, one that affluent men as well as women could respectably suffer from. Initially regarded as an American condition, neurasthenia soon caught on in Europe, as psychiatry offered a new language for intercontinental anxieties and ailments. Since treatment for the condition involved travel and relaxation, prosperous neurasthenics could temporarily exit the iron cage of progress.

By the 1890s, the "pure culture" of hysteria—which involved dramatic bodily contortions as much as it did anaesthesia—had traveled from the back wards of the Salpêtrière hospital in France to the private clinics of Vienna. Jean-Martin Charcot, the charismatic neurologist who assumed command of this women's hospital in the 1870s, as discussed in chapter 6, "secularized" hysteria by drawing parallels between the religious ecstasy of the saints and mystics and clinical displays of hysterical fits. Captivated by the new technology of photography, Charcot prominently displayed his favorite hysterics in various contorted poses, characteristic of the indigenous variety of hysterical fits. These were generally more robust, bodily articulated fits than the fainting spells, vomiting, and facial tics of the bourgeois hysterics.

Charcot was blind to what are today termed "observer effects" as well as to the social solidarity of hysterics themselves in this choreographed madness. Women on the wards trained each other to perform hysterical fits, taking Charcot's lead in what appears, from a historical distance, to be a parody of psychiatric authority. The women of Salpêtrière did undoubtedly suffer from a range of psychiatric and medical problems. But the complexity of their lives and their ailments—the multiplicity of possible narratives of suffering—was "repressed" by the monolingual medical world of Charcot. Women were offered one role in this psychodrama and were able to mesmerize their audience even as they were silenced by the stereotypical script.[43]

The upper-class sisters of these famous Salpêtrière patients—the hysterics who found their way to the psychiatric parlors of Breuer and Freud in Vienna—were able to articulate their hysteria, mesmerizing men with speech as well as with the language of the body. Charcot had demonstrated the essentially psychological basis of the bodily contortions and mysterious anaesthesia that were the hallmark of late-nineteenth-century hysteria. But he had no interest in listening to his women patients, who were typically poor and uneducated.[44] The Salpêtrière was an institution, and it had a culture different from that of the intimate psychoanalytic parlor. For women as well as for men, modernity created impersonal, public institutions at one end of the social stratum and highly privatized, claustrophobic ones at the other.

THE FEMINIZING OF THE UNCONSCIOUS

Feminism, throughout its history, has struggled with ambivalences in relation to the powerful fathers in cultural legacies and with separating the repressive and the emancipatory aspects of traditions. One way of disengaging from the seductive fathers, and from their abusive or repressive legacies, has been to refuse the Law of the Father, embracing as recuperative strategy the Law of the Mother (or Sisters). As Benjamin argues, the interplay of engagement and disengagement with powerful others is the basis of enlarging human capacities, and this interplay inevitably involves aggression.[45] From this standpoint, we may view the collective daughters' refusal to grant the fathers any emancipatory role in the drama as a necessary moment of self-differentiation.

We may want to linger at this threshold of feminist ambivalence, neither capitulating to nor refusing engagement with the powerful fathers in the psychiatric past, and see how we may make use of conflicting paternal identifications. In exploring the "maternal" side of various surrogate father/daughter relationships in our collective history, we may still "refuse" patriarchal control, even as we bring a fuller picture of the symbolic father into view.

In the previous chapter, I argued that nineteenth-century female mediumship ushered in an era when women held increased control over the trance state, even though this control was orchestrated within the confines of prevailing gender codes. Much of the movement to secularize religious ecstasy—facilitated by the anticlerical Charcot—took the form of challenges to unorthodox, "alternative" practices, such as magnetism and spiritualism, rather than to the practices of the church.[46] In a sense, the debate over both mediumship and hysteria contained a critique of religious authority, displaced onto predominantly female patients and research subjects.

In the early experimentalist movement in Europe, no less than in the United States, laboratory-based science was infused with similar spiritual yearnings and implicit identifications with the feminine. Indeed, much of the late-nineteenth-century psychophysiological research that focused on stimulus intensities and perceptual thresholds was intimately tied to the subliminal-psychology movement's intrigue with female spiritism.

Take, for example, the work of the French psychometrician Alfred Binet, father of intelligence testing. Published in 1896, Binet's *Alterations of Personality* reviews the competing claims of French schools of thought concerning hypnosis, hysteria, and "double consciousness." In mediating competing claims that hysteria is either the product of suggestion or a disease of the mind, Binet argues that hysteria has some of the properties of normal consciousness, evident in the discontinuities of everyday awareness, even though it manifests a pathological magnification of these discontinuities. In defending the study of consciousness against the rising tide of an antimentalist psychology—"the hypothesis which considers man a machine"—Binet invests consciousness itself with femininity, implicitly acknowledging that traversing states of consciousness carries theorists across a gender divide. We must recognize, he exclaims, that "consciousness does not renounce her rights as easily as has been sometimes admitted, and that she can exist even when psychological activity is very low."[47]

Binet's "filter-exhaustion" theory of dual consciousness and dual personality is infused with Victorian ideas, both in its neurasthenic conception of neurosis as a by-product of mental exhaustion and in its view that the female mind is particularly prone to ecstatic states. Much along the lines of Janet and James, Binet conceptualized the hysteric as lacking the strength of will to impose unity on consciousness, so that her dreamlike states inevitably seep into normal consciousness. Summoning Janet's pronouncement that hysterics suffer from "a contraction of the field of consciousness," Binet concurs that hysterics are highly distractible and prone to unstable states.[48]

The theorizing that emerges out of what Binet terms his "little facts" points to a crucial absence within the hysteric of a countergravitational field, an ego, that would resist the influence of various powerful stimuli, either external or internal. The hysteric, it seems, is captive to whatever appears in her field of perception, whether it be spirits, hypnotic suggestions, the rumblings of her own unconscious, or the trivial preoccupations of daily life. Binet notes that hysterics are able to sew, knit, or write—the main activities permitted Victorian women—even as they display insensibility—that is, lack of sensation—in the trance state. And Binet was quite correct, in a sense, even though both his interest in establishing the "lawfulness" of mental phenomena and his own social assumptions work against any real insight into the descriptive material he reviews.

In looking back on a hysterical crisis during late adolescence, Alice James, who manifested more debilitating symptoms than did her neurasthenic, successful brothers, William and Henry, offers a poignant account of female bodily estrangement.[49] She describes her own "insensibility" and the fluctuating states of consciousness that imprisoned her:

> When all one's moral & natural stock in trade is a temperament
> forbidding the abandonment of an inch or the relaxation of
> a muscle 'tis a never ending fight. When the fancy took me of a
> morning at school to *study* my lessons by way of variety instead
> of shirking or wiggling thro' the most impossible sensations of
> upheaval violent revolt in my head overtook me so that I had to
> "abandon" my brains as it were. So it has always been, anything
> that sticks of itself is free to do so, but conscious & continuous
> cerebration is an impossible exercise & from just behind the eyes
> my head feels like a dense jungle into wh. no ray of light has ever
> penetrated. So with the rest, you abandon the pit of yr. stomach
> the palms of yr. hands the soles of yr. feet & refuse to keep them
> sane when you find in turn one moral impression after another
> producing despair in the one, terror in the other anxiety in the
> third & so on until life becomes one long flight from remote
> suggestion & complicated eluding of the multifold traps set for
> your undoing.[50]

In this personal account of the hysterical condition, Alice James articulates the feeling of disconnectedness of her body parts and of her body as both the location and the enemy of a tortured consciousness. Having internalized the rigid constraints of Victorian sensibilities, James finds no passage out, no means of revolt, no access to the mental sublimations afforded to men of her social class. "Continuous cerebration" eludes her, and her illness registers this violent division between her own urgent, inchoate desires and the impotence such desires generate. James quite literally devours herself through her illness, even as this same illness insistently registers the gender inequality of emotional suffering.

This passage movingly chronicles the emergence in late adolescence of a female selfhood that fails to bridge the realm of childhood—with its associated strivings for independence and its anxieties over dependence—and an adult world beyond it. This emergent selfhood is experienced as a fragile container, perpetually threatened by rupture from the internal forces it tenuously holds in check. Victorian femininity required an artful cultivation of a state of perpetual receptivity, childlike innocence, and airy purity of mind. As Alice James describes it, this cultivated serenity conceals a "dense jungle," an impenetrable inner reality. She experiences her mind as intensely private, a kind of unreachable island, and simultaneously as a phallic, aggressive force that threatens to annihilate her.

A decade later, adolescence would come to be articulated as a specific stage of development, with unstable mental properties and latent potentialities, and Alice describes her own transitional state in similar terms. Whereas male adolescence normalizes experimentation and mobility, female adolescence cultivates febrile internal states.[51] G. Stanley Hall, who introduced the concept of adolescence in 1904 with his two-volume work, notes the problematic nature of this transitional period in the United States, and the cultural transformations required in this bridge between childhood and adulthood.[52] Hall writes that "our immigrants have often passed the best years of youth or leave it behind when they reach our shores, and their memories of it are in other lands."[53] This collective repression and amnesia seems to be heightened for girls who, like perennial immigrants, find themselves stalled at the cultural borders.

In a journal entry on October 26, 1890, Alice James describes the conditions women face in middle life, as menopause recapitulates menarche.[54] For James, the adolescent torrents have subsided, only to leave a cumulative fatigue and chronic sense of impotence. As her own diagnostician, James takes a certain defiant pride in her hopeless assessment, her refusal to be persuaded by the "mind curers" of her day. In her own view, women confront "a collection simply of unproductive emotions enclosed within tissue paper walls, rent equally by pleasure as by pain; animated by a never ceasing belief in and longing for *action,* relentlessly denied, all safety valves shut in the way of the 'busy ineffectiveness' of women."[55]

If empirical psychology sought to establish the lawfulness of mental effects on the tabula rasa of the mind, Victorian women were, indeed, ready subjects.[56] And yet these same blank tablets, these pools of sustained inattentiveness, resisted their interlocutors. Alice James describes the immobility and translucency of womanhood as a kind of death—"absorbing into the bone that the better part is to clothe one's self in neutral tints, walk by still waters, and possess one's soul in silence."[57] These silent souls stirred considerable discomfort, however, as authorities helplessly intervened, looking intently without really seeing.

It would be a mistake to characterize the psychological treatment of hysteria as merely a strategy of social control, however, or as simply a colonization of the female mind. Scientific psychology implicitly served as midwife to an emerging, robust female selfhood, even as it "naturalized" the course of feminine illness. Through his lengthy descriptions of alternating states, Binet advances the idea of the intelligent unconscious. Even in the apparent reflexivity of automatic handwriting, Binet discerns the presence of an active observer.[58] Much more than do normal subjects, hysterical patients demonstrate a duality of consciousness in the sensory realm, Binet concludes, and "this stigma—formerly called the *brand* of the possessed, or the *clutch mark* of the devil—is *insensibility*" (94).

While Binet probes "the intelligence that may lie in the subconscious movements of an hysterical patient" (111), his mappings of this highly female sensorium are, in many respects, as blind as those of the medieval clerics. As he ponders the mysterious, disembodied movements of the hysteric, Binet fails to consider the perverse physical and social constraints on women in the Victorian world. Girls and women not only were prohibited from mental pursuits, as Alice James so insightfully recognizes in analyzing her own nervous condition, but were also bound by restrictive clothing and by a cult of female illness that invested femininity with an ethereal fragility. While Binet noted that female hysterics were far more likely to exhibit automatized movements and fluctuating sensations and insensibility than were male hysterics, his inquiry did not extend into the everyday basis of this female bodily estrangement.

In establishing the lawfulness of the phenomena observed, then, Binet and other experimentalists overlooked the culture-bound character of these phenomena. We may wonder, for example, about the prevalence of blood spitting as a hallmark sign of hysteria, frequently noted by Binet in his review of cases of hysteria. In the late nineteenth century, "consumptive" illness, or tuberculosis, assumed a cult status, particularly in women's literature.[59] The consumptive woman drew her inspirational strength from the idea that the withering of the female body joined her intimately with the burning power of the soul. Jean Strouse describes this eroticizing of female illness in the late nineteenth century. "Romantic ladies in the literature and art of the period often had pale cheeks, sunken, glittering eyes, painfully thin limbs, and nameless, vaguely glamorous diseases. The refined female spirits inhabited a feverish realm of keen perception and subtle response far above the plane of the body."[60]

The dying heroine, spitting blood and fading passively into eternity, embodied this sentimentalized, tragic view of femininity.[61] We may suspect in the many clinical reports of inexplicable blood spitting, the operation of these romanticized, consumptive images of women, in addition to possible indications of psychiatric and physical infirmities. Medical interventions in hysterical illness likely exacerbated the poor health of many Victorian women, as "rest cures" and passive treatments such as electrical stimulation and massages came into vogue.[62] At the same time, out of the ambiguity of bodily located distress, women likely produced many of the requisite symptoms sought by the medical profession, even as such symptoms perpetually migrated from one bodily zone to another.

RECOVERING THE MEMORIES
OF A CREATIVE MADWOMAN

At a 1995 conference on treating sexual abuse survivors, Lenore Terr cautioned the audience about the pitfalls of dwelling too extensively on past sexual trauma.[63] While she did not probe alternative meanings that may be derived from recovered memories of sexual abuse, she did suggest that therapists may linger unproductively in the realm of past abuses. Citing Virginia Woolf as an inspirational example of an incest survivor, Terr pointed out that many survivors go on to accomplish glorious things in spite of the scars of childhood trauma. She exhorted women to get up off their incestuous sickbeds, like modern-day Lazaruses, and walk. While there was a brief period of time when women could nurse their sexual wounds, the climate of the 1990s seemed to have turned resoundingly in the direction of insisting that survivors "get over it."[64]

This typically American-style advice offers no real understanding, of course, of the various forces that may shape selective uses of memory, nor does it offer insight into the specific role that child sexual abuse may play in female madness. Returning to the example of Virginia Woolf, this final section of the chapter looks at how modern feminist sensibilities have "recovered" memories of incest in her work and some of the problematic aspects of this project of linking childhood sexual abuse, female madness, and creativity.

Woolf was born in London in 1882, into a large, affluent, Victorian family—a social and historical milieu similar to that of Bertha Pappenheim.[65] Much like Pappenheim, Woolf grew up with an intense awareness of the privileges granted to males and of the power exercised by fathers over women and children. Coming into consciousness during an era of activist feminism, both Pappenheim and Woolf struggled to overcome debilitating emotional problems and went on to identify strongly with the women's rights movement. Woolf is considered one of the important writers of the twentieth century, and her novels, essays, and autobiographical works are informed by an astute sensitivity to women's oppression. While Woolf did not make use of the "talking cure," she was treated for nervous illness with the "rest cure," the most common turn-of-the-century method of managing female maladies.[66]

It has long been recognized, in various biographies, that Woolf was sexually abused by her older half-brother, Gerald Duckworth, although the extent of this abuse has been subject to more recent debate. In a controversial biography, Louise DeSalvo brings this incestuous relationship to center stage in explaining the tragic events of Woolf's life, including her final act of suicide.[67] DeSalvo claims that shortly before her death Woolf recovered memories of Duckworth's abuse of her that extended further back into childhood than her earlier recollections, and, DeSalvo continues, this abuse began to figure prominently in the "auto-analysis" Woolf undertook in 1939, several years before her death. Under the threat of what she and her husband, Leonard, felt to be an imminent Nazi invasion of England, Woolf undertook the writing of her autobiography, *A Sketch of the Past*. As a contemporary feminist text, DeSalvo's biography raises important questions, both about the life that she so compassionately portrays and about the legendary use of that life. We may recognize the importance of historical recon-structions—both for Woolf individually and for feminism collectively—while also critically examining the basis of these various reconstructions.

In her first argument, DeSalvo decisively rejects the view that Woolf was mad, reframing her debilitating symptoms as a normal response to early trauma, par-ticularly sexual trauma. In part, DeSalvo is countering earlier biographers who explain Woolf's lifelong mental anguish as the result of early, "excessive depen-dence" or inborn eccentricity.[68] DeSalvo is certainly correct in pointing out how the notion of "artistic temperament" conceals the suffering born of real, lived experience. For women, this mystique converges with the ancient notion, embedded in popular conceptions of hysteria, that women are by nature sen-sitive creatures, easily overwhelmed by the vicissitudes of life. Debunking this idea of an inherent, female fragility means demonstrating the magnitude of what women often endure and of the rationality of women's emotional reactions. (See chapter 3.)

At the same time, this repudiation of madness does have its costs. There is a phobic response toward madness operating in DeSalvo's analysis that accepts a narrow conception of sanity and rationality. Her attempt to "normalize" female madness limits the range of injurious experiences women may address to those readily derived from external events. Further, it accepts the premise that a more generalized madness, which may overtake women as an effect of the demoralizing constraints imposed by patriarchal authority or by the historical contingencies of existence, is less convincing than a more "localized" madness, born of discrete events.

This problem of madness leads to the second of DeSalvo's arguments: that childhood sexual abuse is more traumatic and determinative of adult suffering than are other life experiences.[69] DeSalvo's work follows in the tradition of var-ious literary and feminist projects exposing the private tyranny of fathers within the family and revealing the cold inhumanity that may be hidden behind bourgeois respectability.[70] The Stephen family, Virginia's family of origin, con-forms to this prototype, including the various disguises employed to repress emo-tional distress.

Drawing on trauma/dissociation theory, DeSalvo assumes that recovered, repressed memories are more revelatory of the trauma they signify than are more continuous memories. She notes, for example, Woolf's struggle with turbulent upsurges of memory as she writes her autobiography. Forbidden memories seem to have a will of their own, a magnificent force, that overrides the will of the rememberer. DeSalvo draws on Woolf herself in characterizing this work of remembering, which appears in elusive fragments: "no words"; "very apprehensive"; "something cold & horrible"; "I am powerless to ward it off: I have no protection."[71] DeSalvo points out that traumatic memory often emerges in disconnected fragments, lacking a coherent, meaningful story. Yet even in Woolf's state of intensive introspection, DeSalvo concludes, she is not able to locate the origin of her madness in her relationship with her half-brother.

Like many contemporary trauma therapists, DeSalvo forecloses on this unsettling ambiguity by filling in the gaps of memory, bringing these diffuse states of female anguish to a decisive denouement. At the same time, she does note that rape and incest may serve as metaphors for various disturbing, invasive experiences. For example, "when she [Woolf] wrote of her rage at him [her father], she used a rape image: how 'deep they drove themselves in me, the things it was impossible to say aloud'" (112). Yet Woolf's metaphorical use of such imagery is deployed in DeSalvo's analysis as "hints" that Woolf was becoming increasingly aware of the extent of her early sexual abuse.

Putting sexual abuse in the foreground in DeSalvo's reading of Woolf also serves to "repress" the conflictive currents of Woolf's relationship with her mother. In her own autobiographical writings and essays, Woolf stresses the emotional unavailability and coldness of her mother, Julia Stephen, even as she sympathetically portrays the harsh, demanding aspects of her mother's life. As a feminist, Woolf was attuned to the demands made on women to cater to men, often at the cost of their own children's needs. DeSalvo gives some weight to this unsatisfying mother/daughter relationship, even as she shifts the axis of causality to the sexual incursions of the half-brother. In one passage, DeSalvo notes the intense "repressed hostility" Woolf likely felt toward her mother, a hostility infusing her story entitled "Professions for Women." Here, Woolf murders "the image of the Angel in the House," a figure bearing a remarkable likeness to Julia Stephen. DeSalvo offers a description of this work. "She [Woolf] writes that the Angel was 'intensely sympathetic. . . . She sacrificed herself daily; . . . she was pure.' The Angel, however, is not life-enhancing; she stunts her symbolic daughter's growth. In an exceedingly violent sequence, she describes the murder. It is the only place where she allowed her rage to surface, although through the controlled vehicle of art: 'I turned upon her and caught her by the throat. I did my best to kill her. My excuse if I were to be had up in a court of law, would be that I acted in self-defence. Had I not killed her she would have killed me'" (118).

The next passage in DeSalvo's book turns to Woolf's correspondence, shortly before her death, with a woman friend; in this correspondence Woolf addresses the problems women confront in writing about their sexuality. Writing, for Woolf, is like "breaking the hymen," which DeSalvo interprets as a veiled reference to Gerald's sexual invasion. "Gerald had injured her; he had broken her membrane, an event over which she should have had control; he had robbed her of her virginity" (78).

While DeSalvo may be correct in this interpretation, what is striking about this sequence of topics is the biographer's "flight" from the theme of mother/daughter aggression to the terrain she maps as more primary and determinative: incestuous abuse. The legacy of maternal neglect and abandonment, including Woolf's loss of both her mother and an older sister through death during her adolescence, is cast to the margins of this portrait of Woolf's tragic life. The sins of male relatives—which, indeed, are often omitted in accounts of female madness—are retrieved in this project of remembering the life of Woolf. In this turn to the primacy of the father figures, the ambivalences that pervade mother/daughter relationships weigh in as secondary and peripheral. Ironically, men remain the central protagonists in this portrait of a woman's life, and recovered memory of male perpetrators dominates the vantage point on the past.

Introduction of the maternal determinants of or precursors to states of female madness raises yet another question—the relationship between fantasy and abuse. DeSalvo cites the psychoanalyst Alice Miller in rejecting Freud's position that hysteria is the result of internal conflict rather than of overt abuse. Indeed, DeSalvo credits Freud with demoralizing Woolf during her period of autoanalysis, as Woolf was beginning to examine her own emerging memories. She had visited Freud shortly after he emigrated to London in 1939, and she subsequently immersed herself in his writings. DeSalvo comments on this generative period for Woolf and places considerable emphasis on the pernicious effects of her turn to Freudianism (127):

> At some point, she must have realized that she and Freud would
> describe the etiology of depression in completely different ways.
> She was ascribing her depression and her "madness" to abuse.
> He was describing reports of incest as fantasies and wish-fulfillment.
> She wondered whose view was correct and there is evidence that,
> after a lifetime of struggle to establish the view that I have
> described here, she wavered, reconsidered, and accepted Freud.
> This meant that she would have to see herself as mad. I believe
> that it contributed to her suicide and there is evidence to support
> my view. On 9 December 1939 she wrote: "Freud is upsetting:
> reducing one to whirlpool; & I daresay truly. If we're all instinct,
> the unconscious, what's all this about civilization, the whole man,
> freedom."

DeSalvo goes on to argue that Woolf was trying to establish that her madness was caused by early incest and that Freud's theorizing, with its emphasis on the unreliability of early memories, worked against this newfound insight.

Yet we may draw quite different conclusions from Woolf's encounter with Freud. Freud's own deep pessimism over the prospects for human progress was heightened by his progressive illness and flight from Nazi Germany, as he was spirited away by his daughter Anna. More likely an influence than Freud's position on the accuracy of memory was his dark despair and meager hope for humanity, an angst that may have reinforced Woolf's own long-standing lone-

liness and dark pessimism. Psychoanalysis, after all, only offered the modest consolation of everyday unhappiness over the more unproductive misery of neurosis.
And, at this particular juncture in history, separating the course of individual and
collective madness was difficult indeed.

Woolf's journey into madness concluded more tragically than did Pappenheim's. The story of the transformation of Anna O offers a more triumphant portrait of feminism than that of Woolf. Yet both women suffered and created in
ways that remained, throughout their lives, inscribed by a madness that eludes
precise causal determinants. And both women failed to achieve "recovery," in
part because they continued to live and work in a world that too readily reactivated the injuries of childhood. If hysteria is the prototypical female madness,
its migratory symptoms may map the contours of the migratory insanity of the
modern world.

CONCLUSIONS

How do we answer the question, posed at the beginning of the
chapter, of who is really mad in Huxley's tale of group hysteria, Sister Jeanne or
her interrogators? Just as the trance works both ways, so does hysterical illness.
As I have previously argued, hysteria is often an interactively created illness, emerging out of a social field where emotion and rationality are split off from one
another. And in this gendered interactive field, male authorities, whether spiritual or secular, may dispose of their own disturbing mental states by projecting
them onto women. In this cultural transfer, women become a repository for men's
own "excessive" emotions and ambiguous disturbances. Yet in retelling the hysteric's story from a feminist perspective and in turning the tables on her male
observers, we may readily overlook the complexity of hysterical narratives. And
in countering the ambiguity and irrationality imposed on the prototypical hysteric, we may defensively overstate the clarity and lucidity of her tales. Further,
once we strip our hysterical heroine of fantasy, transgressive sexual desire, moral
conflict, or other disturbing currents, there may be little left of her or her stories
beyond the afterglow of a disturbing sexual revelation.

Hysteria, like hypnosis, is a heterogeneous, ambiguous phenomenon, subject to various interpretations. Both of these phenomena signify, in the broadest sense, the problematic threshold between mind and body, a threshold often
represented culturally by a dreamy-eyed female subject. Throughout much of the
history of Western conversations over the relationship between hysteria and hypnosis, the female subject has been a cultural container for hidden potentialities,
on the one hand, and concealed pathologies on the other.

My emphasis on the essential ambiguity of hysteria—an ambiguity that
gives rise to storytelling and transformative remembering—does not imply that
hysteria is simply an artifact of the imagination. Such interpretations can be distancing and a means of minimizing the pain of women, particularly pain that
is judged to originate in psychic as opposed to physical states. Nor should my

emphasis on the ambiguity of hysteria lead us to conclude that somatic conditions with an emotional component are reducible to the idea of culturally orchestrated "idioms of distress." Such sweeping categories may readily collapse psychosomatic and related conditions under crude rubrics, without sufficient attention to their psychological or cultural specificity. Rather, I mean to suggest that the embodied emotional conditions associated with women, whatever their material or immediate cause, often acquire social symbolic loadings as they traverse the cultural landscape. If human intelligence includes the capacity to create new uses for familiar objects, then it is not surprising that women, no less than men, make creative and transformative use of the inherited legacy of hysteria, whether through the cultural lens of religion or science.

PART III

CLINICAL STORYTELLING AND CONTEMPORARY SOCIAL DILEMMAS

I hadn't so much forgot as I couldn't bring myself to remember. Other things were more important.
—Maya Angelou, *I Know Why the Caged Bird Sings*

And they were filled with the Holy Ghost, and began to speak with other tongues, as the Spirit gave them utterance.   —Acts 2:4

IN RETURNING to the contemporary scene, this part of the book works through the dilemmas of women storytellers from the vantage point of clinical practice. In American culture, psychology and psychotherapy are powerful disciplines for the creation of knowledge about the self and for transformative remembering. As a feminist and psychotherapist, I am intimately engaged in this project of emancipatory knowledge—that is, the struggle for knowledge that expands the range of human freedom.

The inquiry into memory and authoritative influences in part 1 established that clinical storytelling is an interactive process and that experts play a vital role in shaping the past that is "discovered" in the therapeutic journey. But this insight has not been readily integrated into feminist-informed clinical practice, in part because it may so readily be used to cast doubt on the veracity of women's stories. The legacy of the hysterical woman haunts the modern house of clinical practice, just as it does that of feminism. And, in response, there is a tendency in feminist clinical practice to insist that women's remembrances be taken literally as imprints of past events.

This part unfolds through contemporary clinical accounts that have remembered sexual abuse as the dominant motif. In this genre, clinicians who seek to uncover the culturally repressed effects of sexual abuse make use of one of the oldest ideas in psychology—the notion of hidden selves within. As I have previously argued, feminism has a deep affinity with this enchanting notion of concealed knowledge because women, themselves, have been hidden from history and denied an independent vantage point on the past.

In making use of the concept of the hidden self and of the affiliated idea of the revelatory power of the trance state, clinicians in the 1980s and early 1990s came to be mediums for a genre of spellbinding tales about the past, from stories about father/daughter incest to Gothic narratives of familial barbarism and sadistic, orgiastic encounters. In entering into these stories, this part makes use of the interpretive lenses introduced in part 1 and the historical and cultural motifs introduced in part 2. Most specifically, the focus is on what is old and what is new in this recent era of revelatory stories where an embattled female protagonist takes center stage. The part concludes with an alternative reading of clinical material, showing how sexual storytelling traverses the symbolic and the "real" in female narratives of distress.

<table>
<tr><td>Chapter 8</td><td>

TESTIFYING TO TRAUMA

The Sexual Abuse Recovery Movement and Feminist Clinical Practice

</td></tr>
</table>

I REMEMBER STANDING, at the age of twelve, on a street corner in downtown Seattle with my grandmother, distributing tracts entitled "Repent!" to passersby. My fervently evangelical grandmother had insisted that the salvation of souls transcended in importance any youthful embarrassment on my part about being part of such a spectacle. As we thrust our Holy newsprint into the hands of reluctant strangers, I silently made a pact with myself: if discovered by any classmates, I would simply change schools to preempt my inevitable ostracism. Fortunately, the anonymity of the city permitted me to spread the light with my grandmother in total darkness.

Witnessing—the practice of imparting the Good News to the unsaved—was a sacred obligation, one that marked the boundary between those who possessed the truth and those in need of it, the godly and the ungodly. The primary craft of this spiritual trade was developing a compelling testimony, honed and modified according to local and generational tastes. As choreographed contact with outsiders, witnessing protected believers from dreaded worldly contamination by assuring that interactions would be a one-way affair.

Actually, my childhood evangelism was a vital training ground for my later political radicalism. Distributing leaflets protesting a violently sexist film, occupying a building to demonstrate against a war, marching in a picket line during a strike—all these activities require a capacity for oppositional and moral engagement. As Mom so often said, "Being popular is less important than standing up for your convictions."

These were the associations that flooded me—like flashbacks—when I discovered a new army of witnesses in the late 1980s and early 1990s, one quite unlike the army of Christian soldiers of my youth. Witnessing and testifying emerged as idioms in the burgeoning trauma literature, invoking a similarly apocalyptic world of good and evil, yet one grounded in more earthly concerns. War and sexual abuse were the dramatic focus of this new era of testimonials, which followed in the wake of the powerful literature on Holocaust survivors.[1]

Testifiers invariably anticipate resistances on the part of their audiences but these resistances—the unwillingness of others to submit to the testimony—must be understood within their specific social contexts. We may suspect that some testimonies are attempts to control audiences, manipulating guilt and fear in order to achieve some sort of submission. Other testimonials stir respect and receptivity, and we sense that we must try to overcome something within ourselves in taking in the message, in spite of the discomfort it engenders.

Between these two poles, of course, stands a vast range of ambivalent possibilities. For some, invoking a past trauma can be a means of justifying some current cruelty or of minimizing the suffering of others. Reactionary and neofascist groups regularly justify their acts of aggression in the name of avenging past trauma, and wars are routinely fought under this same justificatory banner. More commonly and benignly, references to past suffering enable claims to be made on others, as reminders of binding loyalties or as a method of silencing protests. For example, when I complained as a child about walking to school on rainy days, I often heard the story of my mother's own wretched childhood, her dreary fate of being forced to walk through frozen tundra in northern Alberta to a drafty one-room schoolhouse.

Finding a way of thinking clearly about these various contexts and meanings of testimonials often eludes us. The blurriness of contemporary terms such as *trauma, survivor, witnessing,* and *testimonial* leaves us either thinking of each example of human suffering, one at a time, granting each its due, or imposing a diffuse sameness onto the scene, erasing vital differences. The first of these tendencies particularizes human suffering but lacks a framework for grasping larger commonalities, while the second offers universality while eliminating crucial differences. Collective anxiety over whether the grievances of so many victims now outstrips any possible means of redress may exacerbate this bifurcation of trauma into absolute sameness and absolute difference.

Those who bear witness to the historical reality of the Holocaust continually confront its insidious slide into the realm of the symbolic. Metaphorical use of this collective trauma—Operation Rescue's condemnation of abortion as a "holocaust" or sexual abuse survivor groups' descriptions of their childhoods as a "private holocaust"—becomes a strategy for conveying both moral horror and absolute victimization. Some critics are enraged over the banalizing of the Holocaust, insisting that reducing it to a metaphor or to merely one example of crimes against humanity among many denies the scope of the Nazi program of genocide.[2]

Yet this invoking of the Holocaust to vivify various expressions of collective suffering is symptomatic of a deep cultural crisis. As a hysterical elaboration of suffering, employment of the Holocaust as a rhetorical device is an effort to break through a social barrier, a numbing wall of silence, and to stir responsiveness in others. More pervasive than the invoking of the Holocaust in trauma testimonials is the invoking of the sacral function of memory. The corrective to silent complicity in human suffering, according to a number of texts on trauma witnessing, is to "bear witness" to the trauma, to "remember it," to "refuse to forget it."

But what is actually being said in this ecclesiastical conception of politics? Is there something missing, something out of focus, in this call to witness evil? If witnessing and remembering are reconstructive activities, as psychological research suggests, how do we take into account the distortions and motivations that attend each? Further, how do we distinguish between the virtuous and the voyeuristic, the liberatory and the perverse, in such morally infused acts of looking and speaking?

In analyzing feminist testimonials to sexual trauma, this chapter focuses on one of the "master" narratives of the late 1980s, Ellen Bass and Laura Davis's *The Courage to Heal,* and on its inspirational meanings for women.[3] Its progressive insights and its blind spots are explored, particularly in explaining the complex, conflicting currents of female sexuality. Further examined is the convergence of political and therapeutic conceptions of trauma in feminist-informed clinical practice.

HERETICAL INFLUENCES

"The world has split open. Women have broken the silence." These were the exhortatory opening words of Ellen Bass before a rapt audience of therapists at a 1993 conference on treating sexual abuse survivors.[4] After two days of tedious clinical presentations by several male therapists who have colonized the field of sexual abuse recovery training, Bass spoke from the heart of the survivors' movement and from its soul in feminism. As the first woman during the five-day conference to address the audience—made up predominantly of female therapists—Bass projected a mixture of feminine softness and commanding authority. She called us to arms, to political activism, in countering the pernicious project of silencing survivors, spearheaded by the False Memory Syndrome Foundation and its allies. The FMSF had mobilized against what its members claimed was an epidemic of false allegations of sexual abuse, based on therapeutically "implanted" memories. (See chapter 1.) Bass told of threats against her, even letters calling for her death. But she spoke with steady calm, with warm intonations that comforted the audience of worried therapists, shell-shocked by the memory war. I could not help noticing how her soft brown curls and heart-shaped face belied the venomous portrayals of her critics.

Many critics describe Bass and Davis—the authors of the "bible" of the survivors' movement—as promoters of hate. For some, these women are wolves in sheep's clothing, wooing women away from loving families. Bass mocks this demonizing of her, pointing out that the fact that she and Laura Davis are lesbians underlies much of the contempt for the book. And, in a sense, coming out of the closet about sexual abuse is related to other transgressive acts for women—other strivings for sexual independence from men. The influence of feminist sexual politics within the survivors' movement has not escaped the notice of the FMSF, whose literature often draws a careful line between "radical lesbians" and more "reasonable" feminists.[5] Here as elsewhere, lesbian baiting is at the forefront of reactions to female rebellion.

Bass continues, speaking in a populist tone. "Survivors are the real experts," she insists. It is an expertise that she has assumed in moving from the ranks of Every Woman to stellar oracle of the movement. In the preface to the second edition of *The Courage to Heal,* Bass and Davis underscore the transformative power of their heretical text. Excoriating the mental health industry, endorsements include survivors' scathing indictments of professionals. "I've been in treatment since I was six. I've been in mental hospitals. I've been given shock treatments. I've been on meds. I've seen counselors up the wazoo, but [your book] is the first real help I've ever received."[6]

Offering testimonials attesting to the book's lifesaving powers is not merely self-promotion or grandstanding on the part of its authors. A best-seller for years, *The Courage to Heal* strikes a responsive chord in vast numbers of women. Like so much of the self-help recovery literature that flooded the market in the 1980s, *The Courage to Heal* combines personal accounts, presented in a confessional vernacular, and a step-by-step path to recovery, peppered with common-sense psychology. Much like the booming codependence literature of the late 1980s, which similarly addresses the weariness and emotional binds of modern women, *The Courage to Heal* is an inspirational text.[7] And, like the healing manuals dealing with the aftermath of growing up in alcoholic, dysfunctional families, Bass and Davis's book encourages sexual abuse survivors to disengage from excessive preoccupation with the needs of others. To women who continue to bear primary responsibility for the household while often working long hours in low-status, underpaid jobs, such prescriptive advice feels like welcome medicine. While many self-diagnosed survivors who recover new memories of sexual abuse may not have been literally abused by their fathers, they are likely to find some of the truth of their experiences embedded in the narratives in this lengthy text. This feminist apocrypha inspires and comforts, and grants believers heroic powers. And, indeed, for women to speak up about their own oppression, to refuse to continue as guardians of fathers' and husbands' secrets, does require courage and solidarity.

Bass and Davis fail to understand, however, that once sexual survivorship moves from the realm of the particular abuses of women to that of legendary truth, it speaks to a broad set of female grievances. The incest survivor stands for every woman's seductions under patriarchy, for the myriad, daily violations of her sense

of self, and for the estrangement so many women experience from their own bodies. In locating the source of a range of emotional ailments such as depression
and eating disorders in a forgotten sexual trauma, Bass and Davis grant dramatic
force to the discontents of women. "When you were abused, your boundaries,
your right to say no, your sense of control in the world, were violated. You were
powerless. The abuse humiliated you, gave you the message that you were of little
value. Nothing you did could stop it."[8] Bass and Davis's recuperative message is
moving to many women because it affirms the depths of female grievances. In
an era when child sexual abuse has come to represent the violation of the self
at the deepest level, this same imagery may be employed to objectify a pervasive
sense of anguish.

Take, for example, the belief—widely circulated in the mental health community in the 1980s—that eating disorders are an indicator of repressed memories of sexual abuse. While empirical studies indicate no clear causal connection
between a history of child sexual abuse and eating disorders, the link between
them does have a certain ring of truth.[9] It is difficult to disentangle empirically
single background factors from the web of determinants that contribute to difficulties in adult womanhood.[10] Phenomenologically, however, sexual abuse
assumes priority as a causal factor in female disturbances because it symbolizes
dilemmas common to women—specifically, vulnerability to masculine invasions
and subjugation to male assertions of sexual entitlement. Unlike the "acting-out"
disorders common among men, which are expressed in aggressive or antisocial
behavior, women's ailments are likely to be carried privately, hidden behind the
domesticated behavior cultivated in female development. If incest is the secret
crime, it would seem to explain the sense of private shame that often accompanies the female journey out of childhood and the extent to which women's maladies, such as eating disorders, center on the body.

In the third edition of *The Courage to Heal,* Bass and Davis qualify their earlier,
controversial statement that "if you think you were abused, then you were." In this
new edition the authors reiterate the message while conceding some ground to the
opposition, replacing the definitive "you were" with the qualified "strong likelihood." "It is rare that someone thinks she was sexually abused and then later discovers she wasn't. The progression usually goes the other way, from suspicion to
confirmation. If you genuinely think you were abused and your life shows the symptoms, there's a strong likelihood that you were."[11] The gripping stories of survivors'
journeys into remembering—which include the genre of satanic ritual abuse
accounts—are granted authority by the authors because they "feel true." Women's
own subjective sense of truth—the emotional conviction attached to a personal
discovery—emerges as the final arbiter in the memory war. And for women, who
have lacked authority in adjudicating claims in so many public arenas, emotional
conviction may seem like the only weapon available for fighting back.

Bass and Davis fail to extend the power of their legendary discovery, however, into the far reaches of feminine development. If, as the authors assert, women
experience a range of personal violations in the course of development—from
sexual harassment to neglect and deprecating treatment—might the identity of

child sexual abuse survivor provide an organizing theme for and bring a vivid urgency to the quiet assaults of everyday life? And might the repression of female sexuality—the other side of patriarchal oppression—heighten anxieties organized around the body, so that the "return of the repressed" takes the form of a disturbing sexual memory?

Transformative Remembering

Many of the stories of sexual survivorship in *The Courage to Heal* may be employed to illustrate the process of transformative remembering. They include a dramatic turning point where a recovered memory of sexual abuse becomes a means of escaping diffuse forms of suffering and the troubling binds of growing up female. The new memory provides a developmental landmark, a movement out of the darkness of feminine madness to the new light generated by the recovered trauma scene.

The story of Gizelle, included in *The Courage to Heal,* exemplifies the power of this transformative remembering. A forty-year-old woman from an Irish Catholic family, Gizelle remembers, during the course of therapy, a violent rape by her father at the age of three. Prior to the recovery of this memory, she had suffered various psychiatric and physical ailments. Hospitalized for a series of tests, "with needles in my back" and under heavy sedation, Gizelle begins to have flashbacks. In a state of mental crisis, she calls her therapist, who then conducts a five-hour session during which he administers MDMA, more commonly known as Ecstasy, a drug initially designed and prescribed by some sex therapists for enhancement of lovemaking. Gizelle's therapist uses the drug to "lower the level of fear" in cases such as hers, which indicated "severe repression" (466). Like the devil himself, the repressed truth is a formidable opponent that the therapist now exorcizes. Gizelle describes the marathon therapy scene where she wrestles with the emerging memories. "But, even then, the denial was so strong. . . . And then I'd go into hysteria where I couldn't breathe. And then I'd start choking. And then I would be numb and I wouldn't feel anything. We went around like that for three hours. I said to Frank [the therapist], 'You know what I'm feeling? I feel like I'm lying.'"[12]

Lying is a complicated matter. Truth may be conveyed through a conscious fiction, or a truth may be told with a deceiving intent. Here, we are led to believe that Gizelle feels as though she is lying, even as the truth wells up from the bowels of her unconscious. There may be, however, a complex interplay of fact and fiction, truth telling and deception, embedded in this narrative of memory retrieval. The memory that results from this therapeutic trial by fire may have elements of historical truth, but much of its emotional power may derive from the context of the discovery—both the hospitalization that produced the flashbacks and the marathon therapy session that followed. Gizelle reports that she had felt invaded by the medical procedures, which she had also experienced frequently in her early years in her bouts with illness. Her father, we learn early on in the narrative, is a surgeon and was involved in her medical care as a child. Gizelle's hospitalization may have evoked childhood memories of invasive procedures, with her father as the fantasied or real agent of her pain. Young children often do experience frightening procedures as sadistic assaults, which may be woven into the fabric of memory as abuse. The memory of the father's rape at the age of three may vivify and concretize more ambiguous struggles with a father who let his daughter down in countless unarticulated ways. In a striking parallel, her present therapist administers a drug during an extensive session, which is, itself, an intimate invasion. And the therapeutic probing for a dramatic revelation—and the special treatment of a five-hour session in a drug-induced state—may give incest memories a metaphorical immediacy. Like Daddy having his way with his "special girl," many therapists make exceptions to their own rules in meeting the "unique needs" of suspected incest survivors.

These influences may or may not be important to the meaning of this recovered memory. But, in presenting the testimonial as a straightforward account of a recovered memory of sexual abuse, Bass and Davis fail to appreciate the rich, textured nature of memory or the multiple meanings and interpretations of representations of the past.

Conversion Memories

As a didactic text, *The Courage to Heal* actually blunts the critical edge of feminism, even as it advances feminist aims. Its portrayals of therapeutic ventures are mesmerizing and unreflective. The assumption in the story of Gizelle is that the source of truth lies in the depths of the unconscious and that this emerging truth may be trusted more than any rational processes of mind. Through this resurrection of the buried past, remembering takes on the power of a conversion experience. Gizelle describes her own recovered memory in these terms. "Since it's come out, it's been the difference of night and day, of living in hell and living on the earth. Everything in me has changed—my perception of myself, of others, of the earth, of my power, of my strength, of my abilities, of my sanity—of everything. It's been so fast. I can't believe it. In just three and a half months, there's incredible healing."[13]

Like any conversion experience, the creation of a transformative memory grows out of real human suffering and out of efforts to overcome it. Taking the everyday assaults on the human spirit and elevating them to the realm of the diabolical or the divine ennobles the human quest for solace and meaning. In many "born-again" stories, the former life of degradation—of a descent into hell—serves as dramatic counterpoint to the conversion experience. The most convincing of evangelists have wrestled with the devil, and this devil is cast as a full rival of God in the spiritual cosmology. Within this religious worldview, rebellion and transgressive impulses are central motifs, even though they are experienced as the "work of the devil," requiring the transmutative taming of a supreme power.

For many women, recovered memory narratives offer a powerful mythology because they contain many of these same elements. This mythology is particularly compelling when female storytelling is culturally restricted, an issue I explored in part 2. One dynamic operating in the history of female storytelling, also pursued in part 2, involves women's subversive use of conventional scripts in their efforts to break out of societal constraints. Similarly, if the concepts of God and Satan are the heirs of the child's ambivalence toward the father, as Freud once asserted, the shift from father worship to demonology in Bass and Davis's feminist mythology operates as a deidealization of paternal authority. Indeed, Gizelle's journey is from an idealized love for her father (her recovered memory begins with shouts of "I love you, Daddy; I love you, Daddy") to a rupture in this emotional tie, brought about by the new memory. Since raping one's child is the most egregious of parental violations, it permits a definitive, morally sanctioned bridge out of the father's world.

The Courage to Heal is, then, the "bible" of a fundamentalist feminism, but it has some of the same costs for believers as those exacted by religious fundamentalism. Both provide an emotionally vivid, dramatic encounter with evil and righteousness that breaks through the deadening effects of everyday life. As cosmologies, they unify believers around an emotionally gratifying but simplified universe. All the bad, disturbing aspects of oneself and one's group of believers can be reassuringly placed beyond the gate of the new kingdom, protecting the faithful from both real and imagined threats. The Courage to Heal provides women with a reassuring message that nothing problematic in their own reactions or mental life must be taken into account in understanding life's dilemmas.

Like the preacher who claims to be simply reading directly from the Word, eschewing the vagaries of symbolic meanings and interpretive uncertainty, Bass and Davis approach the feminine unconscious as though it speaks directly to women in an entirely literal way. This "repression" of the role of professional translators, of the multiple meanings in the "text" of memory, and of the influence of drugs on mental states leaves women without any means of understanding the operations of power in the production of their own stories. For Bass and Davis, "honoring the truth" means holding the ground around a literal interpretation of memory while conceding, in their revised edition, that there may be a few "false positives" (449). Such a vision offers an impoverished view of mental life. Much of the complexity of the mind—with its imaginative, symbolic capacities—is rendered away in a one-dimensional tale of feminine innocence lost and regained.

MEMOROPHILIA

In her keynote address at the meeting of the American Psychological Association in 1995, Gloria Steinem began her talk with an interesting comment: "I must say, now that I am sixty-one years old myself, that I sometimes think I've reached the age when remembering something right away is as good as an orgasm."[14] While she went on to review the history of the sexual survivor movement, her statement signaled an underanalyzed area of the recovered memory movement. In many of the popular and clinical reports, there is, indeed, allusion to an orgasmic release in storytelling, although the clinical term for this is *abreaction*. While most therapists in the trauma field stress the painful affects associated with remembering sexual abuse, the pleasurable aspects of remembering, whether in the reporting of women's "war stories" or in the intimacy established in the telling of them, tend to be neglected.

One need not minimize the anguish of recalling sexual abuse in order to recognize how such recollections may serve multiple functions for and arouse myriad responses in tellers and listeners alike. There is an interpersonal dimension—a "call-and-response" exchange—to the telling of an arousing story. The art of storytelling is not based merely on chronicling a sequence of facts but on the artful juxtaposition of dramatic elements. The power of the story to stir others, to communicate shared tribulations and victorious moments, depends on its felt truth and plausibility rather than on its mere facticity. Further, trauma stories, like legends of collective trauma, may have many functions. By preserving a collective memory of past injuries, they may, for example, serve as reminders of the necessity of continual struggle. Trauma legends may also renew collective identity by reestablishing the group's entitlement—the rewards of suffering and righteousness—as well as the group's mourned losses.

Sexual Differences

Whether "recovered" or continuous, memories of childhood sexual encounters have been transformed in recent decades through insurgent social scripts—means of registering and interpreting events—that were unavailable to previous generations. Yet, as I have previously argued, movements advancing new social ideals inevitably contain unresolved conflicts and dilemmas. While the right of children to resist adult authority has been one of the most progressive advances in recent times, this right has been won largely by restoring "pre-Freudian" conceptions of childhood. Cultural discomfort with childhood sexuality, and particularly with the sexuality of girls, intensifies the moral outrage in campaigns against child sexual abuse, an issue confronted again in the next two chapters. Female chastity, as a cultural ideal, has a long, ambivalent history within feminism, no less than in reactionary politics. One of the implicit, subtextual differences between the trauma stories of men and those of women in the sexual abuse recovery literature is in the degree of "license" to convey a mixture of horror and pleasure in the telling of the trauma story. Men can share their war stories with a certain nostalgic longing and can even import moments of homoerotic desire into the "buddy" story while preserving their claims as bona fide trauma survivors.[15]

In the male sexual abuse survivor literature, sexual arousal is recognized as a feature of the experience—to such an extent that it is often framed as the source of the shame attached to the abuse.[16] Further, adolescent males are far more likely than adolescent females to describe sexual contacts with older persons as predominantly positive.[17] Working through sexual abuse for male survivors often means confronting the complex currents of their own desire, including its homoerotic and "feminine" (passive, receptive) elements. Gay men often recall adolescent experiences with adult males quite fondly, and these encounters are understood to be integral to the experience of coming out.[18]

As practitioners in the sexual abuse field so often point out, males are less likely to identify themselves as victims of sexual abuse because the position of victim is so feminized in the culture. To some extent, societal beliefs about the "durability" of boys may protect them from the traumatic effects of childhood sexual encounters. But this same belief operates repressively, in reinscribing gender codes, particularly the idea of male invulnerability. The new genre of male sexual abuse stories in the 1980s, much like the posttraumatic-stress-disorder literature on the effects of combat, signified male resistance to the culture of manhood and an alliance with feminist critiques of sexual domination.[19]

Nonetheless, gender differences in accessing sexual abuse memories are embedded in a cultural vocabulary that runs deeper than identification with the position of victim. Sexual victimization is a far more pervasive theme in female than in male development, from lewd comments on the part of males, "bra snapping," and pinched bottoms, through male sexual exhibitionism, rape, and incest. The mingling in "social memory" of normative, unwanted sexual encounters and more traumatic ones makes the sexual abuse recovery narrative emotionally compelling. For many girls and women, the concept of sexual invasion infiltrates and colors autobiographical recall, inscribed further by various fairy tales and the "folk wisdom" of childhood. (See chapter 5.) As a social script, sexual abuse is readily mobilized in various memory-making contexts.

We may decipher areas of "leakage" within this dominant feminine narrative. For example, one survivor in *The Courage to Heal* describes the agony and ecstasy of recovering memory of early abuse. Initially, she presents excruciating flashbacks: "I'd be driving home from my therapist's office, and I'd start having flashes for things—just segments, like bloody sheets, or taking a bath, or throwing away my nightgown. For a long time, I remembered all the things around being raped, but not the rape itself."[20] While recovered memory is typically described as having this unbidden character—the force of an external agency breaking through consciousness in a fragmented form—such imagery can result from various sources. Some women may recover memories of actual abuse in this way, as psychotherapy or other intensive self-exploration stimulates focused attention on the past. Yet one of the legacies of patriarchal oppression for women involves the suppression and repression of sexual and aggressive fantasies. Violent sexual imagery can be particularly frightening to women, both because it may signal actual memories of abuse and because it departs from domesticated versions of the feminine mind. Nice girls do not have dirty thoughts. In much of the clinical literature, narratives of childhood sexual abuse broaden the range of sexual imagery for women as long as this chain of mental signifiers is stabilized through the recovery of a discrete traumatic scene. (See chapter 4.)

Seductive Mothers

For many survivors, the absent mother, her failure to protect her daughter from abuse, emerges as a dominant motif.[21] And, for feminists, the issue of the mother's culpability has always been a thorny one. Davis does address this issue in her own story, even though there is no discussion of the complex verities of memories of the mother—or of the problematic interplay of real and fantasied maternal failures. Davis's story, titled "I'm Saying No, Mama," centers on "weaning" from her mother and on the rocky road to feminine exile from the family. Guilt over the struggle to separate from the mother is palpable in contemporary feminist discourse. Davis poses the question of how she is able to keep her mother out of her life. "I'll tell you how, Momma, I'll tell you how. Brick by careful brick, that's how. Momma, I've built this wall between us with careful, conscious precision. It is thick, my wall. Thick and nontransparent. I stand behind it and you cannot reach me. Its walls are smooth, Momma, flattened by ancient anger."[22]

The narrative then moves to an assertion of the freedom that this new wall permits, including the freedom to "set boundaries" and to break from the past. The deidealization of the father in the recovered memory narratives finds its parallel in this deidealization of the mother. "I'm not the daughter you wanted, Momma. I've always known that. But with my wall close around me, I can see you're not the mother I wanted either, all-knowing, all-giving, all-protective" (302).

The recovered memory often serves as the decisive break from parental binds that are ensnaring, particularly for daughters. Daughters, more than sons, are expected to preserve intergenerational ties and to care for aging parents. Feminists, however, cannot easily equate the sins of the father and those of the mother. It is true that daughters may be let down by their mothers in irremediable ways and that women who have the freedom to sever ties with destructive or controlling mothers may feel the need to do so. It is an odd oversight, however, for a feminist text to omit commentary on recovered memory of maternal abuse while simultaneously explaining paternal abuse as a direct expression of patriarchal oppression. In other words, there is no attentiveness in the recovered memory debate to claims that require careful feminist scrutiny.

One of the liberating aspects of feminism is in its laying claim to a much larger world than that known by prior generations of women. Girls often discover, first-hand, their mothers' rage and disappointment, although these discoveries may not be informed by understandings of a larger social world of determinants. The daughter may encounter the mother's destructive side, as the mother takes out her own frustrated longings and aggression on a vulnerable, female counterpart. Mothers may minimize the daughters' distress, just as they minimize their own, and look the other way in order to maintain the peace.

But other dimensions of remembering the mother, as I argued in chapters 3 and 4, are intimately tied to primitive fantasies. Since the first object of dependence is typically the mother, the first struggles for independence also are with her. The powerful ambivalence generated by this attachment—often heightened by the social isolation of the nuclear family—infuses later imagery of the mother with infantile conflicts. Memories of the real failures of the mother mingle with fantasy representations of her, infused by the rage, disappointment, and desire that are the lingering legacy of childhood. The disavowal of fantasy elements of memory removes this troubling uncertainty in defining the "boundaries" of self and (m)other in the internal world. So too, sexual desire is dissociated from its emotional origins in various developmental conflicts, including sensual longings for the mother.

Sex for Survivors

In one of the few stories that restores some sexual agency to the survivor, Davis offers an account of her own vacillating movement in and out of sexual passion as she makes love with her partner. The story speaks to female ambivalence around sexuality—on the part of both abuse survivors and nonsurvivors, both lesbians and straights. In this modern narrative Davis retreats from a moment of sexual awakening—from "the sudden jolt of passion"—as genital desire vanishes inexplicably. In a reversal of the traditional story, this modern Sleeping Beauty is awakened by the kiss, only to fall back into a somnambulant state. While Davis's story reverberates with female ambivalence over sexuality, it also registers the complexity of what is awakened through sexual desire. The dread of abandonment and the confusing merger of aggression and pleasure that comes with the mingling of body parts make sexual desire the realm of both the imaginary and the real.

Davis's story reaches its denouement in a final explanation for the torturous ambivalence of this sexual encounter: "I was molested," she utters in a "tiny child's voice" (87). And while we may recognize in this revelation an expression of self-understanding and intimacy, this narrative, like the others in *The Courage to Heal,* tends inexorably to narrow the explanation down to a woman-child with no history or sexual knowledge to draw on beyond that of the trauma memory. This pervasive infantilizing of female sexuality seems to waver uneasily at the threshold of its own subject matter.

In discussing survivors' efforts to come to terms with sex, *The Courage to Heal* maps out the minefield that many women—whether abuse victims or not—encounter in discovering their own active desires and separating them from the invasions of past abusers. Bass and Davis introduce their chapter on "Sex" by noting the formidable obstacles women face in achieving sexual agency in a patriarchal and phallocentric society such as ours. And they affirm the right of survivors to assert control in the area of sexuality and to reclaim their bodies as their own. While women may feel "damaged beyond repair" (250), the message is one of hope and encouragement. Women are advised to masturbate as a means of relearning what feels good and to "start slowly and with awareness" (251). Lesbian relationships are affirmed, and examples of sexual explorations in the course of women's healing are equally divided between female and male lovers.

While Bass and Davis advance a conception of liberated sexuality based on women's own self-conscious explorations, their views also understate the complex, conflicting currents of sexuality. Much of their advice is standard 1990s, liberal fare: sex in moderation is "fun" and important, but it can also be "addictive" or a "reenactment" of childhood abuse. Women are cautioned that one result of incest or other childhood sexual abuse may be"excessive" sex, an ambiguous category that seems to include sexual encounters outside committed relationships.

Being a sexual abuse survivor also permits women to account for feelings of revulsion toward male genitals, without having to explore too fully the various implications of such feelings. Gizelle's story, discussed earlier, includes this theme. "You know, in my fantasies, when I imagine having a lover, I'm making love to him and everything is going along beautifully until he takes out his penis. And then I vomit all over the floor. Literally, in my fantasy, I vomit all over the floor!"[23] This mixture of interest in and revulsion toward male genitals is normalized through the sexual survivor narrative, and the source of these feelings is located in an abuse scene in the past. While some women may have difficulty separating their current lover's genitals from "the genitals that violated you as a child" (266), the framework of sexual abuse survivorship excludes a range of conflicts not inevitably attributable to abuse. More pervasive sources of female ambivalence toward heterosexuality, including the impulse to orally "ejaculate" on the man, are overlooked by the singular focus on sexual abuse.

Sexual abuse survivors, we learn, should educate their partners about their special needs and ensure that the partner is responsive to the survivor's need to "take it slow." Implicitly, nonabused women have fewer claims in this area—fewer rights to insist on a partner's adaptations to their special needs. When all ambiguous and disturbing sexual material is constructed as a sign of a wounded femininity in need of "healing," women are able to make claims on lovers only within a discourse of illness.

Such a "journey to recovery" takes women on a narrow, constricted path of discovery, where disturbing sexual images are understood preemptively as flashbacks of the abuse. One survivor, who describes her intense shame and terror over sadomasochistic fantasies, is offered the redemptive power of the abuse narrative. "If abuse and sadism turn you on, you aren't to blame. You did not create these fantasies out of nothing. They were forced on you just as intrusively as those hands, penises, and leers were forced on you during the original abuse" (272–273).

It is true that sadistic sexual fantasies can result from abuse and that perpetrators invade the imaginations as well as the bodies of their victims. But such fantasies can also have other sources. Just as small children may squeal with delight in being "captured" by their parents as they playfully flee, images of being tied up or forcefully held during sex may be infused with infantile forms of pleasure. The sexual excitement associated with the fantasy of rape must be distinguished from the experience of actual rape. Rape fantasies may draw on motifs that predominate in our "rape culture"—providing a sense of mastery over threatening aspects of the social world—and simultaneously may draw on a range of aggressive sensations and impulses that mingle with sexual ones.

Arousing Memories

One of the subtextual themes in Bass and Davis's account of sexual healing concerns the sexualizing of memory itself. One survivor describes the mixture of pleasure and pain that emerges in the course of recovering abuse memories. "It seems to me that the memories are stored at the same level the passion is. If I don't make love, I don't connect with them. But whenever I open myself to feelings of passion, the memories are right there. It's a little like opening Pandora's box."[24] When disturbing mental imagery is defined as literal memory, women are permitted to experience it as a normal upsurge of traumatic material and as part of the healing process. When this same imagery is identified as fantasy—that is, as internally generated material—its fate is less certain. In *The Courage to Heal* women do describe aggressive sexual fantasies, but these are assumed to be merely echoes of a past abuse. There is even one reference—exceedingly rare in the survivor literature—to how sexually stimulating reading about sexual abuse may be for women. As one survivor confesses, "For weeks on end I compulsively read about incest—*If I Should Die before I Wake* in one hand and my vibrator in the other" (272).

While such experiences are recognized to be unusual—and most likely are—they are embraced within the welcoming arms of the sexual survivor movement as part of the recovery process. There is no recognition on the part of Bass and Davis that some incestuous fantasies may not derive from explicit abuse and that they may be a part of normal female experience. It is only the survivor who is "allowed" such imagery, and this same survivor is instructed to understand her forbidden memories as an essential part of the healing process.

THERAPEUTIC SEDUCTIONS

Published in the same year as the first edition of *The Courage to Heal,* Martha Baldwin's *Beyond Victim* is a prototypical example of the recovery therapy genre of popular literature.[25] Baldwin places her own autobiographical account of remembering sexual abuse alongside those of other women who recount similar experiences, women who found their way into her clinical practice. Following in the footsteps of her masters—various therapists practicing "hypnotic regression, voice dialogue, dream work, Gestalt work, psychodrama, and Rolfing"—Baldwin embarks on her own version of hypnotic regression work with clients.

In the foreword to *Beyond Victim,* Warren Cremer allegorizes the journey charted by the book, underscoring the profound longings that inspire the contemporary genre of incest narratives, of which Baldwin's book is a part:

> The pioneers who conquered the Western wilderness have become so mythologized in our time that we may have forgotten that they were people much like ourselves. The frontiersmen who led them have become Legends transcending mortality. . . .
> Today we are facing the social wilderness that is not only unfamiliar to us but growing more chaotic and threatening each day. Social and institutional reforms continually fail, leaving us angry and frustrated—with no apparent solution in sight. Nor have we found a Legend in our time to lead the way.[26]

The journey into the past in *Beyond Victim* is cast in the context of a broad search for mythic truths. Quite unlike previous guides, Baldwin is described as a "new kind of frontiersman." "No longer God-the-Doctor, aloof, detached, and antiseptically perfect," Baldwin brings us a reassuring sense of her own humanity and authenticity. The problematic mingling of autobiographical and mythic memory, of literal and legendary truth, is "repressed" in the text, however, as journeys into unknown lands seem to require unambiguous markers.

Baldwin is a clinical social worker whose memories of childhood prior to the period of insurgent remembering at the age of forty-one were quite docile, with lifelong trouble centering on her overly controlling, protective, and doting parents. Her book maps the course of her own disillusionment, as the dormant, dark secret she had carried for decades flourished into a dramatic rewriting of her own history. First remembering her father having sex with her and then remembering sexual abuse by her mother, Baldwin works her way back to the black hole in her previously understood to be enchanted early years.

Baldwin presents herself as an ally of the many women who entered her clinical practice in the early 1980s, women who were experiencing mysterious body memories and flashbacks that were thought uniformly to be the echoes of early sexual invasions. Baldwin seeks a new, independent vision of authority unlike the authority of the parents, therapists, husbands, and teachers whom she had followed unquestioningly throughout her life. As she finds her own "voice," establishing herself as an expert on healing from the wounds of sexual abuse, she finds that monstrous memories well up inside her, even as her expertise grows through their gestation.

Therapists do learn from their patients and, ideally, develop new self-understanding and a stronger capacity for relatedness through their clinical experience. So, too, therapists must be able work through issues of professional authority, both in making positive use of it and in confronting its destructive side. Yet Baldwin's highly romantic conception of her own clinical authority, her sense of an unfolding, inner wisdom and goodness emerging out of her newfound memories, brings a certain blindness to the problematic aspects of this same authority.

A critical moment in Baldwin's history, one that opens the floodgates of memory, is her father's death. She had adored her father, felt slavishly dependent on him, and, as he was dying, sensed a glimmer of freedom dangerously within reach. Always the good daughter, Baldwin wearily and dutifully visits her ailing parent, unable to register any real emotion other than fatigue colored with some resentment. In the avalanche of memory that follows several years after his death, she finally achieves the means to free herself of debilitating dependence and guilt, as both her mother and father emerge from the wonder years of her childhood memories as sexual perpetrators.

With various body therapies and meditative practices as aids, a new personal history is born that is nothing short of transformative. As in so many of the self-help manuals, Baldwin's own newfound authority is based primarily on direct experience—transformation through inner knowledge and unmediated revelation. Consistent with this same genre, Baldwin introduces her sense of authority as emerging out of a fellowship of common experience rather than through her schooling and formal credentials. Like the women mystics, spiritualists, and mediums of earlier eras, Baldwin claims a direct, quasimystical connection to a source of transcendent knowledge as she struggles to free herself from the controlling presence of her various male mentors.

Noting that "abuse-by-mother issues are much more buried, and difficult to face than abuse by father," Baldwin takes this struggle to its ultimate conclusion (20). As disturbing feelings search for their moorings in memory, the mother increasingly surfaces in sexual abuse literature as a perpetrator prior to the father. A broad range of sexual abuse texts in the 1990s include mothers as sexual perpetrators, a form of abuse that was thought in the decades prior to be extremely rare.[27] Much like Bass and Davis, Baldwin receives emergent memories with absolute certainty.

One might expect that a clinical movement so deeply indebted to feminist insights would pause at the sight of this new development, reassessing the ground that has been won. As I have previously argued, memories from the earliest years of life are not likely to be true in the veridical sense but may still convey narrative "truth." The "recovered" memory of a sexually invasive mother may signify the daughter's ambivalent struggle with the mother and her strivings for a differentiated sense of self. Further, the recovered memory of the malevolent mother, prior to the invasive father, suggests a "return of the repressed" within feminist-informed therapies, specifically in registering the difficulties in integrating mother/daughter hostilities and conflicts into feminist analysis.

POLITICS AND THERAPY: WITNESSING FOR SURVIVORS

All progressive social movements work to place the "bad" back onto the oppressors in reclaiming the goodness and creative power of the group. Rallying slogans such as "sisterhood is powerful" and "black is beautiful" facilitate this necessary reclamation of an idealized goodness from under the shadow of the oppressor. The work of any liberation movement inevitably proceeds on two fronts: it must confront the sustained injuries the group suffers at the hands of its oppressors, and it must engender healthy capacities to act and intervene in the world. If there is too much emphasis on the injurious side of oppression, a movement loses its sense of strength and agency. But if there is too much emphasis on the transcendent powers of the group—on its own inherent strength and goodness—its claims of having been damaged may be weakened. Further, an overly romantic view of the oppressed—even one asserted by the oppressed themselves through the struggle for liberation—may work against complex understandings of its painful legacy. Breaking free of the seductive aspects of domination is never as fully achieved as is imagined. The most successful liberation movements have shown some capacity to move beyond the early conversion experience—the transformative power of righteous insurgency—to incorporate means of critically reflecting on their own practices and of recognizing destructive capacities as part of both their legacy and the human condition.

An important difference between progressive and regressive social movements—between groups asserting the rights of women, minorities, gays, and workers and reactionary groups—is in whether the enemy is a real or imagined one and in whether the group is able to go beyond collective trauma to envision a more humane social world, one based on human commonalities as well as on unique differences. Progressive as well as reactionary groups, however, may defensively employ a social identity based on opposition to an other at various times. Mobilizing against even genuine enemies or oppressors may serve to ward off internal conflict within the group. A larger issue—one underlying feminist participation in the recovered memory controversy—is the degree to which oppressed groups defensively distort their perceptions of empirically genuine enemies. Women who recover memories of sexual abuse are, I believe, expressing real grievances, although there is, inevitably, a range of distortions, displacements, and other defensive processes involved. At the same time, the sexual abuse recovery movement has made defensive use of its insights and discoveries, sacrificing the conflicting currents in women's experiences and desires.

In this regard, therapists who "bear witness" to sexual trauma walk a much rockier road than those who bear witness to the Holocaust. As the trauma moves from the indisputable terrain of war and the Holocaust to the truly "witnessless" crimes of private life and the family and as it shifts from the numbingly horrific to titillating areas of violence, the meanings attached to such trauma (and their witnessing) seem less and less transparent. Further, once a person introduces her or his position as being that of a witness, invoking the moral and sacral discourse of the testimonial, questions about both the veracity of the testimony and the motivations of the witness are silenced. Those who express skepticism or uncertainty are equated with Holocaust deniers, guilty by association of the same blindness to injustice evidenced by those who have failed to learn the bitter lessons of history. This may be the age of testimonial, as Elie Wiesel suggests, but testifiers do not inevitably speak the truth, as virtuous as they may perceive themselves to be.[28]

Herman invokes the testimonial in her 1992 book, *Trauma and Recovery*, which was discussed in chapter 4 in the context of developments within feminist-informed therapies. Alluding to the motifs of her book, Herman prefaces it with a quote from Salman Rushdie's *Shame*, written in 1983.

> I had thought, before I began, that what I had on my hands was an almost excessively masculine tale, a saga of sexual rivalry, ambition, power, patronage, betrayal, death, revenge. But the women seem to have taken over, they marched in from the peripheries of the story to demand the inclusion of their own tragedies, histories, and comedies, obliging me to couch my narrative in all manner of sinuous complexities, to see my "male" plot refracted, so to speak,

through the prisms of its reverse and "female" side. It occurs to me that the women knew precisely what they were up to—their stories explain, and even subsume, the men's. . . . So it turns out that my "male" and "female" plots are the same story after all.[29]

Throughout *Trauma and Recovery,* Herman places the accounts of sexual survivors within the political landscape of the atrocities of war and the Holocaust, as well as within the small-scale tragic dramas of inner-city violence and domestic battering. In each case, there is an inevitable tension between the "will to deny horrible events and the will to proclaim them aloud" (1). And, in each case, the recovery of the individual and of society depends jointly on the recuperative power of storytelling.

The question of how these stories get told, however, is not her central concern. We may recognize in the project of vivifying the trauma of women, as did Rushdie, a deeply engraved cultural problem, more profound in its implications than Herman seems to recognize. Women have been forced to smuggle tales of their own suffering into public discourse, bootstrapped onto male encounters with evil. Women are, of course, survivors of the same wars, political torture, and institutional violence that men endure. But the sexual abuse testimonials of women often focus on the "intimate enemy," the highly privatized violence that often takes place within close relationships. Here, the defender/protector turns enemy, and the distinction between enemies and allies is often murky.

But are male and female plots really "the same story"? And if there are elements of similarity, are there also crucial differences? Herman works the similarity side of the equation, weaving together an elaborate and compelling tapestry of evils, even as she abruptly reverses herself, placing male and female positions in opposition to one another. It is a story of absolute evil and virtue and of female resistance born of valiant motives. There are no morally conflicted, irrational women in the plot, an understandable corrective to the legacy of women blaming but one that carries its own freight of problems. If Eve is assigned responsibility for the Fall and Western man has persisted in the masculine habit of projecting his own guilt onto her, then modern Eves must project the bad back onto its source and reclaim their virtue and honor. For if "women learn that in rape they are not only violated but dishonored" and suffer "greater contempt than defeated soldiers," then they must learn new strategies of honorable combat (67).

Beyond this strategic issue, Herman's project of identifying common elements in traumatic victimization is important in finding a unifying ground of human experience. There are commonalities in the methods employed by perpetrators in various social contexts of tyranny, as Herman suggests, methods that have as their primary aim the domination of the other. "The accounts of hostages, political prisoners, and survivors of concentration camps from every corner of the globe have an uncanny sameness. Drawing upon the testimony of political prisoners from widely differing cultures, Amnesty International in 1973 published a 'chart of coercion,' describing these methods in detail. These same techniques are used to subjugate women, in prostitution, in pornography, and in the home" (76).

What are these methods of coercive control that are practiced and circulated by perpetrators? Some of the methods clearly do have "an uncanny sameness," particularly when we leave out the degree of violence and sadism. Much like prisoners of war, survivors of domestic violence and sexual abuse describe their loss of personal privacy, how their husbands, fathers, or boyfriends control and regulate their movements and contacts with the outside world. Herman also points out how perpetrators of domestic violence seek to destroy the woman's sense of autonomy by depriving her of food, sleep, or exercise (77). From this perspective of analogous tyrannies, even women's wearisome responsibilities in the family may be framed as a labor-camp experience of induced exhaustion.

Beyond these sadistic privations, victims of various forms of violence may come to identify with the aggressor, who is the precarious link in what remains of the social chain of survival. "Once the perpetrator has succeeded in establishing day-to-day bodily control of the victim," Herman notes, "he becomes a source not only of fear and humiliation but also of solace" (78). He will court the victim, who loses her final sense of separateness through this intimate invasion, with its mingling of pleasure and pain.

Absent in Herman's project, however, is attention to the misuse of trauma stories—their employment in various problematic struggles or their displacements from one field of injury to another. While Herman does recognize how the combat survivor may act out his past war trauma on some present domestic front—displacing rage onto the women and children nearest and thus most captive to his pain—this same insight is not extended to sexual abuse survivors. Women survivors, it seems, are spared these displacements and vengeful uses of history.

We might counter that this neglect of inquiry into female aggression, revenge, or irrationality associated with traumatic memory is a result of the fact that most violence is perpetrated by males. Female victims are likely to engage in self-destructive behavior, whereas male victims are likely to act out against others, as well as to engage in self-destructive behavior.[30] Yet the history of child abuse and domestic violence indicates that while women are less likely to abuse children than men proportionate to the time they spend with them, they do engage in abuse with considerable frequency.[31] And because aggressive impulses are more domesticated and denied in women, female aggression may be expressed in more privatized ways, disguised behind prevailing gender codes.

The use of clinical indicators to register the magnitude of political repression contributes to a worrisome slippage in the use of categories; in politically resisting abusive or exploitive behavior, the victim must demonstrate a corollary level of psychic damage. Yet there is no one-to-one relationship between the level of psychological suffering and the extent of psychic damage, particularly in psychological effects manifested over a long period of time.[32] Trauma experienced early in life, within crucial dependence relationships, may be formative in a way that even more extreme trauma later in life is not. But survivors of early childhood abuse vary in their subsequent emotional adjustment and relational capacities depending, in part, on the extent of positive affective ties in the course of development. So too, some concentration-camp survivors, in spite of unimaginable suffering, have healthy capacities for living and loving, even though they may be haunted by their memories.

Herman understands, to her credit, the political dimensions of much of what occurs in the area of psychological trauma and how power relationships shape whose story gets told and the apportionment of blame and responsibility. "Those who bear witness are caught between victim and perpetrator. It is morally impossible to remain neutral in this conflict. The bystander is forced to take sides."[33] Yet, who are the victims and the perpetrators in this cosmology of evil? The "rights of victims" may be employed in various conservative campaigns, including campaigns to adopt highly punitive legislation, such as "three strikes and you're out." When Herman is describing the posttraumatic stress disorder of Vietnam veterans, she is on the side of male victims of war. When she is describing these same damaged men in the context of domestic violence, she places these male victims in the role of archetypal perpetrator, the oppressive dominators of a female victim. These two positions are dynamically related, of course, as the literature on "cycles of violence" has long claimed. Victimized children often grow up to victimize their own children; soldiers often return home and continue the war on the domestic front. These are truisms of our time, repeated so often that they appear as predictable as natural laws, even though the "reenactment" of traumatic experiences later in life is mediated by many factors.

Herman may be suggesting that in any particular contest between a victim and a perpetrator, one must take the side of the less powerful person, the victim, rather than the more powerful perpetrator. We may grant some credence to this stance as a general principle or orienting value, while still recognizing the pitfalls in applying it to an individual case. Exalting the word of the victim is a problematic strategy, particularly as victim stories come to serve as banners for various crusades and for the self-advancement of others on the cultural scene. Further, we may acknowledge degrees of victimization and perpetration as well as dynamic interplays and situational reversals between victim and perpetrator and, simultaneously, recognize specific situations where lines need to be decisively drawn between the guilty and the innocent, the oppressor and the oppressed.[34] Herman does force us to consider commonalities in victimization experiences, advancing women's grievances through a feminist discourse of trauma and recovery. But this widening of the lens is accompanied by a tremendous loss of acuity, particularly as the solidarity of victims comes to involve the renunciation of internal conflict, destructive capacities, or moral complexity.

CONCLUSIONS

This chapter began with a problem: how do we search out commonalities in female suffering while preserving the vital notion of degrees of harm endured and differences in the effects of destructive experiences? The trauma testimonial literature advances the notion of commonalities in placing a broad range of abusive and harmful experiences women endure under the banner of trauma. Yet in focusing on extreme brutality and absolute subjugation as prototype of women's oppression generally, the trauma testimonial literature advances the idea that suffering must be highly dramatic for it to be socially or therapeutically registered.

Critics of recovered memories often refer disparagingly to Bass and Davis's *The Courage to Heal* as the "bible" of the sexual abuse recovery movement. My own exegesis of this feminist text stresses three main points. First, *The Courage to Heal* is based on the idea that women's difficulties have a common origin in sexually invasive experiences in childhood. Given the pervasiveness of sexual intrusions in female development—ranging from the "sexual gaze," disparaging remarks, unwelcome touching, to overt rape and incest—it is not surprising that women find common cause in the identity of sexual abuse survivor. Second, Bass and Davis offer a "fundamentalist" version of feminism, an inspirational and comforting treatise that incurs some of the same costs as religious fundamentalism. By ignoring the social context of memory retrieval and by treating memory as a sacral function that "reveals" itself in an unmediated fashion, the authors suspend critical awareness of the various influences shaping how women's stories get told. Third, the conflicting aspects of female sexual desire are too wedded to a model of trauma and injury in Bass and Davis's account. While the identity of sexual abuse survivor does permit women to express a broad range of sexual imagery and rebellious impulses, their "redemption" requires the recovery of a childhood sexual abuse scene. There is little recognition of sexuality as an area of inhibition or conflict for women, short of overt sexual abuse, nor is their recognition of alternative interpretations of ambiguous sexual imagery.

In the clinical portraits of sexual abuse in the works of Baldwin and Herman, these same problems prevail. "Remembering trauma" and "refusing to forget" are vital to understanding the persisting impact of history and how what has happened in the past continues to affect the present. Just as psychic trauma reduces the space available for fantasy or mental play, trauma testimonials evoke—and rightfully so—a sense of profound, unspeakable suffering. Yet trauma testimonials may be employed for various motives, some of which enlarge human understanding and some of which restrict awareness of how social influences operate in the telling of an emotionally compelling story.

In approaching the trauma testimonial literature as feminist mythology, I am not reducing it to "untruth" but, rather, attempting to understand the basis of its inspirational value for women as well as its constraints, particularly as it reduces the range of stories and interpretations available to women in fighting for social recognition. The next chapter moves further into the labyrinth of clinical remembering, venturing into the world of multiple personality disorder and mapping out the various competing claims surrounding this mesmerizing female condition.

Chapter 9

SPEAKING IN TONGUES

Multiplicity and Psychiatric Influence

ONE OF MY EARLIEST encounters with altered personality states occurred when I visited a Pentecostal church with my aunt and uncle while on a summer visit. I had, the prior evening, furtively learned to shave my legs, guided by my coconspirator and cousin Lois, who was, at thirteen, a year ahead of me. The next morning, as I rubbed my smooth legs together while we drove on the bumpy country road to the Assembly of God church, the fear of discovery—and the hellfire and brimstone regularly dispensed by my godly uncle—was alloyed with a peculiar sense of pleasure. My smooth legs were my talisman as I, along with my many cousins, marched compliantly up the steps to the dreaded holy sanctuary.

Once inside, my stern elder kin slowly transformed themselves. They entered what we might today call a trance, or dissociated state, and in rhythmic concert with the writhing movements of the congregation cried out in otherworldly voices. The frightening power of the experience—the sheer emotionality and bodily spirituality of the drama—felt transgressive, mesmerizing, in spite of its roots in my own Christian revivalist upbringing. My parents viewed such ecstatic displays warily, with the ambivalence of believers with one foot in religion's id and the other in its superego. Giving oneself over too fully to the spiritual domain, it seemed, threatened the tenuous but necessary balance between the otherworldliness of emotional surrender and the this-worldliness of emotional control. Pentecostals, I came to learn, were backward primitives in the eyes of those evangelicals who sought a more modern, less "bodily" articulated faith. While the Son evoked the humility of fleshly suffering for Pentecostals, the Holy

Ghost—that mysterious third godhead—carried believers into a state of triumphant rapture. Speaking in tongues, being filled with the Spirit, made the divine seem palpably real, viscerally immediate, yet dangerously awesome.

A similar kind of phenomenon—a secular form of glossolalia—rose like a flood tide in clinical settings in the 1980s, as growing numbers of therapists found themselves captured by the dramatic display of multiple personality disorder (MPD), which reemerged from the annals of psychiatric history, like a ghost from the past. It captured the imagination of a new generation of therapists, schooled in trauma theory and post-Freudian correctives. If Freud's error was in not listening sensitively enough to his hysterical patients, his modern heirs listened with acute sensitivity to the noises in the darkness of the unconscious, determined to atone for Freud's deafness.

In striving for a new mode of listening, clinicians in the MPD field have reworked psychiatric understandings of female mental disorders. While there are scattered examples of male MPD in the literature, 90 percent of patients diagnosed as multiples have been women.[1] This gender dynamic is rarely explored in depth, even though it is one of the most striking, historically stable features of the disorder. Unlike other disorders associated with women historically, such as hysteria and borderline personality disorder, MPD has acquired a heroic meaning and a kind of exquisite dignity. Many contemporary theorists describe the capacity to dissociate—the high hypnotizability that is characteristic of MPD patients—as a "gift."[2] Specialists in the field often link dissociative predispositions to intelligence and creativity, an association that has its roots in the thinking of nineteenth-century theorists of multiple personality and hysteria such as Binet, James, and Breuer.[3] (Also, see chapter 7.)

Therapists are often captured by the dramatic imaginativeness of these patients, which is expressed in the creation of a complex cast of characters, or alters. Psychoanalyst George Ganaway notes that alters may take the form of children, adolescents, or adults of either sex. They also may be "demons, angels, sages, lobsters, chickens, tigers, a gorilla, a unicorn, and 'God,' to name a few," and that "inscapes in which they exist have ranged from labyrinthine tunnels and mazes to castles in enchanted forests, high-rise office buildings, and even a separate galaxy."[4]

This chapter explores the MPD movement and the cast of characters involved in the creation of this predominantly female disorder. A number of issues are taken up that span the clinical and cultural dimensions of the phenomenon. The first question is whether the disorder is "real." If we accept the diagnostic criteria currently available in *The Diagnostic and Statistical Manual of Mental Disorders (DSM)*, it is quite evident that many contemporary women do suffer from a scientifically recognized disorder—a "real" condition—since they meet the criteria.[5] But this narrow approach to the question of clinical validity misses the complex interplay of presenting symptoms and clinical and social factors mediating their expression. A second question concerns etiology, in this case widely held beliefs that child sexual abuse, particularly incest, leads to multiplicity. One may accept the disorder as a legitimate clinical entity without endorsing the prevailing explanation of causality in the MPD literature. A third and related question concerns the iatrogenic aspects of the disorder—that is, whether clinicians inadvertently contribute to the conditions they purport to treat. MPD may be a special case of iatrogenic illness, but it also may be no different from myriad other disorders in this regard. A fourth issue centers on the meaning of MPD as a social identity for women and on the question of why so many women in the 1980s embraced this particular explanation for their suffering. Here, the problem of whether the disorder is "real" takes us beyond clinical or scientific criteria and into the social symbolic loading of multiplicity and its meaning as a female "idiom of distress."[6] A fifth and final question involves the fascination MPD held for vast numbers of clinicians in the 1980s. At that time the most inflated estimates of the incidence of this disorder placed it at only 5 percent of clinical populations, raising the puzzling question of why it came to capture the psychiatric "gaze" during this era.[7]

THE CONTEMPORARY MPD MOVEMENT

After a flurry of intense psychiatric interest in "double personality" at the turn of the century, MPD lapsed into obscurity until its robust revival in the 1980s. Indeed, a mere hundred or so of the tens of thousands of documented cases were diagnosed prior to 1980, when MPD was transferred from the category of hysterical neuroses—where it was listed as a subtype thought to be extremely rare—to the newly expanded cluster of dissociative disorders.[8] This migration of MPD across categories was no mere recataloging. It was part of a broad movement to shed the cultural baggage of hysteria, specifically its sexist associations with female emotional "excess" and fantasy-proneness, and to extend the clinical applications of the trauma/dissociation model. (See chapter 3.)

While clinicians in the MPD field are divided on many issues, there is near-universal agreement that this condition is a dissociative reaction to childhood trauma. In the flurry of turn-of-the-century cases, this trauma could be of varying degrees and forms, typically involving early death or loss. Severity of trauma is thought to be a key factor in the etiology of MPD, and early losses or deaths in the family, as well as physical abuse and neglect, continue to be mentioned. But, as leading MPD theorist Richard Kluft puts it, "MPD is primarily a disorder of sexually abused women; in this atmosphere, its recognition has soared."[9]

Multiplicity is most often described as a pathological elaboration of normal dissociation—the mind's capacity for altered states of consciousness and for parallel processing of information.[10] Dissociation theorists argue that in response to severe childhood trauma, and particularly sexual abuse, some children come to rely on dissociative mechanisms to defend against the emotional pain. Pretending she is someone else, assuming the position of an outside observer, or simply spacing out, the victim of childhood sexual assault develops whole systems of identity that operate independently of one another. The child creates a separate persona, coexisting with the original personality, with this second self taking on the emotional task of managing knowledge of the traumatic experience. As repeated trauma occur, further splits in consciousness may develop, as new "alter" selves or personalities are formed. These balkanized states within carry on a secret life. While the dominant, conscious personality, in the majority of patients, is not aware of the alter or alters, these others within the self are often described as inner observers or "inner helpers," assisting the host personality by assuming control during times of emotional distress. Other alters are destructive, rebellious, or defiant, carrying on a guerrilla warfare with the host personality or with the more compliant alters.

Within the MPD movement, the battle for professional legitimacy rests on establishing clear criteria within the procedural rules of medical science. First, conventional clinical indicators must be established to wrest the category from its moorings in spiritualism—that atmosphere of parapsychological mysticism that surrounded late-nineteenth-century inquiry into hypnosis and "double personality." (See chapter 6.) Second, the condition must be separable from related disorders. Without this second criterion—that of differential diagnosis—clinical judgment becomes a situation where "all cows are black in the night sky." Frank Putnam, a leader in the MPD field, led the movement to tighten criteria in the 1994 revision of the *DSM* as a means of dealing with professional skepticism.[11] Given the crusade mentality that has enveloped MPD loyalists, this assertion of scientific objectivity is a necessary strategy.

The clinical validity of this dramatic, mutating condition rests on establishing the presence of an amnesic barrier between at least two of the personalities. While the importance of amnesia as a diagnostic criterion has been the subject of ongoing, intense debates in the MPD field, most of the leading writers agree that amnesia convincingly separates the "true" MPD cases from their various look-alikes. Amnesia includes both periods of lost time—of blackouts or fugue states—and failure to remember the presence of alter personalities. In the clinical cases reported, the host personality is typically unaware of all the alters, particularly at the onset of treatment, whereas the alters may exhibit co-conscious properties. The therapist, more often than the patient, is the one who first discovers these latent, parasitic agencies within and who facilitates their entry onto the stage of consciousness. At the time of diagnosis, two to three personalities are generally discovered. Over the course of treatment, an average of thirteen to seventeen alters are identified, although many cases report over a hundred.[12]

Skeptics argue that psychogenic amnesia does not generally take the form of whole personality constellations. Although traumatogenic events may be forgotten, this amnesia is likely to be ephemeral and specific to details of events rather than to entire domains of experience. Further, critics argue that it is an enormous leap from the specific effects of psychogenic amnesia and fugue states to the elaboration of entire systems of personalities, with their corresponding memories, identities (specific sexes, races, and ages), modes of relating, and unique physiological responses.[13]

In shedding the aura of the paranormal surrounding MPD phenomena, a number of theorists strive for a middle ground. Ernest Hilgard, whose research on the hidden-observer effect provided the MPD field with one of its more scientifically compelling metaphors, cautions against facile overgeneralizations. Much like the automatic handwriting experiments of the late nineteenth century, research on the hidden observer revealed a capacity among some subjects for dissociated mental activity. In experimental studies, Hilgard points out, the hidden observers' memories are matter-of-fact and time-bound, unlike the emotionally charged, historically remote characters and memories recovered in treatment with multiples. While Hilgard tends to accept the clinical validity of MPD—those "unstable personality structures that result from unintegrated childhood identifications"— he calls for additional careful research bridging clinical and experimental phenomena.[14] In a similar vein, Phillip Coons, one of the more cautious proponents of MPD treatment, suggests that "it is a mistake to consider each personality totally separate, whole or autonomous. The other personalities might best be described as personality states, other selves, or personality fragments."[15]

Yet the implications of these murky distinctions for treatment are anything but clear. MPD therapy focuses on ferreting out hidden alters and "mapping" their various names, ages, trauma memories, and relationships with one another. In this mix of genealogy and sociogram, the distinction between personality fragments and alter personalities may be elusive indeed. This problem is compounded by the assumption, widely held in the field, that most alters are masters at camouflage, requiring intensive efforts on the part of clinicians in exposing them.

Clinical Critiques

According to Ganaway, a dissident within the dissociative disorders field with respect to MPD, the various alters that emerge in full-blown multiplicity are a clinically induced reification of conflicting self-states. Women diagnosed as multiples do lack a cohesive, stable sense of self, he asserts, and they readily respond to the intense emotional engagement of therapists who become captured by their fluctuating mental states. From a psychoanalytic perspective, alter personalities may be understood as "alien introjects," or part-object representations, which have not been integrated into a stable psychological structure.[16]

In understanding clinically this proliferation of unstable mental states and flights of imagery, psychoanalytic therapists such as Ganaway stress the importance of helping the patient "hold" fluctuating states of mind. If the therapist becomes engrossed in ferreting out the origins of one particular thread of consciousness, Ganaway cautions, the patient's sense of a stable, holding, therapeutic environment may collapse. In assigning names to fluctuating states and conducting conversations with them, therapists make the existence of separate personalities increasingly real to the patient.

In its retreat from the mystical aura surrounding dissociative disorders, Ganaway's theoretical turn does provide a more conventional psychological explanation. But his analysis fails to explain the narrative content and communicative meaning of multiplicity within either the therapeutic encounter or the broader culture. While he rejects the near-universal assertion in the MPD literature that incest or early sexual abuse is the primary cause of severe dissociative disorders, Ganaway also leaves unexamined the recurring appearance of memories of sexual abuse in MPD narratives.

Like my Christian parents, who sought to distance themselves from the "wild" emotional roots of their own religious tradition, many contemporary therapists find the MPD movement an acute embarrassment. Critics argue that the various personalities—the coordinated systems of thought, behavior, and personal characteristics that lack co-consciousness—are not caused by childhood trauma, as many MPD adherents assert, but rather are the result of the hypnotic or quasi-hypnotic procedures commonly used to diagnose the condition. As evidence, these critics point out that MPD usually develops over many years of contact with mental health professionals, particularly those trained in the diagnostic procedures, hypnotic techniques, and intense personal sense of mission characteristic of MPD specialists.[17]

While defenders of the diagnosis claim that hypnotic susceptibility and dissociative symptoms can be an indication of an underlying dissociative identity disorder (or DID, the term for MPD introduced in 1994), skeptics counter that these same symptoms make some patients vulnerable to therapeutic suggestion. Therapists, as the argument continues, find what they seek. And the engrossing commitment to ferreting out various hidden personalities finds its match in the compliance to authority so characteristic of highly hypnotizable women patients. Put more bluntly, hysterics are good mimics and lack a secure enough sense of self to counter the influence of evangelical therapists.

Cultural Critiques

The resurrection of multiplicity from its turn-of-the-century grave was achieved, according to Hacking, primarily through the anima of the contemporary child abuse movement.[18] Hacking argues that throughout its labile history, the condition of multiplicity has always required a cultural "host." In other words, it emerges through a dominant societal concern. In the nineteenth century, that host was cultural anxiety over the incursions of science into the religious realm; in the late twentieth century, it was cultural concern over child sexual abuse.

Hacking's notion of multiplicity in search of a host anthropomorphizes multiplicity, however, in implying that it stands ready and waiting in the wings of the cultural stage, emerging at opportune moments. We may want to reverse Hacking's formulation, while retaining his insight, by exploring how the suffering of women often requires a "host" for its entry into public consciousness. In this context, MPD may be understood as a predominantly female enactment of distress, one which, like mediumship in the late nineteenth century, simultaneously expresses and mystifies the sources of female misery.[19]

The idea of latent subpersonalities within the female psyche took hold within psychiatry during the late nineteenth century because female identity was in a state of crisis, much as it is today. One of the most deeply rooted divisions in cultural consciousness centers on the Madonna/whore dichotomy—

irreconcilable images of maternal purity and sexual defilement. Throughout the history of multiplicity, a dominant "good-girl" personality—chaste, inhibited, and moralistic—contends with a subsidiary "bad-girl" personality, sexually adventurous and intent on destroying her timid "host" and on wreaking havoc on the host's domesticated world.[20] In the contemporary period, this female "double personality" has proliferated into a phenomenal array of alters. Most women experience such conflicts and disjunctures in their phenomenological world without recourse to multiplicity, even though the gulf between good girl/bad girl self-representations, as previous chapters have illustrated, is a predominate theme in women's narratives. In the classical understanding of neurotic conditions, such as hysteria, the anguished divisions between various self and self-other representations emerge as a source of conflict and anxiety, although the self retains a basic psychological coherence and stability over time.

We may wonder whether symptoms of multiplicity develop as a condition of women when rebellious currents within the female self contend in some new way with the social or cultural terrain. The multiple "selves" and "ego states" that are described in the literature on dissociation may express not only the dilemmas of identity but also a historically emergent set of female possibilities for identity. In the contemporary period, there is an awakening of the feminine imagination, a refusal to be silenced, but these assertions of self remain a chaotic, unrealized potential for many women. Like late-nineteenth-century hysterics and double personalities, the modern multiple registers unrealized potential in the realm of the imaginary. A cast of characters is created: alters at one end of the dissociative continuum and various ego states at the other. Multiplicity may very well describe this state of emotional and imagistic flooding, this groundless place between the refusal of old constraints and the discovery of new possibilities for self-representations.

The discussion of dissociation and trauma in previous chapters focused on problems that have emerged historically in disengaging female emotional suffering from the psychiatric legacy of hysteria. Defending the legitimacy of women's complaints—that is, taking women seriously—required a strategy for confronting the cultural readiness to view women as fantasy-prone and emotionally unstable. The trauma disorders, such as posttraumatic stress disorder (PTSD), provided a psychiatric language for making claims concerning the mental damage suffered by women while retaining emphasis on women's essential rationality. Since women, historically, have served as psychological receptacles for disavowed male anxieties and have been vulnerable to various intrusions and violations, models that permit the "reprojection" of disturbing conflict back onto the oppressor seem to serve a recuperative function. Yet, as I have previously argued, the trauma/dissociation model overexternalizes conflict, stripping women of psychological complexity.

Within this trauma/dissociation framework, why did MPD emerge, even displacing interest in PTSD as the riveting diagnosis of the 1980s? One factor may

be the historical emergence of PTSD out of the Vietnam veterans' rights movement.[21] PTSD, for the most part, was thought to be a reaction to the immediate
aftermath of trauma, particularly combat. Further, the gender-neutral language
of PTSD failed to convey the phenomenology and particularity of female suffering
within the family.[22]

THE MOTHER OF ALL MULTIPLES

In the contemporary MPD movement, Cornelia Wilbur, a
psychiatrist and psychoanalyst, is recognized as having been the leading
theorist in the immediate postwar period.[23] Along with Richard Kluft, Bennett
Braun, Ralph Allison, and others, Wilbur promoted interest in MPD through an
"oral tradition" within psychiatry.[24] While these psychiatrists presented workshops at American Psychiatric Association meetings, their work was marginal
to the field until interest in dissociation and multiplicity reached a fever pitch
in the 1980s.

The case of Sybil, the basis of a book published in 1973 and a film released
in 1976, also initiated a new genre of psychiatric docudrama—books collabo-
ratively written or jointly authored by women patients and their therapists.
Sybil—the book and the film—was significant in bridging clinical discourse and
popular culture and in granting women patients a historically unprecedented
role in co-narrating the clinical encounter. By the late 1980s, this genre—including titles such as *When Rabbit Howls, The Flock,* and *The Magic Daughter*—had
displaced the prior female genre of codependence literature on many bookstore
shelves throughout the country.

Sybil as Cultural Text

Wilbur treated Sybil over an eleven-year period—from 1954 to
1965—and invited Flora Schreiber, a professional writer, to chronicle the development of the treatment. However, Schreiber wanted to be assured of a cure. She
took on the Sybil case in 1962 after being told by Wilbur that a happy ending
was in sight. Such an ending placed the case within the tradition of American
success stories, stories of overcoming unhappiness—stories, in other words, with
a large market potential. Like Wilbur, Schreiber became intimately involved in
Sybil's life, and the three of them remained close friends as the preparation of
the book followed the completion of treatment.

Sybil charts the troubled waters of a female identity in flux, both expanding
and uncertain.[25] Unlike the 1950s case portrayed in *The Three Faces of Eve,*[26] Sybil
displayed a plethora of alters—seventeen by the end of treatment—a trend that
accelerated into the dizzying cast of alters that became commonplace by the 1980s.
The historical significance of the case at the time was that she was "the only
multiple personality to have crossed the borders of sexual difference to develop
personalities of the opposite sex" (291). Since *Sybil*, male alters have become
commonplace. The case also is considered significant because it raised public

awareness of early child abuse, particularly of sexual abuse. Unlike the many cases of sexual abuse that emerged in the clinical literature in the decades to follow, where the perpetrator was typically a father figure, Sybil was presented as the victim of a sexually sadistic, psychotic mother.

The case of Sybil and Wilbur was of historical significance for other reasons as well. As an explicitly feminine narrative, the case of Sybil represents a modern mother/daughter clinical dialogue that grew out of the transformative events of the postwar era. Sybil's own dissociative episodes unfold like an epoch saga of U.S. history. An identity forged in the confining security of a small town is shattered as the Great Depression and World War II mark Sybil's passage to the cosmopolitan world of New York City. The book opens with "flashbacks" to the summer of 1945, during Sybil's adolescence, with her quiet "war of nerves"—an inexplicable nervousness—festering as silent, feminine counterpart to the cataclysmic events being played out on the world stage.

While much of the history that emerges in the course of treatment is undoubtedly based on actual events in Sybil's life, it is still important to recognize what was at stake for Wilbur in unearthing traumatic memory. It is not a matter of whether Sybil was telling the truth about the past. Understanding the new history Sybil found—the clinically recovered trauma memories and various alter personalities—requires that we consider the powerful context in which this clinical subject came to life.

The Presenting Picture

As Sybil crosses the threshold into adulthood, she becomes entranced by trains, by their power to carry her away. At twenty-two years of age, when she enters treatment with Wilbur, she is unable to emotionally separate from what she experiences as the suffocating control of her mother. Unlike the hysterics and multiples at the turn of the century, whose symptoms commonly included paralysis, Sybil catches glimmers of freedom on the horizon and frequently finds herself lost in strange places. She is a woman of the night, finding herself in seedy hotels, without place or identity.

Wilbur became increasingly obsessed with her mysterious patient, a condition among therapists that has become as much a standard feature of MPD as have the patients' amnesic states. For Wilbur, this absorbing preoccupation was tied to the power of a pioneering discovery. Beyond the intrigue associated with fugue states, which made these cases akin to a good detective story, the postwar era was enthralled with the general possibility of medical "breakthroughs" through the redemptive power of science.

Sybil's problems initially took the form of a lack of interest in sex or marriage—a clear sign of "feminine maladjustment"—and difficulties in fulfilling her considerable intellectual promise. The trouble centered on inexplicable fits of rage. In a chemistry class at Columbia University, Sybil had abruptly smashed some glassware during what we later learn to be one of her frequent fugue states. Something is clearly wrong. We have learned in the book's introduction, however, that Sybil's madness is not schizophrenia—that dreaded disorder that overtakes its victims early in adulthood. We are informed that Sybil is possessed with "grand hysteria"—a condition that has a long history as a mysterious disturbance of women.

Postwar Psychiatry

Wilbur's formulation of this case unfolds during a time when the psychiatric understanding and treatment of schizophrenia were undergoing revolutionary change. With the development of the major tranquilizers in the 1950s, schizophrenia no longer meant an inevitable downward spiral into mental deterioration and institutionalization. But this same chemical breakthrough transformed treatment regimes governing mental illness. While psychoanalysis had long been recognized as more suitable for neurotics than for psychotics, many therapists believed that early trauma caused conditions such as schizophrenia and that psychoanalytic techniques could be effectively used. The work of Frieda Fromm Reichmann—the psychoanalyst who treated the young schizophrenic woman in *I Never Promised You a Rose Garden*—illustrated this pioneering tradition, which came to a close in the wake of the pharmaceutical revolution.[27]

Within this context of transformations within psychiatry, specifically the shift toward drug management of the mentally ill, the Sybil case becomes a new chapter—a kind of apocrypha—in postwar psychiatry. Wilbur is staking new ground within the lost terrain of psychiatry, and this venture requires that she establish the essential differences between grand hysteria and its ominous lookalike, schizophrenia. Just as Freud minimized the extent of illness among his early patients in advancing the effectiveness of the "talking cure," Wilbur continued to insist that Sybil was "not crazy" even as her condition steadily worsened.

A seemingly devoted and caring therapist, Wilbur was also driven by her own determination to cure Sybil through excavating trauma memories. Unlike a schizophrenic, whose loss of contact with reality and tortured hallucinatory visions compromise the capacity to speak coherently about the past, Sybil, Wilbur believed, had symptoms that were a rational response to an irrational situation. The essential wisdom and sanity of the patient's mental strategy for survival separated her from the psychotic. And this diagnosis required the establishment of a corollary set of early experiences that would logically explain and provide sufficient cause for the severe, debilitating symptoms that plagued her young patient in the present.

In the postwar period, the movement within psychoanalysis toward object relations theory—with its emphasis on early attachments and the tie to the mother—replaced the father-oriented, Freudian emphasis on sexual and aggressive drives. (See chapter 3.) The seed of later pathology was not to be found in the child's nature but rather in early nurture. While this new environmentalism in psychology broke from the older, more conservative idea that traits were hereditary, it did have its downside in that the pathogenic environment was near-exclusively defined in terms of bad mothering. In explaining the hidden cruelty in Sybil's life, Schreiber cites an essay from *Parents* magazine entitled "Can a

Loving Mother Be Dangerous?" The problem, according to the article, was in the mother's ambivalence. Schreiber notes that "this consistently inconsistent love is dangerous to the trusting child" (372).

Female Autonomy

Breakthrough discoveries often involve heightening, even grossly exaggerating, distinctions between the old findings and the new ones. For Wilbur, the secondary personalities of earlier multiples in psychiatric history "exhibited very little independence in voluntarily moving about in a social world—working, acting, and playing. Clearly, this was not true of Sybil. Her alternating personalities were obviously autonomous" (109). This theme of feminine autonomy was important in several respects. First, the emphasis on the autonomy of the personalities countered the conventional psychiatric view that MPD is merely a hysterical elaboration of different sides of the self; women who are in a state of role conflict or who are caught between the demands of a strict upbringing and rebellious impulses may enact the conflict through alternating states of mind. In MPD, the amnesia or partial amnesia of at least one personality or alter in regard to the others is clinically central. But Wilbur's own engrossing engagement in the drama may have contributed to the patient's experience of distinctive states. Like Morton Prince, whose pioneering work on multiplicity made psychiatric history during the early years of the century,[28] Wilbur engaged in dialogue with various alters, treating them as though they were separate persons within the patient.[29]

Second, Wilbur's claim of autonomous personalities worked to counter the inevitable suspicion that therapy may have induced these dissociative states. The question of therapeutic influence, looming on the horizon since MPD's psychiatric birth in the late nineteenth century, has always been threatening to the profession because it undermines the ideal of scientific objectivity that is assumed to be foundational in any applied science. But if the alter personalities are understood to resist discovery, Wilbur could feel reassured that they were discovered rather than created. Indeed, the MPD literature tends to stress the alters' resistance to manifesting themselves. It is as though both patient and therapist are drawn, unwillingly, into a drama whose magnitude overtakes them with the force of a tidal wave.

A third aspect to this claim of autonomous personalities is once again related to the cultural and historical contours of MPD. The postwar multiples are, like so many of their contemporary female therapists, struggling to achieve a level of independence that had not been conceivable during earlier eras. Wilbur failed to recognize that she, as a woman in battle with her own profession, might be midwife to the autonomous, glorious selves that occupied her prized patient. While the turn-of-the-century raft of cases may have similarly followed in the wake of profound cultural changes, including the emergence of new claims for women's rights, the post–World War II era signaled a turning point, accompanied by large-scale anxieties, on the one hand, and rising expectations on the other.

The Prototypical Postwar Daughter and the New Mother

Child of rural parents and a bitterly unhappy mother, Sybil moves to the city in search of a more promising life. She rejects marriage and family and is unable to separate from the inexorable pull of her strict religious upbringing. The "independence" of the various alters—their assertions of will and rebellious actions—stands in stark contrast to the dependence of the cowering Sybil, who fails to recognize her own strivings in this otherness within her. Wilbur did have a keen sensitivity to the profound influence of social constraints on women's lives and aligned herself with those "personalities" within Sybil fighting for freedom. A thoroughly modern woman and New York analyst, Wilbur was engaged in a crusade against the parochial, fundamentalist Christian upbringing of her tortured patient. In 1957, she offered Sybil a dual freedom: "I want you to be free not only of your mother and your ambivalent feelings about your father but also of the religious conflicts and distortions that divide you."[30]

Sybil—this postwar daughter full of creativity, intelligence, and ambition—was in need of a new mother. And here, too, one may speculate that this powerful New Mother drew some of her majestic power from the disintegration of the Old Mother. In other words, the idealization of this female therapeutic relationship is achieved through the deidealization and devaluation of the original mother/daughter tie. The trauma scenes that unfold over the eleven years of treatment become increasingly graphic and horrific, shifting from conventional losses—the death of a beloved grandmother, the emotional breakdown and withdrawal of a psychotic mother, the rigidity of a strict religious family—to chilling scenes of sadistic torture. With the unwavering belief that her patient will get well only if the original trauma is excavated and released, Wilbur presses for the pernicious source of her patient's deteriorating condition. Strikingly absent in *Sybil,* as well as in Wilbur's own published accounts, is any reflection on the pitfalls of this aggressive search for trauma memory.

As a rebel against the orthodox practices of psychoanalysis—particularly against the practice of maintaining emotional distance, or "abstinence," from patients—Wilbur becomes the apotheosis of the "good mother." She purchases clothing for Sybil, and they go on long drives together in the country. They even live together for a period of time. By the close of *Sybil,* we learn that, after treatment ended, Wilbur loaned Sybil money for a down payment on a house and that they continued to spend intimate time together.

The *Sybil* narrative reveals an eery parallel between the sadomasochistic memories of childhood torture and the ritualized encounters of therapy itself. Wilbur moves from conventional therapeutic listening to hypnosis and then to the use of sodium pentothal as she becomes increasingly worried about the worsening condition of her patient. Wilbur comes to Sybil's apartment regularly to administer pentothal intravenously. Even though she previously emphasized the value of "straight psychoanalysis" for Sybil, Wilbur reasons that her patient's deteriorating mental health requires more aggressive methods (355).

Although "pentothal brought to the surface the deeply buried, debilitating hatred of her mother," Sybil also became highly addicted to the treatment. The drug provided a euphoric release from the unending nightmare that had become Sybil's wakening state of mind. But Wilbur's frequent visits to her apartment also "brought additional comfort" (357). "Feeling more alive, more interested, Sybil redecorated the apartment, made it more attractive for her doctor-guest. The jab in the vein, the occasional inability to find a new vein after months had passed and so many veins had been pressed into service, the not-infrequent swelling of the injected part of the anatomy, the feeling of chill that sometimes ran through the patient . . . none of it mattered, however, in the light of the bright new day sodium pentothal had brought" (357).

These treatments may have been associated, for Sybil, with a regressive return to the womb of the "good mother." But, conversely, these treatments seemed to have the character of a sadistic, sexual encounter. Just as the memories of being essentially raped by her mother with an enema bag included the rationalization that "this is for your own good," the intravenous administration of pentothal was similarly justified as "for your own good." The memories of early sexual torture at the hands of her mother may have been stimulated by the introduction of hypnosis and, later, pentothal and may have symbolically communicated distress over the invasiveness of the treatment itself.

Transformative Remembering

As new personalities and trauma memories emerge, the material becomes increasingly sadistic and sexual, and this trajectory has its parallel in the movement of therapy. Sybil produces new memories of her mother that feature "horsey games" involving mutual masturbation with young girls in the woods outside her hometown. "Finger moving. Palms stroking. Bodies gyrating. Ecstatic expressions. Everybody seemed to be holding somebody. Her mother was holding Hilda. Her mother's hands were at Hilda's crotch" (207).

This pornographic material involving "secret rituals," sexual games, and "atrocities" foreshadows the satanic ritual abuse theme that emerged in the trauma stories of multiples in the 1980s. (See chapter 10.) And it also signifies a continuing blindness to how the therapeutic relationship casts its own indelible shadow on the past that is recovered. The talk of "secret rituals" of childhood finds a peculiar echo in the search-and-seizure rituals of treatment itself. The scenes that emerge during these therapy sessions are unspeakably chilling. And we have no way of knowing the degree to which they represent fact or fantasy. Making sense of this material, however, does require that we attend to how it was obtained.

Wilbur acknowledges the need for a dramatic breakthrough in the case. And we can only imagine her anxiety as she fails, for many years, to find the path that she has, with steadfast confidence, assured her patient will lead ultimately out of the wilderness to the promised land. Wilbur's fixation on finding the "taproot" of Sybil's dissociations blinds her to her own demand for a performance. At one point Sybil confronts Wilbur. "I came to New York with five thousand dollars in savings. Three thousand have been spent on paying for the analysis and buying a few extras" (349). After Wilbur ends the pentothal treatment because of the worry over addiction, Sybil charges that "you want me to dissociate. If I didn't, you'd miss seeing Vicky [one of her alters] and all those other people you're so fond of" (363). While Wilbur encourages Sybil to express her rage against her mother freely, this freedom does not extend to raging against Wilbur herself. Wilbur chastises Sybil for her drug dependence, failing to acknowledge that it was she, the therapist, who had convinced the patient to pursue these treatments.

It is inescapably ironic that Joanne Woodward, who played the role of the patient in *Three Faces of Eve*, released in 1957, is cast as Wilbur in the film version of *Sybil*, the next generation's multiple story. Woodward's Dr. Wilbur has cast off the traditional restraints of the dowdy Eve White, emerging in resplendent powers as a modern maternal authority. In one final scene, Wilbur and Sybil, played by Sally Fields, are picnicking in a bucolic setting. While birds chirp joyously in the background, Sybil reveals the deeply buried trauma memory that has imprisoned her since childhood. The scene begins with Wilbur and Sybil sitting at the base of a forked tree shaped like massive, open legs. The imagery strongly evokes childbirth, with Wilbur holding the daughter she has given psychological birth to and Sybil expelling, like afterbirth, the final memory of her traumatizing mother.

The entire *mise en scène* may be understood as a cultural fantasy—a collective, female fantasy—of the New Mother and the New Daughter, the wish for unity free of the pain of conflict or disappointment. In representing this fantasy of a relatively whole, intact, maternal other, *Sybil* hypnotizes us, suspending critical awareness of the defensive side of such fantasies. While many women do struggle to work their way through the effects of destructive mothers, *Sybil*, like much of the trauma discourse, disavows both the daughter's own aggression toward the mother and the possibility of unholy alliances among women in overthrowing pernicious legacies.

THE CRISIS OF THE THERAPEUTIC

Until her death in 1992, Wilbur continued her work as champion of the MPD cause and as mother of the movement.[31] Professional journals routinely rejected her manuscripts, although she held a position at the medical school in Lexington, Kentucky. While the MPD "interest group" was marginal to mainstream psychiatry throughout the 1970s, by the mid-1980s it had made significant incursions into the professional ranks; it boasted a new journal, a professional organization, and a host of training seminars. With these advancements and the "upgrading" of MPD in the 1980 edition of the *DSM*, MPD specialists clearly emerged as a force with which to be reckoned.

In a sense, MPD emerged as the alter of psychiatry, its romantic soul, returning from its turn-of-the-century grave to awaken and haunt a profession that was in a state of crisis. For unlike other of the diagnostic categories that have proliferated over the past few decades, MPD—as the glorious blossom of the trauma tree—resists normal psychiatric intervention. Indeed, the *DSM* symptom profile has an unusual criterion. "The patient has long been diagnosed with many other psychiatric disorders. The average number of years a multiple [spends] in the mental health system prior to diagnosis is almost seven."[32] The MPD patient, in other words, is a kind of feminine Munchausen (that other psychiatric wanderer in search of a cure). Her journey tells an embarrassing story of the therapeutic employment of various diagnoses and treatments while the patient's condition worsens. Indeed, part of the folk wisdom of MPD speaks to an acquired knowledge of psychiatric stigmatization. "Never tell the hospital you hear voices; otherwise they'll say you are schizophrenic. If you must talk about voices, make clear they are *inside* your head!"[33]

In reaction to contemporary psychiatry's focus on symptom management and behavioral control, MPD specialists assert the communicative meaning of psychic disturbances. Psychoanalytic clinicians most certainly would agree, as I argued in chapter 3, that symptoms tell an unconscious story and that the clinical project is one of deciphering disguised communications within the configuration of symptoms. But there is a mystical aura surrounding MPD, with its dramatic appearances and disappearances of latent selves, which only "highly sensitive" experts are able to decipher. Psychologist Ray Aldridge-Morris, a passionate critic of MPD, attempts to recuperate an old category—the grand hysteria initially employed by Wilbur, a term he translates into the more banal "psychotic hysteria."[34] While he makes a compelling case that the MPD field obfuscates ordinary aspects of mental illness through its exalted categories, we may also wonder what is at stake in Aldridge-Morris's renaming of MPD. The dissociative disorders field had tried to accomplish a domestication of multiplicity by renaming it dissociative identity disorder (DID) in the 1994 edition of the *DSM*. MPD is still the preferred term for many, including myself, perhaps because it preserves the populist roots of this unruly female condition.

Behind debates over renaming, we often find countervailing ways of looking at the world. In this case, we may wonder about the implications of viewing alters as hallucinations, delusions, metaphors, or part-object representations. In contrast, we also may wonder what is at stake in viewing them as autonomous agencies within, powerful and clever enough to break through the thresholds of consciousness at opportune moments. It is quite clear that many critics sense a theology at work in the autonomous-agent formulations, even in their secular, psychiatric vestments of trauma/dissociation theory. At the same time, neither the more conventional psychiatric viewpoint nor this more evangelical one seems quite adequate.

Just as Protestantism grew in part out of a deep crisis within the Catholic Church, the MPD movement is also partially a reaction to real problems in how psychiatry operates as a "normalizing" discipline—that is, as adjudicator of the boundary between normalcy and madness. One of these problems involves the increased bureaucratizing of diagnostic categories and mental health practices. Of the many hundreds of categories currently available, MPD has the glorious distinction of often parading as many other disorders. Bennett Braun, a leading writer in the MPD field, notes that "every diagnosis in the *Diagnostic and Statis-*

tical Manual of Mental Disorders (1980) has at one time or another been applied to MPD."[35] Even more elastic and chameleonlike than hysteria, MPD is described as being easily confused with manic depression, the schizophrenias, histrionic disorders, and various psychosomatic disorders and neurological conditions. While skeptics argue that MPD is "really" one of these other conditions, defenders assert that these other conditions are "really" MPD.

Without diluting the importance of differential diagnoses, we may recognize a curious agreement in these two positions concerning the refractoriness of MPD to normal psychiatric classification. In her fragmentation, the multiple encompasses the mutating state of psychiatric nosologies. Searching for unity out of the multiple's psychiatric heterogeneity may be fascinating for clinicians because she embodies the wandering soul of psychiatry itself.

In attempting to recuperate this "soul," MPD specialists also strive to reduce the emotional distance between healer and sufferer. The folklore of MPD includes the caveat that multiplicity cannot be readily diagnosed—it takes considerable time with the patient—and that it requires new standards of care. In the professional literature, there are also caveats concerning overinvolvement and excessive fascination with multiples. But Putnam and Kluft stress the importance of more frequent and longer sessions—for example, ninety minutes rather than the standard fifty.[36] It is true that patients often are diagnosed too quickly, particularly in institutional settings. Even in outpatient settings, evaluation, diagnosis, and prescription of medication often take less than an hour. Like attacks against the church's selling of indulgences during the Reformation, the MPD movement's attack on quickly dispensed diagnoses and treatments reverberates with deeper grievances. Central to these grievances is the sense among many therapists of diminished professional autonomy and of intensified pressure to produce symptom relief.

Uncoupling this severe dissociative condition from the legacy of schizophrenia and the psychoses is a means of reviving interest in madness, in recouping the ground lost to biological psychiatry, and of resisting pragmatic interventions that have as their principal aim the elimination of abnormal symptoms. Throughout the 1980s, inpatient units specializing in dissociative disorders sprang up throughout the country, based on the principle that medication was largely ineffective in the treatment of trauma-related conditions.[37] In resisting the tide of psychopharmaceutical control over the field, programs specializing in dissociative disorders relegitimized psychotherapeutic inquiry into madness.

REBELLIONS IN PSYCHIATRY

Multiplicity has displaced schizophrenia as the malady of social protest within the mental health field. The origins of the MPD movement can be traced to the radical psychiatry movement of the 1960s and 1970s, even though there are crucial differences in the two worldviews. More than a revolt against the medical model and scientific expertise, the radical psychiatry movement advanced a trenchant critique of society.[38] While often embracing the schizophrenic as a folk hero—as protester against conventionally constituted reality—this movement rarely lost sight of the fact that delusions and hallucinations were only loosely tied to consensual reality. It was a movement committed to humanistic reform of psychiatric institutions and to analysis of the social origins of madness, including those fostered by the helping professions.[39]

The MPD movement contains some of these same critical perspectives and romantic currents. The work of Chris Sizemore is illustrative of the contradictory elements of the MPD movement, including its roots in radical psychiatry.[40] In tracing the history of her own public education and advocacy work as a multiple, Sizemore tells a moving story of battling the establishment. The famous patient in Corbett Thigpen and Hervey Cleckley's *The Three Faces of Eve* (1957), popularized in the subsequent film, Sizemore went public in 1977 with *I'm Eve*. In this autobiography she contradicts many of the claims made by her psychiatrist, Thigpen, and his cowriter, expressing outrage over the course of her own treatment. In her more recent book, *A Mind of My Own*, published in 1989, understandings of multiplicity are filtered through the developments of the preceding decade. Sizemore claims nineteen additional personalities beyond the three identified by her psychiatrist. In *A Mind of My Own*, Sizemore also embraces paranormal explanations for her dissociative abilities, reframing multiplicity as a spiritual gift.

Noting the hysterical and self-aggrandizing character of these claims, her critics tend to overlook the insights and lucidity in Sizemore's autobiographical works.[41] Like many of the autobiographical accounts of multiplicity of the 1980s, Sizemore's story centers on aggressive, creative "selves" in perpetual combat with a predominating, inhibited, people-pleasing persona. Yet she frames her struggle to achieve an always fragile health and wholeness within the patients' rights movement.

In describing this movement, Sizemore observes that "some advocates called for an investigation of patients allegedly being over-medicated in psychiatric institutions." Further, she cites one former mental patient and advocate who calls for a broad analysis of the plight of the mentally ill. "The lack of adequate income is a serious problem for most mental patients. Not only are they poor before institutionalization, but the chances for improving their economic situation are greatly reduced by the discrimination (in employment, housing, etc.) they suffer once released."[42]

As a successful writer, artist, and consultant, Sizemore clearly has benefited from the release of multiplicity from the literal and figurative back wards of psychiatry. The stories of the chronically mentally ill are far less dramatic, less riveting in their daily struggles with reality, than are those of the more normal-appearing and lively multiple. Yet Sizemore's historical account links the fate of multiples to broad cultural dramas and reforms. Sizemore traces the trajectory of reform efforts to the defeats of the early 1980s, as President Ronald Reagan reversed many of the gains of the community mental health movement, slashing public funding for mental health services. In asserting her alliances with feminism, she notes that the defeat of the Equal Rights Amendment during this same period was demoralizing for women. Further, she recognizes in her own multiplicity a struggle over female identity and a rebellion against cultural constraints on women's self-expression.

If multiplicity has been a suitable "host" for the revival of the radical psychiatry movement, it also is a medium for broad social critiques. In recovering the insights of the radical psychiatry movement, James Glass, a clinical researcher at Sheppard Pratt Hospital outside Baltimore, employs MPD to advance his own indictment of modern life. In *Shattered Selves: Multiple Personality in a Postmodern World*, Glass draws on clinical accounts of multiplicity to argue against what he views as the emotional detachment of postmodernist theorizing.[43] In identifying parallels between postmodernism and the phenomenology of MPD—indeed, that the multiple could be understood as the archetypal postmodern subject— Glass goes on to argue that the suffering of the multiple vivifies the perils of downplaying the costs of "decentered" subjectivity. Whereas postmodernists play with fragmentation, multiples live it.

Unlike the postmodernists, who critique the very foundation of authority, Glass presents a highly valorized portrait of therapists. In their engaged, empathic capacities, therapists stand as polar opposite to emotionally detached postmodernists. "Postmodernism's dalliance with disconnection and chaos may be either trivial, a just plain false interpretation, or, more likely, dangerously irresponsible. To suggest that persons have no connection, no histories, no cohesive selves, is literally to throw the self into a psychologically contingent world."[44]

Glass describes the inner world of the multiple as an ungrounded place, where the constant switching of personalities forecloses possibilities for achieving any degree of certainty or coherence. Out of Glass's portrayals of the disorienting confusion of the multiple's inner world, however, emerges a quite definitively drawn father figure, the destroyer of the self's unity. Unlike the archetypal delusional patient described in Glass's previous book,[45] whose illness spoke of ambiguous origins, the archetypal multiple in *Shattered Selves* is notably sane and rational in her madness.

The recovery of trauma memories described by Glass, most of which center on sexual abuse, was part of an aggressive treatment instituted at Sheppard Pratt Hospital in 1987, with the arrival of Richard Lowenstein, an MPD expert.[46] The problematic implications of this change of the psychiatric guard remain outside the scope of Glass's moral lens, as he focuses on the apocalyptic revelations of the multiple.

> Is this evil not the father who habitually and traumatically abuses, both physically and sexually, his daughter? Is this not evil in its pure form, a man who acts as God within the confines of the regime of desire, who transgresses not only the primordial laws of incest but the very patriarchal power that creates the authority, the very canons of the civilization that gives his life its structure, meaning, and existence? . . .
> Father/phallocrat/God imposes himself as tyrant on the body of his child; her body and consciousness become his fiefdom; his

tyranny, his incest, is bound only by the limits of her flesh and the depth of her suffering. The psychological process of disconnection which follows—discrete personalities occupying the same body—is the direct consequence of his terrorizing.[47]

Clearly aligned with feminism and its resistance to patriarchal abuses, Glass rejects socially removed, "agnostic" theorizing, and he advances, instead, quite decisive convictions concerning the locus of the trouble. In his social explication of MPD, there is scant interest in the question of whether the diagnosis of MPD and its army of practitioners are themselves reactions to a modern disorientation—of anxiety-ridden efforts to anchor identity in a secure relationship to the past. Glass grasps the existential emptiness of some of postmodernism, while remaining seemingly oblivious to postmodern theory's quite valid critique of the costs of an excessive drive for certainty, including certainty within the professions.

Psychiatrist Donald Ross, also at Sheppard Pratt, offers a social-psychological account of the MPD culture that overtook the unit. He notes the vulnerability of patients with insecure identities and "permeable ego boundaries" to the dramaturgy of MPD. The psychiatric staff, who often felt helpless and overwhelmed by the difficulties in achieving real therapeutic gains, also embraced the revolutionary promise of MPD treatment. "The conceptual framework of trauma theory, with its emphasis on dissociation and the use of . . . hypnosis, offers some promise of helping our patients and reducing anxiety. . . . It gives the patients a dramatic language to express their identity diffusion and their massive internal conflicts or 'parts.' Besides, it engages us in a way that is exciting and reinforcing."[48]

1980s POPULIST PSYCHIATRY

In awakening the consciences of professionals and in advancing a new vision of therapeutic authority, the MPD movement also registers the influence of various religious groups—Christian and New Age—that gained a foothold in the mental health field in the 1980s. New Age psychology—with its emphasis on the wisdom of the body and its resistance to the scientific paradigm—filtered into clinical practice during this decade. The MPD movement also dovetailed with the recovery movement of the 1980s, where self-help groups drew on psychological theory and members self-diagnosed as Adult Children of Alcoholics (ACOAs) or codependents.[49] Cross-fertilization between MPD professional groups and self-help groups reduced the gap between healers and sufferers. For many formerly diagnosed as codependent, the multiple label offered a heroic reading of feminine suffering.

These populist currents in the MPD crusade have precursors in the human potential movement of the 1970s. Also termed humanistic psychology, self-actualization, and Third Force psychology, this earlier movement inspired many therapists who sought an alternative to behavioral and psychoanalytic approaches. One of the guiding principles of this movement, which straddled the mental health field and popular culture, was that there is a core self buried under the layers of culture and beneath the various roles imposed in the socialization process. Further, this core self may be accessed and released through therapeutic techniques. In Gestalt and psychodrama exercises, patients were invited to act out dialogues among these various "parts"—for example, to place the critical-parent part on a chair and to speak to it from the child part of the self. The core self—the "inner child"—was conceived as essentially good: spontaneous, loving, and able to know its own needs. Anger and hostility originated in the core self's need for protective defenses, and these defenses were thought to correspond directly to actual threats to well-being. Like peeling away the layers of an onion, therapeutic interventions aimed at retrieving this core self from the suffocating personas that disguised its essence.

There is a progressive dimension to this humanistic tradition, with its emphasis on the growth-seeking aspects of human strivings and on human capacities that become distorted or damaged in the course of socialization. Yet its romantic currents—its insistence on an essential, unproblematic selfhood—create a therapeutic situation where destructive feelings or impulses are perpetually placed at the margins of subjectivity. Identifications with others are not understood as constitutive aspects of the self or its structure but rather as a distorting overlay on its basic nature.

The Parts Model and MPD

Humanistic psychology found its way into the MPD movement through its creation of a discourse for the various dialogues among "parts" of the self. Theoretical or clinical interest in the structure of the self, mechanisms for organizing internal experience, and developmental processes—the groundwork of traditional psychodynamic approaches—were cast aside. Advanced as an alternative to mechanistic, scientific models within psychology, humanistic psychology offered a palatable stew of ideas and practices, such as psychodrama, "body work," and personal-growth groups, consistent with an action-oriented culture.

Paradoxically, humanistic psychology's rebellion against mechanistic models within psychology produced its own highly mechanistic ideas about the mind and therapeutic technique. Various "parts" of the mind could be orchestrated in a psychodrama on command, with the bad "parts" of the inner world discharged through cathartic exercises. Therapeutic exercises intended to release individuals from the constraints of the past took on a quasimagical meaning, without regard for the enduring structural forces, internal or external, anchoring identity. Transformations in the self could be rapidly induced, the influence of the past could be negated, and reality could be created anew.[50]

In the context of the social movements of the 1960s and 1970s, this was a heady and compelling vision of human possibilities. Unlike the radical psychiatry of this same period, however, humanistic psychology advanced an implicitly conservative worldview even in its protest against social constraints: the valiant, powerful individual stood in solitary opposition to a social order whose only function was a distorting one.

The Troops

In the MPD movement, the construction of a psychodrama involving various alter personalities follows from this tradition, as does the romantic search for the essential self. In Trudi Chase's widely read autobiographical account of treatment, *When Rabbit Howls,* written in consultation with her therapist, these themes are pervasive. In the introduction, her psychologist, Robert Phillips, informs us that Chase's earlier treatment by an analyst had been futile. The condition of multiplicity, he asserts, breaks existing theoretical molds for understanding the human mind. As the story unfolds, we learn that the purpose of multiplicity "is to protect the core, the original, first-born entity."[51]

In this same account we learn that Chase's birth personality died at the age of two, after spawning an alter identity that mutated into the ninety or so personalities that emerge by the end of treatment. Unlike earlier accounts of multiplicity, the therapist excitedly reports, this case reveals a fundamental fracture in the core self. In observing that "nowhere in other multiple case studies had there been more than one core," the therapist goes on to make what for him is the obvious, horrifying inference. "What kind of parental guidance, under what guise, from what corner of hell, produced damage so severe?" (147). Chase's memories of incest with her stepfather and of sex with animals anchor the vertiginous proliferation of personages, as treatment centers on tracing emerging alters to their roots in the past. The therapist attempts to break through the barriers of memory by thrusting sexual terms at the patient. Writing from the therapist's perspective, Chase describes one such "breakthrough" session. "When he [Phillips] launched vehemently into pronouncing the words 'penis' and 'vagina' and describing sex acts, perverted and otherwise, in an attempt to blast away some of her mental cotton batting, she merely stared at the floor. It was apparent that while she acknowledged the words on one level, she couldn't repeat them" (141–142).

Therapy becomes a kind of perpetual hell, where the patient's condition and capacity to function steadily worsen. As fragmentation becomes increasingly severe, with new alters materializing on every horizon, the therapist looks to the patient to deliver him from the mounting confusion. "In all the case histories I've read on multiplicity," he reasons, "there is one among the other selves who knows everything" (151). Other scenes of sexual invasion emerge out of the fragments of childhood, and, emboldened by this breakthrough, the therapist presses on. "There is one among you who knows everything, who remembers it all. Would that person come forward?" he commands (157).

We may wonder whether the fragmentation of the patient operates defensively in managing this highly stimulating, intrusive therapist. Chase seems to marshal various fantasy personas—collectively termed "the Troops"—as ego scaffolding. The alters who stand guard at the gates of her labyrinthine inner world also seem to evoke her father. A military man frequently away on missions during her childhood, her father had been a beloved figure in her early life.

Blind to these or other potential dynamics, Phillips forges ahead in pursuit of early trauma memories. In responding to the patient's mounting confusion and turmoil, Phillips emphatically insists on her normalcy, frequently pointing out that multiples are brilliant and creative. Further, he extolls, multiples have an indestructible resilience. "If the world blew up tomorrow, guess who'd walk out of the rubble?" (138).

As in other accounts of MPD, the therapist assumes that incest is the "breeding ground" of Chase's multiplicity. It is quite possible that this patient did suffer sexual abuse at the hands of her stepfather, and it is likely that the recovered memories reported here contain elements of her lived experience. The elaborate mythology she produces, however, with its medieval cast of characters engaged in military maneuvers, may reveal a more immediate set of dynamics than those that emerge out of whatever happened in the past. What manifests itself most vividly in these passages is the interactive dynamics between this woman patient and her therapist, particularly the mesmerizing power that her fluctuating personae have for him. He frequently describes, with fervent, childlike wonder, the frenetic energy and excitement that fill him following their sessions.

PSYCHIATRIC NOIR: MULTIPLICITY AND THE GENDER CRISIS

There is a noir element to the psychiatric discourse on MPD, which bears a striking resemblance to the "woman of the night" in this film genre. Like the detective who moves between the masculine, rational world of the day and the feminine, irrational world of the night, modern MPD therapists are arbiters of the changing boundaries of gendered identity. In the noir convention, the detective is voyeuristically captured by the fantasy of a concealed, nocturnal world where female powers operate. Feminist film critics have argued that this male pursuit of the woman of the night, who is ultimately brought under control, mobilizes collective anxieties over a maleness readily overwhelmed by a culturally emergent female authority.[52] Not reducible to empirical men and women, these masculine and feminine positions in the narrative are unstable, fluctuating identifications and fantasies for both sexes. Similarly, MPD is "a pathology of hiddenness," requiring intensive efforts on the part of the therapist to ferret out the layers of concealed alters.[53] For male and female clinicians alike, there is a highly paranoid aspect to this psychiatric gaze, a preoccupation with dangers lurking in hidden enclaves of the psyche. For women therapists, the sexual aspects of this anxiety-ridden, voyeuristic gaze are concealed in a protective, maternalized authority. Clinicians—male and female—focus on missing time or gaps in the life narrative. Their reports of patient histories are filled with intrigue—with mysterious clothing and meetings with strangers. The multiple, then, is the woman with a secret life, the woman who finds herself in unexpected places, arousing suspicion in others.

The MPD movement thus enacts broad cultural anxieties over sexuality and female rebellion, translating these anxieties through the moral authority of the sexual abuse recovery movement. Multiplicity may emerge, as many practitioners claim, out of the desperate, creative efforts of girls who are attempting to escape sexual invasions. But the chronic demands and neglects girls and women endure in daily life may also be experienced as a form of captivity, and these more mundane forms of bondage are more difficult to dramatize, less amenable to psychiatric intrigue. Through the new mythology that is permitted her, the MPD patient expresses a creativity and rebelliousness that are much less evident in clinical portraits of the past. The clinical discourse of MPD permits women to express socially prohibited feelings—murderous rage, lesbian fantasies, grandiosity. This clinical permissiveness does have its limits, however: the patient must produce the requisite trauma memories, which anchor and redeem the clinical project. In MPD treatment approaches, the preoccupation with mapping the feminine psyche and linking various alters to their corresponding trauma memories wards off exploration of the therapist's own desires and anxieties in relation to feminine disturbances. It may be that a fragmented feminine subject is easier to manage in the therapeutic encounter than the whole of what these combined parts suggest about female conflict. Within the clinical setting, the patient may respond to the therapist's anxieties by producing a narrative in manageable units. The frequent "switching" between alternating personas may be an unconscious effort to protect the therapist. As both patient and therapist search in the remote areas of the psyche for a hidden memory of sexual abuse, both are spared the difficulty of confronting the intrusive invasions immediately at hand.

On a cultural level, a number of forces may contribute to both this emerging clinical configuration of female conflict and the clinical construction of these conflicts. Different historical periods may create a tendency toward particular defenses and disorders, and historical factors may influence how therapists shape and interpret clinical material. Women have made significant advances into public life that permit new sublimational possibilities and avenues of identity formation. It may be that the disorganizing experiences of women that are associated with childhood abuse or environmental deficits are more effectively contained or dissociated through multiple identity states than was possible in the past. The vivid imagery available to women—the possible selves—is much vaster than it was in times past, but the barriers to self-realization remain daunting, especially for women who find their way into the folds of MPD specialists.

CONCLUSIONS

The chapter began with the question of whether MPD is a "real" diagnosis. But beyond the debate over the validity of the disorder is the question of how historical processes mediate both the clinical construction of human suffering and the kinds of defenses available in the intrapsychic elaboration of traumatic events. Whatever conclusions one might draw about the validity of the diagnosis, it seems likely that the fascination with MPD in the mental health field extends far beyond its numerical frequency.

One picture that I have assembled centers on multiplicity as a vehicle for rebellion within the mental health profession and for the struggle to recapture its own soul. Women patients with histories of various injuries and deprivations, including those inflicted by psychiatric authorities, find common cause with rebels in the mental health system who themselves feel fragmented and under siege. But there is a companion story in the affinity between multiplicity—as a female idiom of distress—and contemporary dilemmas of women. The MPD diagnosis permits the expression of the aggressive and sexual "personalities" of women within a trauma/dissociation model that locates the meaning of these powerful enactments in discrete events of the past. Women can express promiscuous, vengeful, and infantile selves because these selves are clinically constructed as visitations of the traumatic past. The female imagination is unleashed, finding a rapt audience in the person of the therapist, but this permissive stance toward feminine transgressions is conditional on producing sexual abuse scenes.

The 1950s story of *The Three Faces of Eve*—the woman caught between the stifling safety of the home and the wild abandon of the streets—has given way to more complex feminine narratives, a wider Street of Dreams than was formerly imaginable. While the worlds of women are undoubtedly larger and freer than in the past, many women continue to find themselves harnessed with domestic responsibilities, trapped in lower-status occupations, and without the engine of an activist women's movement to break through the barriers. More than in the past, the roadblocks must be negotiated one by one as discrete daily dramas. For countless contemporary women, the disappointments can seem unbearable and insurmountable.

MPD may be viewed as a modern variant of hysteria, that ambiguous feminine malady of migratory symptoms. The multiple is an empowered hysteric, one who is no longer paralyzed. The woman who takes to her bed and, as Freud put it, "cannot put one foot in front of the other" now wanders aimlessly.

Because defenders of MPD are so clearly mesmerized by the productivity of the multiple's imagination, many critics respond fearfully, dismissing its rich significance. Yet between the poles of exalting and degrading the MPD narrative, we must recognize the painful dilemmas women face in making integrative use of the rich potentiality of their inner worlds. There continues to be less recognition and less "holding" of female potentiality, both within families and within the larger society. If MPD treatment takes this potentiality down the dead-end street of a messianic psychiatry, this route may be attractive to many women because the present alternatives are so limited.

BETWEEN THE DEVIL AND THE DEEP

Chapter 10

Satanic Ritual Abuse Narratives and Cultural Crises

IT WAS 1967 and feminism was yet a glimmer in the eye of most young women. *Rosemary's Baby* was the film that held audiences spellbound throughout the country. Played by a waiflike, anorexic Mia Farrow, the female protagonist comes to the dawning realization, as the film progresses, that she is carrying the child of the devil. In a Faustian bargain, her husband had offered her up as sacrificial lamb, exchanging the soul of his unborn child for the promise of career advancement. Bound and drugged, Rosemary is impregnated during an orgiastic Black Mass on a dim-lit altar surrounded by elderly worshipers of Satan.

Rosemary, we learn, is a lapsed Catholic, uncertain of her stand with respect to matters of faith. As the satanic seed gestates into what the cult hopes to be its future anti-Christ, we find that Rosemary, lacking firm opinions of her own, is utterly defenseless against the forces of darkness surrounding her. During the rape scene, a priest appears and Rosemary appeals for his forgiveness for unnamed sins. Seduced into mothering the child of the devil, Rosemary nonetheless remains the embodiment of absolute virtue. Even in her degradation and ruination, she is somehow untouched by the evil that envelops her. Rosemary is part Christ figure, part Virgin Mary.

In 1973, the devil appeared again in a blockbuster film as the antithesis of feminine chastity, but this time the Cartesian divide shifts from good mother/bad fetus to a complex configuration of oppositions. *The Exorcist* centers on the demonic possession of a young girl, daughter of a single mother, with an absent father as backdrop to the emerging trouble. Early scenes stress the sensuous intimacy and serene plenitude of the mother/daughter pair, with the oedipally positioned father away in Europe, inaccessible because of his own selfishness and neglect. This Edenic vision of female mutuality—with scenes of girlish tickling—soon takes a disturbing turn as the pubescent daughter becomes a wild child. Eventually, fathers do step in, however, as two priests preside over an exorcism, providing the redemptive restoration of female chastity and patriarchal order by the film's conclusion.

As the film unfolds, scenes alternate between the world of a young priest and that of the possessed girl's mother, a successful actress. The priest, who is also a psychiatrist, is tormented by existential doubt and is suffering a deep crisis of faith. Sexually celibate, he is impotent in his spiritual powers, surrounded by suffering that he cannot touch. After a series of failed psychiatric interventions, the girl's mother searches out this demoralized priest, who implicitly confronts his own demons as he recovers an ancient craft of the priesthood—exorcism.

The possessed girl is mediator of several cultural crises. First, there is the struggle between religion and psychiatry, the priest embodying the dual personalities of these contemporary redemptive authorities. Psychiatry proves to be utterly ineffectual in combating malevolent forces battling for control over the human soul. Second, there is a crisis over the rebellion of youth, with resistance to authority on college campuses serving as a critical backdrop to the drama. The puberty-aged girl is on the threshold of a new age; she is signifier of the eruption of an androgynized youth movement that will overtake civil and familial quietude. There is no father on the scene to restore order, and the mother struggles futilely to save her daughter from diabolical convulsions.

The horror operates through the theme of the female double, with psychiatry accessing the disturbing otherness within the feminine self but lacking the ability to control the forces it unleashes. Religion steps in where psychiatry fails, introducing a decisive means of containment. Wrestling with the devil also enacts a deeper crisis within the church, for this palpable devil, in the person of the young girl, revivifies the collapsing faith of the priest. In his moment of ultimate sacrifice, as he takes on the devil and carries him to his grave, the priest vanquishes evil. The film affirms the church as tragic protagonist by pitting it triumphantly against psychiatric authority and, secondarily, against youthful rebellion.

Several decades later, women were reporting similarly horrific scenes, scripted eerily along the lines of *Rosemary's Baby* and *The Exorcist,* in therapy offices around the country. And much like the heroic priest, women in combat with the devil affirmed the triumph of woman over the forces of darkness, even as it signaled a profound yet ambiguous cultural crisis.

Michelle Remembers, by Michelle Smith and her psychiatrist (and later husband) Lawrence Pazder, published in 1980, marked the transition from the admitted fiction of accounts of satanic ritual abuse (SRA) to the gripping realism of a new genre of clinical literature.[1] While the terror evoked by *Rosemary's Baby,* like many films of the horror genre, centered on the failure of those most intimate with the protagonist to grasp the gravity of the situation, *Michelle Remembers* found a receptive audience in the trauma therapy field, where the readiness to believe had become axiomatic.

This shift toward psychiatric realism virtually ignored the role of cultural imagery in clinical storytelling. Yet since source memory—recall of the source of retained knowledge—is particularly vulnerable to deterioration, there may be a human tendency to incorporate a broad range of vivid imagery into the text of autobiographical recall. Films and television provide representations of the world that mesmerize the subject with their lifelike imagery. Under the influence of hypnotic media, the boundary between that which is experienced directly and that which is known vicariously may be imprecise, particularly for those whom Hilgard terms "hypnotic virtuosos," individuals who are capable of intense imaginative involvement and absorption.[2] (See chapter 6.)

The question of whether powerful filmic experiences are incorporated into memory has not been systematically studied, although films are suggested as an influence on MPD and SRA material by a number of critics.[3] Contemporary narratives of SRA contain unmistakable echoes of horror classics. But it would be crudely causal to suggest that films—cult classics or others—are passively registered in mind and surface later in the form of a trauma memory. This suggestion mirrors the problematic reasoning that has so limited the field of trauma therapy—its emphasis on singular causes of disturbing states.

Bearing in mind that both events in question—horror films and trauma memories—may be the product of some yet-unknown determinant or set of determinants, we may still introduce potential lines of influence, or mediating factors, in exploring the cultural context of SRA narratives. Other fanciful tales that emerged in the clinical storytelling of the 1980s and early 1990s were similarly inscribed with broad cultural preoccupations and motifs. In *Abduction,* Harvard psychiatrist John Mack describes his own clinical practice involving recovered memories of alien abductions, stories he came to accept as literal accounts.[4] Mack's book joined a growing genre of descriptions of clinically mediated mystical encounters, with channeling and past-life regression coming into vogue as therapeutic techniques for accessing the beyond. None of these implausible tales captured the mental health community with the same force as did SRA stories, however, even though they share much of the same dissatisfaction with "normal" science and with conventional storytelling.

This chapter seeks, first, to understand how cultural and psychological factors intervened in the production of and receptivity to satanic abuse imagery in mental health culture in the 1980s and early 1990s . A second problem taken up concerns the relationship between the psychology of women and the SRA narrative. Specifically explored is the possibility that cultural factors in female development may create a particular affinity for such "satanic verses." (Also, see chapter 4.) Third, the chapter addresses the receptivity to SRA accounts within grassroots feminist organizations in the 1980s and 1990s and how these accounts permitted a kind of ritual violation of taboos within feminism.

BELIEVING THE VICTIM

In a letter to Wilhelm Fliess in 1897, Freud posed questions that continue to echo in the controversy over SRA a century later:

> What would you say, by the way, if I told you that all of my brand-new prehistory of hysteria is already known and was published a hundred times over, though several centuries ago? Do you remember that I always said that the medieval theory of possession held by the ecclesiastical courts was identical with our theory of a foreign body and the splitting of consciousness? But why did the devil who took possession of the poor things invariably abuse them sexually and in a loathsome manner? Why are their confessions under torture so like the communications made by my patients in psychic treatment? Sometime soon I must delve into the literature on this subject.[5]

In the fledgling field of dissociative disorders in the 1980s, a passionate sub-culture emerged as many clinicians unified around a shared belief in the literal meaning of reports of SRA. Many came to see in the hysterical possession states described by Freud the literal devil at work; others inferred a secular, mortal domain of devil worshipers who, by their very numbers and the magnitude of their influence, assume supranatural proportions. And for those converted to the literal reality of SRA stories, the answer to Freud's questions came in the form of an apocalyptic psychiatry. The patient that Freud describes is, many therapists would assert, the oracle of a profound reality; she is exposing a maniacal movement afoot that aims at world domination in the name of evil.[6]

There are, by now, a range of elements in and variations on the satanic abuse tale, even though still-recognizable key elements distinguish these accounts from "ordinary" memories of child abuse.[7] In addition, a typology has emerged in the literature, separating relatively benign or limited occult practitioners, such as New Agers, "teenage Satanist dabblers," and "isolated psychopaths," from "orthodox" satanic ritual abusers. In practice, however, these distinctions blur, and groups with culturally unorthodox practices are often the targets of SRA campaigns, particularly in communities experiencing tensions over cultural differences.[8] Day-care workers were a frequent target, many of them poor women.[9] Countercultural practices were also frequently cited—for example, pagan holidays celebrated as part of goddess worship or witchcraft ceremonies. Caribbean-influenced practices involving ritual uses of animal blood were suspect. Another common target was teenage, heavy-metal culture, with its rebellious uses of images associated with satanism.[10]

In the clinical literature, SRA is described as multigenerational, multi-perpetrator assaults on children.[11] According to believers, these satanic cults are elaborately organized networks of adults who engage in cannibalism, ritual sacrifice of babies and animals, sexual torture of children, and parody of the Christian religion through the Black Mass.

While the establishment of a wide child-pornography ring is sometimes
given as the motive behind such barbarism, this explanation does not explain
the highly ritualized torture that prevails. The primary aim, believers insist, is
a simple dedication to evil. Many clinicians speak of how listening to such stories
changed their worldview: how they have, through the accounts of survivors,
seen the face of the absolute, unredeemable corruption of the human spirit.[12]
Beliefs in these conspiratorial, large-scale cults remain unwavering for many in
spite of the lack of material evidence to support such claims beyond the stories
of "survivors."[13]

Patients diagnosed as suffering from MPD are a primary source of SRA
accounts.[14] In the therapeutic uncovering of deeper layers of trauma memory,
often under hypnosis, the personalities, or alters, that surface are like visitors
returning from foreign lands with shocking tales of distant tribal practices. As
these stories become increasingly elaborate, they often extend beyond the ritualized torture of children to include the "programming" of cult members, which
leaves them like walking time bombs. This development brought a new subcategory into the differential diagnosis of MPD: some alters were designated as
reactions to childhood trauma, whereas others now were regarded as having been
implanted by the cult for maintenance of control over the survivor into adulthood. The distinction between "reactive" and "structured" MPD codified this
new discovery.[15]

In *Manchurian Candidate* fashion, cult survivors suffering from structured MPD
were believed to be programmed to commit suicide on particular dates or were
implanted with cryptic cues that prompted self-mutilation, particularly when
the victim sought help from a mental health professional. Generally, the triggers
for these malevolent alters to surface corresponded to particular dates that
had significance for the cult, such as pagan holidays, or to idiosyncratic symbols—for example, hidden messages deciphered from greeting cards. Much of the
self-destructive behavior of these patients came to be understood as part of
the labyrinthine programming of the cult. Vampirelike, the cult was believed to
operate in the realm of the hidden, under the cloak of various disguises, dreading the redemptive light of mental health practitioners who were committed to
unveiling their nefarious deeds.[16]

These accounts seem hysterical at best and psychotically paranoid at
worst. How, then, could otherwise sensible therapists become convinced of
their literal truth? The field of trauma therapy has created a culture of belief
that is a potent incubator of such florid, quasipsychotic reactions. Since one
of the axiomatic principles in work with sexual abuse survivors in the 1980s
was creating a climate of "belief" and working against the culture of "denial,"
these graphic reports of childhood torture found a receptive clinical audience.
Many clinicians in the sexual survivor movement maintained, and correctly

so, that victims, particularly women and children, suffered as much from social silencing as they did from injuries inflicted by their perpetrators.[17] For many clinicians schooled in trauma theory, erasing the line between imaginative reconstructions of reality and authoritative reports about the past became a morally and politically inscribed one. In adjudicating this boundary, many clinicians felt it was better to err on the side of belief than on that of disbelief since the dangers of retraumatizing patients by questioning the authenticity of their reports seemed a pressing one. Indeed, treatment protocols codified "believing the survivor" as an essential element of healing. The patient's memory of trauma, too horrific to reveal to conventional practitioners, could emerge only in a therapeutic environment of absolute receptivity to the "unthinkable."

This clinical mandate to "believe the victim" is, however, a misleading one. In their analysis of reports of SRA in dozens of day-care centers throughout the United States in the 1980s, Debbie Nathan and Michael Snedeker conclude that these stories did not originate with the children.[18] In a ventriloquial fashion, the children began to report sexual abuse after hours of intensive police interrogation, with their stories escalating over a period of months into grueling tales of killing and eating animals and babies, sacrificial ceremonies, and pornographic encounters with devil worshipers. In the McMartin case in Manhattan Beach, California, police investigators and therapists who conducted the investigation held prior beliefs in satanic practices and were seeking evidence in support of them. Nathan and Snedeker's interpretation of the SRA accounts emphasizes the convergence of Christian beliefs, ambient anxieties in the culture over public care of children, and rank opportunism on the part of investigators and clinicians.

While we can grant credence to Nathan and Snedeker's insightful analysis, they did not go on to explore the phenomenon of recovered memories of SRA. While the fantasy world of children may be highly permeable to adult directives and unconscious cues, do these same processes explain the many accounts that emerged in the treatment of adult women during this same period? Even though therapy may have effects similar to those obtained in interrogative interviews, there are many examples in the clinical literature of more subtle, complex interactions.

While SRA accounts are patently irrational, they may contain a concealed story of actual abuses or terrors. Just as stories of alien abduction are not plausible as veridical accounts of past experience, they, like stories of ritual abuse, communicate meanings—symbolic truths—that require interpretation. The tendency in the debate over SRA, like that over recovered memory generally, is to inscribe the boundary between truth and falsehood too definitively. Once the literal credibility of recovered memories—including those of satanic orgies, past lives, and other fantastical tales—has been debunked, critics often smugly turn away from their defeated opponents, declaring a decisive victory.

SRA ACCOUNTS AND CULTURAL CRISIS

Many social scientists argue that demonology has a long history, emerging with particular forcefulness during periods of social transition or acute cultural stress.[19] This imagery may be more floridly manifested in disturbed individuals, who are barometers of broader, disequilibrating cultural forces. From this vantage point, we may view dissociative patients as highly susceptible not only to clinical suggestion but to ambient anxieties in the culture. Just as the paranoid may weave cultural imagery and real social brutalities into their delusional systems, less disturbed individuals may similarly merge personal history with broad cultural motifs.

Social constructionist and sociological explanations of SRA typically establish too much distance, however, from the vivid suffering of individuals reporting such terror. These approaches locate SRA stories within socially organized belief systems, such as Christianity, focusing on collective representations of ambiguous threats to well-being. More attuned to the psychological and phenomenological world than to the sociological or historical context, clinicians have access to forms of personal anguish that cannot be easily reconciled with these distancing frameworks. Further, the concept of "urban legend," commonly invoked in explaining the circulation of SRA accounts in the 1980s, does not explain the phenomenon of firsthand accounts or their specific structural elements.[20]

Unlike more benign or socially innocuous legends, SRA stories contain currents of aggression and sadism. Disturbing to many skeptical of SRA accounts is the tendency of defenders to abandon traditional rules of evidence and to accept the fixed idea of ineradicable human evil. Yet defenders' exhortative claim that barbarism has always existed and that villainy operates in various cultural disguises does find a responsive chord in modern sensibilities, as does rejection of the notion of historical progress. Implicit in the clinical rhetoric of SRA and its millennialism is a recognition that individual psychopaths and incidences of violence and brutality are part of an organized process of collaboration. The notion of cults, conspiracies, and multiperpetrator abuse invokes a highly social and institutionalized vision of human destructiveness.

There is some basis to this claim of socially orchestrated evil, particularly if we consider the role of both the church and the state in protecting powerful interests and in concealing their own role in human villainy. The problem, here, is that the SRA critique is mythically elaborated into a cosmology, a religious worldview that is impervious to the complexities of actual experience and to conflicting sources of evidence. As such, it both engages and evades the ramifications of human destructiveness. It engages the real harm done to children, pervasive not merely in families but throughout U.S. society and the world. Such inhumanity is evident in the United States in the erosion of public education and social-welfare institutions in the 1980s, including services to children and families. Much like religious revivalism, the SRA movement transports this social crisis into the metaphysical realm, enlisting believers in a displaced struggle against fantastically elaborated and reified enemies.

In defending SRA accounts, Craig Lockwood—editor of *Beyond Survival,* a journal for ritual abuse survivors—chronicles the history of various evils in the name of Satan. In concluding his book, *Other Alters,* which rails against Marxist humanists and other cultural "relativists," Lockwood describes a modern variant of what he describes as "Mexico's long tradition of human sacrifice and cannibalism." Lockwood summarizes a case involving a Chicano, Jesus Constanzo, who took a group of middle-class Mexicans and Americans under the spell of his charismatic influence on a crime spree in the 1980s, culminating in the murder and cannibalism of children. While there was no evidence of satanism, Lockwood uses this example to make the point that "an international conspiracy, predicated on committing human sacrifice to ensure personal gain through crime, can flourish undetected."[21]

The larger point, beyond that of weaving together a plausible account to shore up the claims of beleaguered SRA defenders, is that rampant evil requires some form of spiritual renewal. Like many defenders of SRA, Lockwood concludes with a call to bear witness to the eternal power of evil, implicitly condemning the failure of secular methods to contain such power. For his message to be compelling, Lockwood's analysis must be filtered through a Christian millennialism:

> This is the face of a human evil that has been called a thousand names, over thousands of years. Dismissing it, discounting the power of those who practice whatever form of it they learn, is a mistake. These are very dangerous people. Whatever it is that people such as Constanzo learn to worship and serve is not a part of some culture. It is its own culture—has always been its own culture, and can be found in bits and pieces here and there in every human society. This kind of evil forms the darkest corner of the underground of rejected occult knowledge.[22]

In this alpha and omega of evil, oppressed and vulnerable groups are easily ensnared in the conspiratorial net. This reliance on moral categories to grasp human problems readily slides into drawing lines between the more or less human among us. There are flagrant hints of the blood libel in these accounts—the charges, advanced by Catholic theologians in anti-Semitic campaigns in Europe for centuries, that Jews killed Christian children, drained their blood, and baked it into holiday matzos.[23]

As symptomatic of a cultural crisis, however, this apocalyptic vision points to real difficulties in the contemporary world: the failure of the social sciences to adequately intervene in problematic moral areas; the sense that many modern institutions are irredeemably corrupt; and the loss of traditional institutions that have provided protective, humanizing public functions. As sociologist Jeffrey Victor puts it, "The satanic cult legend is an expression of people's shared feelings of powerlessness to change our society for the better."[24]

Demonic Institutions

Throughout the history of Western incursions into concealed aspects of mind, the female subject has served as a medium—literally and figuratively—for alternative storytelling, for communications that deviate from dominant cultural scripts. Part 2 pursued the history of female storytelling through key historical junctures, showing how male clinicians and scientists periodically made use of the "receptive" mental states of women to transport their own imaginings and subversive ideas. The other side of this history of hypnotic encounters is that women sometimes have made use of the trance state to stage their own disguised rebellion, mesmerizing the audience with communications from "beyond the normal." Just as female mediumship in the nineteenth century permitted the emergence of a more authoritative feminine voice, many contemporary "alternative" therapies augment female authority by investing it with mystical powers. And in both eras women struggle to find their places on the margins of dominant institutions, neither fully inside nor entirely outside of the kingdom. While male practitioners led the SRA crusade, just as they did the MPD crusade, the foot soldiers in these interlocking movements were largely female practitioners.

In the 1980s, therapists were faced with reconciling the Byzantine system of modern psychiatry and the humanistic project of therapeutic recovery. The massive trend toward short-term treatment in the 1980s, including rapid turnover in overburdened institutions, created a situation where many clinicians struggled to sustain some emotional engagement and purpose in their work. In such a situation, the patient who tells the most riveting tale of horror may be most effective in enlisting helpers on her or his behalf. And in the ward or in the therapy office, horror stories may "warm the soul," warding off the chill of coldly calculating institutions. Therapists may identify with stories that traverse the Christian legends of childhood and the brutalities of institutional life, particularly if such motifs are displaced from the immediate scene—one that seems impervious to intervention—to a remote sphere of cosmic influence.

If the size of our gods and devils must inevitably match the magnitude of our internal longings and fears, we may recognize in the social psychology of satanic imagery a subtext of the enormity of social anxiety concerning institutional controls. It is not only that blatant evil is rampant in the contemporary world, as SRA defenders assert, but that so many feel impotent in the face of everyday problems, including their own struggles with the "programming" of workplaces, including mental health settings. More pervasive than barbarism and savagery are these mundane, everyday forms of human alienation. The SRA story—combining the detective thriller, the Gothic horror story, and the Bible—amplifies those currents of suffering that had previously fallen beneath institutional thresholds of perception.

Demonic Threats to Saintly Therapists

Dramas over bodily control—imagery centering on surrender to a powerful other—register infantile ambivalences, even as they do a history

of traumatic invasions and other assaults on the self. The body is the early location of the infant's struggles over engagement and disengagement with a powerful (m)other. Childhood games of tag and capture—of escape and forceful
surrender—include this dynamic of engagement and disengagement, of a to-
and-fro interplay of binding closeness and social distance. (See chapter 4.) So too,
pleasure in loss of control, of being taken over by a strong other, may be identified in a broad range of cultural situations and practices, particularly those
centering on ritualized loss of ego controls.

The unmistakable sadism and terror in the clinical literature on SRA, however, seems to overtake various participants on the clinical scene. From a Kleinian perspective, satanic abuse narratives may signify a social alliance based on
paranoid/schizoid anxieties. (See chapter 4.) The aggressively devouring imagery
of forced acts of eating flesh and drinking blood under the maniacal control of
an other is suggestive of a deeply disturbing aspect of the interpersonal field. From
a psychoanalytic perspective, this oral incorporative imagery is a psychologically
primitive defense, involving the fantasy of engulfing a dangerous object in
order to eliminate it as an external threat. (For example, the partaking in the Holy
Communion of the body of Christ, or God the Son, protects the believer from
the wrath of God the Father.) We may wonder, then, whether an interpersonal
dynamic operating in these therapies may contribute to the production of such
primitive defenses and imagery.

In the SRA clinical literature, metaphors often have a decisively regressive
quality, suggesting a merger of therapist and patient against threats of cosmic proportions. Robert McFarland and Grace Lockerbie, for example, describe the long
and "exhausting" process of treating satanic abuse and what it entails: "the
therapist must be like a nurturing placenta, removing toxins and providing
nourishment for a badly damaged child."[25]

Robert Rockwell, a Jungian psychiatrist, describes his own conversion to the
reality of SRA accounts, presenting a case of multiple personality where increasing numbers of alters began reporting ritual abuse memories. One session centers on sexual material that emerged prior to the SRA memories.

> Several months into therapy, "Gloria" (an alter) began to appear.
> She was warm and aggressively seductive. She wanted to be sexual
> with me. She explained that she came into being to do the "sexual
> work" that "Sara" had been required to do. . . . While we were
> talking, a dog barked outside of my office. Her demeanor changed;
> she look terrified; she shrieked, ran back to my rear office and
> smashed the window. . . . The next session, the dog barked again.
> She again became terrified and started to run back to the rear office.
> I restrained her and tried to reassure her that she was safe.[26]

At this point, the patient begins to tell a story involving a pet monkey; the
story is set in a rural mansion where she and other young girls were taken for sexual orgies under the command of "wealthy New England businessmen."[27] The
patient worsens after this revelation, requiring hospitalization for suicidal gestures. Rather than exploring his own reactions to this demand for "sexual work"

and its potential clinical meanings, Rockwell embarked on a ritual abuse expedition. After attending the 1988 meetings of the American Psychiatric Association and hearing a presentation on the issue, he began networking with therapists in the dissociative disorders field who were suspecting "well organized satanic cults" in the backgrounds of MPD patients. Subsequently, he heard more and more reports of them from patients.

Such clinical vignettes unfold as a conspiratorial enclosure of the therapeutic relationship, where the patient and therapist forge an alliance around a menacing, external threat. As the patient becomes increasingly ill, the therapist searches for an explanation that may account for it. Just as the imagery of the therapeutic "placenta" suggests a regressive fantasy of the relationship, Rockwell's account portrays a siege mentality, where the source of distress is perpetually projected outward, onto the "cult."

What is "detoxified" in the therapeutic "placental" barrier may be the therapist's own unconscious hostility. Therapists' reliance on primitive defenses in the management of hostility and aggression may be exacerbated by the overuse of the trauma model. The literature on hysteria and borderline disorders, generally rejected by therapists in the trauma field, acknowledges the intense, negative emotions that often emerge in the therapeutic relationship, including in the countertransference responses of therapists.[28] The best of the literature on borderline disorders emphasizes both the developmental conflicts and unmet needs that contribute to a provocative way of relating to others and the various dynamic and defensive meanings of aggression.[29] In the trauma literature, however, aggressive impulses and fantasies are assumed to be entirely derived from past abuse experiences. Within this context, the SRA story may become the vehicle through which various disturbing emotions are permissibly expressed and externalized, particularly those that are felt to be threatening to the idealized tie between therapist and patient.

SRA AS A FEMININE NARRATIVE

We don't have to look far in cultural life to recognize the symbolic potency of imagery of bodily invasion. Horror films are replete with them. But how are particular images selected from some broad storehouse of cultural symbols to form the SRA narrative? Further, why are women so often the creators of these tales, which may combine actual and mythic events? While we may recognize how SRA dramatizes female suffering, hysterically elaborating on less culturally decipherable forms of anguish, how do we understand SRA as an idiom of female distress and rebellion located at the nexus of religious and sexual abuse imagery?

Thus far, I have considered factors within both the broader culture and the mental health field that may serve as incubators of such dramatic portrayals of suffering. Yet such factors do not readily explain why women came to be a common source of SRA stories. Much of the heated controversy over both MPD and SRA centers on whether these "syndromes" are clinically or culturally created (or both) and, further, whether trauma memories are veridical accounts of past events. While such questions are important, there has been relatively little exploration of how SRA imagery may operate within the context of female development and cultural life.

If SRA is akin to a "possession" state, a hypnotic, choreographed engagement with a powerful other, it may enact the dilemmas of women in reconciling traditional ideals of female purity and the vicissitudes of modern life. The SRA story registers a sense of invasive corruption, represented in the imagery of bodily contamination. In that the structure of the narrative includes both a confession of corruption—of being forced to do the work of the devil—as well as a resistance to overpowering, socially orchestrated expressions of evil, it may signify the conflicts of contemporary women located at the threshold between private and public life.

Even in adult life, recollections of past experiences may be infused with the uncertainties and inhibitions that are prototypical in female development. (See chapter 4.) Girls entering adolescence are more likely than boys to "stall" in their intellectual achievement, as if there is some loss of steam, some critical blunting of the drives and psychic structures necessary to traverse the border between childhood and adulthood. This diffuse female malaise is most certainly mediated by cultural factors that lead to the social invisibility of girls and the idealization of female emotional receptivity, especially to males. Beyond such factors, this developmental vulnerability also may be a product of pervasive anxiety projected onto girls—the tendency of various authorities on the scene to anxiously scrutinize young women and to convey to them a sense of their fragility and vulnerability.

The Social Symbolic Uses of the Body

British anthropologist Mary Douglas, whose cross-cultural work centers on ritual uses of the body and bodily imagery, suggests that transition states, such as that between childhood and adulthood, are considered "hot" and dangerous in many cultures.[30] Rites of passage serve to manage the inherent instability and ambiguity of these states.

> Danger lies in transitional states, simply because transition is
> neither one state nor the next, it is undefinable. The person [boy]
> who must pass from one to another is himself in danger and
> emanates danger to others. The danger is controlled by ritual which
> precisely separates him from his old status, segregates him for a
> time and then publicly declares his entry to his new status. Not
> only is transition itself dangerous, but also the rituals of segregation
> are the most dangerous phase of the rites. So often do we read that
> boys die in initiation ceremonies, or that their sisters and mothers
> are told to fear for their safety, or that they used in the old days to
> die from hardship or fright, or by supernatural punishment for
> their misdeeds. Then somewhat timely come the accounts of the
> actual ceremonies which are so safe that the threats of danger
> sound like a hoax.[31]

A subtextual element of the SRA narrative is the idea of sexual sacrifice, of a virgin maiden who undergoes a horrific voyage into a Miltonian underworld. This plot structure resembles the initiation rites described by Douglas—rites that maintain their legendary power through dramatization of events—that is, through rumors of feats endured.

Dramatization plays an important role in storytelling, although its role in trauma narratives is decisively downplayed in the clinical literature. Women have been denied the position of central protagonist in many cultural legends, performing mostly as cheerleaders for the main action. The SRA drama is, at base, a tale of female heroic transfiguration in the face of evil, even though it draws heavily on ideas of female chastity and childlike innocence. In surviving the ravages of the cult, the girl child is anointed with special powers. As Ganaway has pointed out, it is remarkable how many of the stories of the cult center on the female protagonist's preparation or training for the high priesthood.[32]

According to Douglas, transitional-status conditions grant special license to individuals to behave in ways otherwise restricted in the society. Those who emerge from seclusion carry the powers of having been on the margins and are held to be "hot and dangerous," requiring a "cooling down" period.[33] Douglas argues that pollution rituals—such as menstruation taboos—center on the negotiation of a threatening social boundary, one that often registers the fears of men concerning the threatening powers of women. Women, too, participate in such rituals, sometimes making use of oppressive traditions in registering their own influence. In other words, the very imposition of the ritual codifies the potential within women to subvert male control.

A recognizable motif in the social psychology of SRA is what Douglas describes as the symbolic use of the body in enacting conflicts over social boundaries. In those societies where women are acquiring power or where the sexual difference is an unstable and changing category, the female body may become a focus of collective anxiety. As girls and women traverse the social boundary between private and public life, often stalled at the border, and as public life itself is seen as increasingly dangerous, female body boundaries take on additional symbolic loading.

Indeed, sexual and female reproductive themes are pervasive in SRA imagery: pregnancy, babies, and blood predominate, as do sexual violations. (Similar motifs pervade the alien-abduction literature.) Within this drama, the female victim is sacrificed, quite literally on the altar of parental barbarism. She is forced to commit acts of violent aggression against her will. Yet her immense suffering anoints her, granting her a moral, exhortative voice she would otherwise lack. The oral incorporative imagery of SRA stories—eating babies and drinking blood—may express the role of frustrated rage in female development under patriarchy, particularly in the context of controlling, invasive family dynamics.

Just as the evangelist, in wrestling with the devil, demonstrates the magnitude of his spiritual powers, women survivors and their allies may similarly enlist the devil in dramatizing a transfigurative struggle. Women are granted little cultural license for aggressive feelings or violent outrage, even though they are the frequent objects of it. Women who exhibit nonmaternal feelings are often punished, sometimes severely, and such prohibitions create a state of female anxiety over aggressive impulses generally.

The image of cult possession of the female self objectifies myriad violent feelings. Since cults are, by definition, outsider groups, lacking in cultural legitimacy, the employment of this term permits women to marginalize real foes. Parents, community officials, and religious leaders—frequently targeted as cults in the clinical literature—are dethroned and cast outside the boundaries of "civilized" society.[34] Since everyday families, churches, and workplaces are rarely thought of as cults, in the sense of maintaining control over group members, rebellion against the dominating influence of conventional institutions may be difficult to sustain. The vocabulary of cults registers the effects of intimate invasions of the self, while placing them in a mythologized realm beyond "normal" experience.

The Revolt against Religious Authority

Many of the women patients who have recovered memories of satanic abuse grew up in Christian fundamentalist or Catholic families where icons such as blood sacrifice and cannibalism (eating the body and drinking the blood of Christ), demonic control, and the mysteries of religious surrender take the form of highly concretized, literalized beliefs.[35] Largely unexplored in the work of SRA believers are the disturbing meanings associated with such religious imagery and of the dominant role of Satan in the Christian cosmology. Indeed, for many fundamentalist Christians the devil is the most proximate deity, closer to the fleshly, sinful state of actual human affairs than is the more remote God the Father. Christ, the son, reduces this cosmic gap but not entirely, particularly for women, whose representation is "repressed" in monotheistic cosmologies.

Contemporary women, often ambivalently wavering between a sense of entitlement and rights, on the one hand, and the bondage of religious devotion on the other, may wage symbolic warfare through the SRA story. Since reversals often prevail in the unconscious, religious reversals may reign in the trance state. Emotional surrender plays a central role in many expressions of Christianity, and the experience of conversion—of being "born again"—involves the purification of the self. The rejected, unclean aspects of the self threaten to return, however, in the form of struggles with the devil, the agent of rebellion within this kingdom of the Father.

In an article describing the use of Christian healing rituals in recovery from "organized sadistic abuse,"[36] a woman patient and her female therapist, with the assistance of a female minister, present a modern psychodrama of Christian recovery.[37] The therapist, Lea Nicoll Kramer, asserts that "healing at the spiritual level" is a necessary part of recovering from the severe childhood trauma she describes. The patient, a thirty-two-year-old woman, entered therapy with "feelings of worthlessness, confusion, hurt, and loneliness" as well as suicidal thoughts (40). Initially, the patient conceded to trying therapy for six months with the intent that if she failed to find relief, she would carry out her plan of suicide. The therapy continued for three years, in a stormy progression through various suicidal and self-destructive crises and hospitalizations for alcoholism, a diagnosis of MPD accompanied by therapeutic recovery of ritual abuse memories, and a series of Christian healing rituals.

Early on in treatment, a dialogue ensued between "Little Rebecca," an alter personality that emerged, and the therapist. Little Rebecca, we learn, "believed that she carried 'tainted blood' as a birthright, a belief that led to self-mutilation because she believed that cutting herself to bleed offered her the only way to cleanse herself of her contamination" (41) The therapist takes this disturbing imagery as an indication that the patient has been quite literally infected by the vampirish activity of a cult, as the theme of ritual abuse moves to the center of the clinical drama. We learn almost nothing about the actual history and life circumstances of the patient, other than that she is trying to break from an abusive marriage and to achieve some distance from her family. As the therapist knits together the elements of the organized sadistic abuse story, she enlists the wise Little Rebecca as ally in the therapeutic journey. Little Rebecca holds the knowledge of the horrendous happenings of childhood and lives in dread that anyone who learns of the sadistic abuse will be in "imminent physical danger." "Little Rebecca reported systematic brainwashing and torture that instilled in her the belief that she was a 'child of Satan,' and that she would always be a part of the abusive group. Rebecca reported that her mother held an influential position in this group, and because Rebecca thought of herself as a part of her mother (having come out of her mother's body), she believed that her own body harbored her mother's evil. Thus, though Rebecca wanted to escape, she believed that she'd belonged to the abusive group even before she drew her first breath" (41).

As these reports emerge, therapist and patient, sharing similar religious beliefs, decide to embark on a "spiritual approach to her therapy." This approach includes a series of Christian rites, with a gathering of observers schooled in this syncretic blend of trauma therapy and Christian spiritualism. Unlike most religious observers, however, the female acolyte is able to control the proceedings, exacting elaborate adjustments from the presiding authorities. "The rite wasn't something being *done* to [the patient]. If anything made her feel uncomfortable *at any time,* she was to let Susan [the minister] know immediately" (41–42).

The patient experiences considerable relief, even as Little Rebecca gives "detailed information about her forced participation in abusive acts directed toward both humans and animals." These revelations "devastated her adult self," who was a gentle creature, intent on never hurting "another living being." Such horrific acts introduced particular problems in carrying out the second healing rite, the Holy Communion. Rebecca had participated in bloody rituals, including eating and drinking "various disgusting substances," making the spiritual consumption of the blood and body of Christ a potential reenactment of the trauma (43).

The therapist seems to be blind to the hostility toward religion implicit in this material. Indeed, what the therapist and minister find most difficult throughout the "healing" process is quite revealing: it is Rebecca's feeling "hard and cold and very skeptical about God's power." The aim of reconciling Rebecca to God collides, it seems, with the tenacious forcefulness of her memories and the persisting "mind control" of the abusive group (44).

The healing rituals may indeed have provided some measure of relief from frantic acts of self-destructiveness, as the therapist asserts, just as exorcisms may reduce the terror associated with possession states. There are considerable costs, however, in this reification and externalization of disturbing forces that inhabit the human mind. Relapses are a perpetual danger as dreaded aspects of the self intrude on consciousness, including rebellious impulses incompatible with the ideal state of virtuous believer.

The Revolt against Therapeutic Authority

One potential reading of the SRA story is that it is an expression of unconscious rebellion on the part of the patient against therapeutic authority, as well as against religious and familial authority. The heretical elements of SRA—its inversion and defilement of the Christian icons—may be employed to similarly mock the therapeutic encounter. Like the cleric who is so filled with his own sense of virtue that he is unable to understand the disguised rebellion—the residue of paganism—in the Christian practices of converted natives, therapists may be similarly blind to "occult" revolts against their own sanctioned authority.

Religious and sexual imagery came to a similar boil in the clinical cauldron in a case that involved a secular approach to healing. A husband and wife therapist team and a journalist joined forces in combating SRA in an MPD patient. In *Suffer the Child,* a book heralded in the dissociation field as a landmark study in the links between MPD and satanic ritual abuse, author Judith Spencer presents this tale. Her patient, a thirty-four-year-old woman who had been previously diagnosed as schizophrenic, became the surrogate child of Spencer and her husband, a couple who devoted many hours a day to her care, without expectation of a fee. Citing MPD expert Bennett Braun, who prescribed sessions as long as eight hours and even twenty-four-hour attention, Spencer tells a story of satanic influence that has an eery parallel in the therapists' own sense of being "possessed" by the patient.[38]

The patient, we learn early on, was raised by a fundamentalist Christian woman who was preoccupied with the devil. Devoutly religious yet prone to frequent moral lapses, particularly in her sexual behavior, this mother is relentlessly abusive of her daughter. Beatings and forced enemas emerge as part of childhood recollections, mixed with Bible readings centering on cleansing the body of the devil's influence.

Yet this conventional history of religious and everyday abusiveness is sidelined by the central story. The chronic hardship of the patient's childhood comes to life in the plot that vitalizes the book, as a cult—a shadowy world of devil worshipers—becomes the fascinating, main protagonist in the drama. This alternative scene gives a profound specialness to the woman patient, a sense of her place in a maniacal but purposeful cosmos. Indeed, the cult, we are told, had recognized the special powers of "Jenny"—the assigned childhood name of this patient, who multiplied into a plethora of selves. "They had never seen a child quite like her before. She was a standout among the children. Small for her age, she looked almost cherubic, with strawberry-blond curls framing a pretty, round face. Her fair skin did not freckle, but turned golden in the summer sun. And her skin could not seem to be marked. Burns or cuts healed almost instantly, leaving scars so faint they could barely be seen. She was always clean—as if she just stepped out of a bandbox. She wore pretty little dresses and knee socks and black patent Mary Janes. She looked special" (18).

Throughout the story, virtue and cleanliness are symbolically equated, as the young, blue-eyed virgin enters into her ordeal of ritual defilement. The cult makes her do unspeakable things, forcing the heroine to actively engage in profane acts that are orchestrated from on high. As events turn monstrously sinister—including the protagonist's participation in the murder of a woman—the text takes on a pornographic quality.

> The high priest caressed the woman's face and breasts. Then, concealing his actions, he injected her with a drug to sedate her further. He continued to explore her body with his hands, now exaggerating the moves for the benefit of the observers. He entered her first with the tip of the dagger, then with his hands. He prolonged the sensual play. He presented first a symbolic phallus, then his own for her to fondle and take into her mouth. She offered no resistance to these acts, nor to his final act of coupling. The people became increasingly aroused. They were eager to begin their own parts in the sexual celebration, waiting only for the signal from the priest. But the high priest did not release them, not yet. He waited for the priestesses to replace his robe for him and then to stand ready to serve at his side.[39]

Jenny, who by now had created a number of alter personalities to assist in the management of the cult's pornographic and sadistic practices, emerges as an alternatingly compliant and defiant girl who finds more interesting company in the cult than in the dreary world of her schoolmates. In a commentary on the action that seems to mimic the therapeutic situation, we learn of Jenny's capacity to mesmerize others as she submitted to the cult's continual tests of obedience: "cult leaders who witnessed the extraordinary performances were compelled by what they saw to use this exceptional child to their own advantage" (63).

In advancing the SRA story as the new frontier of women's unspeakable suffering, an expanding audience of professionals in the 1980s became quite blind to the voyeuristic elements of their own clinical gaze. Just as Jenny was "more creative than her abusers" in the past, she may have been more creative than her therapists, whose own imaginations were stunted by some very conservative premises. Unable to recognize the tremendous generativity of the human mind—its capacity to elaborate on everyday misery and to dramatize mundane suffering—many therapists in the trauma field were spellbound by pornographic stories of horror, even as they recounted them with the matter-of-factness of a travelogue. Unable to recognize the profound depths of female conflict over the body and sexuality, or the gripping power of religious imagery, these same therapists overlooked the most obvious dimensions of the pornographic material that emerged from the innocent mouths of virtuous Christian maidens. For these highly civilized therapists, the only plausible explanation was that "the devil made her do it."

GRASSROOTS FEMINISM AND THE SRA LEGEND

A number of historians have described the recurring emergence of satanic conspiracies, which appear particularly during periods of social stress, and their deep roots in Christian demonology. Dominant or insider groups often accuse the outsider group of heretical practices that threaten the destruction of cherished societal values. When a dominant group is threatened by a competing worldview, such as those that beset the church during the late medieval period, accusations of demonic practices may reinvigorate institutional authority and revitalize the commitment and loyalty of followers.[40]

While it is not difficult to grasp the function of demonology in such contexts, there has been little attention in the literature to the varying and complex political uses of such subversion legends. In the contemporary historical context, the SRA legend finds a ready receptivity in conservative Christian groups, with their preoccupation with the Prince of Darkness, defense of majoritarian religious values, and advancement of right-wing politics. Accounts of ritual abuse survivors became standard fare on Christian talk shows in the 1980s, circulated through the expanding cable network channels. These tales of sexual perversion emerged as the Christian pornography of the 1980s, riveting audiences with descriptions of moral degradation.[41]

Less understandable is the receptivity to SRA accounts that flourished in grassroots feminist organizations during this same period. In crisis clinics throughout the country, materials began to circulate on ritual abuse, including elaborate glossaries, checklists of signs and symptoms, and intervention strategies. By 1990, ritual abuse was a standard part of staff training in many feminist crisis facilities throughout the United States.[42] Initially distributed by the Los Angeles County Commission for Women through its task force on ritual abuse, these materials elicited no discernible critical response or skepticism among feminist practitioners. Given the large percentage of suspected female perpetrators of SRA, particularly day-care workers, and the number of feminist "witchcraft" practices implicated in ritual abuse cases, the enthusiastic participation of feminist organizations in circulating news of the "epidemic" is startling.[43]

In 1994, I spoke with dozens of women in feminist crisis organizations in the Pacific Northwest, including therapists who were affiliated with feminist organizations through their training sessions and workshops on SRA (or RA). In addition, I talked with a number of women's studies students who believed in the SRA epidemic; many of them had come to self-identify as cult survivors or had a close relationship with a survivor. A number of themes emerged in these discussions that seem to explain key elements of the social dynamics of SRA within grassroots feminism.

Female Confessionals

As I have argued throughout the book, one of the persisting problems in feminist analyses of women's oppression is in reconciling female agency and victimization. Consciousness raising about sexual abuse, domestic battering, and other forms of violence against women often confronts, at some point, the question of female complicity in such destructive behavior. The various syndromes that explain women's failure to leave abusive situations—such as the battered-wife syndrome—tend to center on limited economic options and other external constraints on women's choices. While such factors are clearly primary and are associated with chronic demoralization, low self-esteem, and depressive withdrawal, by the 1980s psychological factors came also to be recognized as important mediators of women's responses to abuse.[44]

Once a psychology of victimhood was introduced, the separation of political and psychological aspects of abuse became murky. Crisis-center staff increasingly recognized the importance of therapeutic expertise in the area of sexual abuse, while emphasizing the political nature of domestic violence, such as battering. The split between sexual abuse survivors, who were seen as being in need of psychological services, and other categories of female survivors, less likely to be understood as in need of psychological help, found its way into feminist discourse on victimization. The discourse on child sexual abuse permitted many women to articulate the complex emotional valencies of their experiences within the context of the trauma model. Feminist crisis counseling with SRA survivors grew directly out of the trauma model, with its requirement to "believe the victim" and its literal interpretations of memory.

Suspected ritual abuse, like suspected sexual abuse, required an active interventionist stance. One widely circulated manual includes the following guidelines. "First, listen and validate what the caller says. Don't identify a caller as a RA survivor unless she/he presents as such." In practice, however, staff learn that the caller's willingness to self-identify as an RA survivor depends on how the counselor passes various tests, specifically whether the counselor is likely to believe that a person is an RA survivor. The second guideline is that "you must believe that this abuse has happened. Tell the survivor that you believe him/her and why you believe. Let the survivor know why you know about ritual abuse, i.e., you have talked to other ritual abuse survivors and you have had some training sessions, etc." After following guidelines on how to encourage the survivor and after assessing whether helpful alters may be available, counselors are advised to "encourage involvement in therapy" and "educate the survivor about triggers and programming."[45]

The SRA narrative, with its references to the victim's forced participation in sadistic acts, provided a format for a new kind of female testimonial. When I asked staff members at crisis facilities how they came to suspect ritual abuse in listening to callers, the most common response was that the caller expressed horrible guilt over having committed terrible deeds. Over the course of the call, vague references to guilty acts congealed into SRA narratives. Callers would tell of their participation in sexual sadism, of having killed babies, and of having been forced to participate in pornographic orgies. Women could now "confess" and have their antisocial feelings and perverse impulses acknowledged as a "normal" response to an "abnormal situation." It became possible to refer to "female perpetrators," a discourse that would have been unthinkable in the earlier era of feminism, while suggesting that a complex, powerful system—the cult—was the ultimate source of the evil.

The Crisis in Feminist Crisis Services

Many staff members described the context of discovery, the moment of learning about SRA, as revelatory and invigorating, although the more common terms were "horrifying" and "shocking." The staff's descriptions of how they made use of SRA material suggested that it often took the form of galvanizing group activity. One clinic director reported that the staff "devoured everything they could get their hands on," spending considerable hours reviewing materials. This oral incorporative language, it seemed to me at the time, did aptly describe the process: information was "consumed" without being "digested" or integrated into existing knowledge of women's victimization. As a result, one could read, in the same manual, about dozens of pagan holidays that served as "triggers" for the cult and, turning to another part, could read about the rape culture, and further on, the scapegoating of gays and lesbians. Further, the work of right-wing Christians such as James Friesan—an "expert" on ritual abuse—could be circulated in training manuals alongside feminist materials, without any effort to integrate this "dissociative," fragmented feminist theorizing.[46]

Conversion to the SRA stories often came at a time when staff morale was at a low point and community-based organizations were experiencing chronic funding crises. Throughout the 1980s, the decline of an activist women's movement and the rise of political conservatism took a heavy toll on grassroots organizations. Political programs targeting sexual abuse of children survived while other programs, including domestic-battering and poverty-related services, did not because sexuality was the one area where feminists could enlist conservative support and moral outrage.[47]

Feminists and conservative religious groups found a meeting of minds in the SRA controversy in the child-pornography theme. Because it was difficult to argue that large groups of people would organize themselves and invest vast resources to kill their own children out of a simple dedication to evil, child pornography surfaced as a compelling motive. At the same time, the debate over adult pornography had become a divisive one within feminism, particularly because antipornography measures often took a conservative, repressive turn.[48] They tended to draw more of their political ardor from religious, puritanical sentiments than from feminist critiques. Feminist moral crusades, such as the temperance movement, have historically united more effectively when the issue is advanced as a threat to children rather than to adults.[49] Women have been granted political freedom to express outrage and rebellion against men when they have claimed the role of public mothers fighting on behalf of vulnerable youth. (See chapter 1.)

While there is a child-pornography cottage industry in the United States, it is minuscule in comparison with adult pornography. Thus, there was an element of opportunistic victimology at work in feminist organizations' readiness to magnify the threat of child pornographers. In addition, pornography, more than battering, is an issue that evokes strong reactions among young, middle-class women, who are the most likely to be recruited as crisis-center volunteers. The real issue may be the understandable resentment many women have toward male sexual irresponsibility and exploitation and the difficulties for women in separating their own sexual desires from those imposed by a sexist culture.

Further, there is a kind of "return of the repressed" in the feminist erotic imagination. Just as stories of black men raping chaste white women became the folk pornography of the Bible Belt in the early twentieth century,[50] SRA stories emerged as the folk pornography of feminism in the 1980s. Those areas of feminism that foreclose on the sexual imagination of women most forcefully, albeit in the service of combating violence against women, may create a fertile ground for the proliferation of perverse stories of sexual exploitation.

Grievances against Women

For feminist organizations, targeting women as sexual perpetrators seems politically self-defeating, the result of a short-sighted, opportunistic use of whatever issue morally galvanizes the public at the moment. Feminism is no more insulated than other social movements from the desperate impulse to capture the fleeting attention span of the media. It is difficult to sustain movements for social justice during periods when cultural tolerance for human suffering seems to be rising and when fewer and fewer categories of victims are deemed worthy of public assistance. Under such conditions, hysterical reactions are understandable, as is the desire to make use of whatever is at hand to revive demoralized troops in the struggle.

Yet there may be an element of overdetermination, of unconscious motivation, in the failure of feminist organizations to register the irony that so many of the "perpetrators" in SRA allegations were women. As I raised questions about the SRA controversy, expressing some degree of skepticism, a frequent response was that I was an "ivory-tower feminist," whereas those who worked in the crisis centers were in touch with the dismal realities of "real women." Many women in crisis organizations expressed the view that they were the true bearers of an activist feminism and that feminists within academia and the professions were too distant from the daily concerns of women.

There is certainly some basis to this position and to the implicit recognition of the widely divergent fates of women. Some of the resentment is economic, as well as political, and reflects the discrepancies in the fortunes of feminists and awareness of various opportunistic uses of the women's movement by "career feminists." Yet since nurturance and cooperation are unifying values within feminism, in opposition to patriarchal values such as dominance and competition, the emergence of conflict, competition, and hostility among women can feel disquieting. The problem of reconciling female solidarity, on the one hand, and hostility toward other women on the other has always been difficult to integrate into feminist consciousness. There may be an element of "dissociated" feminist consciousness that emerges in stories of female perpetrators. The SRA narrative includes the struggle with a diabolical mother who assumes a commanding role in the operations of the cult. Hostility toward the archetypal powerful mother, less permissible under ordinary circumstances and often chastened by feminism, is notably unleashed in the cosmic drama of the SRA story.

Feminist Pacts with the Devil

Those who have followed the rumor-transmission pattern of SRA allegations emphasize the role of the police in introducing suspected cult abuse into criminal investigations.[51] Indeed, a subculture of SRA believers flourished in police departments throughout the country during the 1980s. During this same period, therapists and feminists developed a historically unprecedented intimacy with police institutions, as workshops and computer networks centering on SRA reports became the primary medium of professional expertise. To some extent, this intimacy was the product of prior alliances and converging pragmatic interests. As reporting laws concerning child abuse were passed (in most states by 1980), the historical distance between mental health workers, including child-protection workers, and policing institutions was reduced. So too, in the women's antiviolence movement, the police were often enlisted to enforce restraining orders and to intervene in situations of domestic violence.[52] Consciousness raising within police departments concerning domestic violence was one of the real feminist gains of the 1980s, as law enforcement became increasingly responsive to community concerns, at least in white communities.

Policing institutions primarily serve the function of social control, enforcing and monitoring the protective boundary between "good folk" and the swelling ranks of imprisoned "bad" elements. Enlisting the police to protect women is often necessary. Yet in relying too heavily on the criminal-justice system to control male behavior, feminists run the risk of legitimizing conservative law-and-order campaigns.[53] Moreover, there may be a vulnerability within grassroots feminism to the captivating paranoia of policing institutions. If a devil of great magnitude is afoot, as SRA believers maintain, emergency measures may be called for. Feminists, demoralized on the long, slow road to emancipation, may find this alliance with crusading police and crusading therapists a most compelling one, but one carrying enormous liabilities, some as yet unforseen.

CONCLUSIONS

One does not have to travel far into the clinical labyrinth of SRA to find that these stories enthrall and capture listeners. If MPD set the stage, introducing a cast of characters, SRA animates these characters within a mythologized universe. This modern drama marks the tremendous distance women patients have traveled, as cultural storytellers, from the borderline-disorder and hysteria categories. Whereas the borderline was known to be "manipulative," "provocative," and savvy in mobilizing enemies and allies, generally creating hysterical chaos, the satanically abused multiple is understood to be eliciting the help of others in a desperate and valiant struggle for survival. The female protagonist's place in the SRA cosmology is part Christ figure, part Virgin Mary, sacrificed on the altar of parental barbarism and transfigured through her suffering.

Possession states—the subjective experience of being involuntarily occupied by an alien presence—are open to various interpretations, contingent in their specific narrative content on the cultural world in which they operate. Clinically, the SRA narrative operates as a kind of "screen memory," in the sense of both concealing and revealing ambiguously experienced threats to the integrity of the self.[54]

While SRA narratives grew out of Christian demonology and its fascination with the rebellious Fallen Angel, they also have an implicitly subversive feminine subtext. Multiplicity introduced conventions for female clinical storytelling, centering on an unstable, fluctuating identity and unrealized female potential, while the SRA story transports these themes into a spiritual realm. Its riveting preoccupation with the devil permits the expression of a transgressive femininity within an overt discourse of female purity and childlike innocence. The narrative facilitates the expression of wild, profane imagery and grandiosity, impulses ordinarily prohibited in female development.

SRA defenders, in the course of validating the external threats faced by women and the reasonableness of their fears, create a majestic universe of terror that ultimately brings women to their knees, impotent before the boundless magnitude of mythologized evils. As a result, these petrified women, like Lot's wife, are less prepared than ever to confront the genuine but mundane problems of everyday existence.

SEX, LIES, AND THERAPY

Chapter 11

OUTFITTED in a bold print dress and matching costume jewelry, "Susan" strode into my office with the air of a woman who still, at fifty, had a strong sense of her sexual powers. As she sat down on the couch, her features darkened. I had come to appreciate the time-worn faces of middle-aged women, faces that could accumulate years and then lose a decade in the course of a conversation.

"I'm furious with you," she stated abruptly, opening our first session after an interim of several years. Susan continued that while our earlier work had been helpful, we had not gotten to the root of her problem. She went on to describe an experience she had during a personal-growth workshop—a childhood memory she had recovered that seemed to explain the stormy relationships and mood swings that continued to trouble her. Rocked in the arms of other group members who aided her in the "birth" of this new memory, Susan had a "flashback" of having been sexually molested at the age of three or four. The sexual imagery was vivid while the identity of the perpetrator was murky. She surmised that it must have been her father.

In the course of her earlier therapy, her conscious memories of her father centered on his emotional seductiveness, and we had explored the possibility of sexual abuse. He was the exciting, idealized, and ultimately disappointing love object of her childhood. Susan was quite seductive as well in her mode of relating to both men and women, and she seemed to identify with her powerful father and his alternating way of being palpably present and chillingly absent. The memory of the father was a part of her object relational world, a presence associated with strivings for recognition. Susan could be socially engaging and provocative but tended to disengage if one got too close. Fiercely independent and ambitious, she also required considerable admiration from others to sustain her precarious sense of self.

Susan and her father were long-standing allies in their mutual contempt for her mother, whom Susan experienced as helpless and childlike as well as physically grotesque. Like many women of her generation, Susan measured her accomplishments by the distance she traveled from her mother's world. The imago of the exciting father, as a "selfobject," represented a union against a more threatening, repressive tie to her mother.[1] For Susan, situations of dependence or vulnerability aroused an emotional free fall into indistinctiveness, a collapsing of vital borders. As Susan confronted me with my failure to assist her in uncovering this early sexual memory, I wondered whether there was some truth to this accusation. While feeling attacked and defensive, I also felt that I may have let her down in some way that needed to be understood, independent of whether the sexual memory was based on an actual past event. Over the years, finding ways of acknowledging my errors as a therapist had become a vital part of my work. The effects of my own therapeutic failings were often difficult to disentangle from the patient's anger or disappointment derived from childhood experiences—feelings that are analyzed and worked through in therapy as transference. But the concept of transference can be protective and self-serving, shielding the therapist from the elements of truth in a patient's confrontations, particularly when these elements seem to be distorted or magnified by the patient's past.[2] Interpreting some disturbing feeling as not really belonging to the present, as actually directed toward someone in the past, can bring both insight and "counterinsight," which involves a defensive resistance to emotional understanding.

Like the parent who feels unappreciated and misunderstood in response to an adult child's accusations of betrayal, I initially was inclined to dismiss Susan's complaints. Had I not, after all, tried hard to provide the therapeutic responsiveness and steadiness that had helped her through various crises? And she had generally improved throughout the several years we had worked together. But like the indignant parent faced with a litany of childhood complaints, I at first responded self-protectively rather than with an objective assessment of Susan's needs or condition.

This defensive restoration of one's own fantasy ideal as the good protector can preempt engagement and self-knowledge. But I was able to shift to a receptive stance, to a willingness to learn something from this angry patient, and she was able to continue telling me what made this new memory feel so transformative. Susan talked about the group members and how she had felt something with them that had always been lacking. Cradled in their arms, she experienced a sense of emotional well-being that seemed to forever elude her. I ventured an interpretation. "Perhaps you wish that I had held you and made you feel so physically and directly cared for in that way." "Yes," Susan responded, "you always seemed to keep some distance between us. There was this reserve about you."

As we proceeded to explore these longings, the content of the memory was less the focus than was the context of its "recovery." The imagery associated with this childhood recollection allowed Susan to feel that her suffering was "real." Further, the process of accessing it signified an active search for a means of grounding her current state of distress. I wondered whether she was bringing back into therapy an old, unresolved longing for a maternal connection that she had fled from as too dangerous and disappointing in relation to her mother and that she had not been able to satisfactorily find in her relationship with me.

Bringing this recovered memory to me was both a hostile demand and a "gift." The hostile demand was apparent in her implication that she had received something from this personal-growth group in a weekend that I had been unable or unwilling to give her over the years we had worked together. Yet, as a gift, the new memory was an expression of both her capacity for self-discovery and her desire to enlist me in understanding the past in a deeper way. Coming back with the prized object—the powerful, transformative memory— seemed, in part, a demand for recognition, which is a frequent motif in the lives of girls and women.[3] For many, recovered memories of sexual abuse are an effort to disengage from familial entrapments, to fortify the blurry boundary between self and others, and to sever binding ties. But for others the new memory is a bridge back into the relational past and a striving for revitalized contact with others.

For Susan, the recovered memory of childhood sexual abuse became a means of engaging her mother, who did confirm that Susan had been fondled as a toddler by a neighbor boy. Whether this childhood incident was related to the new memory is unclear. However, it is evident that the remembrance was associated with the fantasy of restored connection, a search for an intervening image that holds the potential for changing the outcome of an old relational struggle.[4] But, as with the sacred totem, the fascination with the object can blind observers to the rituals and meanings surrounding its use.

This chapter focuses on the therapeutic implications of transformative remembering and explores a range of sexual stories bridging the symbolic and the "real." Through clinical material drawn from my own practice, I discuss the interpersonal conflicts that emerge through imagery of the body and the psychological terrain that such imagery may encompass. In describing clinical cases, I have omitted or altered biographical details that would identify the patients discussed, while attempting to preserve the psychodynamic meanings and integrity of their stories.

CREATIVE ENCOUNTERS

A prototypical drama not uncommon in the lives of many women bears some resemblance to Susan's uncertain path into adulthood. It begins in adolescence as the girl couples early, fleeing a stormy relationship with her mother.[5] But she soon returns, like the prodigal daughter, with a new baby on her hip, to enlist the aid of the mother whom she had left behind. She and Mama now take care of the new baby and vicariously revisit the earlier struggle between the two of them.

This story is less common among middle-class than among poor and working-class women, who often establish cooperative ties with other women through shared care-giving responsibilities.[6] Poverty and blunted opportunities make the sacrifices of early parenthood a more acceptable tradeoff than they may be for young people who are offered promising futures. So too, the vitality of a newborn can warm the soul—and can even create a corporeal barrier against the cold edges of a hostile world. Returning home can be the last refuge after venturing out and searching for something that remains perpetually out of reach.

Internally, this return home also can be prompted by the lingering force of unmet childhood longings. The fantasy of bringing the baby (or the memory, the creative object) to Mama in order to revive her spirit, of carrying back home the gift that opens up new possibilities for mutual exchange, can be a dominating one. Like the memory, the baby is an intervening presence between mother and daughter that protects against dangerous engulfment or dependence.[7]

Although raised in a middle-class family, Susan had also coupled early and brought to young motherhood the fantasy of restored wholeness and connection. And this fantasy had betrayed her, as it has so many other women. In a search for new generative possibilities within herself, she had, in her thirties and forties, pursued various prospects for a satisfying career. Susan's strivings for self-development placed her at odds with the physically and emotionally domineering husband of her first marriage. Even though she was finally able to leave him, she continued to waver between a romanticized idealization of and a profound contempt for and envy of powerful men. Her own sense of personal entitlement—even grandiosity—frequently collapsed as she was overtaken by frustrations and personal defeats that underscored her ancient belief that she was truly not entitled to much and that what she took from life was not legitimately her own.

How are these dynamics related to Susan's recovery of a memory of childhood sexual abuse? We may be tempted to conclude—and correctly, in a sense—that this new memory was an artifact of a hypnotic group experience. The group had employed a cultural script—the search for early sexual abuse as an organizing explanation for diffuse forms of distress in women's lives.[8] And Susan had played her part in the drama, producing the requisite memory that justified the attentive concern she received. Indeed, the sexual memory may have been stimulated by the eroticized nature of the group itself. If there was sexual seduction expressed through this memory, it may have been related more to the immediate encounter than to a past one.

But concluding that Susan's memory was "false" or "implanted" by the group misses the continuity of past and present in this moment of discovery. Indeed, the elaboration of sexual memories into increasingly dramatic tales of childhood horror may be a response to this dismissive devaluation of women's experiences. To devalue an emotional discovery as mere fool's gold can be a form of emotional assault. Many women are accustomed to not being taken seriously, and they may employ hysterical defenses to break through this wall of chilling repudiation. (See chapter 3.)

In my discussions with Susan about the meaning of her recovered memory, two relational themes emerged. One involved Susan's highly ambivalent relationship with her parents, both of whom seemed, on the basis of her reported history, to be quite self-absorbed. The recovered memory seemed related to an effort to break through a sense of emotional deadness and to enlist others in recognizing her needs, just as she had tried so futilely to evoke parental responsiveness in the past. In this sense, recovering the memory was one episode among many in her life where a crisis served to rally others and arouse a vital emotional connection.[9] Sexual abuse of a young child has a particularly evocative power in our culture, vivifying both the potency of the suffering and the right of the victim to make demands upon others.

The other relational theme involved in Susan's bringing the sexual abuse memory to me was her attempt to locate and concretize some difficulty she sensed in our therapeutic relationship. She was correct, in a sense, that I had remained emotionally aloof in ways that I had not fully recognized at the time. In reflecting back, my fear of my own aggression toward her—of my impulse to deflate her grandiosity—resulted in a certain emotional remove, perhaps a counteridentification with the "engulfing" mother. This distance was partly helpful in preserving some stability to our relationship, in providing a holding presence that could withstand the considerable emotional heat she was capable of generating. But my distance was also defensive in a blinding way. Rather than recognizing my own aggressive, destructive impulses, bringing them under some conscious control and making therapeutic use of them, I had internally disavowed such feelings. Like the "good" mother who goes through the motions of parenting, I often resisted genuine, empathic contact while maintaining an interpretive stance.

Many individuals may well have been abused in the ways that are later recalled in "flashbacks" or other intrusions into consciousness, but, as with Susan, the difficult and important questions center on the context in which these images emerge and the various interpersonal uses that may be made of them. Sorting memories into true and false piles obscures this generative, indeterminate place where truth and falsehood meet, entangled in contradictory communicative possibilities.

TRUTH AND LIES

A lie, at times, can be closer to the truth than a fact. I would like to illustrate this indeterminate relationship between truth and falsehood with another patient of mine, a man in his early thirties who entered treatment because of his difficulties with feeling and expressing emotion. Michael was a pleasant, cerebral person, who prided himself on his rational approach to life. His wife was less appreciative of this tendency, often complaining that he was unable to show affection or empathy. Her powerful, emotional outbursts stirred a cool detachment and methodical problem-solving stance in Michael. Hysterics and obsessives, as has frequently been observed, are often intimate companions.

During puberty, Michael had been diagnosed with a serious health condition and was subjected to a series of painful procedures and hospitalizations throughout his adolescence. Although the condition, never successfully treated, threatened to significantly shorten his life, he described this medical history to me with the emotional distance of a surgeon. While the chronic ailment was clearly a distressing preoccupation, his inhibitions seemed to be strengthened by this dreadful knowledge. Michael avoided any state of arousal, much to the detriment of his capacity for emotional closeness or sexual pleasure.

One day, he told me a story, prefacing it by saying sheepishly, "I used to lie to my friends about how I got the surgical scars on my chest." The story involved getting into a knife fight with several older boys while walking to school through a park. They had tried to steal his lunch, and as he fought back, one of them viciously attacked him with a blade. As I listened, I found myself believing quite literally Michael's tale. As he conveyed the terror and aloneness he felt, I experienced some of these feelings with him, forgetting completely that the story was untrue. I was momentarily spellbound. As we discussed this story, I commented that this "lie" had allowed him to feel something that was true, to put into words some of his childhood sense that his body was under attack. Through the lie he was able to convey disturbing feelings to me in a way that he had been unable to do before.

The truth of the lie can be understood on several levels. First, Michael had drawn on a male narrative of combat to explain the prosaic surgical trauma of his childhood. Just as women may draw on sexual abuse as a metaphor for violations of the self, men may similarly draw on battle narratives to symbolically convey myriad conflicts centering on the body or gender identity.[10] Michael pointed out that other children were never able to understand the medical aspects of his life, and so he had found a readily available "script" in explaining his mysterious scars. The physical scars were the lasting reminders of those injuries to his sense of bodily integrity and masculine self that necessitated the creation of an emotionally compelling narrative.

Second, Michael had employed the story to convey his sense of having been aggressively attacked by sadistic others in the course of his illness. While he could rationally comprehend, even as a ten-year-old boy, the necessity of various medical procedures, a part of that experience was not "rational." On an unconscious level, these procedures felt like vicious punishment, with the image of his father—a high school athletic coach and a devoutly religious man—looming on the horizon of his childhood as suspected "assailant." Our discussion of this memory of the lie opened up new exploration of his terror of his father, whose temper was frightening. At the same time, he was terrorized by his own unacknowledged aggression—his impulses to "knife" those on whom he so desperately depended. This transformative remembering became a vehicle for knowledge—

in this case, emotional and relational knowledge of the self. It provided a bridge from the "rational" into the "irrational" aspects of his inner world and from the private to the interpersonal realm of relating to me.

TRANSFORMATIVE REMEMBERING

The interpersonal context of psychotherapy shapes the knowledge that is recovered in complex ways. As the patient tells his or her life story, particular events emerge as prototypical of later conflicts. Events that achieve this status are not inevitably causal in the sense of setting in motion demonstrable effects that result directly from them. Where symptoms follow from specific trauma—such as the loss of a parent, a severe childhood illness, or episodes of abuse—one can speak of originating causes. But more often one finds an array of experiences that feel "determinative" and myriad prior contexts that potentiate their effects. Further, childhood events are retrieved and employed in various ways over time, depending on one's current state of mind and the nature of emerging intrapsychic or interpersonal conflicts.[11] The therapeutic relationship also provides its own complex prompts for engaging the past. The questions asked, the responsivity evoked in relation to particular themes, the coconstructed memories of the patient's past, all mediate the knowledge that is gained. Much like "priming," therapeutic interpretations sensitize the patient to subsequent meanings and associations in looking back on an unfolding personal history.[12]

What truth is contained in the memories of Susan and Michael if the determinative status of memory is so irreducibly ambiguous? A number of considerations come into play that stabilize this apparent infinite regression in meaning. First, episodic memory—memory for personal events—takes on a scriptlike character over time when repeated experiences are integrated into self and object schema. Second, the truth of the memory may reside in underlying themes—what Neisser termed repisodic remembering—rather than in its factual content. (See chapter 2.) For example, a male patient may describe his father as morally severe and unyielding. The therapist asks for examples of experiences that led the patient to this conclusion, or for pictures that come to mind of the judging father. The patient is likely to recall real and imagined scenes vivifying this parental imago. The "gist" of the memory is more likely to be accurate than are the details. Yet details create the sense of vivid, experiential knowledge and are related to accessing the affective coloring of autobiographical memory. Efforts to situate knowledge about relationships in a past scene—whether imagined or actual—open up a field of imagery that may aid in understanding the relational meaning ascribed to life events.

A third finding that may guide our understanding of how experiences are preserved in mind is that source memory—knowledge of when and where one acquired information—tends to be lost, although unique, emotionally significant events are less likely to be disengaged from an original context or source than are repeated ones. One implication of these findings is that ongoing relationships, which are more likely to be constitutive of the self than are episodic encounters, are both the most and the least memorable. They are most memorable in that they are likely to generate stable, representational processes based on a rich reservoir of past experience. They are least memorable in that they are associated with generic, scriptlike recollections, where the details are less crucial to the "truth" of the memory than is its relational structure.

Fourth, ongoing relationships, particularly those originating in early dependence ties, are generative of complex, divergent meanings, encompassing a wider scope of self/other configurations than are relationships of a more limited nature. The effort to identify an originating cause, the source of selfhood as it is presently constituted, out of the contours of these more ambiguous yet determinative vistas of self/other representations becomes a creative act—much like creation mythologies.

There is a dynamic interplay, then, between the factual elements of memory and the interpretive work of remembering. As events recede in time, the interpretive work assumes increased significance, as it does when events take on emotional importance in relation to some central aspect of the self. From a psychoanalytic perspective, clinical investigation centers on what the patient is attempting to evoke through the present telling of a story as much as on the content of past encounters or of deeds done.[13]

How do we understand the contemporary context that shapes the contours of the past that is recovered? Why, we may ask, does the patient try to remember and how might we understand what is involved in the search for episodes in the past that hold explanatory potential? Michael, for example, might recall an image of the judging father because of a current struggle concerning guilt and failure. He feels as though he were standing before the father in the present, condemned for falling short of his standards. Now it both matters and doesn't matter whether this memory is an accurate representation of the father's attitudes. It matters to the extent that the patient is attempting to understand why the activation of conscience—or moral sensibilities—is so paralyzing and why his or her own superego dictates are so unremittingly harsh. Yet, over time, the patient comes to see that a part of the father has become an aspect of the patient's own mental structures. Ideally, the repressive hold of this paternal imago is progressively modified by internalizing the more reasonable, empathic interpretations of the therapist, a process Kohut terms "transmuting internalization."[14]

Thus far, I have emphasized the context invoking memory "work" and the scripts contained in memory schema. The memories described are scriptlike and consciously accessible—they are explicit—even though ideas and affects associated with them may remain unconscious. Yet it is important to recognize that positive, loving feelings may be repressed as readily as negative, hostile ones, for these loving feelings may be associated with unbearable conflict and disappointment. For example, a male patient may remember his punitive father and his hatred of him, offering countless memory reports to support this mental representation, but he may be unable to recollect tender moments or longings for his father's approval. These unconscious wishes may be revealed indirectly, through slavish submission to male authority or through a phobic avoidance of intimacy with other men.

In a therapeutic situation, a recovered memory—that is, a new memory—is suggestive of an important shift, one that carries a range of potential intrapsychic and interpersonal meanings. For example, a male patient's remembering for the first time a tender experience with his father may disrupt the prior imago of the relentlessly harsh father. The stimulus for this new memory may be an emerging tenderness toward a male therapist or feelings of conscious affection toward another man in his life. Once again, the recovered memory signals some emerging or recovered capacity within the self rather than being an autonomous, veridical image of the past that is leaking into awareness. The ability to access a broad range of memories, with variable affective content and differentiated self and other (object) representations, has less to do with the empirical status of past events than with current, shifting self-structures or affective capacities. There is a dynamic, motivational aspect to remembering, just as there is to the process of forgetting.

The sudden intrusion of the past into consciousness—often described as a flashback—can signify a range of phenomena. In the first case I presented, Susan experienced her memory as an emergent truth forcefully impinging on her consciousness. Her subjective conviction of its authenticity sprang from its apparent externality: it appears, unbidden, like a visitation from the gods. This revelatory aspect of the memory gives it a dramatic power, much like an epiphany.

At the same time, Susan's positioning of herself as passive receptor to a communication from her unconscious makes it difficult for her to recognize both the social field of the memory's "discovery" and her own motivational state. For Susan, this revelatory recollection emerged during a period of crisis; her husband and adult children were openly angry with her, charging her with reckless disregard for the needs of others. The group experience, and the associated recovered memory, provided a temporary deliverance from this tortuous situation and a reprieve from her own guilty conscience. The "false" aspect of the memory may be less in its content than in the fantasies about it. Working through its meaning involves understanding the motivational wish—which may involve the desire to be relieved of guilt and to be removed from a terrible situation. For Susan, the criticisms from her family felt like an intolerable assault, eliciting, perhaps, memories of other assaults on the self.

This wish for a clarifying truth is the wellspring of religious experiences and dramatic recovered memories alike. With recovered memories, the vividness and verisimilitude of the memory dispel nagging uncertainty over its origin or meaning. It feels transparent and externally imposed, liberating the sufferer from some oppressive internal experience. An element of projection may be involved in such memories, as dreaded or unwanted aspects of the self are externalized onto a past scene, relieving the individual of anxiety. Since auto-biographical memory involves referencing external events of import to the self, it may be employed to objectify, even overobjectify, elusive processes of mind. The creation of a new memory can be a defensive operation of the ego that involves placing the dilemma "elsewhere"—that is, in the past and outside of core constitutive aspects of the self.

The trauma discourse of the unconscious—which envisions the yet-to-be-known aspects of mind as carefully revealing essential truths through timely and accurate memories—is, in some respects, helpful. Much of the recovered memory literature assumes this stance toward the unconscious. (See chapter 3.) It thus represents an effort to overcome phobic dread of concealed aspects of mind. Yet this concept of the rational, wise-child unconscious carries with it a significant cost. It does not permit the patient to experience confusing, murky internal states or destructive impulses as part of self-experience. The assumption, implicit in much of the recovered memory literature, is that conflict is imported into the psyche from an external source. The memory, it is assumed, is the register of a powerful other on the self, and the subject's own internal states or conflicting desires are not understood to be essential to the "recovery" of the memory's meaning. For women, particularly, intense aggressive and sexual imagery may feel unfamiliar or ego-alien, incongruent with available feminine narratives. Patient and therapist may anxiously foreclose on such intense, ambiguous states, searching for a place in the past to securely deposit what they mutually experience as dangerous and unstable.

One of the central differences between psychoanalytic therapy and various competing approaches, such as trauma therapy, is in the use of the concepts of transference and countertransference. (See chapter 3.) Both terms refer to what is evoked emotionally in the therapeutic encounter and to the transfer of past relational experiences and conflicts into the present. Transference is, of course, a ubiquitous phenomenon. As Szasz once wryly observed, transference is no more a unique product of therapy than are microorganisms forms of life that exist under microscopes.[15] Psychoanalytic therapists analyze the processes by which the past becomes present, making use of responses in the therapeutic encounter to vivify and intervene in the patient's object relational world. Just as the patient's relational conflicts and defenses are unconsciously evoked in the clinical encounter, so too are the therapist's. And just as feelings and conflicts originating in relational struggles of the past may be transferred onto the therapist, so too does the therapist transfer feelings onto the patient. The difference, ideally, is in the therapist's knowledge of her or his own inner world and emotional reactions and in the therapist's ability to make use of them in helping the patient gain new self-understanding.

In the two case examples I presented, childhood memories emerged as communications bridging past and present relational dilemmas. The truth of the memories was located in their interpersonal and affective meaning rather than in their factual content. In this sense, remembering involved an effort to vivify a conflict involving self in relation to an "object," an internal representation of a person or a part of a person. For the therapist, listening to memories requires an attentiveness to multiple meanings and to the position of self in relation to the other embedded in the memory narrative. A childhood recollection may be factually false yet true in the sense that it represents an aspect of selfhood within a relational field.

Subjectively, however, interpreting a mental event as a memory feels quite different from interpreting it as a fantasy, imago, or mental representation. In part, it feels different because the capacity to distinguish between internally and externally generated imagery—between a fantasy and an external event—is a vital part of reality testing. Young children and highly disturbed individuals have more difficulty discriminating between the two, and are more likely to incorporate fantasy material into narrative accounts of external events.[16]

As the literature on hypnotic states suggests (see chapter 6), however, the boundary between externally and internally derived imagery may be less distinct for most individuals than is commonly assumed. Fact and fiction, like history and mythology, infuse one another, making the boundaries between them imprecise. It is not simply that wishes and imaginative processes compromise reality testing, although they certainly may have such effects. The generative and motivational capacities of mind also open up possibilities for seeing reality in a new light, even giving rise to creative discoveries and insights.

It may require either considerable emotional security or social distance to remain untroubled by the uncertainties attached to human consciousness. For women who are striving to emerge out of the shadows and silences of history, the acknowledgment of uncertainty may feel like a retreat. The contemporary movement to focus on the mental traffic in memory, over against other mental representational processes, is itself an effort to stabilize and concretize the activity of the mind. Autobiographical recall carries with it the subjective conviction that "this is how it really happened." The call to remember is a call for certainty, and it has a unifying appeal in women's contemporary refusal to be silenced, as problematic as this triumph may be.

DISSOCIATIVE STATES AND MULTIPLE SELVES

How, then, do we assemble the various fragments of experience in creating a more authentic past while preserving the rich textures and ambiguous borders of female selfhood? In previous chapters I have addressed the costs of therapeutic foreclosure on uncertainty and have focused on cultural anxieties mediating this tendency, particularly in relation to unstable identity states in women. The trauma/dissociation paradigm allows women patients to express a broad array of sexual, aggressive, and rebellious imagery, but it requires the production of a trauma memory in order to redeem and make sense of this therapeutic project. The trauma paradigm has been employed in negotiating a difficult cultural barrier, and the passage through it has involved reconciling older ideals of femininity—as childlike, chaste, and nurturant—and emergent, divergent possibilities. These more culturally transgressive "selves"—which include more aggressive, sexual, defiant awarenesses—evoke ambivalence for many women patients and their therapists, as various unintegrated states surface and retreat dissociatively in the therapeutic encounter.

Dissociation is defined in *The Diagnostic and Statistical Manual* as "a disruption in the usually integrative functions of consciousness, memory, identity, or perception."[17] In applying this definition to clinical practice, we might ask what constitutes "normally integrative functions," particularly for women, who are most often diagnosed as dissociative. Further, what clinical significance may we attach to fluctuating mental states, and when do we assume that they are indicative of trauma, sexual or other? As a defensive response to trauma, dissociation is a means of protecting against anxiety by fragmenting knowledge of overwhelming events. But dissociation also may be understood as encompassing emergent, unassimilated psychological experience more generally—whether memories, imagery, emotions, or desires. It may signify a self in a state of flux, a moment of awareness of some yet-to-be-known aspect of the inner world.

In everyday examples of these incongruencies, a therapist may sense that the patient is unconsciously communicating a disavowed mental state: the woman who pulls her wedding ring on and off as she describes impassively some recent effort to please her husband; the man who describes with an air of emotional detachment a recent episode of being humiliated by a colleague, as though it were happening to someone else. We may recognize this defensive detachment, or divided consciousness, in many forms of disturbance, both normal and pathological. Some aspect of an experience—an affect, an idea, an impulse—is separated off and unintegrated into consciousness.

Repression implies motivated, unconscious forgetting, as does dissociation. A key difference between the repression and dissociation models, as established in chapter 3, is in what is assumed to happen to the material when it is out of consciousness. The repression model elaborated through ego psychology and object relations theory includes a range of defenses, with varying adaptive meanings and psychic costs. For example, internalization, identification, projection, rationalization, sublimation are all based on repression, but they operate as defenses by distorting reality in various ways. Clinicians who rely heavily on the dissociation model adhere to a view of the unconscious based on fragmentation rather than distortion. They stress the mind's capacity to preserve the original source of disturbance, albeit in a fragmented form. A corollary to this stance is that the unconscious can be directly accessed through therapeutic interventions.

The case I present next illustrates some of the critical problems in the clinical interpretation of abuse memories and dissociative states and illustrates as well the shifting valencies in transference and countertransference processes. The woman I describe is not a survivor of father/daughter incest but does meet the current criteria for a sexual abuse survivor. Through this presentation of my work with her over two years of psychodynamic therapy, I hope to illustrate and make salient three central points: first, the ambiguities in clinically differentiating the effects of sexual abuse from the effects of other traumatic childhood events; second, the shifting meanings attached to abuse experiences in the course of treatment; and, third, the variable meanings of dissociation in the patient's intrapsychic and interpersonal worlds.

Lana is a Vietnamese woman who was in her thirties at the time I initially saw her. Born in Vietnam, she had arrived with the first boat lift in 1975 during early adolescence. A slight, soft-spoken woman with large expressive eyes, she sat quite motionless during our first session. There was a tremendous sense of suffering about her, as well as a tenseness. She was still except for her hands: her graceful, long fingers circled the air to assist her in her efforts to speak. She described herself as shy. Yet she dressed in a flamboyant style that suggested another side to her.

Lana sought treatment because of a deteriorating relationship with her husband, Jack, a European/American man with whom she had lived for about five years. She also wondered whether she might have been sexually abused as a child, adding that she recognized herself in many of the self-help portraits of sexual abuse survivors. While she initially reported having no memories of sexual abuse, this "wondering" introduced an important vector into our subsequent therapeutic exploration of the past.

Most immediately distressing to Lana was her sense of emotional numbness and her lack of sexual feeling for her husband. Jack had high standards, she informed me, and he was "always helping me to improve myself, particularly my English." She overtly welcomed his tutoring and agreed with his assessment that she needed "self-improvement," yet she was less able over time to make use of his many suggestions. Lana was in agreement with Jack's observation that she was not improving but, rather, worsening in her professed desire for social independence and cultural literacy.

Toward the end of our first session, Lana described a minor collision with her car a few days prior that had been quite upsetting. When she described having "rear-ended" someone in a dazed state, I wondered where she was during this state. I also wondered about her aggressive feelings—what experiences she was having with aggression that might be disorganizing to her.

I was aware during this first session of my hostility toward her husband, and I also felt sympathy for this oppressed woman. I felt the impulse to protect her and to invoke in her some rage toward this man who seemed to be so undermining of her capacities. At the same time, I knew that Jack might represent some aspect of her own ego ideal, so my impulse to attack him was also directed at a part of my patient.

Many of the elements of Lana's experience—the depressive symptoms and sadomasochistic flavor of her relationship with her husband—were familiar clinically. But my initial feeling was that I would not be able to understand Lana. It was not her English, which was quite fluent, but rather her cultural world that left me uncertain. I was keenly aware of the limitations of my background, as a white person, and my impulse was to retreat in the face of the cultural divide between us. I wondered whether the range of affect or integrative capacities that I assume to be normal or adaptive could be applied to another culture, and I also wondered how to think about the difference between cultural labeling and therapeutic diagnostics. Do categories such as depression, dissociation, or passive-dependent personality really apply? So the problems that are always latent in clinical work—the various assumptions that structure and organize clinical data—were right there before me, mobilizing uncertainty and feelings of inadequacy. Part of this sense of wanting to withdraw, of feeling inadequate to the task, was in response to Lana's own sense of helplessness and emotional isolation. Just as she often lapsed into dissociative distance in her relationships with others, I had, in the course of the hour, experienced some aspects of this emotional retreat.

Over the early months, Lana spoke more and more freely even as she cried softly during most of the sessions. We talked about crying and what she was aware of as she cried. She confessed that crying felt extremely shameful and that it was an expression of submission and defeat. At the same time, she began to understand her crying not simply as an expression of her mute and humiliated state but as an effort to feel and to evoke a feeling within me. The fights with Jack always left her in a state of tears, followed by an inconsolable sense of aloneness. As she cried with me, I felt a vague sense of guilt, of feeling implicated in unnamed transgressions.

We began to explore what these fights and numbing tears evoked historically. Lana talked of growing up in a family where there was a tremendous amount of fighting and warfare, not only in the cultural backdrop of her early childhood but at home between her mother and father. The dissociated states that she connected with the fighting, where she could imagine herself as having vacated her body or as being somewhere else, also evoked the memory of frantic efforts to escape the aggressively charged atmosphere of her early world.

Lana began to construct a picture out of fragments of the past. Her early experience in Vietnam was hazy and not very accessible to her. Her move to the United States also was associated with confusion. Most of what she remembered was her mother crying. Her mother was described as a joyless woman whose hopelessness and grief were deeply inscribed in Lana's memory of emigration. This crossing of the ocean also came to serve as a metaphor for the traumatic loss of childhood and of her own entry into adolescence without a sense of emotional protection. Her crying mother felt useless to her, as she felt useless to herself in alleviating her emotional distress in the present.

The memories of the early years also included recollections of criminal activity. Lana's parents had been involved in some kind of illegal activity in Vietnam that was carried over to the United States. There was a vague memory of the parents being away in jail—one of the parents, maybe both, she was not sure. There was a hazy sense of something having happened when she was little, during this time when someone was in jail. The parents also traveled, and their various comings and goings were cloaked in secrecy. She also remembered relatives and friends taking care of her, providing a quite vital sense of belonging and emotional warmth.

Some therapists would stress the importance of recovering these early traumatic memories, with the clinical assumption that Lana's emotional numbness was a dissociative response to early trauma. Even if this formulation is correct, what is important clinically is understanding how the patient is making use of memory—and what she is communicating of her relational world through emerging memory fragments. I commented, at this point, on the coming and going of people, of her own struggle, even now, to find something to hold on to in those frightening moments when her world seemed as though it were falling apart. She responded by telling me how she comforted herself when she was little by making doll clothes, dressing and undressing her dolls, over and over.

I privately wondered, at this point, whether the "something" that happened" when her parents were away involved sexual abuse. I also wondered whether the vague memory that they may have been in jail was a fantasy—a wish for punishment of the violating parents. I asked what she could recall and asked about her own associations with dressing and undressing dolls. She remembered that as a young girl she had wanted to be someone else and that going to the United States meant that she could transform herself. Looking back, she felt that this doll play centered on remaking herself, a private, ritualized act of transfiguration.

While early images of the parents centered on their criminal activity and the experience of emotional abandonment, memories turned to her mother's powerful temper, which was aroused particularly during Lana's adolescence. She recalled that her mother would become enraged and that she, as the oldest daughter in the family, would be the primary object of the mother's fury. Lana experienced her mother as weak and helpless in her frequent fights with the father but as frighteningly powerful when she turned on her. As Lana moved into adolescence—and American culture—she began to defy her mother and the two of them were in a state of continual escalating combat.

This image of the defiant, aggressive daughter struck me as surprising, initially, six months into therapy. The conflict between her passive, submissive side and her own aggression and narcissistic rage became a central motif in therapy. She recalled a fight with her mother when she had "talked back." Her mother yelled at her and hit her, and Lana gave her mother a wooden spoon, the instrument of her own punishment. In this sense, she aided her mother's aggression—engaging her in a relational struggle that signified Lana's effort to break through her helplessness and numbing isolation.

In working with this kind of material—memories of childhood abuse—the tendency to impose a formulaic or particular moral cast on the events, partly in response to the disturbing feelings evoked in patient and therapist alike, can interfere with therapeutic receptivity to a range of unconscious meanings. Lana was conscious of her hostility and contempt toward both her parents and particularly toward her mother. She had a sense of her own entitlement and of feeling superior to her mother from an early age.[18] We discussed what it felt like to give her mother the spoon and Lana's associations with this active engagement with her tormentor. She described her sense of moral triumph over her mother in this act, of feeling the victor even in this moment of defeat. As the imago of the monstrous mother became increasingly vivid, I wondered whether Lana's own infantile rage had infused these memories of the mother. Over time, we returned to this prototypical struggle with the mother in different ways, with the shifting valencies of our therapeutic relationship allowing new uses of this formative scene. What came to feel particularly troubling to Lana was her discovery, through her own defiance, of some weakness and desperation in her mother. As we explored her hatred of her mother, Lana became concerned that she had destroyed a vital maternal connection through her own rage. In looking back, this act of aiding her mother in her own punishment seemed to be a way of reasserting the corporeal reality of the mother, of resuscitating the defeated mother. She recognized a kind of atonement in the beating and in later sadomasochistic engagements, a strangely comforting sense of being held, of a desperate connection.[19]

Sexuality emerged early on as a concern for Lana, initially expressed through sexual problems with her husband. She described his sexual withdrawal from her and his complaint that she merely wanted a father figure, that she was using sex to be held. He had noticed—unlike other men with whom she had been sexual—that she did not derive much pleasure from sex in the genital sense. Her sexuality was organized around a pregenital longing for some kind of contact with a holding presence. Yet Jack's recognition of her need, his probing gaze, made her fearful that she could not protect herself against the shamefulness of his discovery. Lana's early sexual awarenesses were against the backdrop of her father's sexuality. She recalled that her father and mother fought mainly about his infidelity. He apparently had lovers and occasionally saw prostitutes. The mother would find out about his sexual exploits, and they would fight. The mother's own father—Lana's maternal grandfather—had abandoned her as a young girl. Lana recognized her mother's tremendous sadness, and at the same time she despised her mother for her helplessness in the face of it. In a certain way, she admired her father's capacity to escape the torment of the family's enforced dependence. The father caused the mother pain through his infidelity, but, at the same time, he embodied the prized, masculine other, the one who possessed the freedom to act on his own desires.[20]

Early on in treatment, Lana recalled an experience, during early childhood, when she was fondled and undressed by an older brother. She began to talk about this as we explored her early sexual experiences and feelings. She remembered being quite stimulated by this experience with the brother and having a sense of doing what Daddy was doing. There was some forbidden pleasure in this association with what Daddy had done, a sibling enactment of paternal transgressions. This may have been a later reconstruction of the experience. She also described the shame she felt in seeing herself as being like the prostitutes whom Daddy saw. So the incestuous relationship with the brother seemed to evoke less an awareness of his intrusiveness than it did a sense of a forbidden discovery.

During early adolescence, Lana became sexually involved with a much older man. Her discovery of her own sexuality at this time was for her an important bridge out of her mother's world. She recalled her parents' having card parties where she would serve the guests and feel herself to be in the position of servant. Her responsiveness to this older man, who was a frequent guest at these parties and a kind of avuncular presence in the family, represented a violation of both incest and age taboos. At the same time, her eager interest in him was a flagrant and defiant protest against her own position as servant. She warmed to this man's overtures, and they began a love affair. While this relationship was clearly abusive, Lana's initial memory was that this man did care for her. To characterize these experiences as traumatic or abusive prior to her own explorations of their meanings, would be to rob her of her initial insight: that this man provided a bridge, a kind of transitional object, out of a depressed state. Lana's mother found out about this secret affair, and a new period of warfare between her and her mother began. Lana persisted in seeing this man, sneaking out of the house and making furtive phone calls in defiance of her mother's insistence that she stop. This warfare culminated in Lana's leaving her family and going to live with relatives.

Lana's final expulsion from the family was precipitated by her call to the police after her mother had beaten her. She had some understanding, by then, of the concept of child abuse and of her own legal rights. Calling the police represented both an assertion of her rights and, at the same time, a violation of a cultural taboo.[21] She had shown the ultimate disrespect to her parents by calling in the authorities—white people—to rescue her from her torture. This was a painful conflict for her, one that led her to flee Vietnamese culture entirely. Her intrapsychic experience was of having killed her culture, which carried the memory of stable, maternal objects even as it evoked destructive ones.

Lana was intent on becoming Americanized as she took flight from her family and community. She saw Vietnamese culture as destructive and as repressive of women. "You are a slave," she said, "and if you are a daughter you are more of a slave. Children obey their parents, no matter what." During the first six months of therapy, much of her aggression was directed toward her culture, which she saw as the enemy of her own emotional survival. I began to be aware of my own uneasiness as this aggression mounted. I felt that this warfare against her culture was an effort to free herself from her own harsh, cruel superego. However, I also felt that the devaluing of her "mother culture" was part of the Americanization experience, the demand of enculturation itself, and that it had left her vulnerable to new forms of oppression in the dominant culture she had entered.

About nine months into treatment, Lana suddenly reported matter-of-factly, "I've gone back to my Vietnamese name." Lan was the name she had given up when she had left home as an adolescent. This name change seemed to signal a shift in her engagement with the past. At the same time, she began to express a longing for a deeper closeness with me, a desire for something more. She wanted to know about me and felt resentful of my reserve, asking to hug me at times at the end of sessions. She alternated between idealizing me, as her first woman friend, and feeling an unbearable sense of insufficiency in the relationship. She joined a women's group, which was a way both of recognizing the limits of what I could give her and of acting out her rage toward me. (She would compare my approach to the group approach, often finding me lacking.) At the same time, joining the women's group represented a progressive effort toward knowing women in a more vital and intimate way than in the past.

As she began increasingly to express criticism of me, Lan voiced the suspicion that I held some secret knowledge that allowed me to privately triumph over her (as she had over her mother). At the same time, she began to demand that I tell her what to do, and she seemed to be provoking me to become more "Jack-like." Her sense of failing to find a gratifying, maternal object mobilized aggressive engagement. However, she was no longer in the passive, masochistic position but, rather, in open defiance, even as she wanted to be held and controlled. With this more openly aggressive engagement, Lan began to describe her fear that she was really like her father, that she used sex the way he used it, and that sex was for her a game, a form of currency. Even though she pretended to care for men, she wondered whether she really did. She had a secret sense of triumph, of victory over them, in having their desires aroused and in withholding her own. While men thought women to be the more fragile and vulnerable, she said, it was actually they, with their bulging member, who were ridiculously exposed. Women pretended to be weak in order to make men feel strong. I asked Lan whether she felt there was emotional pretending in our relationship as well. She responded that she was uncertain about whether I would still like her if I knew things she had done in the past or whether I would just "pretend to" for the money.

As we talked about her associations with dirty money and dirty secrets, Lan began to identify what felt like a cruel part of her own sexuality. There were memories that she had never spoken about and had barely thought about. She talked about her guilt over a brother, eight years younger who was important to her as a young girl. Lan had been a mother figure to this younger brother, who was often under her care. As a puberty-aged girl, Lan found herself stimulating her little brother's genitals, and she confessed that at one point she had put his penis inside her to "see what it felt like." She felt tremendous guilt over this experience, of having abused a certain power over this younger brother who loved her. We did explore this memory in the context of both her own sexual abuse by her older brother and her unbearable loneliness. But moving too quickly to redemptive interpretations can be based on the therapist's own fear of some disturbing part of the patient, a retreat from the experience of guilt and from the recognition of her own destructive capacities.

Our exploration of Lan's remembrance of herself in the hurtful, active position—the one who holds the power to dominate vulnerable others—led to associations with the Vietnam War. "I have been reading about Vietnam and the war, lately," Lan said softly and deliberately. "I never wanted to think about it before." I asked her about her recollections of the war, feeling a vague sense of dread and uncertainty. Lan continued. "I don't remember much about the war; mainly I remember stealing and money. A lot of things happened with money that I didn't understand. I don't want to be like my parents who were stealing, but this book I've been reading tells how stealing was a way of dealing with poverty, with surviving. This is true because Vietnamese people are very generous; they are more so than whites."

I commented, "You are finding something again that is good in the Vietnamese world, something that you had forgotten, and yet you are not sure what is stolen and what is legitimately yours." Lan responded, "Well, I've always loved the food. I never felt like you have to steal the food; but the other things of the culture I don't like."

"Food is the good and abundant side of your Vietnamese world," I said, "and this feels so different from the dirty money that is the other side, the destructive side."

Lan responded, "I don't like the whole success part. You know, Vietnamese people have been invaded so much, and yet there is so much emphasis on making money. That is the only important thing, making money. And yet I also know that your country raped my country and before that it was the French. But for my generation, it was the Americans that raped our country."[22]

At this point, I was aware of myself as the rapist, as part of the world that had reduced her country to having to steal. Stealing came to be associated with the rebellious side of her traditions and with her own active strivings to find the lost, valuable objects that had been taken away. I commented that this memory of being back in Vietnam was also a way of looking for some lost part of herself, something that had been taken away from her. I also asked whether there were times when she hated me too, times when she thought of me as the enemy. This moment was unsettling for both of us. She was remembering Vietnam, and feeling loss and longing, while I was located as part of the dominant invading culture, on the other shore. She insisted that it was only for a moment that she felt hate for me. "Maybe it's that we are both women," Lan retreated. "I don't see us as creating war, yet I haven't trusted women before either; I have always turned to men."

"With men, you know how to get something back, you know how to bargain," I responded. "With women, it has been more difficult and maybe more disappointing to not find what you are looking for."

Lan continued, "During the war, the men were in more danger, and we were protected. My mother cried and cried, yet we did win; we stood up to this big country and defeated it. I was talking to Jack about this last night, how we had defeated the United States, even though we were just this little country."

I suggested, "You are sort of like that little country, you had to learn to fight; and you felt like you were stealing something when you made other people pay attention to your needs."

During our last months of therapy, Lan periodically assumed a dominating, teaching stance with me. She began to talk about what she had learned about Vietnamese traditions, and she became critical of American ways, particularly the rudeness. I was aware of being the object of her active desire to teach me something—to assert what she had that I lacked. This criticism was, of course, a means of externalizing her own sense of what was lacking, putting back onto me her burdensome sense of cultural devaluation. But also carried into this cultural divide were earlier developmental struggles and associated experiences of guilt and defeat. Shifting between our female "sameness" and our ethnic differences, Lan was building, out of her own representational past, a new sense of subjective coherence, one that included a less traumatic differentiation between self and other as well as a capacity for idealization and merger of self and other. In many of her relational struggles, there were active, sadistic moments and passive, masochistic ones, but these were less frightening or immobilizing than before. I often found myself rallying in response to Lan's chastisement of American culture, perhaps in an effort to absolve myself of cultural guilt. But beyond this defensive avoidance of guilt, I shared in her pleasurable triumphs, including her moments of triumphing over me.

Therapeutic responsiveness requires entering into a range of shifting states of consciousness while holding the vital connections that are created between present and past. For Lan, dissociated states did signify a numbing response, as a defense against deprivation as well as against overt abuse. In the course of therapy, Lan's discordant self states did seem to be related to traumatic dissociation. But dissociated identity states may also be understood as signifying insurgent awarenesses and capacities for which there was as yet no compelling story or organizing framework. Perhaps one of the most significant countertransference errors, in response to either disorienting states or the loss of a sense of self-continuity, is to dispel the uncertainty by prematurely imposing a story on the moment of felt chaos.

Attending to the sequence of memories, their relational content and emotional quality, is more clinically useful than excavating for dramatic content. In my work with Lan, the murkiness of those memories—like the ocean she crossed in coming to the United States—provided the generative, creative space for self-discovery. This space included recognition of her own powerful desires and fantasies, of the various defensive distortions and operations that shaped the past that was discovered, and of the range of traumatic losses that had to be mourned.

CONCLUSIONS

I began this chapter by approaching the new memory of my patient Susan as a "gift"—an interpersonal exchange oriented toward engaging others in a vital way. While the historical basis of the memory is important in many situations, the therapeutic focus here was on the interpersonal context of both the memory "recovery" and how it permitted engagement with others, including the return to psychotherapy. The truth of the memory, for our purposes, is in the relational dilemmas it transmits and in its affective loading. While women's traumatic sexual memories have been ignored or minimized in the past, these same sexual memories, having once been "won" as a vital marker of a valiant selfhood, may be created unconsciously to convey a process of interpersonal struggle and emerging capacities for self-development.

This emphasis on emerging self-capacities extends to understandings of dissociative phenomena, specifically in considering how dissociative states may signify shifting borders in self-experience. I have introduced this therapeutic turn as a corrective to the tendency in the trauma/dissociation field to overdiagnose trauma on the basis of highly ambiguous states or unintegrated clinical material. Lan made use of memory "scripts" to enlist others, including others within the therapeutic situation. Sexual memories shift in their psychodynamic meanings, conveying a range of self and object representations and interpersonal dilemmas.

Lan's question about being a sexual abuse survivor, posed at the onset of treatment, seemed to be a means of framing her concern about anticipated, disturbing discoveries in the yet-to-be-remembered past as well as of framing an awareness of herself as engaged in a process of personal struggle. The question of sexual abuse also signified her emerging sense of entitlement as a woman and her struggle to negotiate, through the cultural narratives available to her, a widening terrain of possibilities for female identity. Therapeutic attentiveness to such shifting communicative fields—including what is communicated through sexual imagery—is vital in developing a more integrated—that is, less dissociated—sense of self.

CONCLUSIONS

Looking Back and Looking Forward

IN *THE WOMAN'S BIBLE*, written in the mid-1890s, Elizabeth Cady Stanton omits Genesis 19 from her heretical text.[1] For this pioneering feminist, the entire tale of Lot's flight from Sodom and Gomorrah was beyond redemption. Stanton saw how sacred legends conceal cruelty toward women and how the sins of the holy fathers are so often hidden behind robes of piety and the skirts of women. In *Pillar of Salt* I have employed the central metaphors of this biblical passage to map the treacherous process for women of looking back, of creating a past out of the contours of a vaguely discernible history. The mythic fate of Lot's wife—a consequence of her refusal to comply with the Almighty's commandment—registers the tragic side of female rebellion. Yet the petrified figure of this biblical wife introduces a creative space for feminist analysis and for alternative storytelling practices.

If feminists were to create a story for Lot's wife, it might begin with her numbing terror in looking back on the devastation of her homeland. Perhaps she would recall the evening prior to their hasty departure, as she argued with Lot over whether to leave or to stay. Emotional ties were never so binding for Lot as they were for her, she muses, and he was more able to separate himself from the suffering of those around him. As a righteous man, he readily rose above the fate of the less righteous. Always eager to negotiate with the prevailing powers, Lot was known for his keen instincts for survival. Lingering on the scene of the burning city, perhaps Lot's wife has a flashback, remembering being beaten as a young girl by her father with a hot stick. She tries to remember why but is unable to recall the reasons for his bursts of rage. Or perhaps she recollects baking bread with her mother on a cold winter morning, feeling the stinging rush of heat as they prepare the oven stone to receive the rounds of fleshy dough.

And what stories might Lot's daughters have to tell? We may imagine them, scrambling determinedly up the hill with their eyes fixed on their father's broad, stooped back. The younger girl is in lockstep with her older sister, entranced by the rhythmic sound of dry stones underfoot. Safe from danger, they turn around to discover that their mother has vanished. After searching frantically for some sign of her, the daughters break into convulsive sobbing.

We may also picture Lot in his state of drunken grief and sullen withdrawal. Unable to tolerate emotional pain, he turns to his daughters for succorance. By morning, Lot has placed his seed into his first daughter, depositing into her as well his own guilt and sorrow. By the next morning, the second daughter has found herself under her father's body, noticing a feeling of uneasy pleasure alloyed with a deadening loneliness. While the father sleeps like a baby, this second daughter is less able than her sister to rid herself of the sex smells. Perhaps this second daughter remembers the incest while the first one forgets.[2] Separated from the women of their village and struggling for survival in a motherless land, the two daughters have no common memory to bind them. They bicker constantly, finally parting after the sons they have produced lead them out of their respective wildernesses.

The children and grandchildren of these daughters of Lot might have yet other stories to tell, as history evolves into legend and memory gives rise to fantasy. For the less traumatized heirs of Lot, the origins of painful consciousness are less readily located, just as their memories emerge out of more elusive events, part known and part unknown. For the progeny of Lot, the half-sons/half-grandsons, the story of the destroyed city is told as a singular lesson in the rewards of obedience. Yet even as they pay homage to Lot, they are unified in their contempt for this patriarch who did not have the courage to look back. For these bastard sons, shame is transformed into vengeful battles with neighboring villages. Like their father, they also are prone to drunken states of amnesia.

The first daughter of Lot gives birth to a daughter, as does the second, some years after the destruction of the city. For these granddaughters of Lot, the legend generates a profusion of storytelling practices, both compliant and resistive. The more compliant granddaughter suffers from inhibitions, fearful of flames though she has not been burned. The other granddaughter becomes mad, overcome with hallucinatory images of embalmed bodies and persecutory voices. One legend has it that the more compliant granddaughter becomes a mystic, transforming the chaos of forbidden images and unruly passions into a system of ritualized containment. Whereas the madwoman is seized uncontrollably by frenetic daydreaming and is prone to hysterical paralysis, the mystic enters into states of altered consciousness with certainty of purpose. Much like the artist, the mystic manipulates the terrifying objects of her consciousness, monitoring their comings and goings. Unlike the artist's, however, the mystic's demons are too immediate, too real, to permit her much freedom of movement.

What storytelling practices are created by the great-granddaughters of Lot? As tribes break apart and new alliances emerge out of social disorder, fidelity to the old legends is less binding. While some women pay homage to the dying patriarchs, the rebellious ones declare that God is, after all, an illusion. In this heretical act, they defy the patriarchs who summon the power of the Almighty in the enforcement of the Law. Less bound than their mothers to patriarchal rule, these daughters discover the power of exposing the fathers' secrets. In resisting the strategies of survival passed down by their fearful mothers, these defiant ones draw inspiration from the legendary great-grandmother's refusal of the Almighty's commandments.

One version of the legend tells of a sisterhood of Gomorrites, unified and sustained through the social memory of the destroyed city. For these women, the polymorphic perverse Gomorrites—the pagans—signify the generativity and abundance of a world prior to the repressive, patriarchal fathers, a world where mothers, daughters, and sisters work and love in harmony. In this version of the archaic past, Gomorrah evokes a rich landscape of pleasures cultivated by the little gods (and devils), prior to the triumph of the Supreme Being.

We can see how this Edenic vision of a lost maternal world—as a feminist fantasy—must finally yield to complex realities and countervailing currents in women's experience. Once the rebellious granddaughters and great-granddaughters of Lot enter history, they, much like their brothers, inherit a sense of guilt. As they invade the kingdom of the fathers, laying claim to yet-unauthorized freedoms, they encounter the destructive side of their own transgressive desires. Stunned and fearful of arousing the cruel vengeance of the father(s), they initially retreat into old sanctuaries. They insist on the purity of their hearts, their absolute innocence, as a means of escaping damnation and the threat of banishment. Ambivalently defiant, however, they remember together the incestuous act of the old patriarch, agreeing on the necessity of continuing the struggle.

Finally, casting off ancient inhibitions, the rebellious great-granddaughters of Lot do begin to speak freely, placing themselves as protagonists in their own stories. And as they tell their many stories to their own daughters and sons, they find themselves at times fondly repeating the legends of the old patriarchs. Unlike their mothers and grandmothers, however, they are able to explain to the young the power of storytelling—its potency as a tool and a weapon—and how it is that new tales may be crafted out of remnants of the old ones. This reconstruction of the legendary past is not the tribute that the elders have demanded—for much is destroyed and desacralized in the retelling. But it will have to suffice, for these heretical stories are simultaneously loving and destructive acts. The secrets that are told in these tales do, indeed, betray the patriarchs. But rebellious storytellers are also exposed through their telling of secrets, sometimes more than they dare realize. Those gathered smile in recognition of the interplay of fact and fancy in the mesmerizing tales that are told, gripping accounts of valiant struggle that sometimes generate more heat than light. It is important to remember, though, that warmth may feel more vital than light, as confining as the darkness may be.

The stories I have created here for Lot's female kin do not correspond in a point-by-point fashion, of course, to the history of women's storytelling chronicled throughout the book. But these stories offered in conclusion—my feminist apocrypha—do suggest the shifting narrative structure of the dramas that have unfolded historically in prototypical stories about the central dilemmas of the female self. Throughout the book, the movement has been from a female position of "lack of memory" to remembrances bound by the Law of the Father and its inhibiting effects and, finally, to an insistent, insurgent female voice.

One allegorical use of the image of Lot's wife, one familiar to the reader by now, centers on the trauma and losses women have endured throughout history—trauma and losses women have been forbidden to speak about. The second story, interwoven with the first throughout this book, centers on fantasy and the imaginary—processes of mind that require some distance from the troubling scene in question in order to recognize how the mind represents and transforms objects of consciousness. If we remain too close to the disturbing drama, we are unable to decipher what the mind is doing with the action. Further, we may be mesmerized by the horror of the drama, losing sight of how various participants structure the story that gets told. But if we remain too distant, treating the mind as merely a playground for reality, we may miss the terror aroused by the events taking place. And if we grant too much weight to the indeterminacy of all forms of human knowing, we may be inhibited from taking action in the face of genuine threats to human well-being.

From the first of these two storytelling perspectives, the trauma perspective, the daughters of Lot's wife may be viewed as inheritors of a heroic and tragic legend. Remembering Lot's wife and her unfortunate daughters is a call to testify to the continuing assaults on women's bodies and minds and to remain aware of the precariousness of the rights we have achieved. In refusing to forget the nameless and powerless wives and daughters of history, we are not likely to be lulled into complacency or to be seduced by a false sense of progress. Indeed, women continue to be subject to the authority of men in private and public life, and the public perception of female emancipation may even contribute to a certain intolerance of women who remain in a state of bondage.

Still from the trauma perspective, analyzing women's disturbing reactions proceeds from the impact of external events to the immobility and terror they generate. Throughout history, hysterical paralysis for women has been a rational response to an irrational situation, as inescapable terrors are converted into the language of the body. Like Lot's wife, women have suffered from more than "mere" castration anxiety; they have faced the fundamental threat of self-annihilation and loss of self. In witnessing to the traumatic side of women's history, feminists assert the right of women to survive and to speak out. The recovery of subsequent generations—the collective daughters of Lot's wife—may be envisaged as a process of remembering the injurious side of women's history as well as the positive capacities that endure through this same history. Such remembering cannot take place within the cultural space offered by men; it requires a protective maternal fold, beyond the illusory sanctuary of seductive patriarchs.

The second storytelling perspective I have adopted in reworking the story of Lot's wife requires some distance from the effects of actual trauma. This perspective makes use of the story as a cultural fantasy, recognizing in the symbolism of the text the operation of repressed desires, anxieties, and defenses. Fantasy does include the use of imagery to achieve emotional distance, but it encompasses much more. It also facilitates generative aspects of mind, including the process by which representations of disturbing events are transformed over time. Initial perceptions are reshaped and reconfigured by an active human subject engaged in telling various stories about the self in relation to others. If memories were merely the imprints of external events, we would be far less able to envision an alternative world, much less to have the imaginative capacities to bring it about.

Once we enlarge the scope of meanings attached to remembrances, we acquire a more complex subjectivity. In describing this biblical imagery to my analyst, for example, and in being asked to speak about whatever comes to mind, I might generate a series of associations less related to concrete trauma than to diffuse uncertainties and conflicts. The fear of annihilation may emanate from an awakening awareness of the power of internal forces as much as from the magnitude of actual external threats. The image of the destroyed archetypal mother—who is left behind and entombed in memory—also may symbolize the consequences of the daughter's own aggression toward the mother, born of an infantile wish to kill off the mother and to take her place in the affections of the father. Further, the wavering of Lot's wife may be interpreted as signifying female ambivalence. She is torn between the impulse to establish a world apart from past constraints and the desire to hold on to an earlier sphere of attachments. Lot's wife, from this perspective, is overtaken by the terrors of an inner world that has no outer-directedness, no cultural position from which to mount an effective rebellion. She freezes in her tracks because there is no holding position available to her in converting her distress and desires into effective action or emotional catharsis. Lot, as symbolic father, is more able to dis-identify with emotional suffering, to secure a place beyond the scene of terror and to find substitutes for sustained losses.

In viewing Lot's tale through the lens of feminist psychoanalytic theory, it may be useful to regard the drama as a product of the patriarchal unconscious. Placing patriarchy on the couch, we may understand the instructions of the Almighty as a projection of masculine wishes and defenses. Surviving patriarchs wish to be relieved of their guilt in turning away from the destruction left behind. As a result, women are often the bearers of dissociated emotions and memories within the culture. They carry the vulnerability, sorrow, and dependence men refuse to acknowledge in themselves, and, as bearers of such disavowed states, women are often the objects of masculine dread because they embody the threatening possibility of a "return of the repressed." When women internalize these anxieties, they experience their own emotional states and desires as engulfing.

The "correct" interpretation of the story may shift over time, as new circumstances and emerging conflicts guide the process of transformative remembering. Yet the uncertainty attached to the idea of multiple meanings may be destabilizing, both for women themselves and for various presiding authorities. The ambiguous, bodily articulated stories of women have often been the object of a voyeuristic gaze, even as they have generated anxiety in the listener. One response of contemporary therapists, including those guided by feminist insights, has been to foreclose on this uncertainty, preempting the process of discovery through overly decisive pronouncements. Just as fundamentalists may need to believe that Lot's wife really was transformed into a pillar of salt in order for the story to have meaning, many contemporary therapists schooled in trauma theory maintain that memories must be literally correct for them to have therapeutic meaning.

In the 1980s, the cultural circulation of ritual abuse stories echoed the spectacle of nineteenth-century mediumship, in which women mesmerized audiences with similarly prophetic tales. In both historical contexts, the notion of a hidden self, containing unique powers of insight, grew out of women's own restive demands for a cultural voice. Then and now, professional healers import their own disavowed anxieties and preoccupations into the mental domain that is discovered. So too, women continue to respond to the clinical search for a latent self because many of the capacities and desires of women remain culturally repressed. The late-nineteenth-century expressions of female dual consciousness—alternating between a domesticated "good girl" and a rebellious "bad girl"—have mutated into a broad cast of characters even though the underlying script remains much the same.

It would be a mistake to conclude that the historical conversation between female subjects and male authority is one-sided, just as it is simplistic to conclude that therapeutic authority operates only repressively. The modern, dynamic concept of the unconscious (of a hidden realm of desires and strivings) is a product, in a sense, of female marginality, intimately bound to the contradictions of women's experience over the past century. Standing at the threshold between private and public life, the female psychological subject is divided between those internalized structures that constitute the social ego and those insurgent internal forces opposing it. Struggling to emerge out of the suffocating constraints of domesticity, this subject searches for a new mode of self-expression, particularly during eras when the social boundaries of gender are shifting.

Male professionals have periodically aligned themselves with this emerging female selfhood. Sometimes this alliance is empathetic and sometimes it is voyeuristic. Indeed, through the febrile mental states of women, male professionals have been able to express vicariously their own "feminine" emotionality and hysterical reactions. The voyeuristic aspects of the psychiatric "gaze" were more readily apparent in the past, when the roles of women and men were more singularly cast in opposition than they are in the present period.

Yet female therapists today, no less than male therapists, may find the eroticized conditions of women enchanting. In the 1980s, women patients and embattled therapists, who were increasingly likely to be women, found common cause in a Romantic revolt against medical psychiatry. The resurrection of the lost soul of psychiatry—with its assertion of an unproblematic human nature destroyed through a decisive, dramatic rupture of innocence—was a reaction to the increased medicalizing of mental suffering. The woman patient as multiple emerged as modern prophet and conduit for various grievances and anxieties in the mental health field. Yet this vivifying of female suffering reenacted a chronic problem: for the misery of women to be socially recognized, it must burst the bounds of ordinary, everyday discontent. Women patients, no less than their therapists, were constrained in what they felt allowed to complain about. As trauma stories migrated across the cultural terrain, they became loaded with less readily articulated social grievances.

Within feminism, the task of reconciling the distortions, defenses, and disguises that accompanied women's own perceptions and consciousness, on the one hand, and the aim of asserting increased authority for women to speak, on the other, has been perennially daunting. Because women's oppression has been so often justified on the basis of an unruly female tongue—on male assertions of the untrustworthiness of female speech—defensive reactions are understandable, if not inevitable. In this book, I have shown how costly the view that women "always speak the truth" has been for feminism. A stance that celebrates women as single-mindedly virtuous in their motivations does restore a sense of feminine goodness from the negatively colored projections of men. This self-idealization is a vital part of any emancipatory movement, even though it is highly limiting if not tempered with other insights. Defending the virtue of women too often rests on the conservative ideal of female sexual purity. For women in the nineteenth century, for example, the price of public authority was to display a kind of perpetual virginity of mind. The pronouncements of women took on an otherworldly glow, as mediums and spiritualists drew authority from the limited cultural ground available to them. In the contemporary period, many women have similarly made use of the limited authority granted them in advancing grievances. Mobilizing against child sex abuse draws on two areas where women have traditionally exercised some authority: the protection of children and the monitoring of male sexuality. The image of the sexually abused child emerged as a cultural icon in the 1980s because it appeared to convey a human tragedy uniquely devastating in its impact on later life.

The expansion of the sexual abuse survivor movement from victims holding continuous memories to those who came to their memories through a process of therapeutic discovery was both an advance and a retreat for women. As an advance, it signified a broad awareness of the pervasiveness of "boundary violations" in female development. Further, it represented a collective deidealization of fathers in patriarchal families and a search for a morally sanctioned bridge out of binding familial obligations. Once the father is labeled sexual abuser or seducer, he relinquishes any moral claims on the daughter, permitting the daughter her rebellious departure without having to look back. But this galvanizing discovery was also a partial retreat for women. Since this resistance to fathers was harnessed to a stance that all sexually disturbing images were indicative of a history of incestuous abuse, the sexual abuse survivor movement inadvertently heightened women's terror. The broadly accepted clinical and political idea that "innocent" children do not generate sexual fantasies—nor do good girls have dirty thoughts—introduced its own repressive silencing into the storytelling of women. As a result, there was a return of the repressed in the form of increasingly menacing sexual stories, in which sexual perpetrators acquire magnificent powers as objects of women's own projected sexual anxieties.

The contemporary debate over women's recovered memories of sexual abuse is also symptomatic of deeper cultural dilemmas over changing gender roles and normative understandings of the family. Searching for memory of paternal abuse in the murky contours of a forgotten past does signify the distance adult daughters have traveled in their refusal to be the guardians of the fathers' secrets. Uncovering the dreadful legacy of the father's sinful deeds is a vital part of the feminist legacy. Without strong female alliances and storytelling practices, legends of sexually controlling fathers tend to drop from the cultural record. Whether taken literally or metaphorically, sexual abuse stories convey some of the truth of the daughter's seductions under patriarchy. The incest survivor is Every Woman in that her sexual awakening confronts the prior presence of patriarchal authority and her story chronicles an emerging awareness that the Law of the Father circumscribes female desire. The traditional fate of female development has involved the transfer of feminine affections from one father figure to another. Feminism has intervened in this ancient, cultural transfer, refusing both literal and symbolic fathers their traditional right to sexually control daughters.

There is another side of the father/daughter plot—one that has been repressed in much of the contemporary feminist inquiry centering on sexual abuse. In the United States, feminist inquiry has largely banished oedipal desire and fantasy from representations of the daughter's dilemmas. There is a certain irony in this banishment in that contemporary women—the daughters of the women's movement of the 1960s and 1970s—have achieved the conditions for "oedipal" struggle, which did not exist for prior generations of women. They are, indeed, more in a position to fantasize than ever before. In describing the dilemmas of the Victorian women of his time, Freud was quite right in arguing that women were not able to resolve oedipal conflict—that they were unable to transform infantile desire into sublimated, rule-governed activity—because they lacked the phallus, signifier of the sexual difference. Maleness determined the course of the journey out of childhood, including the possibilities for identification with the rights and privileges accorded men in public life. These rights and privileges, offered to sons as substitute for the pain of relinquishing the satisfactions of infancy, were not extended to daughters. In the contemporary period, however, sons no longer hold exclusive rights to the kingdom. Daughters, as well, have achieved entitlement to this kingdom and may, like sons, struggle ambivalently with the desire to displace the powerful fathers (and mothers).

The distinction between paternal seduction as a fantasy and as a literal event should not be taken lightly, even as both are central to the analysis developed in this book. Actual incest collapses the possibilities for creative use of fantasy and imagery. In the early period of the sexual abuse survivor movement, it was common to speak of "emotional incest" along with "physical incest." These two categories introduced the vital idea of a continuum of harmful effects—an idea that tended to be lost in the feminist sexual politics and psychotherapies of the 1980s. Nonetheless, the concept of emotional incest was insufficiently grounded in a theory of female sexuality. It cast the disturbances and bodily anxieties of women as wholly imported from the environment, leaving unexamined the conflicting aspects of sexuality for women, including desire directed toward fathers or father figures.

However, since male abusiveness is deeply implicated in the suffering and constraints of women, we may feel the need to work through these effects before deciding what is left of women's own internally generated conflict. Further, women's fantasies are so intertwined with patriarchal culture that the entire domain of fantasy may feel for women like colonized territory. Because of the intimate association between femininity and fantasy proneness and suggestibility in the patriarchal imagination, feminists have understandably waged war against these two categories. Yet the price of this form of resistance has been tremendous. It has narrowed the possibilities for understanding the rich, complex meanings contained in women's stories. In the turn toward what I call fundamentalist feminism, the stories of women are reduced to literal reflections of external events, stripped of their richly layered meanings.

Only as we increase the freedom to interpret our own remembrances will we more fully become active subjects. And as knowing, speaking subjects, we may both recognize and mis-recognize the nature of threats to our well-being, for this is in the nature of human intelligence. Further, once the story moves from the realm of immediate events to that of the symbolic, we may consider situations where the destruction envisaged is born of our imaginations. Achieving the right to see—a right emerging out of the centuries-old gestation of the women's movement—brings with it a complex interplay of social and psychological processes. As the nameless wives and daughters of history begin to give utterance to what they perceive on the cultural horizon, they acquire an increasingly full subjectivity. And, as a result, perceptions of external threats mingle with imaginary terrors in the theater of consciousness.

In writing this book, I have made extensive use of literary works because through them we can readily appreciate the vital role of fantasy and imaginative processes in women's storytelling. Women's fiction reminds us that there are many plots and subplots contained within a single story and that the female body may be inscribed with various meanings within the contours of shifting cultural possibilities. But in turning from literary works to feminist politics and to feminist-informed psychotherapies, we are on more uncertain ground as to how to understand the inevitable gap between the imaginary and the "real." Yet if feminism is to realize its fullest potential, including the overthrow of the lasting vestiges of patriarchal control, it must take into account the inevitable blind spots and uncertainties that emerge in creating more authentic versions of the past and must recognize, as well, that the pasts that are recovered in individual or collective remembering are transformed by the dilemmas of the present. To conceive of remembering as a transformative process need not imply a minimizing of the historical past and its associated trauma. Rather, it suggests that women's storytelling practices are carved out of a broad cultural and historical landscape—a landscape that is resistive in some places and yielding in others.

The cultural terrain continues to be rocky and uncertain, arousing hopes and fears alike. For some women, it is fear of looking back at the injurious side of the past that predominates, whereas for others it is the inhibiting aspects of the journey. But whatever the future of these emerging female selves, there is no turning back. To that, as mothers and daughters of history, we should all shout "Amen."

Notes

Introduction LOOKING BACK

1. See Rebecca Goldstein, "Looking Back at Lot's Wife," *Commentary* 92, no. 3 (Sept. 1994): 37–41. Goldstein offers a moving account of her own response to this story as a young girl and how she confronts her father with her sense of the unfairness of the Almighty's actions.
2. Ellen Bass and Laura Davis, *The Courage to Heal: A Guide for Women Survivors of Child Sexual Abuse*, 1st ed. (New York: Harper & Row, 1988).
3. Betty Friedan, *The Feminine Mystique* (New York: Norton, 1963).
4. For discussion of the history of the incest recovery movement, see Louise Armstrong, *Rocking the Cradle of Sexual Politics: What Happened When Women Said Incest* (New York: Addison-Wesley, 1994).
5. Naomi H. Rosenblatt and Joshua Horwitz, *Wrestling with Angels: What Genesis Teaches Us about Our Spiritual Identity, Sexuality, & Personal Relationships* (New York: Doubleday, 1996).
6. See Dorothy Zeligs, *Psychoanalysis and the Bible: A Study in Depth of Seven Leaders* (New York: Human Sciences Press, 1974). Zeligs offers a psychoanalytic analysis of the story of Lot and his family. She argues that the city is a maternal symbol and that the punishment for looking back signifies repression of the wish for union with the mother.
7. For examples of this tendency, see Katie Roiphe, *The Morning After: Sex, Fear, and Feminism on Campus* (Boston: Little, Brown, 1993); Christina H. Sommers, *Who Stole Feminism? How Women Have Betrayed Women* (New York: Simon & Schuster, 1995); and Naomi Wolf, *Fire with Fire: The New Female Power and How to Use It* (New York: Fawcett Columbine, 1994). In locating the vestiges of women's oppression primarily in female identification with the victim role, these "postvictimization" feminists minimize the ongoing difficulties of women, particularly the extent to which women continue to be harmed by men.
8. In the 1990s, many of the attacks, on both sides of the memory debate, assumed a highly personal tone. While I emphasize the personal side of science, I also attempt to avoid ad hominem criticisms or reflexive reactions to the varying positions in the debate.

Chapter 1 FAMILY REMEMBRANCES: A Daughter and a Mother Look Back

1. Jane Smiley, *A Thousand Acres* (New York: Fawcett Columbine, 1991), esp. 223–229.
2. Jennifer J. Freyd, "Theoretical and Personal Perspectives on the Delayed Memory Debate" (paper presented at Foote Hospital's continuing-education conference "Controversies around Recovered Memories of Incest and Ritual Abuse," Ann Arbor, Mich., Aug. 7, 1993). For a briefer version of betrayal-trauma theory, see Jennifer J. Freyd, "Betrayal Trauma: Traumatic Amnesia as an Adaptive Response to Childhood Abuse," *Ethics and Behavior* 4, no. 4 (1994): 307–329. For the personal narrative presented at this conference, see Jennifer J. Freyd, "Personal Perspectives on the Delayed Memory Debate," *Treating Abuse Today* 3, no. 5 (1993): 13–20.
3. Jennifer J. Freyd, *Betrayal Trauma: The Logic of Forgetting Childhood Abuse* (Cambridge, Mass.: Harvard University Press, 1996).
4. Jane Doe, "How Could This Happen? Coping with a False Accusation of Incest and Rape," *Issues in Child Abuse Accusations* 3, no. 3 (1991): 154–165.
5. Freyd, "Theoretical and Personal Perspectives," 25–26.
6. See D. Stephen Lindsay, "Contextualizing and Clarifying Criticisms of Memory Work in Psychotherapy," *Consciousness and Cognition* 3 (1994): 426–437; Elizabeth F. Loftus and Katherine Ketcham, *The Myth of Repressed Memory: False Memories and Allegations of Sexual Abuse* (New York:

St. Martin's Press, 1994); D. A. Poole et al., "Psychotherapy and the Recovery of Memories of Child-hood Sexual Abuse: U.S. and British Practitioners' Beliefs, Practices, and Experiences," *Journal of Consulting and Clinical Psychology* 63 (1995): 426–437; and Michael Yapko, "Suggestibility and Repressed Memories of Abuse: A Survey of Psychotherapists' Beliefs," *American Journal of Clinical Hypnosis* 36, no. 3 (1994): 163–171.

7. I was not in attendance at this conference. The description of the tenor of the audience response to Freyd's talk is based on reports from a colleague of mine who was there.

8. For an analysis of the issue of clergy abuse, including this case, see Richard Sipe, *Sex, Priests, and Power: Anatomy of a Crisis* (New York: Brunner/Mazel, 1995).

9. American Psychiatric Association, "Statement on Memories of Sexual Abuse," *International Journal of Clinical and Experimental Hypnosis* 42, no. 4 (1994): 289–303. Also see Johnathan W. Schooler, Miriam Bendiksen, and Zara Ambadar, "Toeing the Middle Line: Can We Accommodate Both Fabricated and Recovered Memories of Sexual Abuse?" in *False and Recovered Memories*, ed. M. Conway (New York: Oxford University Press, in press).

10. See note 6 above.

11. Freyd, "Theoretical and Personal Perspectives," 3.

12. Richard J. Loewenstein, "Psychogenic Amnesia and Psychogenic Fugue: A Comprehensive Review," in *Dissociative Disorders: A Clinical Review*, ed. David Spiegel (Lutherville, Md.: Sidran Press, 1993), 45-52.

13. Kathleen Nelson, "The Psychological and Social Origins of Autobiographical Memory," *Psychological Science* 4, no. 1 (1993): 7–14.

14. Bessel A. van der Kolk, "The Body, Memory, and the Psychobiology of Trauma," in *Sexual Abuse Recalled*, ed. Judith Alpert (New York: Citadel Press, 1995), 29–60.

15. See note 6 above.

16. See D. Stephen Lindsay and J. Don Read, "'Memory Work' and Recovered Memories of Childhood Sexual Abuse: Scientific Evidence and Public, Professional, and Personal Issues," *Psychology, Public Policy, and the Law* (in press).

17. See Judith Lewis Herman and Emily Schatzow, "Recovery and Verification of Memories of Childhood Sexual Trauma," *Psychoanalytic Psychology* 4, no. 1 (1987): 1–14; Linda M. Williams, "Recovered Memories of Abuse in Women with Documented Child Sexual Victimization Histories," *Journal of Traumatic Stress* 8, no. 4 (1995): 649–673; and John N. Briere, *Child Abuse Trauma: Theory and Treatment of the Lasting Effects* (Newbury Park, Calif.: Sage, 1992).

18. For discussion of cognitive explanations for forgetting and remembering, see Schooler, Bendiksen, and Ambadar, "Toeing the Middle Line."

19. Freyd, "Theoretical and Personal Perspectives," 29–30.

20. For discussion of this theme, see Judith Lewis Herman with Lisa Hirschman, *Father- Daughter Incest* (Cambridge, Mass.: Harvard University Press, 1981); Carol Ann Hooper, *Mothers Surviving Child Sexual Abuse* (London: Tavistock/Routledge, 1992); and Janet Liebman Jacobs, *Victimized Daughters: Incest and the Development of the Female Self* (New York: Routledge, 1994).

21. Most of Pamela Freyd's work is published through the *FMS Foundation Newsletter* by the FMSF in Philadelphia. Freyd begins each monthly issue with her "Dear Friends" column.

22. Eleanor Goldstein and Kevin Farmer, *Confabulations: Creating False Memories, Destroying Families* (Boca Raton, Fla.: SIRS Books, 1992).

23. Personal communication in my correspondence with an FMSF member.

24. See Toni Bernay, "Reconciling Nurturance and Aggression: A New Feminine Identity," in *The Psychology of Today's Woman: New Psychoanalytic Visions*, ed. Toni Bernay and Dorothy W. Cantor (Hillsdale, N.J.: Atlantic Press, 1986), 105–120.

25. For discussion of the centrality of care giving in female moral reasoning, see Carol Gilligan, *In a Different Voice: Psychological Theory and Women's Development* (Cambridge, Mass.: Harvard University Press, 1982).

26. Freyd, "Theoretical and Personal Perspectives," 33.

27. Ibid., 23.

28. Doe, "How Could This Happen?" 162.

29. Personal communication, July 1995.

30. Doe, "How Could This Happen?" 161.

31. See Sylvia Fraser, *My Father's House: A Memoir of Incest and of Healing* (New York: Harper & Row, 1987). This autobiographical account of an incest survivor exemplifies the genre, with the theme of the oppressed, passive mother figuring prominently in family dynamics. For discussion of the history of mother blaming in the incest literature, see Armstrong, *Rocking the Cradle of Sexual Politics;* Herman with Hirschman, *Father-Daughter Incest;* and Carol Tavris, *The Mismeasure of Woman* (New York: Simon & Schuster, 1992).

32. Personal communication, July 1995.

33. For discussion of mother/daughter ego boundaries, see Jessica Benjamin, *The Bonds of Love: Psychoanalysis, Feminism, and the Problem of Domination* (New York: Pantheon Books, 1988); Nancy Chodorow, *The Reproduction of Mothering: Psychoanalysis and the Sociology of Gender* (Berkeley: Uni-

versity of California Press, 1978); and Marianne Hirsch, *The Mother/Daughter Plot: Narrative, Psychoanalysis, Feminism* (Bloomington: Indiana University Press, 1989).
34. Personal communication, July 1995.
35. H. Merskey, "What Is a Syndrome?" *FMS Foundation Newsletter,* June 1995, 6.
36. Ibid.
37. See, for example, Laura S. Brown, "Politics of Memory, Politics of Incest: Doing Therapy and Politics That Really Matter," in *A Feminist Clinician's Guide to the Memory Debate,* ed. Susan Contratto and M. Janice Gutfreund (New York: Harrinton Press, 1996), 5–18; Joan C. Golston, "A False Memory Syndrome Conference: Activists Accused and Their Professional Allies Talk about Science, Law and Family Reconciliation," *Treating Abuse Today* 5, no. 1 (Jan./Feb. 1995): 24–30; and Bessel A. van der Kolk, Alexander C. McFarlane, and Lars Weisaeth, eds., *Traumatic Stress: The Effects of Overwhelming Experience on Mind, Body, and Society* (New York: Guilford Press, 1996).
38. Goldstein and Farmer, *Confabulations,* 235.
39. See Debbie Nathan and Michael Snedeker, *Satan's Silence: Ritual Abuse and the Making of a Modern American Witch Hunt* (New York: Basic Books, 1995), 238.
40. Michele Barrett and Mary McIntosh, *The Anti-social Family* (New York: Verso, 1982); and Jan E. Dizard and Howard Gadlin, *The Minimal Family* (Amherst: University of Massachusetts Press, 1990).
41. For discussion of recent integrations of the false memory critique into therapeutic practice, see Elizabeth A. Waites, *Memory Quest: Trauma and the Search for Personal* History (New York: Norton, 1997); and Charlotte Prozan, ed., *Construction and Reconstruction of Memory: Dilemmas of Childhood Sexual Abuse* (Northvale, N.J.: Aronson, 1997).
42. Thomas S. Kuhn, *The Structure of Scientific Revolutions,* 2d ed. (Chicago: University of Chicago Press, 1970/1962).
43. For discussion of methodological issues in psychology, see Janice Haaken, "Field Dependence Research: A Historical Analysis of a Psychological Construct," in *Gender and Scientific Authority,* ed. Barbara Lasslett et al. (Chicago: University of Chicago Press, 1996), 282–301; Stephanie Riger, "Epistemological Debates, Feminist Voices: Science, Social Values, and the Study of Women," *American Psychologist* 47, no. 6 (1992): 730–740; Tavris, *The Mismeasure of Woman;* and Jane Ussher and Paula Nicolson, eds., *Gender Issues in Clinical Psychology* (New York: Routledge, 1992).
44. See Steinkar Kvale, *Psychology and Postmodernism* (London: Sage, 1992). For a feminist perspective, see Sandra Harding, "Feminism, Science and the Anti-Enlightenment Critiques," in *Feminism/Postmodernism,* ed. Linda J. Nicholson (New York: Routledge, 1990).
45. For an overview of the history and politics of child abuse legislation, see Lela Costin, Howard Jacob Karger, and David Stoesz, *The Politics of Child Abuse in America* (New York: Oxford University Press, 1996); and Ian Hacking, "The Making and Molding of Child Abuse," *Critical Inquiry* 17 (winter 1991): 253–288. Also see Nathan and Snedeker, *Satan's Silence;* they discuss problems that emerged for feminists in the "believe-the-child" movement..
46. Costin, Karger, and Stoesz, *The Politics of Child Abuse in America,* 182.
47. See Janice Haaken, "From Al-ANON to ACOA: Co-dependence and the Historical Transformation of Caregiving," *Signs* 18 (1993): 321–345.
48. See Nathan and Snedeker, *Satan's Silence,* 101–102.

Chapter 2 **THE GHOST IN THE MACHINE:**
Emotion and the Science of Memory

1. Ian Hacking, *Rewriting the Soul: Multiple Personality Disorder and the Sciences of Memory* (Princeton, N.J.: Princeton University Press, 1995).
2. For discussion of the political uses of scientific psychology, see Stephen Jay Gould, *The Mismeasure of Man* (New York: Norton, 1981). Tavris plays off this title in *The Mismeasure of Woman,* where she traces the influence of popular culture on scientific representations of women.
3. Hacking, *Rewriting the Soul,* 216.
4. See Lynda Birke, *Women, Feminism, and Biology* (New York: Pergamon Press, 1982); M. Lowe and R. Hubbard, eds., *Women's Nature: Rationalizations of Inequality* (New York: Pergamon Press, 1983); and Alison M. Jaggar and Susan R. Bordo, eds., *Gender/Body/Knowledge: Feminist Reconstructions of Being and Knowing* (New Brunswick, N.J.: Rutgers University Press, 1989).
5. For discussion of differing feminist stances toward scientific truth claims, see Mary Hawkesworth, "Knowing, Knowers, Known: Feminist Theory and Claims of Truth," in *Gender and Scientific Authority,* ed. Barbara Laslett et al. (Chicago: University of Chicago Press, 1996), 75–99.
6. For discussion of the history of the employment of metaphors of mind in psychology, see Dedre Genter and Jonathan Grudin, "The Evolution of Mental Metaphors in Psychology: A 90-Year Retrospective," *American Psychologist* 40 (1985): 181–192; and Henry L. Roediger III, "Memory Metaphors in Cognitive Psychology," *Memory & Cognition* 8, no. 3 (1980): 231–246.
7. See Jerome Bruner, *Acts of Meaning* (Cambridge, Mass.: Harvard University Press, 1990); Theodore Sarbin, ed., *Narrative Psychology: The Storied Nature of Human Conduct* (New York: Praeger, 1986); and Robert S. Wyer, Jr., ed., *Knowledge and Memory: The Real Story* (Hillsdale, N.J.: Erlbaum, 1995).

8. See Ruth Bleier, *Science and Gender* (New York: Pergamon Press, 1984). Bleier argues that positivism in the social sciences has been particularly pronounced in psychology. For a critique of positivist influences on memory research, see Jefferson Singer and Peter Salovey, *The Remembered Self: Emotion and Memory in Personality* (New York: Free Press, 1993).

9. Hermann Ebbinghaus, *Memory* (New York: Dover, 1964/1885).

10. Robert Watson, *Behaviorism* (New York: Norton, 1925), 271.

11. William James, *The Principles of Psychology,* vol. 2 (New York: Dover, 1950/1890), 1064.

12. Ibid., 1065.

13. Sir Frederic C. Bartlett, *Remembering: A Study in Experimental and Social Psychology* (London: Cambridge University Press, 1961/1932). Bartlett's work also is important because it introduces the idea of group memory, suggesting that social processes play an important role in the preservation and transformation of knowledge.

14. Mary Douglas, *How Institutions Think* (London: Routledge, 1987).

15. For discussion of the rediscovery of Bartlett's work within psychology, see David Middleton and Derek Edwards, eds., *Collective Remembering* (Newbury Park, Calif.: Sage, 1990), 133; David Riccio, Vita Rabinowitz, and Shari Atelrod, "Memory: When Less Is More," *American Psychologist* 48 (1994): 917–926; and Roger C. Schank and Robert Abelson, "Knowledge and Memory: The Real Story," in *Knowledge and Memory: The Real Story,* ed. Robert S. Wyer, Jr. (Hillsdale, N.J.: Erlbaum, 1995), 1–85.

16. Antonio Damasio, *Descartes' Error: Emotion, Reason, and the Human Brain* (New York: Avon, 1994).

17. Ibid., 128.

18. For discussion of debates within anthropology over the relationship between emotion and bodily sensation, see Mary Douglas, *Purity and Danger* (New York: Praeger, 1966); and Michelle Zimbalist Rosaldo, "Toward an Anthropology of Self and Feeling," in *Culture Theory,* ed. Richard Shweder and Robert A. LeVine (New York: Cambridge University Press, 1984).

19. Damasio, *Descartes' Error,* 139.

20. For discussion of the influence of social factors on intepretations of ambiguous arousal states, see Stanley Schacter and Jerome Singer, "Cognitive, Social and Psychological Determinants of Emotional State," *Psychological Review* 69 (1969): 379–399.

21. Joseph LeDoux, *The Emotional Brain: The Mysterious Underpinnings of Emotional Life* (New York: Simon & Schuster, 1996).

22. For discussion of how science has represented emotion as an ambiguous aspect of mind, see Alison M. Jaggar, "Love and Knowledge: Emotion in Feminist Epistemology," in *Gender/Body/Knowledge: Feminist Reconstructions of Being and Knowing,* ed. Alison M. Jaggar and Susan R. Bordo (New Brunswick, N.J.: Rutgers University Press, 1989).

23. van der Kolk, McFarlane, and Weisaeth, *Traumatic Stress.* LeDoux, *The Emotional Brain,* exhibits this same tendency—that is, the overobjectifying of emotion in countering the scientific legacy of devaluing emotion.

24. For a review of this issue, see Daniel L. Schacter, *Searching for Memory: The Brain, the Mind, and the Past* (New York: Basic Books, 1996).

25. Daniel L. Schacter, "Understanding Implicit Memory: A Cognitive Neuroscience Approach," *American Psychologist* 47 (1992): 559–569. For an overview of the history of memory research, see Daniel L. Schacter and Endel Tulving, "What Are the Memory Systems of 1994?" in *Memory Systems 1994,* ed. Daniel L. Schacter and Endel Tulving (Cambridge, Mass.: MIT Press, 1994), 1–38.

26. Elizabeth F. Loftus and Mark R. Klinger, "Is the Unconscious Smart or Dumb?" *American Psychologist* 47 (June 1992): 761–765; and John F. Kihlstrom, Terrence M. Barnhardt, and Douglas J. Tataryn, "The Psychological Unconscious: Found, Lost, and Regained," *American Psychologist* 47 (June 1992): 788–791.

27. For discussion of metaphors employed in this distinction, see Jerome Bruner, "Another Look at New Look 1," *American Psychologist* 47 (June 1992): 780–783.

28. American Psychiatric Association, "Statement on Memories of Sexual Abuse," 262.

29. For discussion of this theme, see Arlie Hochschild, *The Managed Heart: Commercialization of Human Feeling* (Berkeley: University of California Press, 1983).

30. For discussion of the role of women in the history of science, see Sandra Harding, *The Science Question in Feminism* (Ithaca, N.Y.: Cornell University Press, 1986); Evelyn Fox Keller, *Reflections on Gender and Science* (New Haven, Conn.: Yale University Press, 1985); and Laurel Furumoto, "Mary Whiton Calkins (1863–1930): Fourteenth President of the American Psychological Association," in *In Our Own Words: Readings on the Psychology of Women and Gender,* ed. M. Crawford and R. Unger (New York: McGraw-Hill, 1997).

31. For discussion of the history of experimental inquiry into the concerns of women, see Haaken, "Field Dependence Research."

32. For the history of women in experimental psychology, see Laurel Furumoto, "Shared Knowledge: The Experimentalists, 1904–1929," in *A History of Psychoanalysis: Original Sources and Contemporary Research,* 2d ed., ed. Ludy T. Benjamin, Jr. (New York: McGraw-Hill, 1997), 188–202. Historically and currently, women concentrate in the social and applied areas of the discipline, such as developmental,

social, and clinical psychology, whereas men concentrate in the hard-science wing: perception and physiological and experimental psychology.

33. For a debate on this topic, see Richard Lazarus, "On the Primacy of Cognition," *American Psychologist* 39 (1984): 124–129; and R. B. Zajonc, "On the Primacy of Affect," *American Psychologist* 39 (1984): 117–123. Also, see Bruner, *Acts of Meaning.*

34. Marcia K. Johnson, "Reality Monitoring: An Experimental Phenomenological Approach," *Journal of Experimental Psychology: General* 117 (1988): 390–394.

35. See Daniel Reisberg and Friderike Heuer, "Remembering the Details of Emotional Events," in *Affect and Accuracy in Recall: Studies of Flashbulb Memories,* ed. Eugen Winograd and Ulric Neisser (Cambridge: Cambridge University Press, 1992).

36. See, for examples, B. J. Baars, *A Cognitive Theory of Consciousness* (Cambridge: Cambridge University Press, 1988); and Gary Lynch and Richard Granger, "Variations in Synaptic Plasticity and Types of Memory in Corticohippocampal Networks," in *Memory Systems 1994,* ed. Daniel L. Schacter and Endel Tulving (Cambridge, Mass.: MIT Press, 1994), 65–86.

37. Schacter, *Searching for Memory,* 179.

38. Elizabeth F. Loftus and Katherine Ketcham, *Witness for the Defense: The Accused, the Eyewitness, and the Expert Who Puts Memory on Trial* (New York: St. Martin's Press, 1991), 20.

39. For similar findings, see Richard Ofshe and Ethan Watters, *Making Monsters: False Memories, Psychotherapy, and Sexual Hysteria* (New York: Scribner, 1994); Schacter, *Searching for Memory;* and Michael Yapko, *Suggestions of Abuse: True and False Memories of Childhood Sexual Trauma* (New York: Simon & Schuster, 1994).

40. The political commitments and worldviews of scientists often do shape their orientations to knowledge. Solomon Asch's research on the importance of social alliances in resisting group pressures to produce erroneous answers, for example, grew out of the involvement of Gestalt psychologists in the antifascist movement. See Irvin Rock, ed., *The Legacy of Solomon Asch: Essays in Cognition and Social Psychology* (Hillsdale, N.J.: Erlbaum, 1990). For discussion of the political commitments of Wolfgang Kohler, a leading figure in the Gestalt movement, see Mary Henle, "One Man against the Nazis: Wolfgang Kohler," in *A History of Psychoanalysis: Original Sources and Contemporary Research,* 2d ed., ed. Ludy T. Benjamin, Jr. (New York: McGraw-Hill, 1997), 538–544.

41. Elizabeth F. Loftus, "The Reality of Repressed Memories," *American Psychologist* 48, no. 5 (1993): 518–537.

42. See Schacter, *Searching for Memory.*

43. Ulric Neisser, "Snapshots or Benchmarks," in *Memory Observed,* ed. Ulric Neisser (San Francisco: Freeman, 1982), 43–48; and Ulric Neisser, "John Dean's Memory: A Case Study," *Cognition* 9 (1988): 1–22.

44. See Jerome Bruner, *Actual Minds, Possible Worlds* (Cambridge, Mass.: Harvard University Press, 1986); and Edward Casey, *Remembering: A Phenomenological Study* (Bloomington: Indiana University Press, 1987).

45. See Schank and Abelson, "Knowledge and Memory."

46. Roger Brown and James Kulik, "Flashbulb Memories," *Cognition* 5 (1977): 73–99.

47. See Reisberg and Heuer, "Remembering the Details of Emotional Events"; and Singer and Salovey, *The Remembered Self.*

48. See William F. Brewer, "What Is Recollective Memory?" in *Remembering Our Past: Studies in Autobiographical Memory,* ed. D. C. Rubin (Cambridge: Cambridge University Press, 1996); Frederick H. Frankel, "The Concept of Flashbacks in Historical Perspective," *International Journal of Clinical and Experimental Hypnosis* 42 (1994): 321–336; and Schacter, *Searching for Memory.*

49. For a cultural analysis of forgetting, see Douglas, *How Institutions Think;* and John Shotter, "The Social Construction of Remembering and Forgetting," in *Collective Remembering,* ed. David Middleton and Derek Edwards (Newbury Park, Calif.: Sage, 1990), 120–138.

50. See Stephen Read and Lynn Miller, "Stories Are Fundamental to Meaning and Memory: For Social Creatures, Could It Be Otherwise?" in *Knowledge and Memory: The Real Story,* ed. Robert S. Wyer, Jr. (Hillsdale, N.J.: Erlbaum, 1995), 139–152. They make this same point—that memory research has focused too narrowly on physical attributes of the environment.

51. See Nelson, "The Psychological and Social Origins of Autobiographical Memory," and Judy Dunn, *The Beginnings of Social Understanding* (Cambridge, Mass.: Harvard University Press, 1988). Both these authors advance a social-interactionist model of memory and early development, stressing the complexity of affective learning.

52. Bruner, *Acts of Meaning,* 101.

53. See Sarbin, *Narrative Psychology.*

54. See Peggy Miller, "Personal Story Telling in Everyday Life: Social and Cultural Perspectives," in *Knowledge and Memory: The Real Story,* ed. Robert S. Wyer, Jr. (Hillsdale, N.J.: Erlbaum, 1995), 177–184. Miller is among the few psychologists who address the political dimensions of remembering and conflicts over what she terms "storytelling rights."

55. Ibid., 181.

56. See Julian E. Orr, "Shared Knowledge, Celebrating Identity: Community Memory in a Service Culture," in *Collective Remembering,* ed. David Middleton and Derek Edwards (Newbury Park, Calif.: Sage, 1990), 169–189.

57. Middleton and Edwards, "Introduction," in *Collective Remembering,* 9.

58. For an analysis of media construction of the Kennedy-assassination story, see Barbi Zelizer, *Covering the Body: The Kennedy Assassination, the Media, and the Shaping of Collective Memory* (Chicago: University of Chicago Press, 1992).

59. Bruner, *Acts of Meaning.*

60. See Reisburg and Heuer, "Remembering the Details of Emotional Events."

61. See Craig Barclay and Thomas S. Smith, "Autobiographical Remembering: Creating Personal Culture," in *Theoretical Perspectives on Autobiographical Memory,* ed. M. A. Conway et al. (Norwell, Mass.: Kluwer, 1992), 75–98. Barclay and Smith discuss a psychodynamic approach to remembering, specifically its functions in the maintenance of self-continuity and object relationships. From this perspective, the "truth" of the memory is in its object relational structure rather than in its factual details—a theme I make use of in discussion of my own clinical case material in chapter 11.

62. See Ken Plummer, *Telling Sexual Stories* (London: Routledge, 1995). He describes the solidarizing and "community-building" functions of sexual abuse stories in contemporary U.S. culture.

63. Schank and Abelson, "Knowledge and Memory."

64. See Eric Mankowski and Julian Rapport, "Stories, Identity, and the Psychological Sense of Community," in *Knowledge and Memory: The Real Story,* ed. Robert S. Wyer, Jr. (Hillsdale, N.J.: Erlbaum, 1995), 211–226. Schank and Abelson's concept of skeleton stories does not explain the cultural basis or origin of such narratives or their dynamic shifts over time. For a critique in this same volume, see John G. Holmes and Sandra L. Murray, "Memory for Events in Close Relationships: Applying Schank and Abelson's Skeleton Story Model," in *Knowledge and Memory: The Real Story,* ed. Robert S. Wyer, Jr. (Hillsdale, N.J.: Erlbaum, 1995), 193–210.

65. Schank and Abelson, "Knowledge and Memory," 46.

66. Kihlstrom, Barnhardt, and Tataryn, "The Psychological Unconscious," 789.

Chapter 3   **THE TRAUMA MODEL: Insights and Hysterical Blind Spots**

1. For a review of the history of the trauma model and its roots in psychiatric understandings of hysteria, see Alan Young, *The Harmony of Illusions: Inventing Post-traumatic Stress Disorder* (Princeton, N.J.: Princeton University Press, 1995); and J. P. Wilson, "The Historical Evolution of PTSD Diagnostic Criteria: From Freud to DSM IV," *Journal of Traumatic Stress* 7 (1994): 681–698.

2. For a review, see Anthony J. Marsella et al., eds., *Ethnocultural Aspects of Posttraumatic Stress Disorder: Issues, Research, and Clinical Applications* (Washington, D.C.: American Psychological Association, 1996); and Zahava Solomon, "Oscillating between Denial and Recognition of PTSD: Why Are Lessons Learned and Forgotten?" *Journal of Traumatic Stress* 8, no. 2 (1995): 271–275. Since the 1980s, the field of posttraumatic stress disorders has expanded to include a broad range of factors, such as cultural context, among those that mediate responses to stress and trauma.

3. Bessel A. van der Kolk and R. Fisler, "Dissociation and the Fragmentary Nature of Traumatic Memories: Overview and Exploratory Study," *Journal of Traumatic Stress* 8, no. 4 (1995): 505–525; and Elizabeth Brett, "The Classification of Posttraumatic Stress Disorder," in *Traumatic Stress: The Effects of Overwhelming Experience on Mind, Body, and Society,* ed. Bessel A. van der Kolk, Alexander C. McFarlane, and Lars Weisaeth (New York: Guilford Press, 1996), 117–128.

4. For discussion of Janet's theory, see Janis Jenkins, "Culture, Emotion, and PTSD," in *Ethnocultural Aspects of Posttraumatic Stress Disorder: Issues, Research, and Clinical Applications,* ed. Anthony J. Marsella et al. (Washington, D.C.: American Psychological Association, 1996); and Bessel A. van der Kolk and Onno van der Hart, "Pierre Janet and the Breakdown of Adaptation in Psychological Trauma," *American Journal of Psychiatry* 146, no. 12 (1989): 1530–1540. Also, see Henri F. Ellenberger, *The Discovery of the Unconscious: The History of the Evolution of the Dynamic Psychiatry* (New York: Basic Books, 1970).

5. Richard B. Ullman and Doris Brothers, *The Shattered Self: A Psychoanalytic Study of Trauma* (Hillsdale, N.J.: Analytic Press, 1988).

6. For a history of the political commitments of the early Freudians, see Russell Jacoby, *The Repression of Psychoanalysis: Otto Fenichel and the Political Freudians* (New York: Basic Books, 1983).

7. See Judith Lewis Herman, *Trauma and Recovery* (New York: Basic Books, 1992); and James M. Glass, *Shattered Selves: Multiple Personality in a Postmodern World* (Ithaca, N.Y.: Cornell University Press, 1993). For discussion of the role of psychiatry in the field of trauma testimonials specifically related to the Holocaust, see Shoshana Felman and Dori Laub, *Testimony: Crises of Witnessing in Literature, Psychoanalysis, and History* (New York: Routledge, 1992).

8. See van der Kolk and Fisler, "Dissociation and the Fragmentary Nature of Traumatic Memories"; and Lenore Terr, *Too Scared to Cry* (New York: HarperCollins, 1990).

9. See Sigmund Freud, "First Lecture on Psychoanalysis at Clark University: Breuer and the Treatment of Hysteria," in *A History of Psychoanalysis: Original Sources and Contemporary Research,* 2d ed., ed.

Ludy T. Benjamin, Jr. (New York: McGraw-Hill, 1997), 493–498. In separating psychoanalysis from the medical model, Freud emphasized how the talking cure required a new approach to illness.

10. Josef Breuer and Sigmund Freud, "Studies on Hysteria," in *The Standard Edition of the Complete Psychological Works of Sigmund Freud* (hereafter, *SE*), trans. and ed. James Strachey, vol. 2 (London: Hogarth Press, 1962/1895).

11. See Jean G. Schimek, "Fact and Fantasy in the Seduction Theory: A Historical Review," *Journal of the American Psychoanalytic Association* 35 (1987): 937–965.

12. Sigmund Freud, "Heredity and the Aetiology of the Neuroses," "Further Remarks on the Neuropsychoses of Defence," and "The Aetiology of Hysteria," in *SE*, vol. 3 (1962/1896).

13. See Herman, *Trauma and Recovery;* Jeffrey Masson, *The Assault on Truth: Freud's Suppression of the Seduction Theory* (New York: Farrar, Straus & Giroux, 1984); Bennett Simon and Christopher Bullock, "Incest and Psychoanalysis: Are We Ready to Fully Acknowledge, Bear, and Understand?" *Journal of the American Psychoanalytic Association* 42 (1994): 1261–1282; and Elaine Westerlund, "Freud on Sexual Trauma: An Historical Review of Seduction and Betrayal," *Psychology of Women Quarterly* 10 (1986): 297–310.

14. Monique David-Menard, *Hysteria from Freud to Lacan: Body and Language in Psychoanalysis* (Ithaca, N.Y.: Cornell University Press, 1989).

15. For discussion of this transition in Freud's thinking, see Stephen A. Mitchell and Margaret J. Black, *Freud and Beyond: A History of Modern Psychoanalytic Thought* (New York: Basic Books, 1995). For a review of psychoanalytic theories of psychic trauma, see Theo L. Dorpact and Michael L. Miller, *Clinical Interaction and the Analysis of Meaning: A New Psychoanalytic Theory* (Hillsdale, N.J.: Analytic Press, 1992).

16. Freud's view of retroactive trauma is compatible with much of the thinking in the contemporary field of memory research, specifically the emphasis on reconstructive processes. See Singer and Salovey, *The Remembered Self;* as they demonstrate, current moods color recall of childhood events, although the extent of this effect is an area of ongoing debate.

17. Sexuality, as Foucault points out, came to define the Victorian subject. Just as Freud viewed desire and prohibition as intimately interlocked, Foucault, too, describes the genesis of the sexualized, modern subject in a discourse of prohibition, heightened in the nineteenth-century pursuit of concealed sexual deviations. Michel Foucault, *The History of Sexuality: An Introduction,* vol. 1 (New York: Pantheon Books, 1978).

18. For discussion of the history of the concepts of transference and countertransference, see Mitchell and Black, *Freud and Beyond.*

19. Many of the classical papers broadening the concept of countertransference, including its positive applications in understanding interactive dimensions of treatment, were written by women. See, for example, Phyllis Greenacre, "The Role of Transference," 17–23; Paula Heimann, "On Countertransference," 139–142; and Margaret Little, "Counter-transference and the Patient's Response to It," 143–151, all in *Classics in Psychoanalytic Technique,* ed. Robert Langs (New York: Aronson, 1981).

20. See Jessica Benjamin, "An Outline of Intersubjectivity: The Development of Recognition," *Psychoanalytic Psychology* 7 (supp.) (1990): 33–46; and Lewis Aron, *A Meeting of Minds: Mutuality in Psychoanalysis* (Hillsdale, N.J.: Analytic Press, 1996). Established in 1991, *Psychoanalytic Dialogues: A Journal of Relational Perspectives* grew specifically out of the intersubjective turn in psychoanalysis.

21. Foucault, *The History of Sexuality,* vol. 1.

22. See Michael Kenny, *The Passion of Ansel Bourne* (Washington, D.C.: Smithsonian, 1986); and Elaine Showalter, *Hystories: Hysterical Epidemics and Modern Media* (New York: Columbia University Press, 1996). Also see Jenkins, "Culture, Emotion, and PTSD"; she attempts to integrate nosological criteria for PTSD and cultural narratives employed in its expression in her case example of Salvadorian women refugees.

23. For discussion, see Schimek, "Fact and Fantasy in the Seduction Theory"; Jean G. Schimek, "The Intepretations of the Past: Childhood Trauma, Psychical Reality, and Historical Truth," *Journal of the American Psychoanalytic Association* 23 (1975): 845–865; and Norman N. Holland, "Massonic Wrongs," *American Imago* 46, no. 4 (winter 1989): 329–352. These authors trace the development of Freud's shift from seduction theory to oedipal theory, including the role of his self-analysis in 1896. Freud came to believe that his own hostile feelings toward his father shaped his interpretations of ambiguous clinical material. Aside from the question of the correctness of this reformulation, Freud's recognition of how the clinician's unconscious conflicts shape the past that is "recovered" in treatment was a conceptual advance.

24. Jean-Martin Charcot, under whom Freud trained in the 1880s, established clinically the relationship between trauma and hysteria. See chapter 7 for a history of hysteria.

25. Sigmund Freud, "The Psychopathology of Everyday Life," *SE*, vol. 6 (1995/1901).

26. See Christopher Bollas, *The Shadow of the Object: Psychoanalysis of the Unthought Known* (New York: Columbia University Press, 1995). Bollas beautifully describes this ineffable aspect of trauma and how it collapses the psychic space available for fantasy.

27. For works bridging psychoanalytic and trauma therapy perspectives, see Jody M. Davies and Mary G. Frawley, *Treating the Adult Survivor of Childhood Sexual Abuse: A Psychoanalytic Perspective*

(New York: Basic Books, 1994); Ethel Spector Person and Howard Klar, "Establishing Trauma: The Difficulty Distinguishing between Memories and Fantasy," *Journal of the American Psychoanalytic Association* 42, no. 4 (1994): 1055–1081; Joan Sarnat, "Working in the Space between Psychoanalytic and Trauma-Oriented Approaches to Stories of Sexual Abuse," *Gender & Psychoanalysis* 2, no. 1 (1977): 79–102; and Ullman and Brothers, *The Shattered Self.*

28. For discussion of the historical development of Freud's thinking concerning trauma, see David Healy, *Images of Trauma: From Hysteria to Post-traumatic Stress Disorder* (London: Faber & Faber, 1993).

29. As Foucault points out, the modern bourgeois family was an emotional hothouse, giving rise to a modern, more "eroticized" subject. See Foucault, *The History of Sexuality,* vol. 1.

30. For discussion of the impact of World War II on the generation of analysts who emigrated, see Janice Haaken, "The Siegfried Bernfeld Conference: Uncovering the Psychoanalytic Political Unconscious," *American Journal of Psychoanalysis* 50 (winter 1990): 289–304; and Jacoby, *The Repression of Psychoanalysis.*

31. For discussion of the contradictory aspects of this development, see chapter 4.

32. Ernst Kris, "The Recovery of Childhood Memories in Psychoanalysis," *Psychoanalytic Study of the Child* 2 (1956): 54–88.

33. Ibid., 71.

34. For discussion of the influence of Fairbairn on object relations theory, see Chodorow, *The Reproduction of Mothering;* and Mitchell and Black, *Freud and Beyond.*

35. Ronald W. Fairbairn, "The War Neuroses: Their Nature and Significance," in *Psychoanalytic Studies of the Personality,* ed. Ronald W. Fairbairn (Boston: Routledge & Kegan Paul Ltd., 1952/1943), 275–276.

36. See Ronald W. Fairbairn, "Psychology as a Prescribed and as a Proscribed Subject," in *Psychoanalytic Studies of the Personality,* ed. Ronald W. Fairbairn (Boston: Routledge, 1952/1939), 247–255.

37. Donald Winnicott, *Playing and Reality* (New York: Routledge, 1982). For a discussion of Winnicott and transitional phenomena, see Gerald I. Fogel, "Winnicott's Antitheory and Winnicott's Art," *Psychoanalytic Study of the Child* 47 (1992): 205–222. For discussion of Winnicott's unintended contribution to feminism, see Elsa First, "Mothering, Hate, and Winnicott," in *Representations of Motherhood,* ed. Donna Bassin, Margaret Honey, and Meryle Mahrer Kaplan (New Haven, Conn.: Yale University Press, 1994), 147–161.

38. For a discussion of this issue, see Miriam Johnson, *Strong Mothers/Weak Wives: The Search for Gender Equality* (Los Angeles: University of California Press, 1988).

39. Leonard Shengold, *Soul Murder: The Effects of Childhood Abuse and Deprivation* (New York: Fawcett Columbine, 1989).

40. Donald P. Spence, *Narrative Truth and Historical Truth: Meaning and Interpretation in Psychoanalysis* (New York: Norton, 1982).

41. Shengold, *Soul Murder,* 307.

42. For discussion of debates surrounding the use of these two terms, see Jerome L. Singer, ed., *Repression and Dissociation: Implications for Personality Theory, Psychopathology, and Health* (Chicago: University of Chicago Press, 1990).

43. See George K. Ganaway, "Hypnosis, Childhood Trauma, and Dissociative Identity Disorder: Toward an Integrative Theory," *International Journal of Clinical and Experimental Hypnosis* 43 (1995): 127–144; and Nicholas P. Spanos et al., "Secondary Identity Enactments during Hypnotic Past-Life Regression: A Sociocognitive Perspective," *Journal of Personality and Social Psychology* 61 (1991): 308–320.

44. See Gail A. Horstein, "The Return of the Repressed: Psychology's Problematic Relations with Psychoanalysis, 1909–1960." *American Psychologist* 47 (1992): 254–263. One issue dividing investigators since the late nineteenth century is the relative discontinuity between conscious and unconscious processes and whether the unconscious operates according to different mental "laws" or mechanisms.

45. Ernest R. Hilgard, *Divided Consciousness: Multiple Controls in Human Thought and Action* (New York: Wiley, 1977).

46. Sigmund Freud, "Screen Memories," in *SE,* vol. 3 (1962/1899).

47. See van der Kolk, "The Body, Memory and the Psychobiology of Trauma"; Herman, *Trauma and Recovery;* Terr, *Too Scared to Cry;* and Hilgard, *Divided Consciousness.*

48. See Bollas, *The Shadow of the Object.*

49. See Kenneth S. Bowers and Peter Farvolden, "Revisiting a Century-Old Freudian Slip—From Suggestion Disavowed to the Truth Repressed," *Psychological Bulletin* 119, no. 3 (1996): 335–380; Lindsay, "Contextualizing and Clarifying Criticisms of Memory Work in Psychotherapy"; Michael R. Nash, "Memory Distortion and Sexual Trauma: The Problem of False Negatives and False Positives," *International Journal of Clinical and Experimental Hypnosis* 42 (1994): 346–362; Greg J. Neimeyer and Margaret B. Rareshide, "Personal Memories and Personal Identity: The Impact of Ego Identity Development on Autobiographical Memory Recall," *Journal of Personality and Social Psychology* 60 (1991): 562–569; and Spence, *Narrative Truth and Historical Truth.* For discussion of therapists' beliefs about the literal accuracy of memory, see Yapko, "Suggestibility and Repressed Memories of Abuse."

50. Assertion cited in Jennifer F. Manlowe, *Faith Born of Seduction: Sexual Trauma, Body Image, and Religion* (New York: New York University Press, 1995), 10.

51. For challenges, see James J. Edwards and Pamela C. Alexander, "The Contribution of Family Background to the Long Term Adjustment of Women Sexually Abused," *Journal of Interpersonal Violence* 7 (1992): 306–320; Michael R. Nash et al., "Long-Term Sequelae of Childhood Sexual Abuse: Perceived Family Environment, Psychopathology, and Dissociation," *Journal of Consulting and Clinical Psychology* 61, no. 2 (1993): 276–283; and Howard Steiger and Maria Zanko, "Sexual Trauma among Eating-Disordered, Psychiatric and Normal Female Groups," *Journal of Interpersonal Violence* 5 (1990): 74–86. These reviews of the research literature conclude that childhood sexual abuse is not predictive, in and of itself, of adult psychopathology. General family pathology, neglect, and physical abuse are more predictive. The argument I advance throughout the book is that childhood sexual abuse holds primacy as a cause of women's difficulty not because of automatic effects that result from it but because of its social symbolic meaning for women.
52. Herman, *Trauma and Recovery,* 52.
53. Ellenberger, *The Discovery of the Unconscious.*
54. See, for example, Herman, *Trauma and Recovery;* and van der Kolk and van der Hart, "Pierre Janet and the Breakdown of Adaptation in Psychological Trauma."
55. For discussion of the influence of managed care on mental health practices, see Janet Pipal, "Managed Care: Is It the Corpse in the Living Room? An Expose," *Psychotherapy* 32 (1995): 323–332.
56. See Ilene Philipson, *On the Shoulders of Women: The Feminization of Psychology* (New York: Guilford Press, 1993).
57. Alice Miller, *Thou Shalt Not Be Aware: Society's Betrayal of the Child* (New York: Farrar, Straus & Giroux, 1984), 318.
58. Ibid., 318.
59. Alice Miller, *The Drama of the Gifted Child* (New York: Farrar, Straus & Giroux, 1983).
60. Heinz Kohut, *The Restoration of the Self* (New York: International Universities Press, 1977).
61. For discussion of clinical literature and research linking childhood sexual abuse and adult psychopathology, see Arne Cornelius Boudewyn and Joan Huser Liem, "Childhood Sexual Abuse as a Precursor to Depression and Self-Destructive Behavior in Adulthood," *Journal of Traumatic Stress* 8 (1995): 445–459; Herman, *Trauma and Recovery;* and B. E. Saunders, L. A. Villeponteaux, and J. Lipovsky, "Child Sexual Assault as a Risk Factor for Mental Disorders among Women," *Journal of Interpersonal Violence* 7 (1992): 189–204.
62. Ganaway, "Hypnosis, Childhood Trauma, and Dissociative Identity Disorder."
63. See Patricia A. Harney, "The Role of Incest in Developmental Theory and Treatment of Women Diagnosed with Borderline Personality Disorder," *Women & Therapy* 12 (1992): 39–57; and Herman, *Trauma and Recovery.*
64. Jacobs, *Victimized Daughters;* and Manlowe, *Faith Born of Seduction.*
65. Jacobs, *Victimized Daughters,* 36.
66. Ibid., 37.
67. See van der Kolk, McFarlane, and Weisaeth, *Traumatic Stress;* and Frank W. Putnam, "Dissociative Phenomena," in *Dissociative Disorders: A Clinical Review,* ed. David Spiegel (Lutherville, Md.: Sidran Press, 1993), 1–16.

Chapter 4 **PSYCHOANALYTIC FEMINISM:**
Bridging Private and Public Remembrances

1. For a feminist analysis of the Twelve-Step recovery and codependence movement, specifically in framing women's dilemmas, see Haaken, "From Al-ANON to ACOA."
2. For discussion of radical traditions and applications of psychoanalysis, see Jacoby, *The Repression of Psychoanalysis;* Michael Rustin, *The Good Society and the Inner World: Psychoanalysis, Politics, and Culture* (New York: Verso, 1991); Joel Whitebook, *Perversion and Utopia: A Study in Psychoanalysis and Critical Theory* (Cambridge, Mass.: MIT Press, 1995); and Eugene Victor Wolfenstein, *Psychoanalytic-Marxism: Groundwork* (New York: Guilford Press, 1993). For feminist interpetations of the politics of psychoanalysis, see Benjamin, *The Bonds of Love;* Judith Butler, *Gender Trouble: Feminism and the Subversion of Identity* (New York: Routledge, 1990); Teresa Brennan, *The Interpretation of the Flesh: Freud and Femininity* (New York: Routledge, 1992); Janice Doane and Devon Hodges, *From Klein to Kristeva: Psychoanalytic Feminism and the Search for the "Good Enough" Mother* (Ann Arbor: University of Michigan Press, 1992); Jane Flax, *Thinking Fragments: Psychoanalysis, Feminism, and Postmodernism in the Contemporary West* (Los Angeles: University of California Press, 1990); and Johnson, *Strong Mothers/Weak Wives.*
3. See Jane Gallop, *The Daughter's Seduction: Feminism and Psychoanalysis* (Ithaca, N.Y.: Cornell University Press, 1982). Gallop uses the phrase "the daughter's seduction" to describe the ambivalent relationship between feminism and Freudianism. For discussion of this same theme, see Rachel Bowlby, "Still Crazy after All These Years," in *Between Feminism and Psychoanalysis,* ed. Teresa Brennan (New York: Routledge, 1989), 40–59; Catherine Clément, *The Weary Sons of Freud* (New York: Verso, 1978); Christiane Olivier, *Jocasta's Children: The Imprint of the Mother* (New York: Routledge, 1989); and Madelon Sprengnether, *The Spectral Mother: Freud, Feminism, and Psychoanalysis* (Ithaca, N.Y.: Cornell

University Press, 1990). For a feminist analysis of Freudian theory and lesbian sexuality, see Butler, *Gender Trouble;* Nancy Chodorow, *Femininities, Masculinities, Sexualities: Freud and Beyond* (Lexington: University Press of Kentucky, 1994); and Teresa de Lauretis, *The Practice of Love: Lesbian Sexuality and Perverse Desire* (Bloomington: Indiana University Press, 1994).

4. For an analysis of this transition, see Szasz, *The Myth of Mental Illness;* Jane Ussher, *Women's Madness: Misogyny or Mental Illness* (Amherst: University of Massachusetts Press, 1991); and Hélène Cixous and Catherine Clément, *The Newly Born Woman* (Minneapolis: University of Minnesota Press, 1975).

5. Sandra M. Gilbert and Susan Gubar, *The Madwoman in the Attic: The Woman Writer and the Nineteenth-Century Literary Imagination,* (New Haven, Conn.: Yale University Press, 1979). Their book has popularized the phrase "madwoman in the attic."

6. Showalter, *Hystories.*

7. See Loftus and Ketcham, *The Myth of Repressed Memories;* Ofshe and Watters, *Making Monsters;* and Mark Pendergrast, *Victims of Memory: Sex Abuse Allegations and Shattered Lives* (Hinesburg, Vt.: Upper Access, 1996). These are among the many critics who draw parallels between the European or Salem witch trials and contemporary sex abuse allegations.

8. Phyllis Chesler, *Women and Madness* (Garden City, N.Y.: Doubleday, 1972).

9. The actual wording in the *DSM-III* is that the disorder is a response to events that would evoke "significant symptoms of distress in most people." American Psychiatric Association, *DSM-III* (Washington, D.C.: American Psychiatric Association, 1980), 236.

10. See Armstrong, *Rocking the Cradle of Sexual Politics.* Armstrong chronicles this history, including the shift from political to therapeutic approaches to incest recovery. Also, see Nathan and Snedeker, *Satan's Silence.* For discussion of generational differences in feminist sexual politics, see Nan Bauer Maglin and Donna Perry, "Introduction," in *"Bad Girls/Good Girls": Women, Sex, & Power in the Nineties,* ed. Nan Bauer Maglin and Donna Perry (New Brunswick, N.J.: Rutgers University Press, 1996).

11. Herman, *Trauma and Recovery,* 110.

12. Ibid., 83.

13. See Johnson, *Strong Mothers/Weak Wives.* She also makes use of the idea of an incest continuum, with one end of the continuum extending into normative or culturally sanctioned patterns in father/daughter relationships.

14. See Plummer, *Telling Sexual Stories.* Plummer explores group influences on sexual storytelling, specifically in describing the "community-building" function of stories.

15. Herman, *Trauma and Recovery,* 223.

16. Ibid., 172.

17. For more extensive discussion of Herman's work and its influence on contemporary feminism, see Janice Haaken, "The Recovery of Memory, Fantasy, and Desire: Feminist Approaches to Sexual Abuse and Psychic Trauma," *Signs* 21, no. 4 (summer 1996): 1069–1094. For more extensive discussion of the concept of fantasy in psychoanalytic thought, see Victor Burgin, James D. Kaplan, and Cora Kaplin, eds., *Formations of Fantasy* (New York: Methuen, 1986); and Stavroula Bertis, "The Personal Myth as a Defence against Internal Primitive Aggression," *International Journal of Psychoanalysis* 69 (1988): 475–482.

18. See Mitchell and Black, Freud and Beyond, a useful overview of the Kleinian tradition. See C. Fred Alford, *Melanie Klein and Critical Social Theory: An Account of Politics, Art, and Reason Based on Her Psychoanalytic Theory* (New Haven, Conn.: Yale University Press, 1989), for discussion of this tradition as social psychology. See Dorothy Dinnerstein, *The Mermaid and the Minotaur: Sexual Arrangements and Human Malaise* (New York: Harper & Row, 1977); Dinnerstein introduced one of the earliest Kleinian interpretations of gender development into feminist psychoanalytic critique. Also see Doane and Hodges, *From Klein to Kristeva,* who also examine the implications of Kleinian theory from a feminist perspective, emphasizing the importance of Klein's concept of unconscious fantasy in understanding primitive currents in representations of women.

19. See Doane and Hodges, *From Klein to Kristeva;* and Flax, *Thinking Fragments.* For a critique of this issue and a feminist argument for an environmental (non-Kleinian) object relations theory, see Chodorow, *The Reproduction of Mothering.* The Stone Center, which includes the pioneering work of Jean Baker Miller, is also associated with a revaluing of relational embeddedness as central to female identity.

20. For discussion of British psychoanalytic views on maternal pathology, see Roy Porter, *A Social History of Madness: Stories of the Insane* (London: Weidenfeld and Nicholson, 1987).

21. See Robert Darnton, *Mesmerism and the End of the Enlightenment in France* (Cambridge, Mass.: Harvard University Press, 1968); Robert Darnton, *The Great Cat Massacre and Other Episodes in French Cultural History* (New York: Basic Books, 1984); and Jack Zipes, *Fairy Tales and the Art of Subversion: The Classical Genre for Children and the Process of Civilization* (New York: Methuen, 1983). These two authors present historical explanations for some of these same themes, and they caution against psychologically reductionist interpretations of folktales.

22. See Joseph Klaits, *Servants of Satan: The Age of the Witch Hunts* (Bloomington: Indiana University Press, 1985); Porter, *A Social History of Madness;* and Ussher, *Women's Madness.*

23. Benjamin, *The Bonds of Love.* Pauline Réage, *Story of O* (New York: Grove Press, 1965/1954).

24. Inquiry into the problem of how the oppressed participate or collaborate in their own domination has a long and diverse history. With the shift toward poststructuralism and postmodernism in the social sciences, power is more likely to be understood as being embedded in language or "discourses" than in institutional structures. I have not taken up these debates directly in this book, although I do make use of some of the poststructuralist arguments, particularly the work of Foucault. For discussion of feminism, psychoanalysis, and poststructuralism, see Butler, *Gender Trouble;* Flax, *Thinking Fragments;* Linda J. Nicholson, ed., *Feminism/Postmodernism* (New York: Routledge, 1990); and Chris Weedon, *Feminist Practice & Poststructuralist Theory* (New York: Blackwell, 1987).

25. See Alford, *Melanie Klein and Critical Social Theory;* and Herman, *Trauma and Recovery.*

26. Tavris, *The Mismeasure of Woman.*

27. Winnicott, *Playing and Reality.*

28. See, especially, Anne Rice, *Interview with the Vampire* (New York: Knopf, 1976); and Anne Rice, *The Witching Hour* (New York: Ballantine, 1990).

29. See Melissa Murphy, "Dorothy Allison: The On Our Backs Interview," *On Our Backs* 40, no. 2 (July/Aug. 1993): 23–24. In this interview, Allison discusses the theme of childhood sexual abuse in her work. She grants that her sadomasochistic sexual practices are influenced by the painful side of her childhood but refuses to frame them, as well as pornography, in clinical terms. Also see Dorothy Allison, *Two or Three Things I Know for Sure* (New York: Penguin Books, 1995). Allison analyzes her own use of stories as a response to a childhood where you "have no loved version of your life but the one you make." For other lesbian perspectives on incest, see JoAnn Loulan, *Lesbian Passion: Loving Ourselves and Each Other* (Minneapolis: Spinsters Ink, 1987), 147–172; and Eileen Starzecpyzel, "The Persephone Complex: Incest Dynamics and the Lesbian Preference," in *Lesbian Psychologies: Explorations and Challenges,* ed. Boston Lesbian Psychologies Collective (Chicago: University of Illinois Press, 1987), 261–282.

30. See Irene Gillman, "An Object-Relations Approach to the Phenomenon and Treatment of Battered Women," *Psychiatry* 43 (1983): 346–358; and Sandra Lee Bartsky, *Femininity and Domination: Studies in the Phenomenology of Oppression* (New York: Routledge, 1990).

31. See Susie Bright, *Sexual Reality: A Virtual Sex World Reader* (Pittsburgh: Cleis Press, 1992). Bright makes use of the *Story of O* to tell a whimsical tale of lesbian S/M pleasures, recasting O as an active sexual agent. See Andrea Dworkin, *Woman Hating* (New York: Dutton, 1974), for a radical feminist interpretation of the *Story of O.*

32. For discussion of debates within feminism on sexual practices, including debates over "vanilla sex" versus more aggressive sexual expressions, see Dorothy Allison, *Skin: Talking about Sex, Class and Literature* (Ithaca, N.Y.: Firebrand Books, 1994); Bartsky, *Femininity and Domination;* Amber Hollibaugh and Cherríe Moraga, "What We're Rollin Around in Bed With: Sexual Silences in Feminism," in *The Powers of Desire: The Politics of Sexuality,* ed. Ann Barr Snitow, Christine Stansell, and Sharon Thompson (New York: Monthly Review Press, 1983); and Carol Vance, ed., *Pleasure and Danger: Exploring Female Sexuality* (London: Pandora, 1989), 394–405.

33. See Naomi Segal, "Echo and Narcissus," in *Between Feminism and Psychoanalysis,* ed. Teresa Brennan (New York: Routledge, 1989), 168–185. Segal makes use of this myth to analyze the "repressed" side of oedipal theory—that is, the origins of the phallic stage in the mirroring functions of the mother.

34. While Chodorow and feminists at the Stone Center stress the stability of gendered personality cross-culturally and trans-historically, other psychoanalytic feminists reject this view as essentialist, arguing for a female identity in flux. See Butler, *Gender Trouble;* Mardy S. Ireland, *Reconceiving Women: Separating Motherhood from Female Identity* (New York: Guilford Press, 1993); and Irene Fast, *Gender Identity: A Differentiation Model,* vol. 2 of *Advances in Psychoanalysis: Theory, Research, and Practice* (Hillsdale, N.J.: Analytic Press, 1984).

35. Sigmund Freud, "Ego and Id," in *SE,* vol. 19 (1962/1923). Freud introduced the idea of the body ego as the earliest psychological structure. Freud's instinct theory emphasized drive derivatives and their role in developmental stages. In this theory, drives are not initally object-seeking—that is, oriented toward attachments. While instinct theory has largely been displaced by object relations theory in contemporary psychoanalysis, I emphasize here the phenomenological tension in female development between the body, as a source of pleasurable sensations, and object relations as it relates to representations of self and other and the regulation of interpersonal engagement.

36. See Chodorow, *The Reproduction of Mothering.*

37. See Benjamin, *The Bonds of Love;* Herman, *Trauma and Recovery;* and David-Menard, *Hysteria from Freud to Lacan.* These authors approach this theme in different ways, but each makes central the problem of the female body as receptive site for male sexuality. See Ann Barr Snitow, "Mass Market Romance: Pornography for Women Is Different," in *The Powers of Desire: The Politics of Sexuality,* ed. Ann Barr Snitow, Christine Stansell, and Sharon Thompson (New York: Monthly Review Press, 1983), 245–263. Snitow explores this theme in the Harlequin romance novel.

38. See Johnson, *Strong Mothers/Weak Wives;* and Barrie Thorne, *Gender Play: Girls and Boys in School* (New Brunswick, N.J.: Rutgers University Press, 1993). Both discuss gender dynamics in the classroom.

39. For discussion of gender differences in impulse regulation and in children's play and fantasies, see Marion Libby and Elizabeth Aries, "Gender Differences in Preschool Children's Narrative Fantasy,"

Psychology of Women Quarterly 13 (1989): 293–306. For discussion of the theme of bodily contain-ment and muted desire in female adolescence, see Constance A. Nathanson, *Dangerous Passage: The Social Control of Sexuality in Women's Adolescence* (Philadelphia: Temple University Press, 1991); Sharon Thompson, *Going All the Way* (New York: Hill & Wang, 1994); Thorne, *Gender Play;* and Deb-orah L. Tolman, "Adolescent Girls, Women and Sexuality: Discerning Dilemmas of Desire," in *Women, Girls & Psychotherapy: Reframing Resistance,* ed. Carol Gilligan, Annie G. Rogers, and Debo-rah L. Tolman (New York: Hawthorne Press, 1991), 55–67.

40. See Adrienne Rich, "Compulsory Heterosexuality and Lesbian Existence," in *The Powers of Desire: The Politics of Sexuality,* ed. Ann Barr Snitow, Christine Stansell, and Sharon Thompson (New York: Monthly Review Press, 1983), 177–205. Rich introduces the idea of a lesbian continuum to describe the broad range of erotic pleasures in female relationships.

41. For discussion of gender and nonverbal cues, see Shirley Weitz, ed., *Nonverbal Communication,* 2d ed. (New York: Oxford University Press, 1979); and Elaine Hatfield, John T. Cacioppo, and Richard L. Rapson, *Emotional Contagion: Studies in Emotion and Social Interaction* (Paris: Cambridge University Press, 1994).

42. Hochschild, *The Managed Heart.*

43. Chodorow, *The Reproduction of Mothering.*

44. Jeanne Perreault, *Writing Selves: Contemporary Feminist Autography* (Minneapolis: University of Min-nesota Press, 1995), 19.

45. *Bad Girls* was an exhibit at the New Museum of Contemporary Art, New York, organized by Marcia Tanner, 1994.

46. See Morag Shiach, "Their 'Symbolic' Exists, It Holds Power—We, the Sowers of Disorder, Know It Only Too Well," in *Between Feminism and Psychoanlaysis,* ed. Teresa Brennan (New York: Routledge, 1989), 153–167. Drawing on French feminist thought, Shiach argues for a discursive approach to the body. From this perspective, the female body is signifier of the unconscious itself in patriarchal society.

47. See Cixous and Clément, *The Newly Born Woman;* Luce Irigaray, "The Gesture in Psychoanalysis," in *Between Feminism and Psychoanalysis,* ed. Teresa Brennan (New York: Routledge, 1989), 127–138. For an overview of French feminism with selected works, see Elaine Marks and Isabelle de Courtivron, eds., *New French Feminism: An Anthology* (New York: Schocken Books, 1981). For discussion of French psychoanalytic thought, see Teresa Brennan, ed., *Between Feminism and Psychoanalysis* (New York: Routledge, 1989); and Doane and Hodges, *From Klein to Kristeva.*

48. See Shiach, "Their 'Symbolic' Exists, It Holds Power."

49. Luce Irigaray, *Speculum of the Other Woman,* trans. Catherine Porter and Carolyn Burke (Ithaca, N.Y.: Cornell University Press, 1985).

50. See Luce Irigaray, "This Sex Which Is Not One," 99–106; Chantel Chawaf, "Linguistic Flesh," 177–178; and Madeleine Cagnon, "Body I," 179–180; all in *New French Feminism: An Anthology,* ed. Elaine Marks and Isabelle de Courtivron (New York: Schocken Books, 1981).

51. Cited in Shiach, "Their 'Symbolic' Exists, It Holds Power," 155.

52. Cited in Perreault, *Writing Selves,* 56.

Chapter 5 **SOCIAL REMEMBERING AND THE LEGENDARY PAST**

1. For a review of research on memory, see chapter 2.

2. Bruner, *Actual Minds, Possible Worlds,* 66.

3. For an articulation of this position, see Bruner, *Acts of Meaning.*

4. For a feminist analysis of this tale, see Karen E. Rowe, "To Spin a Yarn: The Female Voice in Folk-lore and Fairy Tale," in *Fairy Tales and Society: Illusion, Allusion, and Paradigm,* ed. Ruth B. Bottigheimer (Philadelphia: University of Pennsylvania Press, 1986), 53–74.

5. Ibid., 59.

6. Gilbert and Gubar, *The Madwoman in the Attic.*

7. See Helen Block Lewis, "Shame, Repression, Field Dependence, and Psychopathology," in *Repression and Dissociation: Implications for Personality Theory, Psychopathology, and Health,* ed. Jerome L. Singer (Chicago: University of Chicago Press, 1990), 233–257.

8. Sherry Ortner, "Is Female to Male as Nature Is to Culture?" in *Women, Culture and Society,* ed. Michelle Zimbalist Rosaldo and Louise Lamphere (Stanford, Calif.: Stanford University Press, 1974), 67–87.

9. Quoted in Gilbert and Gubar, *The Madwoman in the Attic,* 17.

10. Sam Keen, "Against Forgetting: Without Memory, Stories Die," *Utne Reader,* Mar./Apr. 1994, 112–121.

11. For discussion of the new influence of storytelling in academic psychology, specifically in memory research, see chapter 2.

12. Dworkin, *Woman Hating,* 32.

13. Zipes, *Fairy Tales and the Art of Subversion.*

14. Maria Tatar, "Born Yesterday: Heroes in Grimms' Fairy Tales," 95–114; and Kay F. Stone, "Feminist Approaches to the Interpretation of Fairy Tales," 229–236; both in *Fairy Tales and Society: Illusion, Allusion, and Paradigm,* ed. Ruth B. Bottigheimer (Philadelphia: University of Pennsylvania Press, 1986).

15. Ruth B. Bottigheimer, *Grimms' Bad Girls and Bold Boys: The Moral and Social Vision of the Tales* (New Haven, Conn.: Yale Univerity Press, 1987).

16. Ibid., 87–88.

17. Marina Warner, *From the Beast to the Blonde: On Fairy Tales and Their Tellers* (New York: Farrar, Straus & Giroux, 1994), 336.

18. See Jean M. Goodwin, *Sexual Abuse: Incest Victims and Their Families* (Chicago: Year Book Medical Publishers, 1989).

19. Warner, *From the Beast to the Blonde.*

20. Ibid., 334.

21. E. R. Chamberlin, *The Fall of the House of Borgia* (New York: Dial, 1974); and Michael Mallet, *The Borgias: The Rise and Fall of a Renaissance Dynasty* (Frogmore, St. Albans: Paladin, 1971).

22. Quoted in Warner, *From the Beast to the Blonde,* 346.

23. Ibid.; and Zipes, *Fairy Tales and the Art of Subversion.*

24. Jack Zipes, *The Trials and Tribulations of Little Red Riding Hood* (South Hadley, Mass.: Bergin & Garvey, 1986), 16.

25. For the history of the thousand-year-old Cinderella story, including its domesticated versions in the modern era, see Iona Opie and Peter Opie, *The Classic Fairy Tales* (London: Oxford University Press, 1974).

26. Ibid.

27. See Klaitz, *Servants of Satan,* 172; and Anne Llewellyn Barstow, *Witchcraze: A New History of the European Witch Hunts* (San Francisco: Pandora, 1994). For discussion of the influence of religious and political movements on women's autobiographies during these same historical periods, see Sidonie Smith, *A Poetics of Women's Autobiography: Marginality and the Fictions of Self-Representation* (Bloomington: Indiana University Press, 1987).

28. Zipes, *Fairy Tales and the Art of Subversion,* 57.

29. Jack Zipes, "The Grimms and the German Obsession with Fairy Tales," in *Fairy Tales and Society: Illusion, Allusion, and Paradigm,* ed. Ruth B. Bottigheimer (Philadelphia: University of Pennsylvania Press, 1986), 271–285.

30. Foucault, *The History of Sexuality,* vol. 1.

31. For discussion of this theme, see Herman with Hirschman, *Father-Daughter Incest;* and Gayle Rubin, "The Traffic in Women: Notes on the 'Political Economy' of Sex," in *Toward an Anthropology of Women,* ed. Rayna R. Reiter (New York: Monthly Review Press, 1975), 157–210.

32. For discussion of the emergence of the modern nuclear family, see Dizard and Gadlin, *The Minimal Family;* Mark Poster, *A Critical Theory of the Family* (New York: Seabury Press, 1978); and Eli Zaretsky, *Capitalism, the Family, & Personal Life* (New York: Harper & Row, 1976).

33. One of the historical debates within feminism concerns the contradictory aspects of the modern nuclear family. On the one hand, this family form undermined the kinship basis of the economy, permitting a loosening of patriarchal control over female kin and increased opportunities for female mobility. On the other hand, the nuclear family marginalized women's work, relegating female labor to a private sphere, and strengthened the subordination of women to husbands. For an analysis of these themes, see Barrie Thorne and Marilyn Yalom, eds., *Rethinking the Family: Some Feminist Questions* (Boston: Northeastern University Press, 1992).

34. Goodwin, *Sexual Abuse.*

35. For discussion of cultural splitting of villainy and virtue, see Klaits, *Servants of Satan;* and Bottigheimer, *Grimms' Bad Girls and Bold Boys.*

36. See, for example, Bruno Bettelheim, *The Uses of Enchantment: The Meaning and Importance of Fairy Tales* (New York: Vintage Books, 1975).

37. Ann Sexton, *Transformations* (Boston: Houghton Mifflin, 1971).

38. Ibid., 112.

39. For discussion of the social dynamics underlying the movement to confront clergy abuse, see Elinor Burkett and Frank Bruni, *Gospel of Shame: Children, Sexual Abuse, and the Catholic Church* (New Haven, Conn.: Viking, 1993).

40. Clergy abuse has also emerged as a political issue in the Mormon Church, as has the employment of child sexual abuse to advance a broad critique of patriarchal authority. See April Daniels and Carol Scott, *Paperdolls: A True Story of Childhood Sexual Abuse in Mormon Neighborhoods* (San Diego: Recovery, 1992).

41. See Armstrong, *Rocking the Cradle of Sexual Politics.* Armstrong reviews this and other statistical claims advanced throughout the history of the incest recovery movement.

42. Ibid., 24.

43. Richard Terdiman, *Present Past: Modernity and the Memory Crisis* (Ithaca, N.Y.: Cornell University Press, 1993), 214.

44. Patricia Hill Collins, *Black Feminist Thought* (New York: Routledge, 1990).

45. Melba Wilson, *Crossing the Boundary: Black Women Survive Incest* (Seattle: Seal Press, 1994).

46. See Elliot Butler-Evans, *Race, Gender, and Desire* (Philadelphia: Temple University Press, 1989).

47. Quoted in Wilson, *Crossing the Boundary,* 41.

48. See Thompson, *Going All the Way;* Tolman, "Adolescent Girls, Women and Sexuality"; and Vance, *Pleasure and Danger.*

49. See Vance, *Pleasure and Danger.*

50. Susan Brownmiller, *Against Our Will: Men, Women, and Rape* (New York: Simon & Schuster, 1975).

51. See Alice Walker, "Advancing Luna—and Ida B. Wells," in *You Can't Keep a Good Woman Down* (New York: Harcourt Brace Jovanovich, 1982), 85–104. In this reflective essay on the dilemmas of the writer, Walker describes her own ambivalences in telling the story of a white woman friend who claimed to have been raped by a black man in the civil rights movement. The essay works both sides of the ambivalence, framed by the countervailing demands of racial and sexual solidarity.

52. Jacquelyn Dowd Hall, "'The Mind That Burns in Each Body': Women, Rape, and Racial Violence," in *The Powers of Desire: The Politics of Sexuality,* ed. Ann Barr Snitow, Christine Stansell, and Sharon Thompson (New York: Monthly Review Press, 1983), 328–349.

53. Armstrong, *Rocking the Cradle of Sexual Politics.*

54. See Lenore E. Walker, *The Battered Woman Syndrome* (New York: Springer, 1984); and Daniel J. Sonkin, ed., *Domestic Violence on Trial* (New York: Springer, 1987).

55. I would not want to minimize the frequency of such cases. I am suggesting here and throughout the book, however, that the emergence of father/daughter incest as a "master narrative" grew out of factors far beyond the numerical freqency of overt incest and male violence. See Hacking, "The Making and Molding of Child Abuse," 253–288, which advances this same idea.

56. Wendy Maltz, *The Sexual Healing Journey: A Guide for Survivors of Sexual Abuse* (New York: Harper Perennial, 1992).

57. See Edwards and Alexander, "The Contribution of Family Background to the Long Term Adjustment of Women Sexually Abused."

Chapter 6 **HYPNOTIC ENCOUNTERS:**
Eroticized Remembering and Altered States

1. See Getrude Stein, *Everybody's Autobiography* (New York: Random House, 1937).

2. For discussion of the influence of James on Stein's life and work, see Elizabeth Spirgge, *Gertrude Stein: Her Life and Work* (New York: Harper & Brothers, 1957), esp. 22–41; and James Mellow, *Charmed Circle: Gertrude Stein and Company* (New York: Praeger, 1974), esp. 31–34.

3. There are interesting parallels between late-nineteenth-century automatic handwriting and the facilitated-communication movement in the late twentieth century. Whereas automatic handwriting made use of the planchette to communicate with the dead, facilitated communication employs the computer to make contact with autistic individuals. In both contexts, women play the role of "facilitators" in bridging a silence. And, in both contexts, extraordinary capacities to communicate with the beyond, whether the dead or the mentally isolated, position women as outside orthodox scientific practices. For discussion of this history and controversies surrounding facilitated communication, see John Jacobson, James Mulick, and Allen Schwartz, "A History of Facilitated Communication: Science, Pseudoscience, and Antiscience," *American Psychologist* 50, no. 9 (Sept. 1995): 760–765.

4. Cited in John Malcolm Brinnin, *Third Rose: Gertrude Stein and Her World* (Boston: Atlantic Monthly Press, 1959), 30–31.

5. For discussion of beliefs about hypnosis, see John F. Kihlstrom, "William James and Hypnosis: A Centennial Reflection," *American Psychological Society* 1, no. 3 (1990): 174–178; Nash, "Memory Distortion and Sexual Trauma"; and Yapko, *Suggestions of Abuse.*

6. See Loftus and Ketcham, *The Myth of Repressed Memory;* Ofshe and Watters, *Making Monsters;* Showalter, *Hystories;* and Spanos et al., "Secondary Identity Enactments during Hypnotic Past-Life Regression."

7. See Kenneth S. Pope, "Memory, Abuse, and Science: Questioning Claims about the False Memory Syndrome Epidemic," *American Psychologist* 51 (1996): 957–974.

8. See A. A. Mason, "A Psychoanalyst Looks at a Hypnotist: A Study of Folie à Deux," *Psychoanalytic Quarterly* 43 (1994): 641–679. In this thoughtfully "confessional" essay, the author describes the fantasy of "Svengali-like" power over a female subject as a formative one in shaping his interest in hypnosis and psychiatry.

9. The character of Svengali is taken from George du Maurier, *Trilby* (New York: Oxford University Press, 1995/1894). In an introduction to this edition, Elaine Showalter discusses the historical significance of this popularly successful, turn-of-the-century novel.

10. See George Frederick Drinka, *The Birth of Neurosis: Myth, Malady, and the Victorians* (New York: Simon & Schuster, 1984); Ellenberger, *The Discovery of the Unconscious;* and Jean-Roch Laurence and Perry Campbell, *Hypnosis, Will, and Memory: A Psycho-legal History* (New York: Guilford Press, 1988).

11. The period of the French Revolution also was an era of psychiatric reform, with physician Phillippe Pinel's unchaining of mental patients at the Salpêtrière. See Darnton, *Mesmerism and the End of the Enlightenment in France;* Szasz, *The Myth of Mental Illness;* and Ussher, *Women's Madness.*

12. For a description of the magnetic cure, see Drinka, *The Birth of Neurosis;* Robert C. Fuller, *Mesmerism and the American Cure of Souls* (Philadelphia: University of Pennsylvania Press, 1982); and Laurence and Campbell, *Hypnosis, Will, and Memory.*

13. Laurence and Campbell, *Hypnosis, Will, and Memory.*

14. Quoted in ibid., 117.

15. Ibid., 133.

16. Fuller, *Mesmerism and the American Cure of Souls,* 17.

17. See Ann Braude, *Radical Spirits: Spirtualism and Women's Rights in Nineteenth-Century America* (Boston: Beacon Press, 1989); and Alex Owen, *The Darked Room: Women, Power and Spiritualism in Late Victorian England* (Philadelphia: University of Pennsylvania Press, 1990).

18. Braude, *Radical Spirits.*

19. Janet Oppenheim, *The Other World: Spiritualism and Psychical Research in England, 1850–1914* (New York: Cambridge University Press, 1985).

20. See Fuller, *Mesmerism and the American Cure of Souls;* Oppenheim, *The Other World;* and Owen, *The Darked Room.*

21. For discussion of the influence of mediumship on nineteenth-century psychiatry, see Ellenberger, *The Discovery of the Unconscious.* Also, see Hannah S. Decker, "The Lure of Nonmaterialism in Materialist Europe: Investigations into Dissociative Phenomena, 1880–1915," in *Split Minds/Split Brains: Historical and Current Perspectives,* ed. Jacques M. Quen (New York: New York University Press, 1986), 31–62.

22. Quoted in Owen, *The Darked Room,* 148. For discussion of lunacy charges against spiritualists, see Judith R. Walkowitz, "Science and the Seance: Transgressions of Gender and Genre in Late Victorian London," *Representations* 22 (1988): 3–36.

23. Fuller, *Mesmerism and the American Cure of Souls;* Jeremy Hawthorn, *Multiple Personality and the Disintegration of Literary Character* (New York: St. Martin's Press, 1983); and Kenny, *The Passion of Ansel Bourne.*

24. Oppenheim, *The Other World,* 160.

25. See Sonu Shamdasani, "Encountering Hélène: Théodore Flournoy and the Genesis of Subliminal Psychology," introduction to Théodore Flournoy, *From India to the Planet Mars: A Case of Multiple Personality with Imaginary Languages* (Princeton, N.J.: Princeton University Press, 1994), xi.

26. Fuller, *Mesmerism and the American Cure of Souls,* 95.

27. See Ruth Brandon, *The Spiritualists: The Passion for the Occult in the 19th and 20th Centuries* (New York: Knopf, 1983).

28. Owen, *The Darked Room,* 216.

29. Ibid.

30. William James, *William James on Psychical Research,* comp. and ed. Gardner Murphy and Robert O. Ballou (London: Chatto & Windus, 1961/1909).

31. Cited in Braude, *Radical Spirits,* 3.

32. For discussion of the influence of the Civil War on the spiritualist movement and women's guidance literature, see Howard Kerr, John W. Crowley, and Charles L. Crow, eds., *The Haunted Dusk: American Supernatural Fiction, 1820–1920* (Athens: University of Georgia Press, 1983).

33. See Linda Gordon, *Heroes of Their Own Lives: The Politics and History of Family Violence* (New York: Viking Press, 1988); Ussher, *Women's Madness.*

34. For discussion of Charcot and representations of women, see Daphne deMarneffe, "Looking and Listening: The Construction of Clinical Knowledge in Charcot and Freud," in *Gender and Scientific Authority,* ed. Barbara Laslett et al. (Chicago: University of Chicago Press, 1996), 241–301; Healy, *Images of Trauma;* Szasz, *The Myth of Mental Illness;* and Ussher, *Women's Madness.* Also, see Jean-Martin Charcot, "Hysteria in the Male Subject," in *A History of Psychoanalysis: Original Sources and Contemporary Research,* 2d ed., ed. Ludy T. Benjamin, Jr. (New York: McGraw-Hill, 1997), 97–103. Charcot challenges the cultural association between femininity and hysteria in this paper on male hysteria, refuting the assumption that this condition occurs only in women. Yet Charcot's displays of female hysteria, which predominated in his lecture series, served to reinscribe this association.

35. Ellenberger, *The Discovery of the Unconscious,* 91.

36. Ibid.; and Laurence and Campbell, *Hypnosis, Will, and Memory,* 182.

37. Cited in Laurence and Campbell, *Hypnosis, Will, and Memory,* 202; emphasis in original.

38. Ibid.

39. Cited in Ellenberger, *The Discovery of the Unconscious,* 87.

40. While hypnosis was widely regarded in the 1980s as a means of "refreshing" memory and was frequently used in obtaining information used in eyewitness testimony, by the early 1990s the tide had turned in the legal arena. Because a new wave of research emphasized both the problem of suggestion and the conflation of fantasy and factual events in hypnotically recovered memory, such memories, obtained in psychotherapy or in investigative interviewing, were no longer admissible in court. For discussion of this and other legal issues surrounding recovered memories, see Amanda J. Barnier and Kevin M. McConkey, "Reports of Real and False Memories: The Relevance of Hypnosis, Hypnotizability, and Context of Memory Test," *Journal of Abnormal Psychology* 101 (1992):

521–527; Richard J. Ofshe, "Inadvertent Hypnosis during Interrogation: False Confession due to Dissociative State; Mis-identified Multiple Personality and the Satanic Cult Hypothesis," *International Journal of Clinical and Experimental Hypnosis* 40 (1992): 125–156; Martha Rogers, "Factors to Consider in Assessing Adult Litigants' Complaints of Childhood Sexual Abuse," *Behavioral Sciences and the Law* 12 (1994): 279–298; and Donald R. Tayloe, "The Validity of Repressed Memories and the Accuracy of Their Recall through Hypnosis: A Case Study from the Courtroom," *American Journal of Clinical Hypnosis* 37 (1995): 25–31.

41. See Laurence and Campbell, *Hypnosis, Will, and Memory.*

42. For discussion of the controversies that emerged at the Clark conference, see Nathan G. Hale, Jr., *Freud and the Americans: The Beginnings of Psychoanalysis in the United States, 1876–1917* (New York: Oxford University Press, 1971).

43. For discussion of the exclusion of women in the experimental tradition, including the controversy surrounding the Clark conference, see Furumoto, "Shared Knowledge."

44. G. Stanley Hall, "A Medium in the Bud," *American Journal of Psychology* 29–30 (1918): 152. For discussion of Hall's ambivalent responses to women students and colleagues, see Lesley A. Diehl, "The Paradox of G. Stanley Hall: Foe of Coeducation and Educator of Women," in *A History of Psychoanalysis: Original Sources and Contemporary Research,* 2d ed., ed. Ludy T. Benjamin, Jr. (New York: McGraw-Hill, 1997), 266–281.

45. Hall, "A Medium in the Bud," 153.

46. Sigmund Freud, "An Autobiographical Study," in *SE,* vol. 20 (1962/1925), 7–74.

47. Ruth Leys, "Traumatic Cures: Shell Shock, Janet, and the Question of Memory," *Critical Inquiry* 20 (1994): 623–662.

48. Ibid.

49. Elaine Showalter, *The Female Malady: Women, Madness and Female Culture, 1830–1980* (New York: Penguin Books, 1985).

50. See Pat Barker, *The Ghost Road* (New York: Dutton, 1995). In her novel, Barker introduces psychiatry as a central protagonist in the political contests surrounding World War I. Also, for a history of posttraumatic stress disorder in the diagnosis of "combat neurosis" in the First World War, see Young, *The Harmony of Illusions.*

51. See Showalter, *The Female Malady.*

52. Leys, "Traumatic Cures."

53. Quoted in ibid., 628.

54. In the relegitimizing of clinical hypnosis in the 1980s, when it was emerging out of the legacy of psychedelics, on the one hand, and eroticized submission on the other, hynotherapists once again remasculinized this therapeutic procedure. This time, the hypnotist emerged as "coach." See, for example, John F. Kihlstrom and Irene Hoyt, "Repression, Dissociation, and Hypnosis," in *Repression and Dissociation: Implications for Personality Theory, Psychopathology, and Health,* ed. Jerome L. Singer (Chicago: University of Chicago Press, 1990), 183.

55. Hilgard, *Divided Consciousness.*

56. Ibid., 2.

57. Robert E. Ornstein, *The Psychology of Consciousness* (San Francisco: Freeman, 1972).

58. Hilgard, *Divided Consciousness,* 15.

59. See Lisa S. Lombard, Stephen P. Khan, and Erika Fromm, "The Role of Imagery in Self-Hypnosis: Its Relationship to Personality Characteristics and Gender," *International Journal of Clinical and Experimental Hypnosis* 38, no. 1 (1990): 25–38; Putnam, "Dissociative Phenomena," 4. Also, see Hans de Groot, Gwynn Maxwell, and Nicholas P. Spanos, "The Effects of Contextual Information and Gender on the Prediction of Hypnotic Susceptibility," *Journal of Personality and Social Psychology* 54 (1988): 1049–1053.

60. See Eugene L. Bliss, *Multiple Personality, Allied Disorders, and Hypnosis* (New York: Oxford University Press, 1986).

61. See Judith Butler, *Bodies That Matter: On the Discursive Limits of "Sex"* (New York: Routledge, 1993), and Flax, *Thinking Fragments,* for critiques of unitary and universalist conceptions of gender. These authors draw on poststructuralist discourse, particularly in its deconstruction of the concept of the unitary self. For a psychoanalytic critique along these same lines, see E. A. Lowenstein, "Dissolving the Myth of the Unified Self: The Fate of the Subject in Freudian Analysis," *Psychoanalytic Quarterly* 63 (1994): 715–732.

62. See Bliss, *Multiple Personality, Allied Disorders, and Hypnosis;* Frank W. Putnam, "The Scientific Investigation of Multiple Personality Disorder," in *Split Minds/Split Brains: Historical and Current Perspectives,* ed. Jacques M. Quen (New York: New York University Press, 1986), 109–125; and David Spiegel, "Hypnosis, Dissociation, and Trauma: Hidden and Overt Observers," in *Repression and Dissociation: Implications for Personality Theory, Psychopathology, and Health,* ed. Jerome L. Singer (Chicago: University of Chicago Press, 1990), 121–142.

63. See Haaken, "Field Dependence Research." In this paper, I observe this same trend—that is, the recasting, during an era of feminist critique, of dependence from a negative (feminine) trait to the more positive idea of interactive responsiveness.

64. Hilgard, *Divided Consciousness*, 163.

65. Ibid., 163–164.

66. See Bliss, *Multiple Personality, Allied Disorders, and Hypnosis;* and Eric T. Carlson, "The History of Dissociation until 1880," in *Split Minds/Split Brains: Historical and Current Perspectives,* ed. Jacques M. Quen (New York: New York University Press, 1986), 7–30.

67. For discussion of the problems in separating hypnotic phenomena from other suggestive influences, see Kenneth S. Bowers, "Unconscious Influences and Hypnosis," in *Repression and Dissociation: Implications for Personality Theory, Psychopathology, and Health,* ed. Jerome L. Singer (Chicago: University of Chicago Press, 1990), 143–149.

68. For opposing positions on hypnosis, see Spanos et al., "Secondary Identity Enactments during Past-Life Regression"; and Richard P. Kluft, "The Simulations and Dissimulation of Multiple Personality Disorder," *American Journal of Clinical Hypnosis* 30 (1987): 104–112. Whereas Spanos, a leading researcher in the field of hypnosis, emphasizes the continuity between hypnotic states and mundane psychological processes, such as role playing, others, like Kluft, a leading clinician in the field of dissociative disorders, emphasize the dramatic effects of hypnosis.

69. See Bliss, *Multiple Personality, Allied Disorders, and Hypnosis.* In responding implicitly to the cultural concern over hypnosis and in recovering its positive aspects, Bliss makes a distinction between "primary" suggestibility (hypnosis) and social suggestibility (gullability). While such a distinction may make as much sense as any others in the murky field of hypnosis, it also evades the underlying concern.

70. See Yapko, *Suggestions of Abuse;* and note 40 above.

71. See Ofshe and Watters, *Making Monsters;* and Loftus and Ketcham, *The Myth of Repressed Memory.*

72. See Nathan and Snedeker, *Satan's Silence;* and Ofshe and Watters, *Making Monsters.*

73. D. Cordyn Hammond, ed., *Handbook of Hypnotic Suggestions and Metaphors* (New York: Norton, 1990). Hammond also has played a leading role in advancing a literal interpretation of satanic abuse narratives in the mental health community, a literature addressed in chapter 10. For discussion, see Showalter, *Hystories.*

74. Hammond, *Handbook of Hypnotic Suggestions and Metaphors,* 18.

75. Quoted in Mellow, *Charmed Circle,* 34.

76. Stein, *Everybody's Autobiography.*

Chapter 7 HYSTERICAL HEROINES

1. Aldous Huxley, *The Devils of Loudun* (New York: Harper & Row, 1952).

2. See Rowan Williams, *Teresa of Avila* (Harrisburg, Pa.: Morehouse, 1991).

3. Huxley, *The Devils of Loudun,* 353.

4. Robert C. Carson, James N. Butcher, and Susan Mineka, *Abnormal Psychology and Modern Life,* 10th ed. (New York: HarperCollins, 1996), 40.

5. See Williams, *Teresa of Avila.*

6. For an early, feminist analysis of the historical transition from witchcraft to hysteria, see Barbara Ehrenreich and Deirdre English, *For Her Own Good: 150 Years of the Experts' Advice to Women* (New York: Doubleday, 1978). Also, see Porter, *A Social History of Madness.* Porter also describes the historical transformation of women witches into hysterics, emphasizing the social-control dimension of patriarchal healing practices, whether within the province of religion, psychiatry, or medicine. In addition, see Nancy Theriot, "Women's Voices in Nineteenth Century Medical Discourse: A Step toward Deconstructing Science," in *Gender and Scientific Authority,* ed. Barbara Laslett et al. (Chicago: University of Chicago Press, 1996), 124–154. Theriot emphasizes the mixed motivations of nineteenth-century alienists, including their identifications with the social concerns of women.

7. Freud, "First Lecture on Psychoanalysis at Clark University," 494.

8. See Foucault, *The History of Sexuality,* vol. 1.

9. James, *The Principles of Psychology,* vol. 1, 396–399.

10. See Ellenberger, *The Discovery of the Unconscious;* and Carroll Smith-Rosenberg, *Disorderly Conduct: Visions of Gender in Victorian America* (New York: Knopf, 1985).

11. Quoted in James, *The Principles of Psychology,* vol. 1, 398.

12. Ellenberger, *The Discovery of the Unconscious.*

13. See, for example, Ussher, *Women's Madness.* Many of the French feminists also advance a valorized portrait of hysteria, although the recuperation of the hysteric proceeds through a critique of rationality. See chapter 4.

14. Showalter, *The Female Malady.*

15. In his review of this illustrious case, Ellenberger claims that Breuer knew at the time he coauthored *Studies on Hysteria* that the treatment had been a failure, but he nevertheless claimed it as a success for the "talking cure." Ellenberger also discusses discrepancies in biographical accounts of Pappenheim and the competing legends that have developed around her period of illness. Ellenberger, *The Discovery of the Unconscious.*

16. Breuer and Freud, "Studies on Hysteria," 17.

17. Ann H. Jackowitz, "Anna O/Bertha Pappenheim and Me," in *Between Women: Biographers, Novelists, Critics,* ed. C. Ascher, L. DeSalvo, and S. Ruddick (New York: Beacon Press, 1984), 253–273.

18. See ibid.; Marion A. Kaplan, *The Jewish Feminist Movement in Germany: The Campaigns of the Jüdischer Frauenbund* (Westport, Conn.: Greenwood Press, 1979); and Melinda Given Guttman, "'One Must Be Ready for Time and Eternity,'" *On the Issues* 5, no. 4 (fall 1996): 42–46.

19. See Kaplan, *The Jewish Feminist Movement in Germany.*

20. Cited in Jackowitz, "Anna O/Bertha Pappenheim and Me," 253.

21. See Kenny, *The Passion of Ansel Bourne.*

22. For differing interpretations of Pappenheim's treatment and subsequent adjustment, specifically the question of how a young woman so emotionally debilitated could go on to accomplish so much later in life, see M. Rosenbaum and M. Muroff, eds., *Anna O: Fourteen Contemporary Reinterpretations* (New York: Free Press, 1984).

23. Jackowitz, "Anna O/Bertha Pappenheim and Me," 271.

24. Ibid., 267.

25. Guttman, "'One Must Be Ready for Time and Eternity,'" 42.

26. Ibid., 44.

27. Jackowitz, "Anna O/Bertha Pappenheim and Me," 257.

28. Quoted in ibid.

29. Guttman, "'One Must Be Ready for Time and Eternity,'" 44.

30. Ellenberger, *The Discovery of the Unconscious.*

31. Guttman, "'One Must Be Ready for Time and Eternity'"; Jackowitz, "Anna O/Bertha Pappenheim and Me"; and Kaplan, *The Jewish Feminist Movement in Germany.*

32. Jackowitz, "Anna O/Bertha Pappenheim and Me," 260.

33. Quoted in ibid., 260. For discussion of the white slave trade in early-twentieth-century discourse, see John D'Emilio and Estelle B. Freedman, *Intimate Matters: A History of Sexuality in America* (New York: Harper & Row, 1989); Nathanson, *Dangerous Passage.* Also see Barbara Crosslette, "What Modern Slavery Is, and Isn't," *New York Times,* 27 July 1997, sec. 4, pp.1, 3. Crosslette discusses historical shifts in the concept of slavery, as both a rhetorical device in dramatizing a social grievance and as an economic form of bondage.

34. James T. Richardson, Joel Best, and David G. Bromley, eds., *The Satanism Scare* (New York: Aldine de Gruyter, 1991).

35. See Jackowitz, "Anna O/Bertha Pappenheim and Me"; and Kaplan, *The Jewish Feminist Movement in Germany.*

36. For discussion of Briquet's contribution to the history of hysteria, see Healy, *Images of Trauma;* Edward Shorter, *From Paralysis to Fatigue: A History of Psychosomatic Illness in the Modern Era* (New York: Free Press, 1992); and Edward Shorter, *From the Mind into the Body: The Cultural Origins of Psychosomatic Symptoms* (New York: Free Press, 1994).

37. Ellenberger, *The Discovery of the Unconscious,* 122.

38. Healy, *Images of Trauma,* 10.

39. Quoted in Jean Strouse, *Alice James: A Biography* (New York: Houghton Mifflin, 1991), 104.

40. See Showalter, *The Female Malady;* and Shorter, *From Paralysis to Fatigue.*

41. See Shorter, *From Paralysis to Fatigue;* and Showalter, *Hystories.*

42. See Shorter, *From Paralysis to Fatigue;* and Showalter, *The Female Malady.* Also see Szasz, *The Myth of Mental Illness.* Szasz argues that by medicalizing hysteria, Charcot legitimized inquiry into the problems of lower-class women, even as the social origins of their complaints were obscured. For Szasz, this project of social reform remained bound to a system of institutional control over disruptive elements of society. Also, see Michel Foucault, *Madness and Civilization: A History of Insanity in the Age of Reason* (New York: Random House, 1965).

43. See Drinka, *The Birth of Neurosis;* and Showalter, *The Female Malady.*

44. See deMarneffe, "Looking and Listening"; and Szasz, *The Myth of Mental Illness.*

45. Benjamin, *The Bonds of Love.*

46. For discussion of Charcot's anticlerical sentiments, see Drinka, *The Birth of Neurosis;* Herman, *Trauma and Recovery;* and Healy, *Images of Trauma.*

47. Alfred Binet, "Alterations of Personality," in *Significant Contributions to the History of Psychology, 1750–1920,* ser. C, vol. 5, ed. Daniel N. Robinson (Washington, D.C.: University Publications of America, Inc., 1977/1896), ix; my emphasis.

48. Ibid., 64.

49. For biographical background on Alice James, see Strouse, *Alice James.*

50. Alice James, *Alice James: Her Brothers—Her Journal* (Boston: Milford House, 1972/1934), 182 (entry of Oct. 26, 1890).

51. See Hawthorn, *Multiple Personality and the Disintegration of Literary Character.*

52. G. Stanley Hall, *Adolescence: Its Psychology, and Its Relations to Physiology, Sociology, Sex, Crime, Religion, and Education* (New York: Appleton, 1904).

53. Ibid., xvi.

54. James, *Alice James*, 184 (entry of Oct. 26, 1890).
55. Ibid.
56. The concept of mind as a tabula rasa—as a blank slate—is associated with the British empiricist John Locke, who influenced the early philosophical development of academic psychology, specifically its antimentalist currents.
57. James, *Alice James*, 144 (entry of Feb. 21, 1890).
58. Binet, "Alterations of Personality," 98–99. There are notable parallels between Binet's concept of a concealed active observer and Hilgard's hidden observer, also thought to operate in a trance state. Both concepts have a Romantic thrust and are in reaction to views in psychology that the mind is "nothing but" a bundle of mechanisms.
59. See Susan Sontag, *Illness as Metaphor* (New York: Farrar, Straus & Giroux, 1978).
60. Strouse, *Alice James*, 101.
61. Literary portraits of consumptive illness were not limited to women, of course, although the condition in men was often feminized in its association with "sensitive" characters. See, for example, Thomas Mann, *The Magic Mountain* (New York: Vintage International, 1996/1924).
62. See Showalter, *The Female Malady;* and Ussher, *Women's Madness.*
63. Lenore Terr, "Memory Work in Psychotherapy," paper presented at the Institute for Advanced Clinical Training conference "Advances in Treating Survivors of Sexual Abuse," San Francisco, Mar. 4, 1995.
64. See Rose Kernochan, review of *Between Sisters*, by Nian Vida, *New York Times Book Review*, 12 May 1996, 24.
65. See Louise DeSalvo, *Virginia Woolf: The Impact of Childhood Sexual Abuse on Her Life and Work* (New York: Ballantine, 1989).
66. See Showalter, *The Female Malady.*
67. DeSalvo, *Virginia Woolf.*
68. Ibid., 3.
69. Miller, *Thou Shalt Not Be Aware*, also discusses the role of incest in the life of Woolf and the tendency of biographers to minimize its effects on her later struggles with mental illness.
70. See Herman with Hirschman, *Father/Daughter Incest;* and Poster, *A Critical Theory of the Family.*
71. DeSalvo, *Virginia Woolf*, 110.

Chapter 8   **TESTIFYING TO TRAUMA:**
The Sexual Abuse Recovery Movement and Clinical Practice

1. For discussion of the role of psychiatry in Holocaust trauma testimonials, see Dori Laub, "Knowing and Not Knowing Massive Psychic Trauma: Forms of Traumatic Memory," *International Journal of Psychoanalysis* 74 (1993): 287–302.
2. See Alaine Finkielkraut, *Remembering in Vain: The Klaus Barbie Trial and Crimes against Humanity* (New York: Columbia University Press, 1992).
3. Ellen Bass and Laura Davis, *The Courage to Heal: A Guide for Women Survivors of Child Sexual Abuse*, 3d ed. (New York: HarperCollins, 1994); 1st ed. (New York: Harper & Row, 1988).
4. Ellen Bass, "The Courage to Heal: A Five Year Retrospective with Ellen Bass," paper presented at the Institute for Advanced Clinical Training conference "Advances in Treating Survivors of Sexual Abuse: Empowering the Health Process II," San Diego, Mar. 11, 1993.
5. See Goldstein and Farmer, *Confabulations.*
6. Quoted in Bass and Davis, *The Courage to Heal*, 13.
7. For analysis of the codependence literature, see Janice Haaken, "A Critical Analysis of the Codependence Construct," *Psychiatry: Interpersonal and Biological Processes* 53 (1990): 396–406; and Haaken, "From Al-ANON to ACOA."
8. Bass and Davis, *The Courage to Heal*, 39.
9. See Steiger and Zanko, "Sexual Trauma among Eating-Disordered, Psychiatric and Normal Female Groups."
10. For a review of the research, see Edwards and Alexander, "The Contribution of Family Background to the Long Term Adjustment of Women Sexually Abused."
11. Bass and Davis, *The Courage to Heal*, 15.
12. Quoted in ibid., 467.
13. Quoted in ibid., 471.
14. Gloria Steinem, "Making Connections," *Treating Abuse Today* 5, no. 6 (Nov./Dec. 1995–Jan./Feb. 1996): 7.
15. See Johnathan Shay, *Achilles in Vietnam: Combat Trauma and the Undoing of Character* (New York: Simon & Schuster, 1994).
16. Mic Hunter, *Sexually Abused Boys: The Neglected Victims of Sexual Abuse* (New York: Fawcett Columbine, 1990); David Lisak, "The Psychological Impact of Sexual Abuse: Content Analysis of Interviews with Male Survivors," *Journal of Traumatic Stress* 7, no. 4 (1994): 525–548.

17. See Bruce Rind and Evan Harrington, "A Critical Examination of the Role of Child Sex Abuse in Causing Psychological Maladjustment: A Review of the Literature," in *False Memory Syndrome: Therapeutic and Forensic Perspectives,* ed. D. A. Halperin (Washington, D.C.: American Psychiatric Press, in press).

18. Doug Arey, "Gay Males and Sexual Child Abuse," in *Sexual Abuse in Nine North American Cultures: Treatment and Prevention,* ed. Lisa Aronson Fontes (Thousand Oaks, Calif.: Sage, 1995), 200–235.

19. See Mic Hunter, ed., *The Sexually Abused Male,* vol. 1 (Boston: Lexington Books, 1990).

20. Bass and Davis, *The Courage to Heal,* 79.

21. For a discussion of mother blaming in the incest literature, see Herman with Hirschman, *Father/Daughter Incest;* and Armstrong, *Rocking the Cradle of Sexual Politics.*

22. Bass and Davis, *The Courage to Heal,* 302.

23. Quoted in ibid., 266.

24. Quoted in ibid., 265.

25. Martha Baldwin, *Beyond Victim: You Can Overcome Childhood Abuse . . . Even Sexual Abuse* (Highland City, Fla.: Rainbow Books, 1988).

26. Ibid., ix.

27. See Diana E. H. Russell, *The Secret Trauma: Incest in the Lives of Girls and Women* (New York: Basic Books, 1986). For an example of the recent genre of maternal sexual abuse stories, see Tree A. Borden and Jean D. LaTerz, "Mother/Daughter Incest and Ritual Abuse: The Ultimate Taboos," *Treating Abuse Today* 3, no. 4 (1993): 5–8.

28. Elie Wiesel, "The Holocaust as a Literary Inspiration," in *Dimensions of the Holocaust* (Evanston, Ill.: Northwestern University Press, 1977).

29. Herman, *Trauma and Recovery,* n.p.

30. See Herman, *Trauma and Recovery.*

31. See Gordon, *Heroes of Their Own Lives.*

32. See Alexander C. McFarlane and Rachael Yehuda, "Resilience, Vulnerability, and the Course of Post-traumatic Reactions," in *Traumatic Stress: The Effects of Overwhelming Experience on Mind, Body, and Society,* ed. Bessel A. van der Kolk, Alexander C. McFarlane, and Lars Weisaeth (New York: Guilford Press, 1996), 155–181.

33. Herman, *Trauma and Recovery,* 7.

34. See Sharon Lamb, *The Trouble with Blame: Victims, Perpetrators, and Responsibility* (Cambridge, Mass.: Harvard University Press, 1996).

Chapter 9 **SPEAKING IN TONGUES: Multiplicity and Psychiatric Influence**

1. See Putnam, "Dissociative Phenomena"; and Colin A. Ross, *Multiple Personality Disorder: Diagnosis, Clinical Features, and Treatment* (New York: Wiley-Interscience, 1989).

2. See James Friesan, *Uncovering the Mystery of MP: Its Shocking Origins. Its Surprising Cure* (San Bernardino, Calif.: Here's Life Publishers, 1991); and Ross, *Multiple Personality Disorder.*

3. Romantic currents run through the history of multiple personality disorder. See, for example, Shamdasani, "Encountering Hélène," xi–li. Shamdasani traces the link between multiplicity and both intelligence and creativity in turn-of-the-century psychiatry. Also, see Ellenberger, *The Discovery of the Unconscious.*

4. George K. Ganaway, "Narrative Truth: Clarifying the Role of Exogenous Trauma in the Etiology of MPD and Its Variants," *Dissociation* 2, no. 4 (1989): 209.

5. American Psychiatric Association, *The Diagnostic and Statistical Manual of Mental Disorders,* 4th ed. (Washington, D.C.: American Psychiatric Association, 1994).

6. See Kenny, *The Passion of Ansel Bourne.* Kenny presents a thoughtful analysis of the cultural roots of late-nineteenth-century female multiplicity, including the influence of nineteenth-century Christian revivalism.

7. For population estimates, see Ross, *Multiple Personality Disorder;* and Richard P. Kluft, "Multiple Personality Disorder," in *Dissociative Disorders: A Clinical Review,* ed. David Spiegel (Lutherville, Md.: Sidran Press, 1993), 17–44.

8. For discussion of the politics of DSM classifications more generally, see Stuart A. Kirk and Herbert Kutchins, *The Selling of DSM* (New York: Aldine de Gruyter, 1992).

9. Kluft, "Multiple Personality Disorder," 18.

10. Many MPD experts draw on contemporary developments in neuropsychology and memory research, particularly research on multiple systems in memory and divided consciousness. Most research psychologists regard MPD as an iatrogenic illness, however, or as a problematic clinical category. See, for example, Bennett G. Braun and Edward J. Frischholz, "Remembering and Forgetting in Patients Suffering from Multiple Personality Disorder," in *The Handbook of Emotion and Memory: Research and Theory,* ed. Sven-Ake Christianson (Hillsdale, N.J.: Erlbaum, 1992), 411–427; Hilgard, *Divided Consciousness;* Schacter, *Searching for Memory;* and Spanos et al., "Secondary Identity Enactments during Hypnotic Past-Life Regression." It may be, however, that historical and social forces in "advanced" industrial societies—that is, clinical interest in dissociative phenomena, research on mutiple systems

for information processing, and poststructuralist inquiry on the "decentered" subject—mediate this discourse of the fragmented self. Also, see chapter 3.

11. See Putnam, "The Scientific Investigation of Multiple Personality Disorder."

12. See Kluft, "Multiple Personality Disorder," 21; and Ross, *Multiple Personality Disorder*, 110–111.

13. See Bennett G. Braun, "Psychophysiologic Phenomena in Multiple Personality and Hypnosis," *American Journal of Clinical Hypnosis* 26 (1983): 124–137; and Richard P. Kluft, "Aspects of the Treatment of Multiple Personality Disorder," *Psychiatric Annals* 14 (1984): 51–55.

14. Ernest R. Hilgard, "The Hidden Observer and Multiple Personality," *International Journal of Clinical and Experimental Hypnosis* 32 (1984): 252.

15. Phillip M. Coons, "The Differential Diagnosis of Multiple Personality," *Journal of Clinical Psychiatry* 41 (1980): 330–336.

16. Ganaway, "Narrative Truth"; and Ganaway, "Hypnosis, Childhood Trauma, and Dissociative Identity Disorder."

17. See Ray Aldridge-Morris, *Multiple Personality: An Exercise in Deception* (Hillsdale, N.J.: Erlbaum, 1989); Sherrill Mulhern, "Satanism, Ritual Abuse, and Multiple Personality Disorder: A Sociohistorical Perspective," *International Journal of Clinical and Experimental Hypnosis* 52, no. 4 (1994): 265–288; and Pendergrast, *Victims of Memory.*

18. Hacking, *Rewriting the Soul.*

19. See Kenny, *The Passion of Ansel Bourne;* and Showalter, *Hystories.*

20. For a history of this theme in case studies of female multiplicity, see Hacking, *Rewriting the Soul;* Hawthorn, *Multiple Personality and the Disintegration of Literary Character;* and Kenny, *The Passion of Ansel Bourne.* Also, see Bliss, *Multiple Personality, Allied Disorders, and Hypnosis;* and Colin A. Ross, "Anne Sexton: Iatrogenesis of an Alter Personality in an Undiagnosed Case of MPD," *Dissociation* 4 (1992): 141–148.

21. For an analysis of this history, see Young, *The Harmony of Illusions.*

22. See Herman, *Trauma and Recovery.*

23. See Hacking, *Rewriting the Soul.*

24. Ross, *Multiple Personality Disorder,* 44–45.

25. Flora Rheta Schreiber, *Sybil: The True and Extraordinary Story of a Woman Possessed by Sixteen Separate Personalities* (New York: Warner Books, 1973).

26. Corbett H. Thigpen and Hervey M. Cleckley, *The Three Faces of Eve* (New York: McGraw-Hill, 1957).

27. Joanne Greenberg, *I Never Promised You a Rose Garden, A Novel by Hannah Greene* (New York: Holt, Rinehart and Winston, 1994).

28. Morton Prince, *The Problem of Multiple Personality* (Paris: International Congress of Psychology, 1900).

29. See Mikkel Borch-Jacobsen, "Sybil—The Making of a Disease: An Interview with Dr. Herbert Spiegel," *New York Review,* 24 Apr. 1997, 60–64. In this interview, Spiegel claims to have seen Sybil when Wilbur was on vacation. He dismisses Wilbur's diagnosis of MPD and goes on to assert that it is an iatrogenic disorder. Spiegel states that in a session with Sybil she asked, "Do you want me to be Helen?" When he asked, "Who's Helen?" Sybil replied, "Well, that's a name Dr. Wilbur gave me for this feeling." It is interesting to note that Spiegel's son, David Spiegel, is a prominent psychiatrist in the dissociative disorders field and a defender of the MPD diagnosis. David Spiegel, "Dissociation, Double Binds, and Posttraumatic Stress Disorder," in *Treatment of Multiple Personality Disorder,* ed. Bennett G. Braun (Washington, D.C.: American Psychiatric Press, 1986).

30. Schreiber, *Sybil,* 291.

31. Ross, *Multiple Personality Disorder,* 44–45.

32. American Psychiatric Association, *The Diagnostic and Statistical Manual of Mental Disorders,* 3d ed. (1987).

33. Cited in Hacking, *Rewriting the Soul,* 26.

34. Aldridge-Morris, *Multiple Personality.*

35. Bennett G. Braun, ed., *Treatment of Multiple Personality Disorder* (Washington, D.C.: American Psychiatric Press, 1986), xv.

36. Richard P. Kluft, "High-Functioning Multiple Presonality Patients: Three Cases," *Journal of Nervous and Mental Disease* 174, no. 12 (1986): 722–726; Richard P. Kluft, "An Update on Multiple Personality Disorder," *Hospital and Community Psychiatry* 38, no. 4 (Apr. 1987): 363–372; and Putnam, "The Scientific Investigation of Multiple Personality Disorder."

37. For discussion of the growth of dissociative disorders units in the 1980s, see Glass, *Shattered Selves;* and Pendergrast, *Victims of Memory.* Also, see Kluft, "An Update on Multiple Personality Disorder." Kluft argues that psychopharmacology is not effective in treating the "core" problems in multiple personality disorder, even though medication may play a role in managing the "symptoms."

38. For an example of early essays, see Phil Brown, ed., *Radical Psychology* (New York: Harper & Row, 1973). Psychologists and psychiatrists most associated with the radical psychiatry, or antipsychiatry, movement include R. D. Laing, David Cooper, Naomi Weisstein, and Thomas Szasz. For an analysis of this movement, see David Ingleby, "Understanding 'Mental Illness,'" in *Critical Psychiatry,* ed. David Ingleby (New York: Pantheon Books, 1980), 23–71.

39. For a harsh assessment of the antipsychiatry movement, see Rael Jean Isaac and Virginia C. Armat, *Madness in the Streets: How Psychiatry and the Law Abandoned the Mentally Ill* (New York: Free Press,

1990). These authors rightfully point out that the radical psychiatry movement, in its anti-institution position, overlooked the need for sanctuary for the mentally ill. However, in defending the rationality of the medical model against such radical critics, Isaac and Armat overstate the power of the antipsychiatry movement and dismiss altogether its progressive currents.

40. Chris Costner Sizemore and E. S. Pittillo, *I'm Eve!* (Garden City, N.Y.: Doubleday, 1977); and Chris Costner Sizemore, *A Mind of My Own* (New York: Morrow, 1989).

41. See, for example, the discussion of Sizemore in Hacking, *Rewriting the Soul,* 41; and Pendergrast, *Victims of Memory,* 168.

42. Quoted in Sizemore, *A Mind of My Own,* 170.

43. Glass, *Shattered Selves.*

44. Ibid., 97.

45. James M. Glass, *Delusion: Internal Dimensions of Political Life* (Chicago: University of Chicago Press, 1985).

46. See Pendergrast, *Victims of Memory.*

47. Glass, *Shattered Selves,* 94–95.

48. Cited in Pendergrast, *Victims of Memory,* 169.

49. For discussion of the ACOA movement and mental health culture, see Haaken, "From Al-ANON to ACOA."

50. See Janice Haaken and Richard Adams, "Pathology as Personal Growth: A Participant-Observation Study of Lifespring Training." *Psychiatry* 46 (1983): 270–280.

51. Trudi Chase, *When Rabbit Howls* (New York: Jove Books, 1990), 135.

52. For discussion of gender tensions operating in the noir genre, see Foster Hirsch, *Film Noir: The Dark Side of the Screen* (New York: Da Capo Press, 1981); and Ann Kaplan, ed. *Women in Film Noir* (London: BRI, 1980).

53. Kluft, "Multiple Personality Disorder," 25.

Chapter 10   BETWEEN THE DEVIL AND THE DEEP:
Satanic Ritual Abuse Narratives and Cultural Crises

1. Michelle Smith and Lawrence Pazder, *Michelle Remembers* (New York: Pocket Books, 1980).

2. Hilgard, *Divided Consciousness.*

3. See R. Kampman, "Hypnotically Induced Multiple Personality: An Experimental Study," *International Journal of Clinical and Experimental Hypnosis* 24 (1976): 215–227. For discussion of the impact of films, specifically *The Exorcist,* see Aldridge-Morris, *Multiple Personality,* 101.

4. John Mack, *Abduction: Human Encounters with Aliens* (New York: Ballantine, 1994). For feminist analysis of alien-abduction narratives, see Jodi Dean, "Coming Out as an Alien: Feminists, UFOs, and the 'Oprah Effect,'" in *"Bad Girls/Good Girls": Women, Sex, & Power in the Nineties,* ed. Nan Bauer Maglin and Donna Perry (New Brunswick, N.J.: Rutgers University Press, 1996), 90–105.

5. Sigmund Freud, "Extracts from the Fliess Papers," in *SE,* vol. 1 (1950/1897), 242.

6. See Goodwin, *Sexual Abuse.* Goodwin cites this Freud passage, using it to illustrate the historical origins of SRA and the reality of multigenerational perpetrators.

7. For a review, see Richardson, Best, and Bromley, *The Satanism Scare.*

8. Jeffrey S. Victor, *Satanic Panic: The Creation of a Contemporary Legend* (Chicago: Open Court, 1993).

9. See Nathan and Snedeker, *Satan's Silence.*

10. Richardson, Best, and Bromley, *The Satanism Scare;* and Victor, *Satanic Panic.*

11. See, for example, Sandra Bloom, "Hearing the Survivor's Voice," *Journal of Psychohistory* 21, no. 4 (spring 1994): 461–477; Jean M. Goodwin, "Credibility Problems in Sadistic Abuse," *Journal of Psychohistory* 21, no. 4 (spring 1994): 479–496; and Walter C. Young et al., "Patients Reporting Ritual Abuse in Childhood: A Clinical Syndrome. Report of 37 Cases," *Child Abuse and Neglect* 15 (1991): 181–189.

12. See Bloom, "Hearing the Survivor's Voice"; Glass, *Shattered Selves;* and Matt Johnson, "Fear and Power: From Naivete to a Believer in Cult Abuse," *Journal of Psychohistory* 21, no. 4 (spring 1994): 435–441.

13. See Phillip Jenkins and Daniel Maier-Katkin, "Occult Survivors: The Making of a Myth," in *The Satanism Scare,* ed. James T. Richardson, Joel Best, and David G. Bromley (New York: Aldine de Gruyter, 1991), 127–144.

14. See George K. Ganaway, "Alternative Hypotheses regarding Satanic Ritual Abuse Memories," paper presented at the Ninety-Ninth Annual Convention of the American Psychological Association, San Francisco, Aug. 19, 1991; Mulhern, "Satanism, Ritual Abuse, and Multiple Personality Disorder"; and Colin A. Ross, *Satanic Ritual Abuse: Principles of Treatment* (Toronto: University of Toronto Press, 1995).

15. See, for example, Craig Lockwood, *Other Alters: Roots and Realities of Cultic and Satanic Ritual Abuse and Multiple Personality Disorders* (Minneapolis: ComCare, 1993).

16. Ross, *Satanic Ritual Abuse.*

17. See Roland Summit, "The Child Sexual Abuse Accommodation Syndrome," *Child Abuse and Neglect* 7 (1983): 177–193. Summit introduced the term *abuse accommodation syndrome* to describe the

child victim's psychological response to social silencing. Since it was generally assumed in the mental health field that children would not falsely report sexual abuse, this concept was deployed in aggressively ferreting out abuse memories.

18. Nathan and Snedeker, *Satan's Silence.*
19. For example, it is commonly assumed in the popular imagination that the witch-hunts engulfed Europe during the culturally stagnant "dark ages," while in reality they were contemporaneous with the culturally dynamic period of the Renaissance. For discussion of the cultural contexts of demonology, see Richardson, Best, and Bromley, *The Satanism Scare.*
20. For discussion of the concept of urban legends, see Jan Harold Brunwald, *The Vanishing Hitchhiker: American Urban Legends and Their Meaning* (New York: Norton, 1981); and Victor, *Satanic Panic.*
21. Lockwood, *Other Alters,* 192–193.
22. Ibid., 200.
23. For discussion of the history of the blood libel, see R. Po-Chia Hsia, *The Mystery of Ritual Murder: Jews and Magic in Reformation Germany* (New Haven, Conn.: Yale University Press, 1988).
24. Jeffrey S. Victor, "The Dynamics of Rumor—Panics about Satanic Cults," in *The Satanism Scare,* ed. James T. Richardson, Joel Best, and David G. Bromley (New York: Aldine de Gruyter, 1991), 227.
25. Robert B. McFarland and Grace Lockerbie, "Difficulties in Treating Ritually Abused Children," *Journal of Psychohistory* 21 (1994): 429.
26. R. B. Rockwell, "One Psychiatrist's View of Satanic Ritual Abuse," *Journal of Psychohistory* 21 (1994): 446.
27. Ibid., 447.
28. See, for example, Harold F. Searles, *My Work with Borderline Patients* (Northvale, N.J.: Aronson, 1986).
29. For discussion of developmental conflicts underlying borderline conditions, see Michael Stone, ed., *Essential Papers in Borderline Disorders* (New York: New York University Press, 1986).
30. Douglas, *Purity and Danger.*
31. Ibid., 96.
32. Ganaway, "Alternative Hypotheses Regarding Satanic Ritual Abuse Memories."
33. Douglas, *Purity and Danger,* 97.
34. See, for example, Friesan, *Uncovering the Mystery of MPD;* Ganaway, "Alternative Hypotheses regarding Satanic Ritual Abuse Memories"; and Rockwell, "One Psychiatrist's View of Satanic Ritual Abuse."
35. Sherill Mulhern, "Satanism and Psychotherapy: A Rumor in Search of an Inquisition," in *The Satanism Scare,* ed. James T. Richardson, Joel Best, and David G. Bromley (New York: Aldine de Gruyter, 1991), 145–172.
36. As critiques mounted in the late 1980s and early 1990s, many clinicians began to distance themselves from the religious and fantastical aspects of SRA, preferring the generic, secular term sadistic ritual abuse. This linguistic transfer, like the transformation of MPD to DID, was an effort to bring the "syndrome" back into the folds of a normalizing psychiatry.
37. Rebecca, Lea Nicoll Kramer, and Susan A. Lukey, "Spirit Song: The Use of Christian Healing Rites in Trauma Recovery," *Treating Abuse Today* 5, no. 6 (1995/1996): 39–47.
38. Judith Spencer, *Suffer the Child* (New York: Pocket Books, 1985), 224.
39. Ibid., 19–20.
40. See Hsia, *The Myth of Ritual Murder.*
41. See Nathan and Snedeker, *Satan's Silence;* Nicholas P. Spanos, Cheryl A. Burgess, and Melissa Faith Burgess, "Past Life Identities, UFO Abductions and Satanic Ritual Abuse: The Social Constructions of 'Memories,'" *International Journal of Experimental and Clinical Hypnosis,* in press; and Victor, *Satanic Panic.*
42. Materials in many of the training packets included the following publications: Los Angeles County Commission for Women, *Ritual Abuse: Definitions, Glossary, the Use of Mind Control* (Los Angeles: Los Angeles County Commission for Women, 1989); and David W. Neswald with Catherine Gould and Vicki Graham-Costain, "Common 'Programs' Observed in Survivors of Satanic Ritual Abuse," *California Therapist* (Sept./Oct. 1991): 47–53.
43. For a critique of feminist responses to the SRA issue, see Armstrong, *Rocking the Cradle of Sexual Politics.*
44. See ibid.; and Russell, *The Secret Trauma.*
45. These questions are from a checklist included in the ritual abuse training packet distributed to volunteers at a women's crisis facility in the Portland, Ore., metropolitan area.
46. Friesan, *Uncovering the Mystery of MPD.*
47. For discussion, see Armstrong, *Rocking the Cradle of Sexual Politics;* Pat Califia, *Public Sex: The Culture of Radical Sex* (Pittsburgh: Cleis Press, 1994); and Nathan and Snedeker, *Satan's Silence.*
48. For discussion of the pornography debate within feminism, see Laura Bell, ed., *Good Girls/Bad Girls: Feminists and Sex Trade Workers* (Seattle: Seal Press, 1987); and Ellen Willis, "Feminism, Moralism, and Pornography," in *The Powers of Desire: The Politics of Sexuality,* ed. Ann Barr Snitow, Christine Stansell, and Sharon Thompson (New York: Monthly Review Press, 1983), 460–467.

49. For discussion of the defense of children and family as a strategic issue in crusades for women's rights, see Califia, *Public Sex;* Gordon, *Heroes of Their Own Lives;* and Nathanson, *Dangerous Passage.*
50. See Hall, "'The Mind That Burns in Each Body.'"
51. Ben Crouch and Kelly Damphouse, "Law Enforcement and the Satanic Crime Connection: A Survey of 'Cult Cops,'" in *The Satanism Scare,* ed. James T. Richardson, Joel Best, and David G. Bromley (New York: Aldine de Gruyter, 1991), 191–204.
52. Armstrong, *Rocking the Cradle of Sexual Politics.*
53. With the intensifying of law-and-order campaigns and tough sentencing throughout the United States, this trend seems unlikely to abate.
54. See Ganaway, "Alternative Hypotheses Regarding Satanic Ritual Abuse Memories." Ganaway draws on Freud's concept of screen memories in describing how SRA narratives may conceal prosaic forms of abuse and trauma. Also, see Bertis, "The Personal Myth as a Defence against Internal Primitive Aggression."

Chapter 11   SEX, LIES, AND THERAPY

1. The term *selfobject* was introduced by Heinz Kohut. The term refers to the use of a representation or part representation of another person as a constitutive aspect of the self. For a review, see Mitchell and Black, *Freud and Beyond.*
2. For discussion of the defensive implications of many transference interpretations, see Thomas Szasz, "The Concept of Transference," in *Classics in Psychoanalytic Technique,* ed. Robert Langs (New York: Aronson, 1981), 25–36; and, in this same volume, Robert Langs, "Interventions in the Bipersonal Field," 279–304.
3. See, for example, Felicita Garcia, "I Just Came Out Pregnant," in *The Powers of Desire: The Politics of Sexuality,* ed. Ann Barr Snitow, Christine Stansell, and Sharon Thompson (New York: Monthly Review Press, 1983), 236–244. In this autobiographical story, Garcia's return home is both an interruption of female development, as she must set aside her own ambitions, and a reengagement with previous struggles with her mother.
4. For discussion of the function of remembering in managing loss, specifically in restoring a vital emotional connection, see Hans W. Loewald, "Perspectives on Memory," in *Papers on Psychoanalysis,* ed. Hans W. Loewald (New Haven, Conn.: Yale University Press, 1980), 148–179.
5. See Chodorow, *The Reproduction of Mothering.* Chodorow suggests that many young adolescent girls take flight into heterosexual encounters to escape a troubling or stormy relationship with their mothers.
6. For discussion of social-class differences in women's organization of household labor, see Barrett and McIntosh, *The Anti-social Family;* Stephanie Coontz, *The Way We Never Were: American Families and the Nostalgia Trap* (New York: Basic Books, 1992); and Dizard and Gadlin, *The Minimal Family.* For discussion of this theme in the context of African American families, see Jualynne Dodson, "Conceptualizations of Black Families," in *Black Families,* ed. Harriette Pies McAdoo (Newbury Park, Calif.: Sage, 1988), 77–90; and, in this same volume, Marie Ferguson Peters, "Parenting in Black Families with Young Children: A Historical Perspective," 228–241.
7. See Hirsch, *The Mother/Daughter Plot.* In her analysis of literary works, Hirsch identifies this same motif—the daughter's effort to find a way of reentering the mother's world and accessing "maternal knowledge" while preserving a sense of a differentiated self.
8. See Schacter and Singer, "Cognitive, Social and Psychological Determinants of Emotional State." They established the importance of social influences and schema in interpreting ambiguous states of arousal. Also, see chapter 2.
9. The human tendency to elicit emotion in another person—as a means of establishing a vital sense of connection—is an important theme in psychoanalytic psychology, particularly in the contemporary movement toward interpersonal and intersubjective models.
10. See Yapko, *Suggestions of Abuse.* In his critique of clinically recovered memories of sexual abuse, Yapko presents a case of a man being treated for posttraumatic stress disorder related to his Vietnam War experiences. After his death by suicide, the therapist discovers that this man did not even serve in the military, much less suffer from combat-related trauma. Yapko overlooks in his discussion of the case the metaphorical potency of military imagery in the cultural world of male development.
11. Current motivational and mood states do influence the affective coloring of past events as well as the types of events remembered. The scope of this phenemonon is still subject to considerable debate in psychology, however, as are its implications for clinical practice. For discussion of clinical implications, see Spence, *Narrative Truth and Historical Truth,* and Donald P. Spence, "Narrative Truth and Putative Child Abuse," *International Journal of Clinical and Experimental Hypnosis* 42 (1994): 289–303.
12. For an explanation of priming, see Daniel L. Schacter, "Priming and Multiple Memory Systems: Perceptual Mechanisms of Implicit Memory," in *Memory Systems 1994,* ed. Daniel L. Schacter and Endel Tulving (Cambridge, Mass.: MIT Press, 1994), 233–268. Priming suggests unconscious processes of influence—that is, cues that shape subsequent responses but that escape the notice of the subject.

13. See Loewald, "Perspectives on Memory"; and Spence, *Narrative Truth and Historical Truth.*

14. See Kohut, *The Restoration of the Self;* and Heinz Kohut, *How Does Analysis Cure?* ed. Arnold Goldberg and Paul Stepansky (Chicago: University of Chicago Press, 1984).

15. Szasz, "The Concept of Transference."

16. Martha Rogers, "Factors Influencing Recall of Childhood Sexual Abuse," *Journal of Traumatic Stress* 8, no. 4 (1995): 691–716.

17. American Psychiatric Association, *The Diagnostic and Statistical Manual of Mental Disorders,* 4th ed., 477.

18. This theme of children asserting authority over the parents, including a sense of guilty superiority over them, seems to be quite common in immigrant families because the children often acquire language and cultural proficiency more readily than the parents. For discussion of intergenerational conflict in U.S. immigrant families, see Gordon, *Heroes of Their Own Lives.*

19. See Benjamin, *The Bonds of Love.*

20. Ibid.

21. See Wilson, *Crossing the Boundary.* In her discussion of black incest survivors, Wilson stresses the conflict over "putting your business on the street" and how reporting parental abuses to the police may be experienced as an act of racial betrayal or collaboration with the enemy.

22. It is noteworthy that in spite of the enormous clinical literature focusing on the impact of the Vietnam War and the extent to which the Vietnam vet has emerged as a cultural icon for a wounded manhood and as prototype of male trauma, there is little exploration of the war from the "other side"—that is, through the experiences of Vietnamese immigrants.

Conclusions LOOKING BACK AND LOOKING FORWARD

1. Elizabeth Cady Stanton, *The Woman's Bible* (Boston: Northeastern University Press, 1993/1898).

2. See Zeligs, *Psychoanalysis and the Bible.* Zeligs pursues this same line of psychoanalytic thought in arguing that the cave represents the mother, where Lot acts out his own oedipal temptation.

Bibliography

Aldridge-Morris, Ray. *Multiple Personality: An Exercise in Deception.* Hillsdale, N.J.: Erlbaum, 1989.

Alford, C. Fred. *Melanie Klein and Critical Social Theory: An Account of Politics, Art, and Reason Based on Her Psychoanalytic Theory.* New Haven, Conn.: Yale University Press, 1989.

Allison, Dorothy. *Skin: Talking about Sex, Class and Literature.* Ithaca, N.Y.: Firebrand Books, 1994.

———. *Two or Three Things I Know for Sure.* New York: Penguin Books, 1995.

American Psychiatric Association. *The Diagnostic and Statistical Manual of Mental Disorders.* 3d ed. Washington, D.C.: American Psychiatric Association, 1987; 4th ed., 1994.

———. *DSM-III.* Washington, D.C.: American Psychiatric Association, 1980.

———. "Statement on Memories of Sexual Abuse." *International Journal of Clinical and Experimental Hypnosis* 42, no. 4 (1994): 289–303.

Arey, Doug. "Gay Males and Sexual Child Abuse." In *Sexual Abuse in Nine North American Cultures: Treatment and Prevention,* edited by Lisa Aronson Fontes. Thousand Oaks, Calif.: Sage, 1995.

Armstrong, Louise. *Rocking the Cradle of Sexual Politics: What Happened When Women Said Incest.* New York: Addison-Wesley, 1994.

Aron, Lewis. *A Meeting of Minds: Mutuality in Psychoanalysis.* Hillsdale, N.J.: Analytic Press, 1996.

Baars, B. J. *A Cognitive Theory of Consciousness.* Cambridge: Cambridge University Press, 1988.

Baldwin, Martha. *Beyond Victim: You Can Overcome Childhood Abuse . . . Even Sexual Abuse.* Highland City, Fla.: Rainbow Books, 1988.

Barclay, Craig, and Thomas S. Smith. "Autobiographical Remembering: Creating Personal Culture." In *Theoretical Perspectives on Autobiographical Memory,* edited by M. A. Conway et al. Norwell, Mass.: Kluwer, 1992.

Barker, Pat. *The Ghost Road.* New York: Dutton, 1995.

Barnier, Amanda J., and Kevin M. McConkey. "Reports of Real and False Memories: The Relevance of Hypnosis, Hypnotizability, and Context of Memory Test." *Journal of Abnormal Psychology* 101 (1992): 521–527.

Barrett, Michele, and Mary McIntosh. *The Anti-social Family.* New York: Verso, 1982.

Barstow, Anne Llewellyn. *Witchcraze: A New History of the European Witch Hunts.* San Francisco: Pandora, 1994.

Bartlett, Sir Frederic C. *Remembering: A Study in Experimental and Social Psychology.* London: Cambridge University Press, 1961/1932.

Bartsky, Sandra Lee. *Femininity and Domination: Studies in the Phenomenology of Oppression.* New York: Routledge, 1990.

Bass, Ellen. "The Courage to Heal: A Five Year Retrospective with Ellen Bass." Paper presented at the Institute for Advanced Clinical Training conference "Advances in Treating Survivors of Sexual Abuse: Empowering the Health Process II," San Diego, March 11, 1993.

Bass, Ellen, and Laura Davis. *The Courage to Heal: A Guide for Women Survivors of Child Sexual Abuse.* 3d ed. New York: HarperCollins, 1994; 1st ed., New York: Harper & Row, 1988.

Bell, Laura, ed. *Good Girls/Bad Girls: Feminists and Sex Trade Workers.* Seattle: Seal Press, 1987.

Benjamin, Jessica. *The Bonds of Love: Psychoanalysis, Feminism, and the Problem of Domination.* New York: Pantheon Books, 1988.

———. "An Outline of Intersubjectivity: The Development of Recognition." *Psychoanalytic Psychology* 7 (supp.) (1990): 33–46.

Bernay, Toni. "Reconciling Nurturance and Aggression: A New Feminine Identity." In *The Psychology of Today's Woman: New Psychoanalytic Visions,* edited by Toni Bernay and Dorothy W. Cantor. Hillsdale, N.J.: Atlantic Press, 1986.

Bertis, Stavroula. "The Personal Myth as a Defence against Internal Primitive Aggression." *International Journal of Psychoanalysis* 69 (1988): 475–482.

Bettelheim, Bruno. *The Uses of Enchantment: The Meaning and Importance of Fairy Tales.* New York: Vintage Books, 1975.

Binet, Alfred. "Alterations of Personality." In *Significant Contributions to the History of Psychology, 1750–1920,* ser. C, vol. 5, edited by Daniel N. Robinson. Washington, D.C.: University Publications of America, 1977/1896.

Birke, Lynda. *Women, Feminism, and Biology.* New York: Pergamon Press, 1982.

Bleier, Ruth. *Science and Gender.* New York: Pergamon Press, 1984.

Bliss, Eugene L. *Multiple Personality, Allied Disorders, and Hypnosis.* New York: Oxford University Press, 1986.

Bloom, Sandra. "Hearing the Survivor's Voice." *Journal of Psychohistory* 21, no. 4 (spring 1994): 461–477.

Bollas, Christopher. *The Shadow of the Object: Psychoanalysis of the Unthought Known.* New York: Columbia University Press, 1995.

Borch-Jacobsen, Mikkel. "Sybil—The Making of a Disease: An Interview with Dr. Herbert Spiegel." *New York Review,* 24 April 1997, 60–64.

Borden, Tree A., and Jean D. LaTerz. "Mother/Daughter Incest and Ritual Abuse: The Ultimate Taboos." *Treating Abuse Today* 3, no. 4 (1993): 5–8.

Bottigheimer, Ruth B. *Grimms' Bad Girls and Bold Boys: The Moral and Social Vision of the Tales.* New Haven, Conn.: Yale Univerity Press, 1987.

Boudewyn, Arne Cornelius, and Joan Huser Liem. "Childhood Sexual Abuse as a Precursor to Depression and Self-Destructive Behavior in Adulthood." *Journal of Traumatic Stress* 8 (1995): 445–459.

Bowers, Kenneth S. "Unconscious Influences and Hypnosis." In *Repression and Dissociation: Implications for Personality Theory, Psychopathology, and Health,* edited by Jerome L. Singer. Chicago: University of Chicago Press, 1990.

Bowers, Kenneth S., and Peter Farvolden. "Revisiting a Century-Old Freudian Slip—From Suggestion Disavowed to the Truth Repressed." *Psychological Bulletin* 119, no. 3 (1996): 335–380.

Bowlby, Rachel. "Still Crazy after All These Years." In *Between Feminism and Psychoanalysis,* edited by Teresa Brennan. New York: Routledge, 1989.

Brandon, Ruth. *The Spiritualists: The Passion for the Occult in the 19th and 20th Centuries.* New York: Knopf, 1983.

Braude, Ann. *Radical Spirits: Spirtualism and Women's Rights in Nineteenth-Century America.* Boston: Beacon Press, 1989.

Braun, Bennett G. "Psychophysiologic Phenomena in Multiple Personality and Hypnosis." *American Journal of Clinical Hypnosis* 26 (1983): 124–137.

———, ed. *Treatment of Multiple Personality Disorder.* Washington, D.C.: American Psychiatric Press, 1986.

Braun, Bennett G., and Edward J. Frischholz. "Remembering and Forgetting in Patients Suffering from Multiple Personality Disorder." In *The Handbook of Emotion and Memory: Research and Theory,* edited by Sven-Ake Christianson. Hillsdale, N.J.: Erlbaum, 1992.

Brennan, Teresa, ed. *Between Feminism and Psychoanalysis.* New York: Routledge, 1989.

———. *The Interpretation of the Flesh: Freud and Femininity.* New York: Routledge, 1992.

Brett, Elizabeth. "The Classification of Posttraumatic Stress Disorder." In *Traumatic Stress: The Effects of Overwhelming Experience on Mind, Body, and Society,* edited by Bessel A. van der Kolk, Alexander C. McFarlane, and Lars Weisaeth. New York: Guilford Press, 1996.

Breuer, Josef, and Sigmund Freud. "Studies on Hysteria." In *The Standard Edition of the Complete Psychological Works of Sigmund Freud.* Translated and edited by James Strachey. Vol. 2. London: Hogarth Press, 1962/1895.

Brewer, William F. "What Is Recollective Memory?" In *Remembering Our Past: Studies in Autobiographical Memory,* edited by D. C. Rubin. Cambridge: Cambridge University Press, 1996.

Briere, John N. *Child Abuse Trauma: Theory and Treatment of the Lasting Effects.* Newbury Park, Calif.: Sage, 1992.

Bright, Susie. *Sexual Reality: A Virtual Sex World Reader.* Pittsburgh: Cleis Press, 1992.

Brinnin, John Malcolm. *Third Rose: Gertrude Stein and Her World.* Boston: Atlantic Monthly Press, 1959.

Brown, Laura S. "Politics of Memory, Politics of Incest: Doing Therapy and Politics That Really Matter." In *A Feminist Clinician's Guide to the Memory Debate,* edited by Susan Contratto and M. Janice Gutfreund. New York: Harrinton Press, 1996.

Brown, Phil, ed. *Radical Psychology.* New York: Harper & Row, 1973.

Brown, Roger, and James Kulik. "Flashbulb Memories." *Cognition* 5 (1977): 73–99.

Brownmiller, Susan. *Against Our Will: Men, Women, and Rape.* New York: Simon & Schuster, 1975.

Bruner, Jerome. *Acts of Meaning.* Cambridge, Mass.: Harvard University Press, 1990.

———. *Actual Minds, Possible Worlds.* Cambridge, Mass.: Harvard University Press, 1986.

———. "Another Look at New Look 1." *American Psychologist* 47 (June 1992): 780–783.

Brunwald, Jan Harold. *The Vanishing Hitchhiker: American Urban Legends and Their Meaning.* New York: Norton, 1981.

Burgin, Victor, James D. Kaplan, and Cora Kaplin, eds. *Formations of Fantasy*. New York: Methuen, 1986.

Burkett, Elinor, and Frank Bruni. *Gospel of Shame: Children, Sexual Abuse, and the Catholic Church*. New Haven, Conn.: Viking, 1993.

Butler, Judith. *Bodies That Matter: On the Discursive Limits of "Sex."* New York: Routledge, 1993.

———. *Gender Trouble: Feminism and the Subversion of Identity*. New York: Routledge, 1990.

Butler-Evans, Elliot. *Race, Gender, and Desire*. Philadelphia: Temple University Press, 1989.

Cagnon, Madeleine. "Body I." In *New French Feminism: An Anthology*, edited by Elaine Marks and Isabelle de Courtivron. New York: Schocken Books, 1981.

Califia, Pat. *Public Sex: The Culture of Radical Sex*. Pittsburgh: Cleis Press, 1994.

Carlson, Eric T. "The History of Dissociation until 1880." In *Split Minds/Split Brains: Historical and Current Perspectives*, edited by Jacques M. Quen. New York: New York University Press, 1986.

Carson, Robert C., James N. Butcher, and Susan Mineka. *Abnormal Psychology and Modern Life*. 10th ed. New York: HarperCollins, 1996.

Casey, Edward. *Remembering: A Phenomenological Study*. Bloomington: Indiana University Press, 1987.

Chamberlin, E. R. *The Fall of the House of Borgia*. New York: Dial, 1974.

Charcot, Jean-Martin. "Hysteria in the Male Subject." In *A History of Psychoanalysis: Original Sources and Contemporary Research*, 2d ed., edited by Ludy T. Benjamin, Jr. New York: McGraw-Hill, 1997.

Chase, Trudi. *When Rabbit Howls*. New York: Jove Books, 1990.

Chawaf, Chantel. "Linguistic Flesh." In *New French Feminism: An Anthology*, edited by Elaine Marks and Isabelle de Courtivron. New York: Schocken Books, 1981.

Chesler, Phyllis. *Women and Madness*. Garden City, N.Y.: Doubleday, 1972.

Chodorow, Nancy. *Femininities, Masculinities, Sexualities: Freud and Beyond*. Lexington: University Press of Kentucky, 1994.

———. *The Reproduction of Mothering: Psychoanalysis and the Sociology of Gender*. Berkeley: University of California Press, 1978.

Cixous, Hélène, and Catherine Clément. *The Newly Born Woman*. Minneapolis: University of Minnesota Press, 1975.

Clément, Catherine. *The Weary Sons of Freud*. New York: Verso, 1978.

Collins, Patricia Hill. *Black Feminist Thought*. New York: Routledge, 1990.

Coons, Phillip M. "The Differential Diagnosis of Multiple Personality." *Journal of Clinical Psychiatry* 41 (1980): 330–336.

Coontz, Stephanie. *The Way We Never Were: American Families and the Nostalgia Trap*. New York: Basic Books, 1992.

Costin, Lela, Howard Jacob Karger, and David Stoesz. *The Politics of Child Abuse in America*. New York: Oxford University Press, 1996.

Crouch, Ben, and Kelly Damphouse. "Law Enforcement and the Satanic Crime Connection: A Survey of 'Cult Cops.'" In *The Satanism Scare*, edited by James T. Richardson, Joel Best, and David G. Bromley. New York: Aldine de Gruyter, 1991.

Damasio, Antonio. *Descartes' Error: Emotion, Reason, and the Human Brain*. New York: Avon, 1994.

Daniels, April, and Carol Scott. *Paperdolls: A True Story of Childhood Sexual Abuse in Mormon Neighborhoods*. San Diego: Recovery, 1992.

Darnton, Robert. *The Great Cat Massacre and Other Episodes in French Cultural History*. New York: Basic Books, 1984.

———. *Mesmerism and the End of the Enlightenment in France*. Cambridge: Harvard University Press, 1968.

David-Menard, Monique. *Hysteria from Freud to Lacan: Body and Language in Psychoanalysis*. Ithaca, N.Y.: Cornell University Press, 1989.

Davies, Jody M., and Mary G. Frawley. *Treating the Adult Survivor of Childhood Sexual Abuse: A Psychoanalytic Perspective*. New York: Basic Books, 1994.

Dean, Jodi. "Coming Out as an Alien: Feminists, UFOs, and the 'Oprah Effect.'" In *"Bad Girls/Good Girls": Women, Sex, & Power in the Nineties*, edited by Nan Bauer Maglin and Donna Perry. New Brunswick, N.J.: Rutgers University Press.

Decker, Hannah S. "The Lure of Nonmaterialism in Materialist Europe: Investigations into Dissociative Phenomena, 1880–1915." In *Split Minds/Split Brains: Historical and Current Perspectives*, edited by Jacques M. Quen. New York: New York University Press, 1986.

de Groot, Hans, Gwynn Maxwell, and Nicholas P. Spanos. "The Effects of Contextual Information and Gender on the Prediction of Hypnotic Susceptibility." *Journal of Personality and Social Psychology* 54 (1988): 1049–1053.

de Lauretis, Teresa. *The Practice of Love: Lesbian Sexuality and Perverse Desire*. Bloomington: Indiana University Press, 1994.

deMarneffe, Daphne. "Looking and Listening: The Construction of Clinical Knowledge in Charcot and Freud." In *Gender and Scientific Authority*, edited by Barbara Laslett, Sally Gregory Kohlstedt, Helen Longino, and Evelyn Hammonds. Chicago: University of Chicago Press, 1996.

D'Emilio, John, and Estelle B. Freedman. *Intimate Matters: A History of Sexuality in America*. New York: Harper & Row, 1989.

DeSalvo, Louise. *Virginia Woolf: The Impact of Childhood Sexual Abuse on Her Life and Work.* New York: Ballantine, 1989.

Diehl, Lesley A. "The Paradox of G. Stanley Hall: Foe of Coeducation and Educator of Women." In *A History of Psychoanalysis: Original Sources and Contemporary Research,* 2d ed., edited by Ludy T. Benjamin, Jr. New York: McGraw-Hill, 1997.

Dinnerstein, Dorothy. *The Mermaid and the Minotaur: Sexual Arrangements and Human Malaise.* New York: Harper & Row, 1977.

Dizard, Jan E., and Howard Gadlin. *The Minimal Family.* Amherst: University of Massachusetts Press, 1990.

Doane, Janice, and Devon Hodges. *From Klein to Kristeva: Psychoanalytic Feminism and the Search for the "Good Enough" Mother.* Ann Arbor: University of Michigan Press, 1992.

Dodson, Jualynne. "Conceptualizations of Black Families." In *Black Families,* edited by Harriette Pies McAdoo. Newbury Park, Calif.: Sage, 1988.

Doe, Jane. "How Could This Happen? Coping with a False Accusation of Incest and Rape." *Issues in Child Abuse Accusations* 3, no. 3 (1991): 154–165.

Dorpact, Theo L., and Michael L. Miller. *Clinical Interaction and the Analysis of Meaning: A New Psychoanalytic Theory.* Hillsdale, N.J.: Analytic Press, 1992.

Douglas, Mary. *How Institutions Think.* London: Routledge, 1987.

———. *Purity and Danger.* New York: Praeger, 1966.

Drinka, George Frederick. *The Birth of Neurosis: Myth, Malady, and the Victorians.* New York: Simon & Schuster, 1984.

du Maurier, George. *Trilby.* New York: Oxford University Press, 1995/1894.

Dunn, Judy. *The Beginnings of Social Understanding.* Cambridge, Mass.: Harvard University Press, 1988.

Dworkin, Andrea. *Woman Hating.* New York: Dutton, 1974.

Ebbinghaus, Hermann. *Memory.* New York: Dover, 1964/1885.

Edwards, James J., and Pamela C. Alexander. "The Contribution of Family Background to the Long Term Adjustment of Women Sexually Abused." *Journal of Interpersonal Violence* 7 (1992): 306–320.

Ehrenreich, Barbara, and Deirdre English. *For Her Own Good: 150 Years of the Experts' Advice to Women.* New York: Doubleday, 1978.

Ellenberger, Henri F. *The Discovery of the Unconscious: The History of the Evolution of the Dynamic Psychiatry.* New York: Basic Books, 1970.

Fairbairn, Ronald W. "Psychology as a Prescribed and as a Proscribed Subject." In *Psychoanalytic Studies of the Personality,* edited by Ronald W. Fairbairn. Boston: Routledge, 1952/1939.

———. "The War Neuroses: Their Nature and Significance." In *Psychoanalytic Studies of the Personality,* edited by Ronald W. Fairbairn. Boston: Routledge, 1952/1943.

Fast, Irene. *Gender Identity: A Differentiation Model,* vol. 2 of *Advances in Psychoanalysis: Theory, Research, and Practice.* Hillsdale, N.J.: Analytic Press, 1984.

Felman, Shoshana, and Dori Laub. *Testimony: Crises of Witnessing in Literature, Psychoanalysis, and History.* New York: Routledge, 1992.

Finkielkraut, Alaine. *Remembering in Vain: The Klaus Barbie Trial and Crimes against Humanity.* New York: Columbia University Press, 1992.

First, Elsa. "Mothering, Hate, and Winnicott." In *Representations of Motherhood,* edited by Donna Bassin, Margaret Honey, and Meryle Mahrer Kaplan. New Haven, Conn.: Yale University Press, 1994.

Flax, Jane. *Thinking Fragments: Psychoanalysis, Feminism, and Postmodernism in the Contemporary West.* Los Angeles: University of California Press, 1990.

Fogel, Gerald I. "Winnicott's Antitheory and Winnicott's Art." *Psychoanalytic Study of the Child* 47 (1992): 205–222.

Foucault, Michel. *The History of Sexuality: An Introduction.* Vol. 1. New York: Pantheon Books, 1978.

———. *Madness and Civilization: A History of Insanity in the Age of Reason.* New York: Random House, 1965.

Frankel, Frederick H. "The Concept of Flashbacks in Historical Perspective." *International Journal of Clinical and Experimental Hypnosis* 42 (1994): 321–336.

Fraser, Sylvia. *My Father's House: A Memoir of Incest and of Healing.* New York: Harper & Row, 1987.

Freud, Anna. "Contribution to the Discussion, 'The Theory of the Parent-Infant Relationship.'" *International Journal of Psychoanalysis* 43 (1962): 241.

Freud, Sigmund. "The Aetiology of Hysteria." In *The Standard Edition of the Complete Psychological Works of Sigmund Freud.* Translated and edited by James Strachey. Vol. 3. London: Hogarth Press, 1962/1896.

———. "An Autobiographical Study." In *The Standard Edition of the Complete Psychological Works of Sigmund Freud.* Translated and edited by James Strachey. Vol. 20. London: Hogarth Press, 1962/1925.

———. "Ego and Id." In *The Standard Edition of the Complete Psychological Works of Sigmund Freud.* Translated and edited by James Strachey. Vol. 19. London: Hogarth Press, 1962/1923.

———. "Extracts from the Fliess Papers." In *The Standard Edition of the Complete Psychological Works of Sigmund Freud.* Translated and edited by James Strachey. Vol. 1. London: Hogarth Press, 1950/1897.

———. "First Lecture on Psychoanalysis at Clark University: Breuer and the Treatment of Hysteria." In *A History of Psychoanalysis: Original Sources and Contemporary Research,* 2d ed., edited by Ludy T. Benjamin, Jr. New York: McGraw-Hill, 1997.

———. "Further Remarks on the Neuro-psychoses of Defence." In *The Standard Edition of the Complete Psychological Works of Sigmund Freud*. Translated and edited by James Strachey. Vol. 3. London: Hogarth Press, 1962/1896.

———. "Heredity and the Aetiology of the Neuroses." In *The Standard Edition of the Complete Psychological Works of Sigmund Freud*. Translated and edited by James Strachey. Vol. 3. London: Hogarth Press, 1962/1896.

———. "The Psychopathology of Everyday Life." In *The Standard Edition of the Complete Psychological Works of Sigmund Freud*. Translated and edited by James Strachey. Vol. 6. London: Hogarth Press, 1995/1901.

———. "Screen Memories." In *The Standard Edition of the Complete Psychological Works of Sigmund Freud*. Translated and edited by James Strachey. Vol. 3. London: Hogarth Press, 1962/1899.

Freyd, Jennifer J. *Betrayal Trauma: The Logic of Forgetting Childhood Abuse*. Cambridge, Mass.: Harvard University Press, 1996.

———. "Betrayal Trauma: Traumatic Amnesia as an Adaptive Response to Childhood Abuse." *Ethics and Behavior* 4, no. 4 (1994): 307–329.

———. "Personal Perspectives on the Delayed Memory Debate." *Treating Abuse Today* 3, no. 5 (1993): 13–20.

———. "Theoretical and Personal Perspectives on the Delayed Memory Debate." Paper presented at Foote Hospital's continuing-education conference "Controversies around Recovered Memories of Incest and Ritual Abuse," Ann Arbor, Mich., Aug. 7, 1993.

Friedan, Betty. *The Feminine Mystique*. New York: Norton, 1963.

Friesan, James. *Uncovering the Mystery of MPD: Its Shocking Origins. Its Surprising Cure*. San Bernadino, Calif.: Here's Life Publishers, 1991.

Fuller, Robert C. *Mesmerism and the American Cure of Souls*. Philadelphia: University of Pennsylvania Press, 1982.

Furumoto, Laurel. "Mary Whiton Calkins (1863–1930): Fourteenth President of the American Psychological Association," In *In Our Own Words: Readings on the Psychology of Women and Gender,* edited by M. Crawford and R. Unger. New York: McGraw-Hill, 1997.

———. "Shared Knowledge: The Experimentalists, 1904–1929." In *A History of Psychoanalysis: Original Sources and Contemporary Research,* 2d ed., edited by Ludy T. Benjamin, Jr. New York: McGraw-Hill, 1997.

Gallop, Jane. *The Daughter's Seduction: Feminism and Psychoanalysis*. Ithaca, N.Y.: Cornell University Press, 1982.

Ganaway, George K. "Alternative Hypotheses regarding Satanic Ritual Abuse Memories." Paper presented at the Ninety-Ninth Annual Convention of the American Psychological Association, San Francisco, Aug. 19, 1991.

———. "Hypnosis, Childhood Trauma, and Dissociative Identity Disorder: Toward an Integrative Theory." *International Journal of Clinical and Experimental Hypnosis* 43 (1995): 127–144.

———. "Narrative Truth: Clarifying the Role of Exogenous Trauma in the Etiology of MPD and Its Variants." *Dissociation* 2, no. 4 (1989): 205–220.

Garcia, Felicita. "I Just Came Out Pregnant." In *Powers of Desire: The Politics of Sexuality,* edited by Ann Barr Snitow, Christine Stansell, and Sharon Thompson. New York: Monthly Review Press, 1983.

Genter, Dedre, and Jonathan Grudin. "The Evolution of Mental Metaphors in Psychology: A 90-Year Retrospective." *American Psychologist* 40 (1985): 181–192.

Gilbert, Sandra M., and Susan Gubar. *The Madwoman in the Attic: The Woman Writer and the Nineteenth-Century Literary Imagination*. New Haven, Conn.: Yale University Press, 1979.

Gilligan, Carol. *In a Different Voice: Psychological Theory and Women's Development*. Cambridge, Mass.: Harvard University Press, 1982.

Gillman, Irene. "An Object-Relations Approach to the Phenomenon and Treatment of Battered Women." *Psychiatry* 43 (1983): 346–358.

Glass, James M. *Delusion: Internal Dimensions of Political Life*. Chicago: University of Chicago Press, 1985.

———. *Shattered Selves: Multiple Personality in a Postmodern World*. Ithaca, N.Y.: Cornell University Press, 1993.

Goldstein, Eleanor, and Kevin Farmer. *Confabulations: Creating False Memories, Destroying Families*. Boca Raton, Fla.: SIRS Books, 1992.

Goldstein, Rebecca. "Looking Back at Lot's Wife." *Commentary* 92, no. 3 (Sept. 1994): 37–41.

Golston, Joan C. "A False Memory Syndrome Conference: Activists Accused and Their Professional Allies Talk about Science, Law and Family Reconciliation." *Treating Abuse Today* 5, no. 1 (Jan./Feb. 1995): 24–30.

Goodwin, Jean M. "Credibility Problems in Sadistic Abuse." *Journal of Psychohistory* 21, no. 4 (spring 1994): 479–496.

———. *Sexual Abuse: Incest Victims and Their Families*. Chicago: Year Book Medical Publishers, 1989.

Gordon, Linda. *Heroes of Their Own Lives: The Politics and History of Family Violence*. New York: Viking Press, 1988.

Gould, Stephen Jay. *The Mismeasure of Man.* New York: Norton, 1981.

Greenacre, Phyllis. "The Role of Transference." In *Classics in Psychoanalytic Technique,* edited by Robert Langs. New York: Aronson, 1981.

Greenberg, Joanne. *I Never Promised You a Rose Garden, A Novel by Hannah Greene.* New York: Holt, Rinehart and Winston, 1994.

Guttman, Melinda Given. "'One Must Be Ready for Time and Eternity.'" *On the Issues* 5, no. 4 (fall 1996): 42–46.

Haaken, Janice. "From Al-ANON to ACOA: Co-dependence and the Historical Transformation of Caregiving." *Signs* 18 (1993): 321–345.

———. "A Critical Analysis of the Co-dependence Construct." *Psychiatry: Interpersonal and Biological Processes* 53 (1990): 396–406.

———. "Field Dependence Research: A Historical Analysis of a Psychological Construct." In *Gender and Scientific Authority,* edited by Barbara Lasslett, Sally Gregory Kohlstedt, Helen Longino, and Evelynn Hammonds. Chicago: University of Chicago Press, 1996.

———. "The Recovery of Memory, Fantasy, and Desire: Feminist Approaches to Sexual Abuse and Psychic Trauma." *Signs* 21, no. 4 (summer 1996): 1069–1094.

———. "The Siegfried Bernfeld Conference: Uncovering the Psychoanalytic Political Unconscious." *American Journal of Psychoanalysis* 50 (winter 1990): 289–304.

Haaken, Janice, and Richard Adams. "Pathology as Personal Growth: A Participant-Observation Study of Lifespring Training." *Psychiatry* 46 (1983): 270–280.

Hacking, Ian. "The Making and Molding of Child Abuse." *Critical Inquiry* 17 (winter 1991): 253–288.

———. *Rewriting the Soul: Multiple Personality Disorder and the Sciences of Memory.* Princeton, N.J.: Princeton University Press, 1995.

Hale, Nathan G., Jr. *Freud and the Americans: The Beginnings of Psychoanalysis in the United States, 1876–1917.* New York: Oxford University Press, 1971.

Hall, G. Stanley. *Adolescence: Its Psychology, and Its Relations to Physiology, Anthropology, Sociology, Sex, Crime, Religion, and Education.* New York: Appleton, 1904.

———. "A Medium in the Bud." *American Journal of Psychology* 29–30 (1918): 144–158.

Hall, Jacquelyn Dowd. "'The Mind That Burns in Each Body': Women, Rape, and Racial Violence." In *The Powers of Desire: The Politics of Sexuality,* edited by Ann Barr Snitow, Christine Stansell, and Sharon Thompson. New York: Monthly Review Press, 1983.

Hammond, D. Cordyn, ed. *Handbook of Hypnotic Suggestions and Metaphors.* New York: Norton, 1990.

Harding, Sandra. "Feminism, Science and the Anti-Enlightenment Critiques." In *Feminism/Postmodernism,* edited by Linda J. Nicholson. New York: Routledge, 1990.

———. *The Science Question in Feminism.* Ithaca, N.Y.: Cornell University Press, 1986.

Harney, Patricia A. "The Role of Incest in Developmental Theory and Treatment of Women Diagnosed with Borderline Personality Disorder." *Women & Therapy* 12 (1992): 39–57.

Hatfield, Elaine, John T. Cacioppo, and Richard L. Rapson. *Emotional Contagion: Studies in Emotion and Social Interaction.* Paris: Cambridge University Press, 1994.

Hawkesworth, Mary. "Knowing, Knowers, Known: Feminist Theory and Claims of Truth." In *Gender and Scientific Authority,* edited by Barbara Laslett, Sally Gregory Kohlstedt, Helen Longino, and Evelynn Hammonds. Chicago: University of Chicago Press, 1996.

Hawthorn, Jeremy. *Multiple Personality and the Disintegration of Literary Character.* New York: St. Martin's Press, 1983.

Healy, David. *Images of Trauma: From Hysteria to Post-traumatic Stress Disorder.* London: Faber & Faber, 1993.

Heimann, Paula. "On Countertransference." In *Classics in Psychoanalytic Technique,* edited by Robert Langs. New York: Aronson, 1981.

Henle, Mary. "One Man against the Nazis: Wolfgang Kohler." In *A History of Psychoanalysis: Original Sources and Contemporary Research,* 2d ed., edited by Ludy T. Benjamin, Jr. New York: McGraw-Hill, 1977.

Herman, Judith Lewis. *Trauma and Recovery.* New York: Basic Books, 1992.

Herman, Judith Lewis, with Lisa Hirschman. *Father-Daughter Incest.* Cambridge, Mass.: Harvard University Press, 1981.

Herman, Judith Lewis, and Emily Schatzow. "Recovery and Verification of Memories of Childhood Sexual Trauma." *Psychoanalytic Psychology* 4, no. 1 (1987): 1–14.

Hilgard, Ernest R. *Divided Consciousness: Multiple Controls in Human Thought and Action.* New York: Wiley, 1977.

———. "The Hidden Observer and Multiple Personality." *International Journal of Clinical and Experimental Hypnosis* 32 (1984): 248–253.

Hirsch, Foster. *Film Noir: The Dark Side of the Screen.* New York: Da Capo Press, 1981.

Hirsch, Marianne. *The Mother/Daughter Plot: Narrative, Psychoanalysis, Feminism.* Bloomington: Indiana University Press, 1989.

Hochschild, Arlie. *The Managed Heart: Commercialization of Human Feeling.* Berkeley: University of California Press, 1994.

Hollibaugh, Amber; and Cherríe Moraga. "What We're Rollin Around in Bed With: Sexual Silences in Feminism." In *The Powers of Desire: The Politics of Sexuality,* edited by Ann Barr Snitow, Christine Stansell, and Sharon Thompson. New York: Monthly Review Press, 1983

Holmes, John G., and Sandra L. Murray. "Memory for Events in Close Relationships: Applying Schank and Abelson's Skeleton Story Model." In *Knowledge and Memory: The Real Story,* edited by Robert S. Wyer, Jr. Hillsdale, N.J.: Erlbaum, 1995.

Hooper, Carol Ann. *Mothers Surviving Child Sexual Abuse.* London: Tavistock/Routledge, 1992.

Horstein, Gail A. "The Return of the Repressed: Psychology's Problematic Relations with Psychoanalysis, 1909–1960." *American Psychologist* 47 (1992): 254–263.

Hsia, R. Po-Chia. *The Mystery of Ritual Murder: Jews and Magic in Reformation Germany.* New Haven, Conn.: Yale University Press, 1988.

Hunter, Mic. *Sexually Abused Boys: The Neglected Victims of Sexual Abuse.* New York: Fawcett Columbine, 1990.

———, ed. *The Sexually Abused Male.* Vol. 1. Boston: Lexington Books, 1990.

Huxley, Aldous. *The Devils of Loudun.* New York: Harper & Row, 1952.

Ingleby, David. "Understanding 'Mental Illness.'" In *Critical Psychiatry,* edited by D. Ingleby. New York: Pantheon Books, 1980.

Ireland, Mardy S. *Reconceiving Women: Separating Motherhood from Female Identity.* New York: Guilford Press, 1993.

Irigaray, Luce. "The Gesture in Psychoanalysis." In *Between Feminism and Psychoanalysis,* edited by Teresa Brennan. New York: Routledge, 1989.

———. *Speculum of the Other Woman.* Translated by Catherine Porter and Carolyn Burke. Ithaca, N.Y.: Cornell University Press, 1985.

———. "This Sex Which Is Not One." In *New French Feminism: An Anthology,* edited by Elaine Marks and Isabelle de Courtivron. New York: Schocken Books, 1981.

Isaac, Rael Jean, and Virginia C. Armat. *Madness in the Streets: How Psychiatry and the Law Abandoned the Mentally Ill.* New York: Free Press, 1990.

Jackowitz, Ann H. "Anna O/Bertha Pappenheim and Me." In *Between Women: Biographers, Novelists, Critics,* edited by C. Ascher, L. DeSalvo, and S. Ruddick. New York: Beacon Press, 1984.

Jacobs, Janet Liebman. *Victimized Daughters: Incest and the Development of the Female Self.* New York: Routledge, 1994.

Jacobson, John, James Mulick, and Allen Schwartz. "A History of Facilitated Communication: Science, Pseudoscience, and Antiscience." *American Psychologist* 50, no. 9 (Sept. 1995): 760–765.

Jacoby, Russell. *The Repression of Psychoanalysis: Otto Fenichel and the Political Freudians.* New York: Basic Books, 1983.

Jaggar, Alison M. "Love and Knowledge: Emotion in Feminist Epistemology." In *Gender/Body/Knowledge: Feminist Reconstructions of Being and Knowing,* edited by Alison M. Jaggar and Susan R. Bordo. New Brunswick, N.J.: Rutgers University Press, 1989.

Jaggar, Alison M., and Susan R. Bordo, eds. *Gender/Body/Knowledge: Feminist Reconstructions of Being and Knowing.* New Brunswick, N.J.: Rutgers University Press, 1989.

James, Alice. *Alice James: Her Brothers—Her Journal.* Boston: Milford House, 1972/1934.

James, William. *The Principles of Psychology.* 2 vols. New York: Dover, 1950/1890.

———. *William James on Psychical Research.* Compiled and edited by Gardner Murphy and Robert O. Ballou. London: Chatto & Windus, 1961/1909.

Jenkins, Janis. "Culture, Emotion, and PTSD." In *Ethnocultural Aspects of Posttraumatic Stress Disorder: Issues, Research, and Clinical Applications,* edited by Anthony J. Marsella, Matthew J. Friedman, Ellen T. Gerrity, and Raymond M. Scurfield. Washington, D.C.: American Psychological Association, 1996.

Jenkins, Phillip, and Daniel Maier-Katkin. "Occult Survivors: The Making of a Myth." In *The Satanism Scare,* edited by James T. Richardson, Joel Best, and David G. Bromley. New York: Aldine de Gruyter, 1991.

Johnson, Marcia K. "Reality Monitoring: An Experimental Phenomenological Approach." *Journal of Experimental Psychology: General* 117 (1988): 390–394.

Johnson, Matt. "Fear and Power: From Naivete to a Believer in Cult Abuse." *Journal of Psychohistory* 21, no. 4 (spring 1994): 435–441.

Johnson, Miriam. *Strong Mothers/Weak Wives: The Search for Gender Equality.* Los Angeles: University of California Press, 1988.

Kampman, R. "Hypnotically Induced Multiple Personality: An Experimental Study." *International Journal of Clinical and Experimental Hypnosis* 24 (1976): 215–227.

Kaplan, Ann, ed. *Women in Film Noir.* London: BRI, 1980.

Kaplan, Marion A. *The Jewish Feminist Movement in Germany: The Campaigns of the Jüdischer Frauenbund.* Westport, Conn.: Greenwood Press, 1979.

Keen, Sam. "Against Forgetting: Without Memory, Stories Die." *Utne Reader,* Mar./Apr. 1994, 112–121.

Keller, Evelyn Fox. *Reflections on Gender and Science.* New Haven, Conn.: Yale University Press, 1985.

Kenny, Michael. *The Passion of Ansel Bourne.* Washington, D.C.: Smithsonian, 1986.

Kernochan, Rose. *Review of Between Sisters,* by Nian Vida. *New York Times Book Review,* 12 May 1996, 24.

Kerr, Howard, John W. Crowley, and Charles L. Crow, eds. *The Haunted Dusk: American Supernatural Fiction, 1820–1920.* Athens: University of Georgia Press, 1983.

Kihlstrom, John F. "William James and Hypnosis: A Centennial Reflection." *American Psychological Society* 1, no. 3 (1990): 174–178.

Kihlstrom, John F., Terrence M. Barnhardt, and Douglas J. Tataryn. "The Psychological Unconscious: Found, Lost, and Regained." *American Psychologist* 47 (June 1992): 788–791.

Kihlstrom, John F., and Irene Hoyt. "Repression, Dissociation, and Hypnosis," in *Repression and Dissociation: Implications for Personality Theory, Psychopathology, and Health,* edited by Jerome L. Singer. Chicago: University of Chicago Press, 1990.

Kirk, Stuart A., and Herbert Kutchins. *The Selling of DSM.* New York: Aldine de Gruyter, 1992.

Klaits, Joseph. *Servants of Satan: The Age of the Witch Hunts.* Bloomington: Indiana University Press, 1985.

Kluft, Richard P. "Aspects of the Treatment of Multiple Personality Disorder." *Psychiatric Annals* 14 (1984): 51–55.

———. "High-Functioning Multiple Personality Patients: Three Cases." *Journal of Nervous and Mental Disease* 174, no. 12 (1986): 722–726.

———. "Multiple Personality Disorder." In *Dissociative Disorders: A Clinical Review,* edited by David Spiegel. Lutherville, Md.: Sidran Press, 1993.

———. "The Simulations and Dissimulation of Multiple Personality Disorder." *American Journal of Clinical Hypnosis* 30 (1987): 104–112.

———. "An Update on Multiple Personality Disorder." *Hospital and Community Psychiatry* 38, no. 4 (Apr. 1987): 363–372.

Kohut, Heinz. *How Does Analysis Cure?* Edited by Arnold Goldberg and Paul Stepansky. Chicago: University of Chicago Press, 1984.

———. *The Restoration of the Self.* New York: International Universities Press, 1977.

Kris, Ernst. "The Recovery of Childhood Memories in Psychoanalysis." *Psychoanalytic Study of the Child* 2 (1956): 54–88.

Kuhn, Thomas S. *The Structure of Scientific Revolutions.* 2d ed. Chicago: University of Chicago Press, 1970/1962.

Kvale, Steinkar. *Psychology and Postmodernism.* London: Sage, 1992.

Lamb, Sharon. *The Trouble with Blame: Victims, Perpetrators, and Responsibility.* Cambridge, Mass.: Harvard University Press, 1996.

Langs, Robert. "Interventions in the Bipolar Field." In *Classics in Psychoanalytic Technique,* edited by Robert Langs. New York: Aronson, 1981.

Laub, Dori. "Knowing and Not Knowing Massive Psychic Trauma: Forms of Traumatic Memory." *International Journal of Psychoanalysis* 74 (1993): 287–302.

Laurence, Jean-Roch, and Perry Campbell. *Hypnosis, Will, and Memory: A Psycho-legal History.* New York: Guilford Press, 1988.

Lazarus, Richard. "On the Primacy of Cognition." *American Psychologist* 39 (1984): 124–129.

LeDoux, Joseph. *The Emotional Brain: The Mysterious Underpinnings of Emotional Life.* New York: Simon & Schuster, 1996.

Lewis, Helen Block. "Shame, Repression, Field Dependence, and Psychopathology." In *Repression and Dissociation: Implications for Personality Theory, Psychopathology, and Health,* edited by Jerome L. Singer. Chicago: University of Chicago Press, 1990.

Leys, Ruth. "Traumatic Cures: Shell Shock, Janet, and the Question of Memory." *Critical Inquiry* 20 (1994): 623–662.

Libby, Marion, and Elizabeth Aries. "Gender Differences in Preschool Children's Narrative Fantasy." *Psychology of Women Quarterly* 13 (1989): 293–306.

Lindsay, D. Stephen. "Contextualizing and Clarifying Criticisms of Memory Work in Psychotherapy." *Consciousness and Cognition* 3 (1994): 426–437.

Lindsay, D. Stephen, and J. Don Read. " 'Memory Work' and Recovered Memories of Childhood Sexual Abuse: Scientific Evidence and Public, Professional, and Personal Issues." *Psychology, Public Policy, and the Law,* in press.

Lisak, David. "The Psychological Impact of Sexual Abuse: Content Analysis of Interviews with Male Survivors." *Journal of Traumatic Stress* 7, no. 4 (1994): 525–548.

Little, Margaret. "Counter-transference and the Patient's Response to It." In *Classics in Psychoanalytic Technique,* edited by Robert Langs. New York: Aronson, 1981.

Lockwood, Craig. *Other Alters: Roots and Realities of Cultic and Satanic Ritual Abuse and Multiple Personality Disorders.* Minneapolis: ComCare, 1993.

Loewald, Hans W. "Perspectives on Memory." In *Papers on Psychoanalysis,* edited by Hans W. Loewald. New Haven, Conn.: Yale University Press, 1980.

Loewenstein, Richard J. "Psychogenic Amnesia and Psychogenic Fugue: A Comprehensive Review." In *Dissociative Disorders: A Clinical Review,* edited by David Spiegel. Lutherville, Md.: Sidran Press, 1993.

Loftus, Elizabeth F. "Psychologists in the Eyewitness World." *Science Watch* 48 (1993): 550–553.
———. "The Reality of Repressed Memories." *American Psychologist* 48, no. 5 (1993): 518–537.
Loftus, Elizabeth F., and Katherine Ketcham. *The Myth of Repressed Memory: False Memories and Allegations of Sexual Abuse.* New York: St. Martin's Press, 1994.
———. *Witness for the Defense: The Accused, the Eyewitness, and the Expert Who Puts Memory on Trial.* New York: St. Martin's Press, 1991.
Loftus, Elizabeth F., and Mark R. Klinger. "Is the Unconscious Smart or Dumb?" *American Psychologist* 47 (June 1992): 761–765.
Lombard, Lisa S., Stephen P. Khan, and Erika Fromm. "The Role of Imagery in Self-Hypnosis: Its Relationship to Personality Characteristics and Gender." *International Journal of Clinical and Experimental Hypnosis* 38, no. 1 (1990): 25–38.
Los Angeles County Commission for Women. *Ritual Abuse: Definitions, Glossary, The Use of Mind Control.* Los Angeles: Los Angeles County Commission for Women, 1989.
Loulan, JoAnn. *Lesbian Passion: Loving Ourselves and Each Other.* Minneapolis: Spinsters Ink, 1987.
Lowe, M., and R. Hubbard. *Women's Nature: Rationalizations of Inequality.* New York: Pergamon Press, 1983.
Lowenstein, E. A. "Dissolving the Myth of the Unified Self: The Fate of the Subject in Freudian Analysis." *Psychoanalytic Quarterly* 63 (1994): 715–732.
Lynch, Gary, and Richard Granger. "Variations in Synaptic Plasticity and Types of Memory in Cortico-hippocampal Networks." In *Memory Systems 1994*, edited by Daniel L. Schacter and Endel Tulving. Cambridge, Mass.: MIT Press, 1994.
Mack, John. *Abduction: Human Encounters with Aliens.* New York: Ballantine, 1994.
Maglin, Nan Bauer, and Donna Perry, eds. *"Bad Girls/Good Girls": Women, Sex, & Power in the Nineties.* New Brunswick, N.J.: Rutgers University Press, 1996.
Mallet, Michael. *The Borgias: The Rise and Fall of a Renaissance Dynasty.* Frogmore, St. Albans: Paladin, 1971.
Maltz, Wendy. *The Sexual Healing Journey: A Guide for Survivors of Sexual Abuse.* New York: Harper Perennial, 1992.
Mankowski, Eric, and Julian Rapport. "Stories, Identity, and the Psychological Sense of Community." In *Knowledge and Memory: The Real Story*, edited by Robert S. Wyer, Jr. Hillsdale, N.J.: Erlbaum, 1995.
Manlowe, Jennifer F. *Faith Born of Seduction: Sexual Trauma, Body Image, and Religion.* New York: New York University Press, 1995.
Mann, Thomas. *The Magic Mountain.* New York: Vintage International, 1996/1924.
Marks, Elaine, and Isabelle de Courtivron, eds. *New French Feminism: An Anthology.* New York: Schocken Books, 1981.
Marsella, Anthony, Matthew J. Friedman, Ellen T. Gerrity, and Raymond M. Scurfield, eds. *Ethnocultural Aspects of Posttraumatic Stress Disorder: Issues, Research, and Clinical Applications.* Washington, D.C.: American Psychological Association, 1996.
Mason, A. A. "A Psychoanalyst Looks at a Hypnotist: A Study of Folie à Deux." *Psychoanalytic Quarterly* 43 (1994): 641–679.
Masson, Jeffrey. *The Assault on Truth: Freud's Suppression of the Seduction Theory.* New York: Farrar, Straus & Giroux, 1984.
McFarland, Robert B., and Grace Lockerbie. "Difficulties in Treating Ritually Abused Children." *Journal of Psychohistory* 21 (1994): 429.
McFarlane, Alexander C., and Rachael Yehuda. "Resilience, Vulnerability, and the Course of Posttraumatic Reactions." In *Traumatic Stress: The Effects of Overwhelming Experience on Mind, Body, and Society*, edited by Bessel A. van der Kolk, Alexander C. McFarlane, and Lars Weisaeth. New York: Guilford Press, 1996.
Mellow, James. *Charmed Circle: Gertrude Stein and Company.* New York: Praeger, 1974.
Merskey, H. "What Is a Syndrome?" *FMS Foundation Newsletter*, June 1995: 6.
Middleton, David, and Derek Edwards, eds. *Collective Remembering.* Newbury Park, Calif.: Sage, 1990.
Miller, Alice. *The Drama of the Gifted Child.* New York: Farrar, Straus & Giroux, 1983.
———. *Thou Shalt Not Be Aware: Society's Betrayal of the Child.* New York: Farrar, Straus & Giroux, 1984.
Miller, Peggy. "Personal Story Telling in Everyday Life: Social and Cultural Perspectives." In *Knowledge and Memory: The Real Story*, edited by Robert S. Wyer, Jr. Hillsdale, N.J.: Erlbaum, 1995.
Mitchell, Stephen A., and Margaret J. Black. *Freud and Beyond: A History of Modern Psychoanalytic Thought.* New York: Basic Books, 1995.
Mulhern, Sherill. "Satanism and Psychotherapy: A Rumor in Search of an Inquistion." In *The Satanism Scare*, edited by James T. Richardson, Joel Best, and David G. Bromley. New York: Aldine de Gruyter, 1991.
———. "Satanism, Ritual Abuse, and Multiple Personality Disorder: A Sociohistorical Perspective." *International Journal of Clinical and Experimental Hypnosis* 52, no. 4 (1994): 265–288.
Murphy, Melissa. "Dorothy Allison: The On Our Backs Interview." *On Our Backs* 40, no. 2 (July/August 1993): 23–24.

Nash, Michael R. "Memory Distortion and Sexual Trauma: The Problem of False Negatives and False Positives." *International Journal of Clinical and Experimental Hypnosis* 42 (1994): 346–362.

Nash, Michael R., Timothy L. Hulsey, Mark C. Sexton, Tina L. Harralson, and Warren Lambert. "Long-Term Sequelae of Childhood Sexual Abuse: Perceived Family Environment, Psychopathology, and Dissociation." *Journal of Consulting and Clinical Psychology* 61, no. 2 (1993): 276–283.

Nathan, Debbie, and Michael Snedeker. *Satan's Silence: Ritual Abuse and the Making of a Modern American Witch Hunt.* New York: Basic Books, 1995.

Nathanson, Constance A. *Dangerous Passage: The Social Control of Sexuality in Women's Adolescence.* Philadelphia: Temple University Press, 1991.

Neimeyer, Greg J., and Margaret B. Rareshide. "Personal Memories and Personal Identity: The Impact of Ego Identity Development on Autobiographical Memory Recall." *Journal of Personality and Social Psychology* 60 (1991): 562–569.

Neisser, Ulric. "John Dean's Memory: A Case Study." *Cognition* 9 (1988): 1–22.

———. "Snapshots or Benchmarks." In *Memory Observed,* edited by Ulric Neisser. San Francisco: Freeman, 1982.

Nelson, Kathleen. "The Psychological and Social Origins of Autobiographical Memory." *Psychological Science* 4, no. 1 (1993): 7–14.

Neswald, David W. in collaboration with Catherine Gould and Vicki Graham-Costain. "Common 'Programs' Observed in Survivors of Satanic Ritual Abuse." *California Therapist* (Sept./Oct. 1991): 47–53.

Nicholson, Linda J., ed. *Feminism/Postmodernism.* New York: Routledge, 1990.

Ofshe, Richard J. "Inadvertent Hypnosis during Interrogation: False Confession due to Dissociative State; Mis-identified Multiple Personality and the Satanic Cult Hypothesis." *International Journal of Clinical and Experimental Hypnosis* 40 (1992): 125–156.

Ofshe, Richard J., and Ethan Watters. *Making Monsters: False Memories, Psychotherapy, and Sexual Hysteria.* New York: Scribner, 1994.

Olivier, Christiane. *Jocasta's Children: The Imprint of the Mother.* New York: Routledge, 1989.

Opie, Iona, and Peter Opie. *The Classic Fairy Tales.* London: Oxford University Press, 1974.

Oppenheim, Janet. *The Other World: Spiritualism and Psychical Research in England, 1850–1914.* New York: Cambridge University Press, 1985.

Ornstein, Robert E. *The Psychology of Consciousness.* San Francisco: Freeman, 1972.

Orr, Julian E. "Shared Knowledge, Celebrating Identity: Community Memory in a Service Culture." In *Collective Remembering,* edited by David Middleton and Derek Edwards. Newbury Park, Calif.: Sage, 1990.

Ortner, Sherry. "Is Female to Male as Nature Is to Culture?" In *Women, Culture and Society,* edited by Michelle Zimbalist Rosaldo and Louise Lamphere. Stanford, Calif.: Stanford University Press, 1974.

Owen, Alex. *The Darked Room: Women, Power and Spiritualism in Late Victorian England.* Philadelphia: University of Pennsylvania Press, 1990.

Pendergrast, Mark. *Victims of Memory: Sex Abuse Allegations and Shattered Lives.* Hinesburg, Vt.: Upper Access, 1996.

Perreault, Jeanne. *Writing Selves: Contemporary Feminist Autography.* Minneapolis: University of Minnesota Press, 1995.

Person, Ethel Spector; and Howard Klar. "Establishing Trauma: The Difficulty Distinguishing between Memories and Fantasy." *Journal of the American Psychoanalytic Association* 42, no. 4 (1994): 1055–1081.

Peters, Marie Ferguson. "Parenting in Black Families with Young Children: A Historical Perspective." In *Black Families,* edited by Harriette Pies McAdoo. Newbury Park, Calif.: Sage, 1988.

Philipson, Ilene. *On the Shoulders of Women: The Feminization of Psychology.* New York: Guilford Press, 1993.

Pipal, Janet. "Managed Care: Is It the Corpse in the Living Room? An Expose." *Psychotherapy* 32 (1995): 323–332.

Plummer, Ken. *Telling Sexual Stories.* London: Routledge, 1995.

Poole, D. A., et al. "Psychotherapy and the Recovery of Memories of Childhood Sexual Abuse: U.S. and British Practitioners' Beliefs, Practices, and Experiences." *Journal of Consulting and Clinical Psychology* 63 (1995): 426–437.

Pope, Kenneth S. "Memory, Abuse, and Science: Questioning Claims about the False Memory Syndrome Epidemic." *American Psychologist* 51 (1996): 957–974.

Porter, Roy. *A Social History of Madness: Stories of the Insane.* London: Weidenfeld and Nicholson, 1987.

Poster, Mark. *A Critical Theory of the Family.* New York: Seabury Press, 1978.

Prince, Morton. *The Problem of Multiple Personality.* Paris: International Congress of Psychology, 1900.

Prozan, Charlotte, ed. *Construction and Reconstruction of Memory: Dilemmas of Childhood Sexual Abuse.* Northvale, N.J.: Aronson, 1997.

Putnam, Frank W. "Dissociative Phenomena." In *Dissociative Disorders: A Clinical Review,* edited by David Spiegel. Lutherville, Md.: Sidran Press, 1993.

———. "The Scientific Investigation of Multiple Personality Disorder." In *Split Minds/Split Brains: Historical and Current Perspectives,* edited by Jacques M. Quen. New York: New York University Press, 1986.

Read, Stephen, and Lynn Miller. "Stories Are Fundamental to Meaning and Memory: For Social Creatures, Could It Be Otherwise?" In *Knowledge and Memory: The Real Story,* edited by Robert S. Wyer, Jr. Hillsdale, N.J.: Erlbaum, 1995.

Réage, Pauline. *Story of O.* New York: Grove Press, 1965/1954.

Rebecca, Lea Nicoll Kramer, and Susan A. Lukey. "Spirit Song: The Use of Christian Healing Rites in Trauma Recovery." *Treating Abuse Today* 5, no. 6 (1995/1996): 39–47.

Reisberg, Daniel, and Friderike Heuer. "Remembering the Details of Emotional Events." In *Affect and Accuracy in Recall: Studies of Flashbulb Memories,* edited by Eugen Winograd and Ulric Neisser. Cambridge: Cambridge University Press, 1992.

Riccio, David, Vita Rabinowitz, and Shari Atelrod. "Memory: When Less Is More." *American Psychologist* 48 (1994): 917–926.

Rice, Anne. *Interview with the Vampire.* New York: Knopf, 1976.

———. *The Witching Hour.* New York: Ballantine, 1990.

Rich, Adrienne. "Compulsory Heterosexuality and Lesbian Existence." In *The Powers of Desire: The Politics of Sexuality,* edited by Ann Barr Snitow, Christine Stansell, and Sharon Thompson. New York: Monthly Review Press, 1983.

Richardson, James T., Joel Best, and David G. Bromley, eds. *The Satanism Scare.* New York: Aldine de Gruyter, 1991.

Riger, Stephanie. "Epistemological Debates, Feminist Voices: Science, Social Values, and the Study of Women." *American Psychologist* 47, no. 6 (1992): 730–740.

Rind, Bruce, and Evan Harrington. "A Critical Examination of the Role of Child Sex Abuse in Causing Psychological Maladjustment: A Review of the Literature." In *False Memory Syndrome: Therapeutic and Forensic Perspectives,* edited by D. A. Halperin. Washington, D.C.: American Psychiatric Press, in press.

Rock, Irvin, ed. *The Legacy of Solomon Asch: Essays in Cognition and Social Psychology.* Hillsdale, N.J.: Erlbaum, 1990.

Rockwell, R. B. "One Psychiatrist's View of Satanic Ritual Abuse." *Journal of Psychohistory* 21 (1994): 443–460.

Roediger, Henry L., III. "Memory Metaphors in Cognitive Psychology." *Memory & Cognition* 8, no. 3 (1980): 231–246.

Rogers, Martha. "Factors Influencing Recall of Childhood Sexual Abuse." *Journal of Traumatic Stress* 8, no. 4 (1995): 691–716.

———. "Factors to Consider in Assessing Adult Litigants' Complaints of Childhood Sexual Abuse." *Behavioral Sciences and the Law* 12 (1994): 279–298.

Roiphe, Katie. *The Morning After: Sex, Fear, and Feminism on Campus.* Boston: Little, Brown, 1993.

Rosaldo, Michelle Zimbalist. "Toward an Anthropology of Self and Feeling." In *Culture Theory,* edited by Richard Shweder and Robert A. LeVine. New York: Cambridge University Press, 1984.

Rosenbaum, M., and M. Muroff, eds. *Anna O: Fourteen Contemporary Reinterpretations.* New York: Free Press, 1984.

Rosenblatt, Naomi H., and Joshua Horwitz. *Wrestling with Angels: What Genesis Teaches Us about Our Spiritual Identity, Sexuality, & Personal Relationships.* New York: Doubleday, 1996.

Ross, Colin A. "Anne Sexton: Iatrogenesis of an Alter Personality in an Undiagnosed Case of MPD." *Dissociation* 4 (1992): 141–148.

———. *Multiple Personality Disorder: Diagnosis, Clinical Features, and Treatment.* New York: Wiley-Interscience, 1989.

———. *Satanic Ritual Abuse: Principles of Treatment.* Toronto: University of Toronto Press, 1995.

Rowe, Karen E. "To Spin a Yarn: The Female Voice in Folklore and Fairy Tale." In *Fairy Tales and Society: Illusion, Allusion, and Paradigm,* edited by Ruth B. Bottigheimer. Philadelphia: University of Pennsylvania Press, 1986.

Rubin, Gayle. "The Traffic in Women: Notes on the 'Political Economy' of Sex." In *Toward an Anthropology of Women,* edited by Rayna R. Reiter. New York: Monthly Review Press, 1975.

Russell, Diana E. H. *The Secret Trauma: Incest in the Lives of Girls and Women.* New York: Basic Books, 1986.

Rustin, Michael. *The Good Society and the Inner World: Psychoanalysis, Politics, and Culture.* New York: Verso, 1991.

Sarbin, Theodore, ed. *Narrative Psychology: The Storied Nature of Human Conduct.* New York: Praeger, 1986.

Sarnat, Joan. "Working in the Space between Psychoanalytic and Trauma-Oriented Approaches to Stories of Sexual Abuse." *Gender & Psychoanalysis* 2, no. 1 (1977): 79–102.

Saunders, B. E., L. A. Villeponteauz, and J. Lipovsky. "Child Sexual Assault as a Risk Factor for Mental Disorders among Women." *Journal of Interpersonal Violence* 7 (1992): 189–204.

Schacter, Daniel L. "Priming and Multiple Memory Systems: Perceptual Mechanisms of Implicit Memory." In *Memory Systems 1994,* edited by Daniel L. Schacter and Endel Tulving. Cambridge, Mass.: MIT Press, 1994.

———. *Searching for Memory: The Brain, the Mind, and the Past.* New York: Basic Books, 1996.

———. "Understanding Implicit Memory: A Cognitive Neuroscience Approach." *American Psychologist* 47 (1992): 559–569.

Schacter, Daniel L., and Endel Tulving. "What Are the Memory Systems of 1994?" In *Memory Systems 1994*, edited by Daniel L. Schacter and Endel Tulving. Cambridge, Mass.: MIT Press, 1994.

Schacter, Stanley; and Jerome Singer. "Cognitive, Social and Psychological Determinants of Emotional State." *Psychological Review* 69 (1969): 379–399.

Schank, Roger C., and Robert Abelson. "Knowledge and Memory: The Real Story." In *Knowledge and Memory: The Real Story,* edited by Robert S. Wyer, Jr. Hillsdale, N.J.: Erlbaum, 1995.

Schimek, Jean G. "Fact and Fantasy in the Seduction Theory: A Historical Review." *Journal of the American Psychoanalytic Association* 35 (1987): 937–965.

———. "The Intepretations of the Past: Childhood Trauma, Psychical Reality, and Historical Truth." *Journal of the American Psychoanalytic Association* 23 (1975): 845–865.

Schooler, Johnathan W., Miriam Bendiksen, and Zara Ambadar. "Toeing the Middle Line: Can We Accommodate Both Fabricated and Recovered Memories of Sexual Abuse?" In *False and Recovered Memories,* edited by M. Conway. New York: Oxford University Press, in press.

Schreiber, Flora Rheta. *Sybil: The True and Extraordinary Story of a Woman Possessed by Sixteen Separate Personalities.* New York: Warner Books, 1973.

Searles, Harold F. *My Work with Borderline Patients.* Northvale, N.J.: Aronson, 1986.

Segal, Naomi. "Echo and Narcissus." In *Between Feminism and Psychoanalysis,* edited by Teresa Brennan. New York: Routledge, 1989.

Sexton, Ann. *Transformations.* Boston: Houghton Mifflin, 1971.

Shamdasani, Sonu. "Encountering Hélène: Théodore Flournoy and the Genesis of Subliminal Psychology." Introduction to *Théodore Flournoy, From India to the Planet Mars: A Case of Multiple Personality with Imaginary Languages.* Princeton, N.J.: Princeton University Press, 1994.

Shay, Johnathan. *Achilles in Vietnam: Combat Trauma and the Undoing of Character.* New York: Simon & Schuster, 1994.

Shengold, Leonard. *Soul Murder: The Effects of Childhood Abuse and Deprivation.* New York: Fawcett Columbine, 1989.

Shiach, Morag. "Their 'Symbolic' Exists, It Holds Power—We, the Sowers of Disorder, Know It Only Too Well." In *Between Feminism and Psychoanlaysis,* edited by Teresa Brennan. New York: Routledge, 1989.

Shorter, Edward. *From Paralysis to Fatigue: A History of Psychosomatic Illness in the Modern Era.* New York: Free Press, 1992.

———. *From the Mind into the Body: The Cultural Origins of Psychosomatic Symptoms.* New York: Free Press, 1994.

Shotter, John. "The Social Construction of Remembering and Forgetting." In *Collective Remembering,* edited by David Middleton and Derek Edwards. Newbury Park, Calif.: Sage, 1990.

Showalter, Elaine. *The Female Malady: Women, Madness and Female Culture, 1830–1980.* New York: Penguin Books, 1985.

———. *Hystories: Hysterical Epidemics and Modern Media.* New York: Columbia University Press, 1996.

Simon, Bennett, and Christopher Bullock. "Incest and Psychoanalysis: Are We Ready to Fully Acknowledge, Bear, and Understand?" *Journal of the American Psychoanalytic Association* 42 (1994): 1261–1282.

Singer, Jefferson, and Peter Salovey. *The Remembered Self: Emotion and Memory in Personality.* New York: Free Press, 1993.

Singer, Jerome L., ed. *Repression and Dissociation: Implications for Personality Theory, Psychopathology, and Health.* Chicago: University of Chicago Press, 1990.

Sipe, Richard. *Sex, Priests, and Power: Anatomy of a Crisis.* New York: Brunner/Mazel, 1995.

Sizemore, Chris Costner. *A Mind of My Own.* New York: Morrow, 1989.

Sizemore, Chris Costner, and E. S. Pittillo. *I'm Eve!* Garden City, N.Y.: Doubleday, 1977.

Smiley, Jane. *A Thousand Acres.* New York: Fawcett Columbine, 1991.

Smith, Michelle, and Lawrence Pazder. *Michelle Remembers.* New York: Pocket Books, 1980.

Smith, Sidonie. *A Poetics of Women's Autobiography: Marginality and the Fictions of Self-Representation.* Bloomington: Indiana University Press, 1987.

Smith-Rosenberg, Carroll. *Disorderly Conduct: Visions of Gender in Victorian America.* New York: Knopf, 1985.

Snitow, Ann Barr. "Mass Market Romance: Pornography for Women Is Different." In *The Powers of Desire: The Politics of Sexuality,* edited by Ann Barr Snitow, Christine Stansell, and Sharon Thompson. New York: Monthly Review Press, 1983.

Solomon, Zahava. "Oscillating between Denial and Recognition of PTSD: Why Are Lessons Learned and Forgotten?" *Journal of Traumatic Stress* 8, no. 2 (1995): 271–275.

Sommers, Christina H. *Who Stole Feminism?: How Women Have Betrayed Women.* New York: Simon & Schuster, 1995.

Sonkin, Daniel J., ed. *Domestic Violence on Trial.* New York: Springer, 1987.

Sontag, Susan. *Illness as Metaphor.* New York: Farrar, Straus & Giroux, 1978.

Spanos, Nicholas P., E. Menary, N. J. Gabora, S. C. Dubreuil, and B. Dewhirst. "Secondary Identity Enactments during Hypnotic Past-Life Regression: A Sociocognitive Perspective." *Journal of Personality and Social Psychology* 61 (1991): 308–320.

Spanos, Nicholas P., Cheryl A. Burgess, and Melissa Faith Burgess. "Past Life Identities, UFO Abductions and Satanic Ritual Abuse: The Social Constructions of 'Memories.'" *International Journal of Experimental and Clinical Hypnosis,* in press.

Spence, Donald P. *Narrative Truth and Historical Truth: Meaning and Interpretation in Psychoanalysis.* New York: Norton, 1982.

————. "Narrative Truth and Putative Child Abuse." *International Journal of Clinical and Experimental Hypnosis* 42 (1994): 289–303.

Spencer, Judith. *Suffer the Child.* New York: Pocket Books, 1985.

Spiegel, David. "Dissociation, Double Binds, and Posttraumatic Stress Disorder." In *Treatment of Multiple Personality Disorder,* edited by Bennett G. Braun. Washington, D.C.: American Psychiatric Press, 1986.

————. "Hypnosis, Dissociation, and Trauma: Hidden and Overt Observers." In *Repression and Dissociation: Implications for Personality Theory, Psychopathology, and Health,* edited by Jerome. L. Singer. Chicago: Universtiy of Chicago Press, 1990.

Spirgge, Elizabeth. *Gertrude Stein: Her Life and Work.* New York: Harper & Brothers, 1957.

Sprengnether, Madelon. *The Spectral Mother: Freud, Feminism, and Psychoanalysis.* Ithaca, N.Y.: Cornell University Press, 1990.

Stanton, Elizabeth Cady. *The Woman's Bible.* Boston: Northeastern University Press, 1993/1898.

Starzecpyzel, Eileen. "The Persephone Complex: Incest Dynamics and the Lesbian Preference." In *Lesbian Psychologies: Explorations and Challenges,* edited by Boston Lesbian Psychologies Collective. Chicago: University of Illinois Press, 1987.

Steiger, Howard, and Maria Zanko. "Sexual Trauma among Eating-Disordered, Psychiatric and Normal Female Groups." *Journal of Interpersonal Violence* 5 (1990): 74–86.

Stein, Getrude. *Everybody's Autobiography.* New York: Random House, 1937.

Steinem, Gloria. "Making Connections." *Treating Abuse Today* 5, no. 6 (Nov./Dec. 1995–Jan./Feb. 1996): 7–11.

Stone, Kay F. "Feminist Approaches to the Interpretation of Fairy Tales." In *Fairy Tales and Society: Illusion, Allusion, and Paradigm,* edited by Ruth B. Bottigheimer. Philadelphia: University of Pennsylvania Press, 1986.

Stone, Michael, ed. *Essential Papers in Borderline Disorders.* New York: New York University Press, 1986.

Strouse, Jean. *Alice James: A Biography.* New York: Houghton Mifflin, 1991.

Summit, Roland. "The Child Sexual Abuse Accommodation Syndrome." *Child Abuse and Neglect* 7 (1983): 177–193.

Szasz, Thomas. "The Concept of Transference." In *Classics in Psychoanalytic Technique,* edited by Robert Langs. New York: Aronson, 1981.

Tatar, Maria. "Born Yesterday: Heroes in Grimms' Fairy Tales." In *Fairy Tales and Society: Illusion, Allusion, and Paradigm,* edited by Ruth B. Bottigheimer. Philadelphia: University of Pennsylvania Press, 1986.

Tavris, Carol. *The Mismeasure of Woman.* New York: Simon & Schuster, 1992.

Tayloe, Donald R. "The Validity of Repressed Memories and the Accuracy of Their Recall through Hypnosis: A Case Study from the Courtroom." *American Journal of Clinical Hypnosis* 37 (1995): 25–31.

Terdiman, Richard. *Present Past: Modernity and the Memory Crisis.* Ithaca, N.Y.: Cornell University Press, 1993.

Terr, Lenore. "Memory Work in Psychotherapy." Paper presented at the Institute for Advanced Clinical Training conference "Advances in Treating Survivors of Sexual Abuse," San Francisco, March 4, 1995.

————. *Too Scared to Cry.* New York: HarperCollins, 1990.

Theriot, Nancy. "Women's Voices in Nineteenth Century Medical Discourse: A Step toward Deconstructing Science." In *Gender and Scientific Authority,* edited by Barbara Laslett, Sally Gregory Kohlstedt, Helen Longino, and Evelynn Hammonds. Chicago: University of Chicago Press, 1996.

Thigpen, Corbett H., and Hervey M. Cleckley. *The Three Faces of Eve.* New York: McGraw-Hill, 1957.

Thompson, Sharon. *Going All the Way.* New York: Hill & Wang, 1994.

Thorne, Barrie. *Gender Play: Girls and Boys in School.* New Brunswick, N.J.: Rutgers University Press, 1993.

Thorne, Barrie, and Marilyn Yalom, eds. *Rethinking the Family: Some Feminist Questions.* Boston: Northeastern University Press, 1992.

Tolman, Deborah L. "Adolescent Girls, Women and Sexuality: Discerning Dilemmas of Desire." In *Women, Girls & Psychotherapy: Reframing Resistance,* edited by Carol Gilligan, Annie G. Rogers, and Deborah L. Tolman. New York: Hawthorne Press, 1991.

Ullman, Richard B., and Doris Brothers. *The Shattered Self: A Psychoanalytic Study of Trauma.* Hillsdale, N.J.: Analytic Press, 1988.

Ussher, Jane. *Women's Madness: Misogyny or Mental Illness.* Amherst: University of Massachusetts Press, 1991.

Ussher, Jane, and Paula Nicolson, eds. *Gender Issues in Clinical Psychology.* New York: Routledge, 1992.

van der Kolk, Bessel A. "The Body, Memory, and the Psychobiology of Trauma." In *Sexual Abuse Recalled,* edited by Judith Alpert. New York: Citadel Press, 1995.

van der Kolk, Bessel A., and R. Fisler. "Dissociation and the Fragmentary Nature of Traumatic Memories: Overview and Exploratory Study." *Journal of Traumatic Stress* 8, no. 4 (1995): 505–525.

van de Kolk, Bessel A., Alexander C. McFarlane, and Lars Weisaeth, eds. *Traumatic Stress: The Effects of Overwhelming Experience on Mind, Body, and Society.* New York: Guilford Press, 1996.

van der Kolk, Bessel A., and Onno van der Hart. "Pierre Janet and the Breakdown of Adaptation in Psychological Trauma." *American Journal of Psychiatry* 146, no. 12 (1989): 1530–1540.

Vance, Carol, ed. *Pleasure and Danger: Exploring Female Sexuality.* London: Pandora, 1989.

Victor, Jeffrey S. "The Dynamics of Rumor—Panics about Satanic Cults." In *The Satanism Scare,* edited by James T. Richardson, Joel Best, and David G. Bromley. New York: Aldine de Gruyter, 1991.

———. *Satanic Panic: The Creation of a Contemporary Legend.* Chicago: Open Court, 1993.

Waites, Elizabeth A. *Memory Quest: Trauma and the Search for Personal History.* New York: Norton, 1997.

Walker, Alice. "Advancing Luna—and Ida B. Wells." In *You Can't Keep a Good Woman Down.* New York: Harcourt Brace Jovanovich, 1982.

Walker, Lenore E. *The Battered Woman Syndrome.* New York: Springer, 1984.

Walkowitz, Judith R. "Science and the Seance: Transgressions of Gender and Genre in Late Victorian London." *Representations* 22 (1988): 3–36.

Warner, Marina. *From the Beast to the Blonde: On Fairy Tales and Their Tellers.* New York: Farrar, Straus & Giroux, 1994.

Watson, Robert. *Behaviorism.* New York: Norton, 1925.

Weedon, Chris. *Feminist Practice & Poststructuralist Theory.* New York: Blackwell, 1987.

Weitz, Shirley, ed. *Nonverbal Communication.* 2d ed. New York: Oxford University Press, 1979.

Westerlund, Elaine. "Freud on Sexual Trauma: An Historical Review of Seduction and Betrayal." *Psychology of Women Quarterly* 10 (1986): 297–310.

Whitebook, Joel. *Perversion and Utopia: A Study in Psychoanalysis and Critical Theory.* Cambridge, Mass.: MIT Press, 1995.

Wiesel, Elie. "The Holocaust as a Literary Inspiration." In *Dimensions of the Holocaust.* Evanston, Ill.: Northwestern University Press, 1977.

Williams, Linda M. "Recovered Memories of Abuse in Women with Documented Child Sexual Victimization Histories." *Journal of Traumatic Stress* 8, no. 4 (1995): 649–673.

Williams, Rowan. *Teresa of Avila.* Harrisburg, Pa.: Morehouse, 1991.

Willis, Ellen. "Feminism, Moralism, and Pornography." In *The Powers of Desire: The Politics of Sexuality,* edited by Ann Barr Snitow, Christine Stansell, and Sharon Thompson. New York: Monthly Review Press, 1983.

Wilson, J. P. "The Historical Evolution of PTSD Diagnostic Criteria: From Freud to DSM IV." *Journal of Traumatic Stress* 7 (1994): 681–698.

Wilson, Melba. *Crossing the Boundary: Black Women Survive Incest.* Seattle: Seal Press, 1994.

Winnicott, Donald. *Playing and Reality.* New York: Routledge, 1982.

Wolf, Naomi. *Fire with Fire: The New Female Power and How to Use It.* New York: Fawcett Columbine, 1994.

Wolfenstein, Eugene Victor. *Psychoanalytic-Marxism: Groundwork.* New York: Guilford Press, 1993.

Wyer, Robert S. Jr., ed. *Knowledge and Memory: The Real Story.* Hillsdale, N.J.: Erlbaum, 1995.

Yapko, Michael. "Suggestibility and Repressed Memories of Abuse: A Survey of Psychotherapists' Beliefs." *American Journal of Clinical Hypnosis* 36, no. 3 (1994): 163–171.

———. *Suggestions of Abuse: True and False Memories of Childhood Sexual Trauma.* New York: Simon & Schuster, 1994.

Young, Alan. *The Harmony of Illusions: Inventing Post-traumatic Stress Disorder.* Princeton, N.J.: Princeton University Press, 1995.

Young, Walter C., et al. "Patients Reporting Ritual Abuse in Childhood: A Clinical Syndrome. Report of 37 Cases." *Child Abuse and Neglect* 15 (1991): 181–189.

Zajonc, R. B. "On the Primacy of Affect." *American Psychologist* 39 (1984): 117–123.

Zaretsky, Eli. *Capitalism, the Family, & Personal Life.* New York: Harper & Row, 1976.

Zeligs, Dorothy. *Psychoanalysis and the Bible: A Study in Depth of Seven Leaders.* New York: Human Sciences Press, 1974.

Zelizer, Barbi. *Covering the Body: The Kennedy Assassination, the Media, and the Shaping of Collective Memory.* Chicago: University of Chicago Press, 1992.

Zipes, Jack. *Fairy Tales and the Art of Subversion: The Classical Genre for Children and the Process of Civilization.* New York: Methuen, 1983.

———. "The Grimms and the German Obsession with Fairy Tales." In *Fairy Tales and Society: Illusion, Allusion, and Paradigm,* edited by Ruth B. Bottigheimer. Philadelphia: University of Pennsylvania Press, 1986.

———. *The Trials and Tribulations of Little Red Riding Hood.* South Hadley, Mass.: Bergin & Garvey, 1986.

Index

About the Author

JANICE HAAKEN is a professor of psychology at Portland State University and a psychotherapist in private practice.